MW00805303

THE **FRANKFURT SCHOOL**
REVISITED

Other Books By Richard Wolin

Walter Benjamin, An Aesthetic of Redemption (1982)

The Politics of Being: The Political Thought of Martin Heidegger (1990)

The Heidegger Controversy: A Critical Reader (1991)

The Terms of Cultural Criticism: The Frankfurt School, Existentialism, Poststructuralism (1992)

Labyrinths: Critical Explorations in the History of Ideas (1995)

Karl Löwith, Martin Heidegger and European Nihilism (editor; 1995)

Heidegger's Children: Hannah Arendt, Karl Löwith, Hans Jonas, Herbert Marcuse (2001)

The Seduction of Unreason: The Intellectual Romance with Fascism from Nietzsche to Postmodernism (2004)

Herbert Marcuse, Heideggerian Marxism (co-editor; 2005)

THE FRANKFURT SCHOOL REVISITED

AND OTHER ESSAYS ON POLITICS AND SOCIETY

RICHARD WOLIN

Routledge
Taylor & Francis Group
New York   London

Routledge is an imprint of the
Taylor & Francis Group, an informa business

Published in 2006 by
Routledge
Taylor & Francis Group
270 Madison Avenue
New York, NY 10016

Published in Great Britain by
Routledge
Taylor & Francis Group
2 Park Square
Milton Park, Abingdon
Oxon OX14 4RN

© 2006 by Taylor & Francis Group, LLC
Routledge is an imprint of Taylor & Francis Group

Printed in the United States of America on acid-free paper
10 9 8 7 6 5 4 3 2 1

International Standard Book Number-10: 0-415-95357-X (Softcover)
International Standard Book Number-13: 978-0-415-95357-3 (Softcover)
Library of Congress Card Number 2005031279

No part of this book may be reprinted, reproduced, transmitted, or utilized in any form by any electronic, mechanical, or other means, now known or hereafter invented, including photocopying, microfilming, and recording, or in any information storage or retrieval system, without written permission from the publishers.

Trademark Notice: Product or corporate names may be trademarks or registered trademarks, and are used only for identification and explanation without intent to infringe.

Library of Congress Cataloging-in-Publication Data

Wolin, Richard.
   The Frankfurt school revisited : and other essays on politics and society / Richard Wolin.
      p. cm.
   Includes bibliographical references and index.
   ISBN-13: 978-0-415-95356-6 (hardback)
   ISBN-13: 978-0-415-95357-3 (pbk.)
   1. Frankfurt school of sociology. 2. Critical theory. I. Title.

HM467.W65 2006
301.01--dc22   2005031279

Taylor & Francis Group
is the Academic Division of Informa plc.

Visit the Taylor & Francis Web site at
http://www.taylorandfrancis.com

and the Routledge Web site at
http://www.routledge-ny.com

For K. L.

Contents

Preface

The Frankfurt School has established itself as an inescapable point of reference for debates in a wide variety of fields in the academy and elsewhere. Its contributions to the study of fascism, cultural studies, philosophy of history, and, more recently, the burgeoning field of democratic theory have become integral components of contemporary scholarly and public discourse. Jürgen Habermas's wide-ranging philosophical work on communicative reason, law, and democratic theory — not to mention his timely, polemical political interventions — have had an immense international impact. His ideas have gone far toward ensuring Critical Theory's continued theoretical and political relevance. To summarize: it would be difficult to imagine the landscape of contemporary thought shorn of the influences of Frankfurt School luminaries such as Theodor Adorno, Walter Benjamin, Habermas, Max Horkheimer, and Herbert Marcuse.

One of the problems with Critical Theory's reception has been that, whereas its key ideas — Adorno's concept of a "totally administered world," for example — were formulated during an era of unremitting political dictatorship (the 1940s), the contemporary situation is radically different. We are the distinct beneficiaries of the so-called Third Wave of democratization. Thus, despite the very real problems of "failed states" and massive, neoliberal-induced economic inequality, there also exists an unprecedented international political consensus about the value of human rights, government by consent of the governed, and popular sovereignty. When viewed in this optic, the Frankfurt School's trademark theoretical pessimism seems distinctly misplaced. From the standpoint of logics of democratization, the Federal Republic of Germany is a remarkable political success story, far exceeding the Critical Theorists' own expectations. This example, along with others such as Eastern Europe during the 1990s, suggests that hope for incremental political betterment is hardly a lost cause. In light of these recent successes, one need not rely exclusively on a quasi-theological "longing for the totally Other" as the later Horkheimer once proposed.

The Frankfurt School's reception in North America has experienced various rhythms. The initial wave during the 1970s followed the waning of the New Left and complemented the widespread influence, a decade earlier, of Herbert Marcuse's writings. Since Frankfurt School thinkers like Adorno, Marcuse, and Benjamin made so many landmark contributions to cultural theory, during the 1980s an attempt arose to amalgamate their perspective with the nascent field of "cultural studies." Their work was assimilated to what Fredric Jameson has labeled "The Cultural Turn." Nevertheless, skeptics appropriately wondered whether the turn toward *cultural* politics represented a flight from *movement* politics. One of the major flaws of "identity politics" — the political corollary of the cultural studies movement — is that it was self-marginalizing and unable to form coalitions with those possessing other identities and political interests.

More recently, representatives of the cultural left have sought to reconcile the Frankfurt School's negative philosophy of history, as developed in *Dialectic of Enlightenment* (1947), with poststructuralism. Both theoretical currents subscribe to the narrative of modernity as a story of decline. In the Frankfurt School perspective, modernity signifies the wholesale triumph of *instrumental reason*: the reduction of persons and things to mere "stuff of domination," a process that culminated in totalitarianism. Among the leading poststructuralist thinkers, Foucault's understanding of modernity as the triumph of the "disciplinary society" purveys a parallel narrative. Reason and autonomy, the purported vehicles of our emancipation, have merely inscribed us more deeply in the infernal machine of "carceralism" — or so the argument goes. It is in this sense that the French philosopher's famous — and controversial — dictum, "*Raison, c'est la torture*," must be understood.

The reception of Habermas's work, which I discuss in Part II, has often proceeded at cross-purposes with that of the first-generation Frankfurters. In 1985, he published *The Philosophical Discourse of Modernity* in which he articulated his theoretical differences with the poststructuralists as well as with his Frankfurt School mentors, Horkheimer and Adorno. Habermas's concern was that by denigrating modernity's emancipatory promise, the first-generation Frankfurters, along with their kindred spirits in Paris (Foucault, Derrida, etc.), preempted the possibility of meaningful political intervention. Instead, both groups sought refuge in the realm of "metapolitics": dyspeptic, antimodernist jeremiads that belittled the prospect of progressive social change. After all, from a "totally administered world" — to employ Adorno's pet Kafkaesque epithet — little good can emerge.

Habermas's theory of communicative action, conversely, revolves around the idea of *redeeming* or *fulfilling* modernity's emancipatory potential. He suggests that modernity's egalitarian promise can be discerned in the progression from civil to political to social rights, as outlined in T. H. Marshall's pathbreaking work, *Citizenship and Social Class*. More recently, neoliberalism and globalization have placed the postwar welfare state consensus at risk. Nevertheless, I am convinced that the only way to counteract the depredations of neoliberalism is by extending the logics of democratization, not regressing behind them. Conceptions of global civil society as well as recent developments in the realm of humanitarian international law point hopefully in this direction.

The appearance of this book owes much to the unstinting generosity of colleagues, friends, and associates. Without their support, it is doubtful whether the project would have come to fruition at all.

At the Graduate Center of the City University of New York, President (and former Provost) William Kelly has created a wonderful working environment from which I and other faculty members have benefited greatly. In the history program, Josh Freeman has been an unfailingly understanding and sympathetic department chair. And the encouragement of Ruth O'Brien, chair of political science, has been, at several points, absolutely crucial.

It has been a great pleasure to work with Rob Tempio, my editor at Routledge. Rob's professionalism, dedication, and promptness, at every step of the publishing process, have been extremely welcome. All authors should be so lucky to have an editor like Rob.

In spring 2005 I was fortunate to be invited to teach in the Philosophy Department at the University of Paris-X, Nanterre. I would like to thank my gracious host, Emmanuel Faye, for the wonderful opportunity to teach at Nanterre — a university with a storied political past — and for the nonpareil hospitality that he and Gwenola Sigen lavished upon me throughout my stay. I would additionally like to thank Jean-Pierre and Marie-Odile Faye for a truly memorable dinner on rue de Varennes — in the former apartment of André Gide, no less!

My graduate students — Italia Colabianchi, Brian Fox, Jessica Hammerman, and Edwin Tucker — have always been a source of lively intellectual feedback. Their material and logistical assistance in completing various writing projects has been invaluable. I reserve a special thanks, however, for Martin Woessner, who read a penultimate version of many of these chapters and unfailingly provided constructive and astute commentary.

Four years ago, Jerrold Seigel and I convened the New York Area Seminar in Intellectual and Cultural History. The seminar has proved a bountiful source of intellectual stimulation. Moreover, I have been the grateful beneficiary of Jerry's magnanimous collegiality and boundless theoretical breadth.

Most of the chapters that comprise *The Frankfurt School Revisited* were presented as invited lectures at various university or public venues. The majority have remained, until now, unpublished. All have been revised for this volume — some quite substantially.

Chapter 1, "Between Proust and the *Zohar*: Walter Benjamin's *Arcades Project*," was presented in February 2003 at a seminar in the Comparative Literature Department at Yale University as part of the Baldwin-Dahl lecture series.

Chapter 2, "The Adorno Centennial: The Apotheosis of Negative Dialectics," is published for the first time.

Chapter 3, "What Is Heideggerian Marxism?", was presented at a Heidegger symposium at the University of Kentucky in November 2003.

Chapter 4, "Critical Reflections on Marcuse's Theory of Revolution," was a lecture delivered at the Marcuse Centennial conference at the University of California, Berkeley in November 1998.

Chapter 5, "The Lion in Winter: Leo Lowenthal and the Integrity of the Intellectual," was presented at an April 2003 conference in honor of Leo Lowenthal, also at University of California, Berkeley.

Chapter 6, "Levinas and Heidegger: The Anxiety of Influence", was presented at a November 2004 University of Illinois, Chicago conference on Heidegger's Jewish students.

Chapter 7, "Karl Jaspers: The Paradoxes of Mandarin Humanism," is published for the first time.

Chapter 8, "What We Can Learn from the Revolutions of 1989," appeared in *Common Knowledge* and is reprinted with permission.

Chapter 9, "From the 'Death of Man' to Human Rights: The Paradigm Change in French Intellectual Life, 1968–86," was presented at a September 2004 conference on "Historicizing Postmodernism" hosted by the Department of Political Science, University of California, Berkeley.

Chapter 10, "The Republican Revival: Reflections on French Singularity," was presented at an April 2004 conference on "French Liberalism: New French Thought Now" at Columbia University.

"Postscript Hexagon Fever," appeared in the Winter 2004 issue of *Dissent* and is reprinted with permission.

Chapter 12, "What Is Global Democracy?", was presented at a May 2004 DAAD (German Academic Exchange Service) conference on "Democratization" at the University of Minnesota.

Chapter 13, "Religion and Public Reason: A Contemporary Debate," was presented at a conference on "Religion, Philosophy, and Society" in honor of Jürgen Habermas in Lodz, Poland in April 2005.

Chapter 14, "The Disoriented Left: A Critique of Left Schmittianism," was presented in May 2005 as a lecture in a symposium on political ideologies at the University of Paris-X, Nanterre.

An earlier version of Chapter 15, "Kant at Ground Zero: Philosophers Respond to September 11," appeared in *The New Republic* in January 2004. Thanks are due to TNR Literary Editor Leon Wieseltier for some astute suggestions for revision.

Introduction

I

Could it be that the Frankfurt School's North American reception has been the product of a colossal misunderstanding? Unaccountably, *Dialectic of Enlightenment* — written between 1941–1944, published in 1947 — has become Critical Theory's signature text. Yet, if one closely surveys the Frankfurt School's *oeuvre* — an output spanning four decades — one realizes the degree to which the book's themes are at odds with the School's dominant theoretical tendencies.

Conceived in the 1930s, Critical Theory aimed at a balanced integration of philosophy and the social sciences. In the words of *spiritus rector* Max Horkheimer, its goal was the pursuit of "interdisciplinary materialism." Traditionally, philosophy reasoned about values or ultimate ends. Yet, to its detriment, it neglected the sphere of reality or concrete existence in terms of which alone its ideals might become genuinely meaningful or lived. The social sciences, for their part, squandered their energies in an unreflective pursuit of "facts." Their antipathy to "values" — a legacy of positivism — meant that frequently the data they produced bore little relationship to genuine human needs. Worse still, their fetishization of expertise was often antidemocratic and abetted the forces of political technocracy.

We now know that, on circumstantial grounds, Horkheimer's original program was prevented from coming to fruition. Hitler's January 1933 seizure of power forced the Frankfurt School thinkers into exile. For a time, Horkheimer and company tried to keep the flame of interdisciplinary materialism alive. Critical Theory's original program had been integrally tied to the goals of progressive politics as defined by the idea of democratic socialism. But, given the challenges and rigors of exile, this political edge became increasingly difficult to sustain.

In one of his early writings, Marx poetically described philosophy as the "head" of human emancipation and the proletariat as its "heart." The term Critical Theory itself had been conceived as a euphemism for a reflective, nondogmatic Marxism. But as the 1930s progressed, Critical Theory metamorphosed into a school of social philosophy that was deprived of a political addressee. Its members became radical intellectuals without a following. The Frankfurt School's political expectations had been kindled by the short-lived wave of "council republics" (*Räterepublik*) that mushroomed throughout Central Europe and Russia following the Great War. But the 1930s — W. H. Auden's "low, dishonest decade" — demonstrated that a different political reality, *fascism*, had become the order of the day. At this point it seemed that the best one could do was to prevent the worst.

In this way the idea of Critical Theory as a "message-in-a-bottle" (*Flaschenpost*) originated. Although its themes and concerns might be destined to fall on deaf ears for the time being, perhaps an unnamed future generation would seize the baton — as indeed happened during the 1960s, when student radicals honed their criticisms of advanced industrial society with pirate editions of Frankfurt School texts in hand. By the same token, during the 1930s Horkheimer and company did not go into a holding pattern. Instead, they focused their energies on preserving a level of theoretical cogency and insight that would, in the years to come, serve as a beacon for a broad stratum of intellectuals and opinion-leaders.

In programmatic essays such as "Traditional and Critical Theory" (1937), Horkheimer concluded that, in lieu of viable progressive politics, emancipatory ideals had sought refuge in the concept of Reason. After all, had not philosophy's mission been to adumbrate and project humanity's highest aspirations and goals? Therein lay its utopian dimension. Metaphysics delineated conceptions of "truth," "beauty," "justice," and "goodness" that, at a later point, an informed citizenry would try to realize in practice. Here one can see that Horkheimer's ideas about the relationship between theory and practice were never far removed from Marx's youthful notion of philosophy as the "head" and the proletariat as the "heart" of political emancipation.

What alarmed Horkheimer during the 1930s were "anti-intellectual" theoretical currents that rejected metaphysics outright for along with metaphysics, they seemingly renounced all prospects for human betterment.

One formidable opponent was logical positivism, which sought to reduce valid knowledge to what could be specified in so-called "protocol sentences." Meaning in general was narrowly reduced to circumstances that could be empirically verified. All the rest — poetry, morality, the *summum bonum* or "highest good" — were dismissed as essentially *meaningless*: the stuff of human reverie on a starry night. As Rudolf Carnap observed in what would become one of logical positivism's defining claims: "In the domain of metaphysics, including all philosophy of value and normative theory, logical analysis yields the negative results that *the alleged statements in this domain are entirely meaningless.*"[1] Since they could not be verified by the procedures of logical analysis, evaluative claims concerning justice and morality bore no relationship to "truth." In the concluding aphorism to the *Tractatus-Logico Philosophicus*, Wittgenstein gave consummate expression to this standpoint by declaring that, "*What we cannot speak of, we must pass over in silence.*" The problem was that, by narrowly equating "reason" with scientific procedure, logical positivism deprived human concerns of their truth-relatedness – and, by association, of philosophical seriousness.

The other theoretical current Horkheimer sought to thwart was *Lebensphilosophie* or "philosophy of life" which, since the turn of the century, had made significant inroads in German intellectual life. In certain respects, *Lebensphilosophie* served as a necessary counterweight to the predominant scientistic tendencies of the age. It celebrated "life," intuition, empathy, and mood as possessing an existential superiority that surpassed the capacities of analytical reason. According to this perspective, the unreflected immediacy of "life" contained a plentitude and richness that the intellect merely contaminated. The conceptual opposition at issue was well conveyed by the title of Ludwig Klages' 1932 opus, *The Intellect as Antagonist of the Soul* (*Geist als Widersacher der Seele*).

Philosophy of life harbored an ideological dimension that, for anyone concerned with contemporary politics, remained impossible to ignore. Many of its representatives openly glorified the forces of instinct, blood, and racial belonging. Moreover, following a precedent set by Plato, philosophers of life generally perceived democracy as a degenerate form of political rule — a form appropriate to the decadent West. Little wonder that many members of the right-wing Weimar intelligentsia who were influenced by *Lebensphilosophie* viewed the Nazi seizure of power sympathetically.

Today, when one thinks of Critical Theory's animating spirits, the names of Horkheimer and Theodor Adorno leap to mind. The two co-authored *Dialectic of Enlightenment*. And, following Horkheimer's retirement in 1959, it was Adorno who succeeded him as director of the Institute for Social Research.

By the same token, it is important to realize that Adorno was a relative latecomer to the Institute in its halcyon, prewar period.

Unlike the other Frankfurt School members who, by 1934, had emigrated to the United States, Adorno remained in Germany until 1935. He had hoped — unrealistically, as it turned out — that the political storm unleashed by Nazism might pass quickly. In the mid-1930s, Adorno accepted a fellowship at Oxford University, where he busied himself writing a withering critique of Husserl, *Against Epistemology: A Metacritique*. Although he had already made several important contributions to Critical Theory's theoretical organ, the *Zeitschrift für Sozialforschung*, only belatedly, in 1938, did he finally join up with Horkheimer and other members of the Institute for Social Research in New York.

In 1941, Horkheimer, faced with financial constraints and health concerns, summarily dissolved the Institute. This was also the year that the last issue of the *Zeitschrift* appeared, under a new title (*Studies in Philosophy and Social Science*) and, for the first time, in English. Institute members Otto Kirchheimer, Leo Lowenthal, Herbert Marcuse, and Franz Neumann sought jobs with a new intelligence organ, the Organization of Strategic Services (OSS), to help the American government decipher information received from Nazi-dominated Europe and, thereby, to assist in the struggle against fascism.

Horkheimer, for his part, had long contemplated writing a major work on dialectics. He had always chafed under his burdensome administrative responsibilities as the Institute's director, which he believed interfered with his theoretical work. With the Institute's dissolution, he was free of these duties. He had also long been impressed both by Adorno's philosophical brilliance as well as his limitless capacity for work. In this way the idea developed of repairing with Adorno to Pacific Palisades, California and finally setting to work on the dialectics book, whose content was still under discussion.

Since there exist a number of excellent accounts of *Dialectic of Enlightenment's* main argument, in the context at hand there is little need to recapitulate it in detail. However, it is worth pointing out that Adorno's background differed considerably from the other Institute members. Adorno was philosophically trained, whereas his Institute cohorts were much more favorably disposed toward the social sciences. Unlike Frankfurt School mainstays such as Erich Fromm, Otto Kirchheimer, Franz Neumann, and Friedrich Pollock — to say nothing of Horkheimer himself — Adorno was never attracted to the methods and goals of "interdisciplinary materialism." Instead, following Walter Benjamin's lead, his paratactic approach to philosophizing, which he later termed thinking in "constellations," sought to "explode idealism from within" — that is, intra-philosophically.

Dialectic of Enlightenment is a peculiar book. In fact, it is hardly a "book" in the customary sense, as its subtitle, "Philosophical Fragments," betrays. It opens with a programmatic discussion of Enlightenment, which states the central thesis: Enlightenment seeks to undermine "myth," yet, in doing so, Enlightenment itself rigidifies into a new form of myth: the reduction of "reason" to the claims of "positive science." Two "Excurses" ensue: "The Odyssey or Myth and Enlightenment," and "Juliette or Enlightenment and Morality." There follows the path-breaking chapter on "The Culture Industry: Enlightenment as Mass Deception." Realizing how deadly serious was Nazi anti-Semitism (a phenomenon that most thinkers on the Left preferred to ignore), the authors present a suggestive, if sketchy, theoretical explanation in the last chapter, "Elements of Anti-Semitism." Finally, as almost an after-thought, one finds a series of uncollated and disparate "Notes and Drafts" — thought-provoking material on a wide range of topics that the authors added in rather slapdash fashion.

How precisely the various chapters and excurses are meant to relate to one another is never clearly stated. How one might go about unifying a study that leaps from (1) Homer to (2) the Marquis de Sade to (3) Mickey Mouse (in the "Culture Industry" chapter) to (4) Auschwitz is anybody's guess. Undoubtedly, over the years the text's fragmentary nature has, in Benjaminian fashion, enhanced its mystique or aura. As such, the book is something of a Rorschach test: the thematic purview is so wide-ranging that there is seemingly something for everyone. Among Frankfurt School devotees, it continues to enjoy cult status.

Yet, beyond the book's mesmerizing individual chapters, its basic intellectual demarche implores critical scrutiny. The authors' starting point is Europe's "regression to barbarism" during the 1930s and 1940s — National Socialism. But is the strategy of searching for Nazism's origins in the Age of Enlightenment plausible? Were not in fact Nazism and the Enlightenment *ideological opposites*? As Goebbels remarked following Hitler's seizure of power: "The year 1789 is hereby effaced from history."[2] Whereas the Enlightenment openly embraced cosmo-politanism and kindred values, Nazism was an unregenerate racist dictatorship. Here, it seems, Adorno borrowed too readily from the lexicon and habitudes of 1920s *Kulturkritik*: from the likes of Spengler, Klages, and similar spirits, all of whom displayed a marked antipathy toward "modernity."

Let there be no mistake: trying to saddle the Enlightenment with responsibility for Nazism is an arch-conservative interpretive strategy. According to this optic, Nazism, like the French Revolution, was a product of the dissolution of the ancien regime and the rise of modern "society." All in all, the ancien regime played a positive role insofar as it furnished ruling elites who kept the unwashed masses in their places, at a remove from the corridors of power. Fascism's origins thus lie in the "revolt of the masses" (Ortega y Gassett): their involvement in political rule, for which they are constitutionally unsuited. However, one of the genuine shortcomings of this interpretation is that Nazism's German specificity — the persistence of authoritarian patterns of socialization; a pronounced ideological hostility to Western values (democracy, basic rights, and so forth) — fades from view.

As has often been remarked, *Dialectic of Enlightenment* signifies Critical Theory's passage from Marx to Nietzsche. By the same token, the book represents an abandonment of the methods of immanent criticism in favor of the Nietzschean practice of total critique. In the authors' view, the failings of modern society can no longer be remedied from within. Instead, à la Nietzsche, modernity is viewed as a degenerate social form, a manifestation of decline (*Verfallsform*). The authors of *Dialectic of Enlightenment* unreservedly embrace Nietzsche's "critique of reason." Reason has ceased to be an indispensable ally in the struggle for emancipation. Instead, it has become a mechanism of domination *simpliciter*.

By accepting a Nietzschean view of reason, Horkheimer and Adorno bid adieu prematurely to the project of human self-determination. Ever since Socrates, the idea of human freedom was tied to a *dialectic of insight and emancipation*. This standpoint was expressed in classical Socratic adages such as "The unexamined life is not worth living." In other words: self-knowledge is the key to the "good life" or human flourishing. In the modern age, this skein was taken up by Marx and Freud. Marx perceived "class consciousness," or historical self-awareness, as the prerequisite for working class emancipation. Similarly, Freud viewed self-understanding as the key to individuation or ego autonomy, as in the maxim "Where id was, there ego shall be."

The problem is that once reason is equated with domination as in Nietzsche, one severs the link between insight and emancipation. A radical hermeneutics of suspicion like Nietzsche's or Heidegger's ultimately becomes self-canceling. By denigrating reflexivity and insight, it risks depriving us of the means of our emancipation.

Yet another circumstantial peculiarity of *Dialectic of Enlightenment* bears scrutiny. We have already remarked that, as a collection of disparate philosophical fragments, the work is a torso. But in addition the text in its current form was never meant to stand alone. *Dialectic of Enlightenment* was conceived as part one of a projected two-volume study. It presented a *negative* treatment of the Enlightenment that the authors intended to supplement with a book-length examination of Enlightenment's *positive* side. Unfortunately, the second part remained unwritten. Thus, to accept *Dialectic of Enlightenment's* pessimistic conclusions at face value — standing Hegel on his head, the authors interpret modernity as "progress in domination" rather than "progress in the consciousness of freedom" — is misleading. For the authors' ultimate intentions cannot be discerned unless one simultaneously takes into account the Enlightenment's constructive contributions to human development.

Although *Dialectic of Enlightenment*, Part II, was never written, we do have determinate indications as to its likely content and direction. Horkheimer openly discusses his ideas for Part II in letters. In addition, many of these notions found their way into his 1947 book *The Eclipse of Reason* — a work that possesses a number similarities with *Dialectic of Enlightenment*, but which also contains some crucial differences of emphasis.

The opposition animating *Eclipse of Reason* is one between subjective and objective reason. Subjective or "instrumental" reason is a reason of means. Given a pre-established goal or end, it proceeds to determine the most efficient path of reaching that end. Since subjective reason is agnostic about ends, it is essentially "amoral." In *Eclipse of Reason* Horkheimer's concern is that the dialectic of civilization results in objective reason's displacement at the hands of subjective reason.

Eclipse of Reason differs from *Dialectic of Enlightenment* in one significant respect. Whereas *Dialectic of Enlightenment*, following Nietzsche, associates reason with domination, and thus views it in essence as a mechanism of social control, *Eclipse of Reason* limits this association to the case of *subjective reason alone*. For Horkheimer, "objective reason," or "metaphysics," possesses indubitable positive value. Unlike subjective reason, it is capable of normatively adjudicating among ends: moral and immoral, just and unjust, and so forth. Were humanity to lose sight of this capacity entirely, the result would be unchecked nihilism — the uncontested reign of instrumental reason.

In Horkheimer's view, objective reason's capacity for strong normative evaluation, as well as its ability to articulate meaningful ideals and goals, played a valuable role in keeping the abyss of technological nihilism at bay. Insofar as Adorno's philosophy, conversely, collapsed subjective and objective reason together, rejecting both as vehicles of oppression, he had immense difficulty seeing beyond that abyss. It was, then, hardly an accident that his diagnosis of the age failed to progress beyond the idea of a "totally administered world." Despite its manifest brilliance, Adorno's philosophy prematurely abandoned the idea that reason could adequately think through or conceptualize domination. In his view, reason had become an expression of coercion *simpliciter*.

Adorno's social evolutionary pessimism — his anti-Hegelian notion that the dialectic of civilization may be described as a one-way street leading toward enhanced technological oppression — has achieved a glib currency in postmodern circles in which a radical "critique of reason" (*Vernunftkritik*) of dubious Heideggerian provenance has become fashionable. Yet parroting slogans — even clever ones coined by Adorno — can

readily become an act of intellectual self-renunciation: a refusal to think
through the parameters of a new historical and political situation.
Those who follow unreflectively in Adorno's footsteps risk reproducing
his theoretical contradictions and missteps.

II

In Part I of the volume that follows, "The Frankfurt School Revisited,"
I seek to reflect on and evaluate Critical Theory's contemporary
relevance.

In both Germany and North America, the Frankfurt School enjoys a
remarkable currency. Its contributions remain a touchstone for debates
in a broad array of academic disciplines and public debates. Its influence
on postwar political culture — Horkheimer and Adorno's role in the
reshaping of postwar German politics; Marcuse's sizeable impact on the
international New Left — was in many respects profound. By the same
token, it falls due to interpreters to prevent the Frankfurt School's
legacy from congealing into a body of received wisdom or *idées fixes*.
This means that its doctrines and positions must also be regularly
exposed to the critical spirit.

Strangely, Walter Benjamin, whose own life was fraught with so
many setbacks and hardships, has been the beneficiary of an uncanny
posthumous canonization. Many of his pathbreaking essays were
published in the Frankfurt School annual, the *Zeitschrift für Sozialforschung*. Via Adorno's influence, he played a profound, subterranean role
in the development of Critical Theory. For example, the change in focus
to a "negative" philosophy of history from a progressive, Enlighten-
ment-oriented model may be traced back to Benjamin's historico-philosophical speculations.

As a result of his tragic death fleeing Nazi-dominated Europe, Benjamin
has acquired the persona of the prototypical twentieth-century intellectual
martyr. His *oeuvre* itself is filled with paradoxes and contradictions. Even
today, much of it subsists as unconsummated fragments — above all, his
unfinished masterwork, the *Passagenwerk* or *Arcades Project*, which has
justly become an object of unending scholarly fascination.

In "Between Proust and the *Zohar*: Walter Benjamin's *Arcades
Project*," I pose a series of questions about the *Arcades Project* as it
relates to Benjamin's broader developmental tendencies. How might
one go about making sense of a work that, in many respects, tries to
reconcile Marx with spiritualism? What is one to make of a methodological demarche that, drawing on the Surrealist fascination with
dreams, claims that the experience of "awakening from a dream"
is a "textbook example of dialectical thinking"? And what about

Benjamin's avowed attraction to right-wing authors such as Ludwig Klages, Carl Schmitt, and C. G. Jung, all of whom opted for Nazism during the 1930s. In his surrealism essay, Benjamin declared that his goal was to "win the energies of intoxication for the revolution" — a remark that seemingly anticipated 1960s-style libidinal politics. Only by carefully pursuing the fault lines and contradictions of his work can we hope to truly do justice to it.

Despite their very real intellectual differences (on the value of mass culture, for example), no one was more faithful to Benjamin's legacy than his ally and interlocutor Theodor Adorno. Three years ago, Adorno's centennial took place. Germany was convulsed with commemorative events. That a former left-wing Jewish exile could become a central figure in the cultural life of the Federal Republic — to the point of meriting his own postage stamp — tells us something important about the expansion of the boundaries of tolerance in postwar German political culture.

"The Adorno Centennial: The Apotheosis of Negative Dialectics" reexamines Adorno's legacy and influence through the prism of the centennial events. Like celebrations and anniversaries in general, the centennial brought out both the worst and best among the participants. Among the German right one still encounters the view that critical thinking, especially as practiced by leftists and Jews — to say nothing of "Jewish leftists" — is responsible for a depletion of national substance. Among the left, there remains considerable resentment that, although Adorno supported the German SDS up to a point, at a later juncture he became highly critical of its senseless provocations. However, when all is said and done, it was Adorno who made the idea of "working through the past" a central leitmotif of postwar German political culture. In the aftermath of Auschwitz, it was Germany's commitment to working through the past that became a sign of its commitment to return to the family of nations. In this respect, it would be impossible to write the history of the Federal Republic apart from Adorno's impact and influence.

Late in life Herbert Marcuse became a type of latter-day Tocqueville: a figure who enjoyed enormous intellectual and political prestige on both sides of the Atlantic. But it is rarely discussed or acknowledged that, at an earlier point, he had been a disciple of Heidegger. In 1928 he traveled to Freiburg to sit at the Master's feet. Two years later, he even wrote a habilitation study under Heidegger's supervision. If, today, the idea of "Heideggerian Marxism" has an oxymoronic ring, for the young Marcuse it represented a plausible solution to the "crisis of Marxism": the fact that, although objective conditions for radical social change seemed to be ripe, the subjective factor or "class consciousness" lagged seriously behind.

In 1933, Heidegger boarded the Nazi juggernaut. That same year, Marcuse joined the Frankfurt School. Thereafter, understandably, their paths rarely crossed. Still, their early alliance represents a fascinating chapter in the history of political ideas — a philosophical interlude that reveals much about the intellectual disposition of both men. In "What is Heideggerian Marxism?" I try to reconstruct a little known chapter in the Frankfurt School's prehistory: the short-lived alliance between Critical Theory and Heideggerian *Exisentenzphilosophie*.

To his credit, Marcuse was never one to rest content with half-measures. He possessed deep insight into the failings of advanced industrial society. His 1955 book, *Eros and Civilization*, speculated as to whether, beyond the "performance principle" of late capitalism, there might be a "libidinal" basis for socialism. Thereby he anticipated with uncanny foresight the Dionysian components of the 1960s "counterculture."

But Marcuse's attachment to revolutionary politics also had its costs. In his view the proletariat's integration within the parameters of the "affluent society" meant that late capitalism was becoming increasingly one-dimensional. Amid the omnipresent growth of a well-adjusted, "happy consciousness," prospects for critical contestation diminished significantly. If the revolutionary class, whose numbers were shrinking drastically in any event, was essentially content with its lot, who, then, would make the revolution?

In "Critical Reflections on Marcuse's Theory of Revolution," I examine the consequences of these developments for Marcuse's political thought. In a number of postwar texts, he openly flirted with the idea of "Educational Dictatorship" as a type of deus ex machina solution. In *What is to Be Done?* Lenin had employed similar reasoning. Since the proletariat was incapable of attaining class consciousness of its own accord, it must be imported from without — the job of a revolutionary avant-garde.

On the one hand, Marcuse was acutely aware of the distasteful historical consequences of the vanguard approach. But that did not prevent him from considering it on a number of occasions as a political option that could preserve the viability of revolutionary politics. As Part II of this book, "Exiting Revolution," attempts to show, today, as a result of bitter historical experience, we have lost confidence in the capacity of the revolutionary model to facilitate progressive social change.

In the annals of Critical Theory, Leo Lowenthal's contributions have been seriously underestimated. During the 1930s, he was managing editor of the *Zeitschrift für Sozialforschung*. Its success in soliciting and publishing pathbreaking articles in so many fields is in no small measure due to his foresight and supervision.

The Frankfurt School thinkers were, of course, scholars. But they also excelled in their capacity as critical intellectuals. In this respect, Lowenthal was an extraordinary figure: someone who had a remarkable ability to bring insights from his area of professional expertise, the sociology of literature, to bear on a wide array of contemporary issues and themes. In "The Lion in Winter: Leo Lowenthal and the Integrity of the Intellectual," I reflect on some of his more timely interventions.

Lowenthal's last project, begun when he was well into his eighties, concerned a critique of postmodernism — which, of course, during the 1980s had become a major academic trend. In Lowenthal's view, the radical "critique of reason" that the postmodernists embraced was all too reminiscent of dubious intellectual tendencies he had encountered firsthand during the Weimar Republic's waning years — e.g., *Lebensphilosophie*, whose proximity to fascist intellectual habitudes had been so disturbing. That Lowenthal continued to write and reflect on these themes until late in life exemplifies the ideal of critical intellectual vigilance.

Karl Jaspers was never especially close to the Frankfurt School. Yet, like the Critical Theorists, his philosophy matured during the cultural and political tumult of the interwar years. Trained in medicine, Jaspers was a relative latecomer to philosophy, although he quickly made up for lost time. Following Jacob Burckhardt, he was enamored of the *Bildung* ideal: the lionization of "great men" who establish a standard of cultural excellence for the rest of humanity to follow. But, following the hecatombs of the Great War, this ideal fell into crisis. Thereafter, *Existenzphilosophie*, as inspired by the writings of Kierkegaard and Nietzsche, came into fashion. Jaspers, along with Heidegger, became one of its leading exponents.

Like Heidegger, Jaspers mistrusted democracy. The Weimar Republic's ceaseless ideological turmoil only confirmed him in his well-established, illiberal views.

In 1931, Jaspers wrote a timely book of popular philosophy, *Man in the Modern Age*. Thematically, it stood in close proximity to Heidegger's *Being and Time*. Here, Jaspers' conservative revolutionary leanings — his ideological proximity to the likes of Schmitt, Spengler, and Ernst Jünger — are on full display. *Man in the Modern Age* concludes with a plea for an authoritarian resolution of liberal political "chaos." Two years later, Jaspers' wishes came to fruition in the demonic guise of Hitler. Although Jaspers held the Nazis in low esteem (in 1937, he lost his teaching position because of his Jewish wife), in 1933 he made an attempt to collaborate with the regime in the realm of educational policy. Fortunately, Jaspers' efforts in this regard ultimately came to naught, although the episode in question remains troubling and recasts his early philosophy in a less than charitable light. In "Karl Jaspers: The Paradoxes of Mandarin Humanism," I reassess his legacy with attention to the various positions he took preceding and following the Nazi seizure of power.

The concluding chapter of Part I, "Levinas and Heidegger: The Anxiety of Influence," examines the shock effect that Heidegger's 1933 conversion to Nazism had upon Levinas.

During the waning years of the Weimar Republic, Jaspers and Heidegger stood out as the "titans of existentialism." Although they and the Frankfurt School were miles apart politically, paradoxically, both parties went far toward internalizing the dominant motifs of Weimar-era cultural criticism: above all, a fear that "culture" and "civilization" were mutually exclusive concepts; that civilization's rise went hand-in-hand with cultural decline.

During the last fifteen years, among the partisans of continental philosophy, interest in Emmanuel Levinas's ethical thought has been short of remarkable. In part, the explanation for this phenomenon is simple. Prior eminences in the field, such as Heidegger and Derrida, scorned ethics as an atavism of the Western "metaphysics of subjectivity." However, in the aftermath of the Paul de Man controversy (de Man's exposure as an avid collaborator in Nazi-occupied Belgium), the problem of continental philosophy's ethical deficit could no longer be avoided. Levinas's "ethical foundationalism," based on an awe-inspiring reverence for the "face of the Other," materialized propitiously to fill the void.

During the late 1920s and early 1930s, Levinas was a devout Heideggerian. Yet, following Heidegger's embrace of National Socialism in 1933, Levinas was caught in a type of intellectual no-man's-land. It became very difficult to square his prior, unguarded enthusiasm for Heidegger's existentialism with the philosopher's totalitarian political allegiances. The problem was not simply that Heidegger had made an odious political choice. What was disconcerting was that the Freiburg sage quite explicitly justified that decision in terms of his own philosophy of existence. Although Heidegger's thought, which was formulated during the 1920s, contained few Nazi elements per se, it was nevertheless seriously compromised by the right-radical spirit of the age: a zealous rejection of democracy and basic rights, and a corresponding attraction to authoritarian political ideals. If one traces Levinas's development as a philosopher, one finds that his own Heideggerian ambivalences persisted until the very end.

III

Part II, "Exiting Revolution," focuses less on the history of ideas and more on issues bearing on contemporary politics. The fall of communism opened immense possibilities for political freedom. The September 11 attacks against New York and Washington D.C. may have closed them off. At present, the world seems to be once again polarized between two camps: supporters of fundamentalist Islam and the West. In addition, as a result of the United States' intemperate unilateralism, the North Atlantic Alliance has unraveled. The democratic coalition that, to its credit, defeated communism exists no more.

Although the handwriting was already on the wall at the time of Moscow's 1979 invasion of Afghanistan, Soviet economic stagnation made systemic change inevitable. Mikhail Gorbachev deserves credit for initiating communism's change of course — although at a later point he ceased to control its direction and pace.

In "What We Can Learn from the Revolutions of 1989," I assess communism's demise as a historical caesura. One of the remarkable aspects of these revolutions pertained to their "moral" nature. It was a moment of the dissident, or antihero, as hero. In November 1989, as the Berlin Wall was breached, the various state socialist authorities were, in essence, shamed into self-abdication. One by one they succumbed to the gentle pressure and moral suasion of so-called Velvet Revolutions. Remarkably, by now a new generation of youth has come of age with no memory of communist authoritarianism nor of cold war nuclear brinkmanship.

Communism was delegitimated in theory before it collapsed in reality. The 1960s generation was enamored of revolution. This was especially true in France where indigenous revolutionary traditions could be readily grafted upon the delusive hopes of "third worldism." But such expectations died amid the "killing fields" of Cambodia and the lamentations of the Vietnamese "boat people." The consequences of these developments were not lost among French intellectuals, who belatedly rallied around the cause of "dissidence." But if human rights were the order of the day, then the ideology of "antihumanism," as propounded by poststructuralism's "master thinkers" — Althusser, Derrida, Foucault, and Lacan — was obviously flawed. Today, historians are still trying to answer the question: how could such a talented group of thinkers have been so politically naïve?[3] In "From the 'Death of Man' to Human Rights: The Paradigm Change in French Intellectual Life, 1968–86," I attempt to reconstruct the political itinerary of this influential generation of French intellectuals.

Communism's fall offered new political opportunities. But it also presented new challenges — many of them economic. Revolutionary developments in communications offered the prospect of record-speed, global economic transactions. Throughout the world, governments pursued a hands-off policy vis-à-vis powerful new, transnational economic actors. Many French intellectuals understandably viewed these developments with horror. Since communism had been discredited as a viable option, and since the Socialist Party had openly abandoned socialism, where was one to turn for an antiglobalization political stopgap? For many, "Back to the Republic!" became the response du jour. In "The Republican Revival: Reflections on French Singularity," I examine the rationale and results of these developments.

Yet, the republican revival was beset by memory loss. It selectively recalled the Third Republic's triumphs — over royalism and Catholicism, for example — but conveniently overlooked its failings. Above all, republicanism relied on an assimilationist model of citizenship — the "immigrants into Frenchmen," one-size-fits-all approach — that was radically out of step with the requirements and demands of multiculturalism. Recently the world looked on in astonishment as France's Ministry of Education prevented Islamic girls from wearing headscarves (the foulard) but permitted indigenous French citizens to sport crosses. One of the key questions is whether the republican tradition can be adjusted to accommodate the demands of "difference."

One of globalization theory's analytical deficits is its economic bias. Unquestionably, trends related to the world economy's deregulation merit serious attention. By the same token, we also need to focus on the capacities of global civil society to offset the dislocations and hardships engendered by the free market.

In "What Is Global Democracy?" I seek to highlight globalization's political dimension. With Marxism's demise, democracy has attained a new legitimacy. To his credit, Frankfurt School heir Jürgen Habermas has been in the forefront of this discussion. In the *Postnational Constellation* and other works, Habermas suggests how popular sovereignty and basic rights might offset the "colonization of the lifeworld" by the impersonal forces of economic and administrative rationality. After years of productive struggle, the Left has grudgingly come to accept the inevitability of a regulated market economy. The choice is no longer, as it once seemed, between capitalism and socialism. Instead, everything, hinges on the construction of "capitalism with a human face." Only a vibrant democratic political culture has the capacity to ensure the accountability of managerial elites at the World Bank, the World Trade Organization, and elsewhere, who nowadays have so much influence over the wealth of nations. The present-day renaissance of democratic theory corresponds to the "realism" of an era that has, understandably, wearied of the false promises of political messianism.

In "Religion and Public Reason: A Contemporary Debate," I examine an important societal trend: the religious revival underway both in the third world (e.g., "political Islam") and the United States. For years secularization theorists have been prophesying religion's imminent demise. But the modern age has not brought an end to life's insecurities — far from it. Thus, in many parts of the world the need for religious consolation, as a cushion against fate's injustices, remains as strong as ever. In fact, one might go so far as to agree with sociologist Peter Berger, who, gainsaying Max Weber, contends we are experiencing a "resacralization of the world."

Religion's return raises important questions for democratic theory. What role should religion play in secular polities? For many persons, religion remains the fount of their most deeply held convictions. To extrude such perspectives from public debate would be both unrealistic and unjust. Instead, a delicate balancing act is required. One must permit the expression of religious conviction within the public sphere, while ensuring one does not offend citizens who pray to a different god — or gods. Taking the "perspective of the other" must work both ways. Not only must those who are religiously inclined understand the importance of secularism; secularists must also learn to understand and tolerate the convictions of believers.[4] In sum, one must make room for religion in a way that is consistent with the values of tolerance and fairness. John Rawls' political philosophy, which distinguishes between reasonable and unreasonable "comprehensive views" or ultimate belief systems, makes an important stride in this direction.

In "What is Left Schmittianism?" I examine left-wing intellectuals' growing fascination with the controversial doctrines of the German jurist Carl Schmitt (1888–1985). The Left has never been impervious to the lures of political sectarianism. Nor has it, in times of uncertainty, avoided assimilating ideas from the political right. One question that arises is: how much might the left borrow from the right while continuing to remain "left"?

Schmitt famously glorified the "state of emergency" and notoriously defined politics as the capacity to distinguish friends from enemies. In a post-9/11 world, Schmitt's partisans feel themselves confirmed. For, doesn't America's aggressive, lone-wolf foreign policy confirm Schmitt's cynical view that international law merely provides ideological cover for states to realize their selfish interests? Historically, the left has always had an ambiguous relationship to parliamentarism and "rule of law," two of Schmitt's bêtes noires. The depradations of globalization have made the left skeptical about rule of law, which at times seems like little more than window dressing for the great powers' own selfish designs. Hence, why not in fact borrow criticisms of these institutions from Schmitt, their foremost twentieth-century detractor? The problem is that once the Left embraces the Schmittian doctrine of politics as an *amoral sphere* — the idea that politics is a question of ruthlessly realizing one's ends regardless of the means that are employed — it invites all manner of political licentiousness. From a normative perspective, left-wing dictatorships are in no way superior to dictatorships of the Right.

The events of September 11, 2001, altered world politics in ways that many of us are still actively trying to fathom. The Bush administration seized on the attacks as a pretext to formulate an unprecedented, risky, and open-ended foreign policy doctrine of "preventative war." Yet, its main foe, Saddam Hussein, had nothing to do with Al Qaeda, nor with fundamentalist Islam. Certainly, he was a brutal tyrant who deserved to be removed from power. But doing the right thing for the wrong reasons establishes a dangerous precedent.

Jürgen Habermas, who was Adorno's former assistant in Frankfurt am Main, is widely acknowledged as the rightful inheritor of the Frankfurt School's intellectual legacy. He responded to the September 11 events via a number of timely opinion pieces, as well as a lengthy interview that was published, along with a text by Jacques Derrida, in *Philosophy in a Time of Terror*. What concerned Habermas above all was the fact that American foreign policy proceeded in flagrant disregard of established norms of international governance. Whereas during the 1990s, following communism's collapse and the end of the cold war stalemate, a renewed confidence in international law as a method of dispute resolution began to emerge, America's post-9/11 unilateralism altered the situation radically. In "Kant at Ground Zero: Philosophers Respond to September 11," I review philosophical responses to the attacks, focusing on the Habermas-Derrida dialogue in particular.

* * *

Marxism's demise, as well as social democracy's "neoliberal" turn, has thrown the Left into an identity crisis. In times of doubt, it is tempting to grasp at sectarian solutions — to abandon prospects for incremental betterment and flirt with the all-or-nothing mentality of political messianism. The contemporary vogue of the "theological turn" ("negative theology," "religion without God," "God without Being") — apparently, postmodernism's ideology of last resort — attests to this situation. Who would have believed that Derrida, who spent the better part of three decades denouncing the lures of "onto-theology," would in the end openly profess deconstruction's commitment to "the Messianic"?[5] Yet for the Left to buy into this vogue would be to succumb to a serious judgmental and strategic error. It would mean leaving the field of contemporary political contestation open to the Right.

By the same token, it is important for the Left not to employ the Frankfurt School's "negative" philosophy of history — one that, contra Hegel and Marx, stresses the inevitability of decline instead of progress — to adorn its own misery cum marginalization. After all, these views were formulated at the twentieth-century's political and moral nadir. Since then, humanity has undergone a difficult and hard-won learning process. A tenuous consensus, codified by precepts of international humanitarian law, has formed against dictatorship and in favor of the values of democratic citizenship. Much of this consensus is reflected by recent developments in global civil society and democratic theory. Here, the contributions of Habermas, the rightful heir to the Frankfurt School legacy, have served as an important bellwether. Any attempt to build constructively on the Critical Theory tradition must take into account the moderately encouraging political and social changes that have ensued since the first generation's demise. Adorno's view of late capitalism as a "totally administered world" is theoretically tempting and seductive. But, in the end, it stands too close to the antidemocratic ethos of those right-wing *Zivilisationskritiker* (critics of civilization) to whom he and his cohorts were nominally so opposed: figures like Spengler, Heidegger, and Carl Schmitt. Critical Theory's precepts should not be turned into a new dogma or treated as articles of faith. The best way to remain faithful to the Frankfurt School legacy is not to follow it mechanically or unreflectively.

Part I
The Frankfurt School Revisited

1

Between Proust and the *Zohar*: Walter Benjamin's *Arcades Project*

What the child (and, through faint reminiscence, the man) discovers in the pleats of the old material to which it clings while trailing at its mother's skirts — that's what these pages should contain.

Walter Benjamin, describing his intentions for the
Arcades Project during the 1930s

To great writers, finished works weigh lighter than those fragments on which they work throughout their lives.

Benjamin, *One-Way Street* (1928)

The Perils of Montage

For years an aura of mystery has surrounded Benjamin's *Arcades Project*, the chef d'oeuvre on which he labored fitfully during the last thirteen years of his life, from 1927 to 1940. His letters of the period furtively allude to a projected magnum opus that aimed at expounding a novel "materialist philosophy of history," a "primal history of the nineteenth century." Yet, precisely what Benjamin intended by these pithy, elusive descriptions has been the source of enormous speculation and controversy.

That the work survived at all is something of a miracle. With the fall of France in 1940, Benjamin, fleeing the rapidly advancing *Wehrmacht* and fearing the worst, hastily entrusted his precious manuscripts to his friend Georges Bataille, who concealed them in the bowels of the Bibliothèque Nationale. A few months later, Benjamin met with an untimely end, taking his own life on the Franco–Spanish frontier rather than fall into the hands of the pro-Nazi Vichy authorities. After the war another French acquaintance, Pierre Missac, following Benjamin's wishes, contacted Theodor Adorno with the information that Benjamin's manuscripts had indeed survived. Adorno, who had been devastated by his friend's death, could barely conceal his exhilaration: "The decisive theoretical sketches for the *Arcades Project*," he wrote to Missac in 1946, "go back to a relatively early date: Benjamin read the first important excerpts aloud to me in Königstein [outside of Frankfurt] in 1928. Among these excerpts was a metaphysical theory of the gambler. These things were doubtlessly among the most ingenious Benjamin ever wrote; it would be extremely important for me to know precisely how much has been saved." And in uncanny anticipation of the enormous philological difficulties Benjamin's thick packet of notes would incite, he went on to remark: "Everything depends on whether the material in your possession consists in large part of theoretical formulations and sketches, or whether it mostly contains excerpted citations that may have had theoretical significance for Benjamin, yet which would, even for me, remain *uninterpretable*."[1]

Three years later, Adorno had come to a preliminary conclusion about the nature of the materials in his possession, and the verdict did not bode well. In a detailed letter to Gershom Scholem, he expressed the fear that his deep-seated methodological reservations concerning the *Arcades Project* had been borne out. Benjamin had long flirted with an experimental method of composition he referred to as the "dialectical image."[2] Under the influence of montage techniques that had been used with such success during the 1920s by both surrealists and *cinéastes*, Benjamin had turned away from the idea of laborious theoretical exposition, preferring instead an uncommented construction of so-called material elements. These "material elements" consisted of either citations or stark empirical observations. When the method was successful — as, for example, in his brilliant, surrealist-inspired collection of aphorisms, *One-Way Street* — the results were magisterial. As a stylist and social critic, Benjamin, when he was on his game, was a nonpareil. However, when this antitheoretical bent was carried to an extreme, the final result could prove infuriating: contra Benjamin's own pantheistic expectations — he was prone to reading both nature and society as inspired palimpsests or "texts" (as he remarks in the *Arcades Project*, "The expression

'the book of nature' indicates that one can read the real like a text";
PW, 574) — the types of empirical observations he had in mind were
rarely self-explanatory.

Upon receiving the manuscript for which his hopes had been
so keen, Adorno believed that his worst fears had been confirmed.
In essence, the "manuscript" for the *Arcades Project* consisted of
Benjamin's working notebooks. It contained thousands of fascinating and suggestive citations culled from predominantly French
sources Benjamin had consulted during years of painstaking research
at the Bibliothèque Nationale. Yet, the theoretical "glue" that would
allow the *membra disjecta* of the *Arcades* to cohere into a meaningful whole seemed all but absent. Adorno articulated these
concerns as follows:

At the beginning of the previous year [1948] I finally received the
arcades material that had been hidden in the Bibliothèque
Nationale. Last summer I worked through the material exhaus-
tively, and problems arose that I must discuss with you. The most
difficult aspect is the *extraordinary inattention to theoretically
formulated ideas as opposed to the enormous store of excerpts.* That
may in part be explained from the idea that was explicitly expressed
on one occasion (and which to me is problematical) that the work
should be merely "assembled" [*montieren*]; that is, compiled from
citations, such that the theory leaps forth without one having to
append it as interpretation. Were that to have been possible, only
Benjamin himself would have been able to accomplish it; whereas I
have always been faithful to the standpoint of the Hegelian
Phenomenology of Spirit, according to which the movement of the
concept, of the matter itself, is coincident with the explicit thought
process of the reflecting subject. Only the authority of sacred texts
would stand as a refutation of this conception, and the *Arcades
Project* has avoided precisely this idea. If one takes, as I would like,
the montage idea not entirely *à la lettre*, it might have easily turned
out that Benjamin's ideas could have been formed from countless
citations (PW, 1072)

One can well imagine Adorno's heart sinking when he came across the
following bold declaration of intent in *Arcades* Convolute (file) N, "On
the Theory of Knowledge, Theory of Progress": "Method of this
project: literary montage. I needn't *say* anything. Merely show. I will
purloin no valuables, appropriate no ingenious formulations. But the
rags, the refuse — these I will not inventory but allow, in the only way
possible, to come into their own: by making use of them" (574).

Yet, in one sense Adorno was wrong: it does not seem that Benjamin, whatever his methodological eccentricities, seriously contemplated fashioning the *Arcades Project* from a montage of citations. At the same time, the interpretive misgivings Adorno expresses in the remarks just cited remain legitimate and troubling. In the *Arcades Project* one encounters the occasional, characteristically brilliant *aperçu*; yet the contours and proportions of the finished whole remain to this day an object of conjecture. In their foreword to the English edition, translators Howard Eiland and Kevin McLaughlin — whose prodigious labors merit unstinting gratitude and admiration — implicitly take a stand against Adorno's theoretical skepticism. Instead, they perceive a positive "compositional principle at work," the aforementioned precept of montage. Correspondingly, they proceed to compare the *Arcades Project* with kindred works from the same period such as *One-Way Street* and *A Berlin Childhood Around Nineteen-Hundred*. "What is distinctive about *The Arcades Project*," they suggest, "is the working of quotations within the framework of montage, so much so that they eventually far outnumber the commentaries."). Though the translators' *bona fides* are certainly above suspicion, here they have attempted, rather transparently, to make a virtue out of a necessity — thereby following the precedent of Benjamin's German publisher, Suhrkamp Verlag, which wishfully sought to compare the *Arcades Project* with Friedrich Schlegel's *Philosophical Fragments* and Nietzsche's *Will to Power*.

The problem is that, in contrast to the two aforementioned Benjamin volumes, in which the montage principle is consummately employed, with the *Arcades Project* the citations remain entirely *unintegrated*: try as one might, one searches in vain for an organizing principle or guiding precept. As Susan Buck-Morss has observed in her exhaustive survey of the *Arcades Project*, *The Dialectics of Seeing*, the 900 pages of fragments, organized into 36 "Convolutes," provide "insufficient evidence as to the overall conception that guided Benjamin's research." In sum, "the *Passagen-Werk* itself *does not exist*."[3]

Of course, the preceding remarks stand in need of qualification. Existence or nonexistence can often be a matter of degree. To declare that the *Arcades Project* is neither a book nor a meaningful arrangement of fragments begs the question of precisely *what it is*, or what Benjamin intended it to be. But an additional obstacle to reaching an understanding concerning the nature of the *Arcades Project* lies in the fact that Benjamin's own conception underwent a number of crucial transformations. Buffeted about the continent during the "low, dishonest decade" prior to the European catastrophe, his methodological conception for the *Arcades Project* seemed to alter in accordance with his own changing existential and political fortunes.

"The Primacy of Politics"

Benjamin described the *Arcades Project* as "the theater of all my struggles and all my ideas." As he once wrote to Scholem: work on the *Arcades* begins to "howl ... in my nights in the manner of a small beast if I do not take it to drink at the most distant sources."[4] The question arises: why was it that Benjamin elected to endow the "material culture" of nineteenth-century Paris — railroads, panoramas, barricades, exhibitions, city streets, gas lighting, the stock exchange, and so forth — with such world-historical import and meaning? Moreover, what relevance would his peculiar obsession with a quaint, yet antiquated nineteenth-century building form — the arcades — have for the momentous political struggles of the Popular Front era, with which Benjamin was so concerned during this period of his life? After all, Benjamin viewed the *Arcades* primarily as a political intervention. Speaking of his intentions for the *Arcades*, he observes: "The Copernican revolution in historical perception is as follows ... *Politics* attains primacy over *history*" (PW, 490–91). Benjamin was not attempting to recoup the past for its own sake, but as a part of an ongoing discourse of progressive social and cultural contestation. A few years earlier in *One-Way Street*, he felicitously characterized his new identity as a writer and critic as a "strategist in the literary struggle."[5]

A quick glance at the headings for the various files simultaneously piques one's curiosity and adds to the confusion. On the one hand, there are the "methodological" Convolutes in which Benjamin reflects on his various theoretical objectives. These files are concerned with the writings of Fourier, Baudelaire, Proust, Marx, C. J. Jung, and the surrealists, all of whom provided major sources of conceptual inspiration. However, the most important methodological file is clearly Convolute "N," "Theory of Knowledge, Theory of Progress." There, Benjamin discusses the cryptic relationship between "dreaming" and "awakening," underlines the importance of the visual or "imagistic" component of the project, and, with disarming frankness, concedes the epistemological centrality of "theology" to its overall success. An examination of Convolute "N" makes it clear that Benjamin was pursuing above all *a utopian-eschatological revitalization of Marxism*. In Benjamin's view, insofar as orthodox Marxism had itself succumbed to a host of economic and scientific prejudices (rendering Marxism itself "bourgeois," as it were), only a massive infusion of utopian and aesthetic concepts could redeem it from its current state of advanced senescence.

The following musings from Convolute "N" are representative of Benjamin's theoretical concerns, as well as of his patented technique of philosophical "micrology" — the art of discerning the major tendencies of an epoch from its apparently most trivial phenomenal manifestations. As Benjamin puts it: "In what way is it possible to conjoin a heightened 'graphicness' [*Anschaulichkeit*] to the realization of the Marxist method? The first stage in this undertaking will be to carry over the principle of montage into history. That is, to assemble large-scale constructions out of *the smallest and most precisely cut components*. Indeed, to discover in the analysis of the small individual moment *the crystal of the total event*" (PW, 575).

Yet the bulk of the *Arcades* Convolutes contain the so-called material elements for Benjamin's study — citations and empirical observations pertaining to the material culture of nineteenth-century Paris. These meticulously culled passages embody the aforementioned "smallest and most precisely cut components," which, through the technique of montage, would ultimately coalesce to form the *Arcades Project* itself. A partial list of the file names provides a good idea of Benjamin's thematic preoccupations: "Arcades"; "Fashion"; "Exhibitions"; "The Interior"; "Haussmannization"; "Dream City and Dream House, Dreams of the Future"; "The Flaneur"; "Prostitution, Gambling"; "Panorama"; "Photography."

In these files Benjamin was at pains to establish a meaningful correlation between the phenomenal manifestations of nineteenth-century Parisian life and the economic sphere — or, bluntly put, "capital." Thereby, he wished to amplify a fundamental Marxian insight: industrial capitalism heralded an age of leisure and abundance; yet, this utopian potential remained distorted and repressed owing to retrograde "relations of production" — the injustices of "class society." This is one of the reasons that Benjamin took the writings of the utopian socialists — Charles Fourier, Robert Owen, Saint-Simon — so seriously. He believed that their doctrines contained, quite literally, "wish images" (*Wunschbilder*) and "dream fantasies" (*Traumphantasien*) of a future classless society. To its detriment, orthodox Marxism — which, under Stalin, had congealed into a "science of domination" — trivialized these thinkers as "merely" utopian.

Aware of the pitfalls of "vulgar Marxism," Benjamin was also at pains to avoid a deterministic reading of nineteenth-century material culture — that is, an interpretation that linked culture too directly with economic developments. One of his keys to avoiding this standard Marxist trap was the category of "expression" (*Ausdruck*). As he remarks in the *Arcades Project*: "On the doctrine of the ideological superstructure: ... if the infrastructure in a certain way determines the superstructure, but if such determination is not reducible to simple *reflection*, how is it then ... to be characterized? As its *expression*. The superstructure is the expression of the infrastructure." But, as we shall see, in practice Benjamin's efforts were often indistinguishable from the vulgar Marxism he otherwise scorned.

A few illustrations culled from the "material" (as opposed to "methodological") Convolutes will help to exemplify what Benjamin had in mind. In the Convolute on the "Arcades," for example, Benjamin observes: "People associated the 'genius of the Jacobins with the genius of the industrials,' but they also attributed to Louis-Philippe the saying: 'God be praised, and my shops too.' The arcades as temples of commodity capital." In this way, Benjamin sought to highlight the fact that the "use-value" of the arcades, as a potential locus of material plenty, has been vitiated by considerations of "exchange value" or profit maximization. A few pages later, he appended a related insight that was also meant to illustrate the destructive predominance of the commodity form: "[Siegfried] Giedion shows (*Building in France*, p. 35) how the axiom, 'Welcome the crowd and keep it seduced,' leads to corrupt architectural practices in the construction of the department store Au Printemps (1881–1889). *Function of commodity capital!*"

In the course of his discussion of "Prostitution and Gambling" (Convolute "O"), Benjamin proffers a number of analogous observations. In his view, the dramatic upsurge in prostitution during the Second Empire derives from the way that, under capitalism, "love" had been systematically reduced to a commodity: "Regarding the influence of fashion on erotic life, a telling observation by Eduard Fuchs: 'Women of the Second Empire' do not say, 'I love him,' but rather, 'I fancy him' — *J'ai un caprice pour lui.*" And, a few pages later, more pithily and directly: "Love for the prostitute is the apotheosis of empathy with the commodity."

The proliferation of gambling during Louis Philippe's reign moves Benjamin (somewhat predictably) to stress a similar set of themes. For Benjamin, gambling was illustrative — both literally and metaphorically — of the degradation of experience in modern commodity culture. To demonstrate this point, he cites the following observations by the French philosopher Alain:

The basic principle ... of gambling ... consists in this: ... that each round is independent of the one preceding .... Gambling strenuously denies all acquired conditions, all antecedents ... pointing to previous actions; and that is what distinguishes it from work. Gambling rejects ... this weighty past which is the mainstay of work, and which makes for seriousness of purpose, for attention to the long term, for right, and for power.

Gambling is thus merely another instance of industrial capitalism's tendency to supplant qualitative with quantitative experience, a point that was driven home in Georg Simmel's magisterial 1900 opus *The Philosophy of Money* — a work that bears rereading a century later. For Benjamin, gambling possessed a certain paradigmatic status and import. With games of chance, experience and tradition count for nil. Accumulated "wisdom" — today, an antiquated word — is useless and pointless. With every roll of the dice, the gambler must begin anew. Thus, for Benjamin, gambling becomes a parable of a more general disintegration of experience — as well as of the capacity to "have experiences" — under modern capitalism. Wage labor (and, ultimately, assembly-line production) replaces craftsmanship; art becomes a commodity or "kitsch"; and "information," as purveyed by journalists, supplants the art of storytelling.

As becomes clear from the preceding examples, the immediate correlations between culture and economics that Benjamin sought to avoid in fact came back to haunt his analyses, with a vengeance, on numerous occasions. The concept of "expression" (*Ausdruck*) he had developed failed to ensure that the mediations between "superstructure" and "base" were sufficiently subtle and complex. Instead, too often, the citations or "material elements" of the *Arcades*, which predominate, serve as knee-jerk exemplifications of preconceived economic concepts. It was this practice, moreover, that wholly alienated Adorno from Benjamin's most substantial draft for the *Arcades Project*, "Paris of the Second Empire in Baudelaire." "Unless I am very much mistaken," comments Adorno,

> your dialectic lacks one thing: *mediation*. Throughout your text there is a tendency to relate the pragmatic contents of Baudelaire's work directly to adjacent features in the social history of his time, preferably economic features. I have in mind the passage about the duty on wine, certain statements about the barricades, or the ... passage about the arcades, which I find particularly problematic .... I regard it as methodologically unfortunate to give conspicuous individual features from the realm of the superstructure a "materialistic" turn by relating them immediately and perhaps even causally to corresponding features of the infrastructure. Materialist determination of cultural traits is only possible if it is mediated through the *total social process*.[6]

By relying on a "wide-eyed presentation of facts," concludes Adorno, Benjamin risked depriving the phenomena of their "real historico-philosophical weight." "If one wished to put it very drastically, one could say that your study is located at the crossroads of magic and positivism. That spot is bewitched. Only theory could break the spell."[7]

"Human Aquaria"

In a 1935 letter to Adorno, Benjamin reflected on the genesis of the *Arcades Project*: "There stands [Louis] Aragon at the very beginning — *Le Paysan de Paris*, of which I could never read more than two or three pages in bed at night before my heart started to beat so strongly that I had to lay the book aside. What a warning! .... And yet my first sketches for the Arcades date from that time."[8] In vintage surrealist fashion, Aragon had transformed Paris into a locus of magical occurrences and chance encounters; with its topographical allure, the city itself became one of the novel's main personae. Inanimate locations assumed an enchanted precedence over the novel's somnambulant human characters. Moreover, the first half of the novel takes place in an arcade that was slated for demolition (a fact that is crucial, given Benjamin's preoccupation with "ruins"), the *passage de l'opéra*. "Our cities are populated with unrecognized sphinxes," declares Aragon, "who will not stop the passing dreamer to ask him life and death questions unless he directs his distracted meditations toward them." Among these "sphinxes," continues Aragon, are the *passages* or arcades: "human aquaria, already stripped of their original life, [that] merit consideration as *repositories of modern myths*."[9]

Following the rejection of his postdoctoral study, *The Origin of German Tragic Drama*, Benjamin announced he was abandoning his interest in German studies. It was the French literary avant-garde that now captured his imagination. As he put it in a 1927 letter: "whereas in Germany I feel entirely isolated among the men of my generation, there are isolated presences in France — especially Aragon and the surrealist movement — in which I see things at work that concern me."[10] Given Benjamin's new political orientation — inspired by a reading of Georg Lukács's *History and Class Consciousness*, he had recently declared his interest in "radical communism" — as well as his fascination with cultural modernism, this change of intellectual focus made perfect sense.

Aragon's celebration of the arcades and astute surrealist eye for the stuff of "modern myth" provided the catalyst for Benjamin's decision to produce a work on the Paris arcades. Its leitmotif would be "the primal history of the nineteenth century," which really meant: the nineteenth century as "primal history." Benjamin was concerned not with the reemergence of "prehistoric elements" in the modern period. Instead he sought to highlight the way that modern commodity culture assumed a mythological — or, as he sometimes called it, "phantasmagorical" — cast, mesmerizing the masses into a trancelike stupor that effectively sapped their will to revolt. As Benjamin observes in Convolute "K" of the *Arcades* ("Dream City and Dream House, Dreams of the Future"):

"Capitalism was a natural phenomenon with which a new dream-filled sleep came over Europe, and, through it, a *reactivation of mythic forces*" (PW, 494). History's regression to a rigid and lifeless "natural history" or "myth" — a conception Benjamin had first developed in his book on German tragic drama — thus became one of the *Arcades Project*'s central themes. From this perspective, the arcades themselves, which primarily stocked luxury items and anticipated the modern department store, embodied for him the apotheosis of consumerist divertissement or socially engendered "false consciousness." They signified, as he felicitously puts it in one of his early notes, a "primordial landscape of consumption" (PW, 994). "Architecture as the most important testimony to latent mythology," remarks Benjamin in the "First Sketches" for the *Arcades* circa the late 1920s. "And the most important architecture of the nineteenth century is the arcades" (PW, 998).

With the *Arcades Project* Benjamin attempted to combine André Breton and Karl Marx. Sifting through Marx's juvenilia, he discovered an aside in an 1843 letter that suggested telling elective affinities between Marxism and the surrealist celebration of dream experience. "The world has long been dreaming of something which it can acquire if it becomes conscious of it," observes Marx.[11] The dialectical interrelationship between these two states, dreaming and awakening, would become the *Arcades Project*'s methodological signature. As Benjamin would declare in a revealing passage: "The utilization of dream elements upon awaking is the canon of dialectics" (PW, 580).

Marx had brilliantly described capitalism's mythological, phantasmagorical side in his discussion of "commodity fetishism." Commodity production engendered an inverted world in which "things," qua commodities, functioned as the prime movers; men and women were, conversely, degraded to personifications of economic categories — as in the Orwellian phrase, so popular among managerial types, "human capital." Whereas a commodity, observes Marx in *Capital* I, initially appears as "a very trivial thing [that] is easily understood," upon closer scrutiny, it abounds in "theological subtleties and metaphysical niceties." For under conditions of advanced capitalism, in which commodity production is the rule, "the relation of the producers to the product of their labor is presented to them as a social relation, existing not between themselves, but between the products of their labor .... There it is a definite relation between men, that assumes, in their eyes, *the fantastic form of a relation between things*."[12]

In the passages just cited, Marx propounded the classical definition of "reification" (literally: to turn into a thing), which would become one of the guiding concepts for the Frankfurt School. During the 1930s

Benjamin would publish many of his key studies in its journal, the *Zeitschrift für Sozialforschung.* The Frankfurt School in turn supported him financially throughout his difficult years of exile. Both Benjamin and the Frankfurt School were "cultural Marxists," a description that is less problematic than it may appear on first view. Orthodox Marxism, with which Benjamin shared few affinities, understood itself as an empirical science based on economics. Following World War I, it succumbed to a crisis: although all the "objective" conditions for revolutionary change seemed to be present, revolution itself succeeded only in backward Russia — a far cry from the scenario Marx had envisioned. In order to better understand the nonrevolutionary nature of the European proletariat, the Frankfurt School elected to focus on the so-called subjective factor or the "reification of consciousness." For thinkers like Max Horkheimer, Adorno, and Benjamin, it was the blandishments of bourgeois culture — phenomena that fell beneath the radar scope of Marxism qua economic science — that had seduced the masses into passively accepting their condition of voluntary narcosis. The "unhappy consciousness" of the nineteenth-century industrial proletariat had been supplanted by the "happy consciousness" of twentieth-century consumer society.

Benjamin's attempt to marry Marx and Breton was far from unproblematical. Moreover, his own attitudes toward both legacies were characterized by extreme ambivalence. For Benjamin, who once declared the worthlessness of "any theory that cannot deduce the nature of the absolute from reading coffee grounds" (!), the temperamental abyss separating him from the reigning variants of Marxist orthodoxy remained profound.[13] During the late 1920s he was keenly interested in progressive developments among the Soviet cultural avant-garde film, theater, and experiments in proletarian literature. Yet, in many ways the *Arcades Project* sought, through the intermediary of surrealism, to reinvent Marxist philosophy in toto. Given its current deficiencies, in his eyes nothing less than a wholesale transfiguration would do. Little wonder, then, that his thought during this period found so few echoes among fellow leftists.

Benjamin also harbored strong political and theoretical misgivings vis-à-vis surrealism. His political reservations had already surfaced in his 1929 "Surrealism" essay, whose centrality for the *Arcades Project* would be difficult to exaggerate. (Benjamin once aptly described it as a "prolegomenon to the *Arcades Project.*")[14] One of the reasons Benjamin was attracted to surrealism pertained to its efforts to surmount the illusions of bourgeois aestheticism, or art for art's sake. Surrealism had sought, in the manner of earlier avant-gardes, to merge art with everyday life. "The writings of this circle are not literature," Benjamin proclaimed approvingly, "but something else: demonstrations, watchwords, documents, bluffs, forgeries." "*To win the powers of intoxication for the revolution* — this is the project around which surrealism circles in all its books and enterprises."[15] This characterization is important, for it shows how, for Benjamin, the meaning of "revolution" (and, ultimately, of the *Arcades Project* itself) was inextricably bound to the notion of "experience" (*Erfahrung*), which, since his youth, had been one of the defining terms of his philosophical lexicon. In his estimation, after the revolution, everyday life would consist of a series of "profane illuminations" — at which point, one could throw away the hash pipe, as it were (following Baudelaire's fascination with "artificial paradise," Benjamin experimented with hashish and mescaline, and kept a detailed record of his experiences). Yet Benjamin feared — and in this surmise he was correct — that surrealism remained enmeshed in the ethereal reaches of bourgeois aestheticism. Ultimately, it would prove unable to accommodate itself to what he somewhat ominously described as the "constructive, dictatorial side of revolution."

The "theoretical" disagreement between Benjamin and the surrealists concerned the status of "modern mythology." Whereas surrealism tended to venerate the phantasmagoria of modern life for its own sake, Benjamin's attitude was more ambivalent and "dialectical": in his view the cultural superstructure of late capitalism served up riddles and enigmas that could become fruitful only once they had been critically decoded. Only upon decipherment could their latent utopian potential be redeemed. Such demystification was the task of "materialist criticism," as Benjamin understood it. In his view the surrealists remained overly satisfied with the enchanted veneer of modern life, failing to penetrate to the level of essence, or "disenchantment." As he observes in the *Arcades Project*: "whereas Aragon persists within the realm of the dream, here the concern is to find the constellation of *awakening*. While in Aragon there remains an impressionistic element ... here it is a question of the *dissolution of mythology into the space of history*" (PW, 571).

In addition to the surrealists, Benjamin found two additional literary sources of inspiration for the *Arcades Project*. The first was Proust, portions of whose *A La Recherche du temps perdu* Benjamin had translated into German during the early 1920s. Proust's theory of remembrance provided Benjamin with a powerful model for the redemption of past experience, albeit, in individual rather than collective terms (the *Arcades Project*, of course, focused primarily on the problem of *collective experience*). Benjamin had employed Proust's doctrines to marvelous effect in his inspired collection of childhood reminiscences and reflections, *A Berlin Childhood Around 1900*. In Proust, Benjamin thought he had discovered a kindred spirit: someone who, starting from the most seemingly trivial everyday circumstances and events, could, through the magic of remembrance, approximate a state of happiness or fulfillment — *temps vécu*. In notes for the *Arcades Project* Benjamin underlines the relationship between Proust's theory of memory and his own utopian historiographical intentions. To begin with, observes Benjamn, "facts [are] something that just now happened to us, first struck us; to establish them is the affair of memory." "Awakening," he continues, "is the great exemplar of memory: the occasion on which it is given us to remember what is closest, tritest, most obvious. What Proust intends with the experimental rearrangement of furniture in matinal half slumber, what [Ernst] Bloch recognizes as the 'darkness of the lived moment,' is nothing other than what here is to be secured on the level of the historical, and collectively" (PW, 491).

Yet, of even greater moment than Proust was the influence of Baudelaire, whom Benjamin lionized as "a lyric poet in the era of high capitalism." As a consummate allegorist of the modern metropolis, Baudelaire, like the surrealists, was able to transform scenes of urban dilapidation into the stuff of inspired reverie. By imaginatively transfiguring the commonplaces of daily life — its detritus and vagabonds — he was able to redeem modernity's tantalizing, yet jealously guarded, *promesse de bonheur*. The oblique relationship between destitution and the sublime that so preoccupied Baudelaire also represented one of Benjamin's foremost obsessions. Whereas the "mythologist" remained ensnared by modernity qua phantasmagoria, as allegorist, Baudelaire was able to surmount the immediacy of bourgeois decay in the direction of transcendent images and visions. As Benjamin observes in "Paris, Capital of the Nineteenth Century":

> Baudelaire's genius, which drew its nourishment from melancholy, was an allegorical one. With Baudelaire, Paris for the first time became the subject of lyrical poetry. This poetry is no local folklore; the allegorist's gaze which falls upon the city is rather the gaze of alienated man. It is the gaze of the *flaneur*, whose way of living still bestowed a conciliatory gleam over the growing destitution of men in the great city.

In "The Painter of Modern Life," Baudelaire stressed that the modernist's task must be "to extract from fashion whatever element it may contain of poetry within history, to distill the eternal from the transitory" — a statement that in great measure corresponded to Benjamin's agenda for the *Arcades Project*. One indication of Baudelaire's importance for the *Arcades Project* is the fact that the Convolute devoted to him is by far the largest: whereas Benjamin allocated 180 pages to Baudelaire, a mere thirty or so are concerned with Marx. In the late 1930s, Benjamin seriously considered devoting a separate monograph to Baudelaire. The drafts for this study, "Paris of the Second Empire in Baudelaire" (published separately in the volume *Charles Baudelaire: A Lyric Poet in the Era of High Capitalism*) are probably the best example of what the *Arcades Project*, had it ever been consummated, may have looked like.

"A Dialectical Fairy Tale"

Throughout the 1920s and 1930s Adorno represented a type of privileged interlocutor for the *Arcades Project*. Born in 1903, he was Benjamin's junior by nine years. The two first met in Frankfurt in the early 1920s. The younger man, destined to become one of the major philosophers of postwar Germany — his *Negative Dialectics* and *Aesthetic Theory* remain unsurpassed models of German philosophical prose — was quick to recognize Benjamin's mercurial brilliance. Several years after Benjamin's 1925 postdoctoral study had been summarily rejected by the Frankfurt University philosophy faculty (with one uncomprehending professor remarking that he "hadn't understood a word of it"), Adorno, as a young *Privatdozent*, sought to avenge his friend's ill treatment by offering a seminar on the *Trauerspiel* book over the course of not one but two semesters.

But the experience that solidified their bond was a 1928 meeting in Frankfurt, where, in the company of Max Horkheimer, the Latvian director Asja Lacis, and Gretel Karplus (Adorno's future wife), Benjamin read aloud excerpts from the early drafts for the *Arcades Project*, which at the time bore the fanciful subtitle: "A Dialectical Fairy Tale." The notes Benjamin read on that occasion sketched the conceptual foundations of the *Arcades*: the kinship between "modernity" and "myth"; the image of the nineteenth century as "hell"; and, most important, Benjamin's provocative reflections on the relationship between "dreaming" and "awakening" that would become the theoretical cornerstone of the *Arcades Project* in its later form. Yet, as Benjamin would remark to Adorno seven years later in a pivotal epistolary reassessment, this early conception displayed a number of telling methodological deficiencies: it betrayed an overly "rhapsodic character," as indicated by the enchanted subtitle; and it was guilty of employing an "archaic form of philosophizing naively caught up in nature" (PW, 1117). According to Benjamin, their "historic" 1928 meeting changed all that: "There would henceforth be no more rhapsodic naiveté," he confidently declared. Instead, Adorno's sober counsel, which urged a more historical focus, motivated Benjamin to propel "the entire conceptual mass of this material ... towards a final shape in which the world of dialectical images is immune to all objections that can be raised by metaphysics" (PW, 1118). At Adorno's urging, the project would abandon its original mythological cast and evolve into a genuinely materialist endeavor as "the primal history of the nineteenth century."

For Benjamin the 1930s were years of extreme hardship. On his fortieth birthday, faced with a variety of intellectual and personal setbacks, he seriously contemplated taking his own life. Forced into exile following the Nazi seizure of power, for a time he continued to publish in German under various pseudonyms. But his publishing mishaps seemed to outweigh his few successes, and his slim hopes of establishing a niche in the Parisian literary avant-garde also came to naught.[16] Increasingly, his subsistence depended on a precarious stipend he received from Horkheimer's New York–based Institute for Social Research. The recently published correspondence with Adorno reveals what a selfless and instrumental role "Teddie" played in keeping Benjamin afloat during these difficult times. As the precipice of war neared, Adorno repeatedly intervened in timely fashion with Horkheimer and potential benefactors on Benjamin's behalf. In many cases his efforts were remarkably successful.

The bulk of their philosophical colloquy concerned the *Arcades Project*. At times, it seemed that Adorno had more invested in the project than Benjamin himself did. As he wrote to Benjamin in 1935: "I view the Arcades project as not only the center of your philosophy, but the decisive standard of what can be articulated philosophically today; as a *chef d'oeuvre*, nothing else, and so decisive in every way ... that I would view as catastrophic and absolutely incorrigible any lessening of the inner promise of this work and any sacrifice of your own categories" (CC, 84). For his part, Benjamin was forced, time and again, to stave off a variety of intellectual and material distractions in order to concentrate on the work he once aptly described as "the theater of all my struggles and all my ideas."

In 1935, material considerations of a non-Marxist variety motivated Benjamin to formulate the first substantial outline of the *Arcades Project*, "Paris, The Capital of the Nineteenth Century." He drafted this text, which is frequently referred to as the Arcades Exposé, at Adorno's urging in order to shore up his financial support from Horkheimer's Institute-in-Exile. Hence, for a short time, Benjamin ceased filling his precious "Convolutes" with enticing citations and began to delineate his major ideas. But the end result — whose fundamental richness was beyond dispute — was a decidedly mixed bag. Adorno, who had been urging its composition, felt intellectually betrayed. To be sure, many of the provocative, central ideas from the late 1920s remained.

Yet, Benjamin had superimposed on these ideas a network of new categories drawn from some extremely dubious intellectual sources: the reactionary doctrines of C. G. Jung and Ludwig Klages.

Here, one must affirm that Adorno's theoretical instincts proved surer than did Benjamin's: Within a few years' time both Jung and Klages would disgrace themselves by becoming vigorous supporters of Germany's Brown Revolution.[17] It had long been one of Benjamin's central (if unadvertised) philosophical goals to reformulate approaches to "experience" popular among right-wing thinkers for the ends of the political left. But as the 1935 version of the Arcades Exposé clearly demonstrates (Benjamin would draft a very different, less myth-laden version in 1939), this approach harbored considerable perils and risks.

The most controversial elements of the 1935 Exposé — and the passages to which Adorno reacted most negatively — appear in the opening section, "Fourier, or the Arcades." After citing Michelet's claim, "Each epoch dreams the one to follow," Benjamin continues:

> Corresponding to the form of the new means of production, which in the beginning is ruled by the old (Marx), are images in the collective consciousness in which the old and the new interpenetrate. These images are wish images; in them the collective seeks both to overcome and to transfigure the immaturity of the social product and the inadequacies in the social organization of production. At the same time, what emerges in these wish images is the resolute effort to distance oneself from all that is antiquated — which includes the most recent past. These tendencies deflect the imagination (which is given impetus by the new) back upon the primal past. In the dream in which each epoch entertains images of its successor, the latter appears wedded to elements of primal history (*Urgeschichte*) — that is, to elements of a classless society. And the experiences of such a society — as stored in the collective unconscious — engender, through interpenetration with what is new, the utopia that has left its trace in a thousand configurations of life, from enduring edifices to passing fashions. (PW, 46–47)

Upon reading these lines Adorno felt that Benjamin had rashly abandoned the materialist and historical program for the *Arcades* that had formed the crux of their philosophical partnership. Benjamin's reckless speculation concerning "wish images" (Klages) from the "primal past" that had been deposited in the "collective unconscious" (Jung), and which then mysteriously mutated into visions of a "classless society," convinced Adorno that his valued interlocutor was in danger of losing his focus — not to mention his grip. In Adorno's view, Benjamin had replaced the original, historical concept of "dialectical images" with the static notion of "archaic images" (*Urbilder*) borrowed from Klages. By the same token, he had substituted Jung's idealistic notion of the "collective unconscious" for the Marxian notion of "class consciousness," which alone could legitimate the *Arcades* in "materialist" terms and thus surmount the avowedly mythological, earlier approach of "A Dialectical Fairy Tale."

Benjamin was indeed an avid reader of Klages, whom he visited in Munich in 1922. As early as 1926, he termed an intellectual confrontation with Klages "indispensable." Four years later, writing to Scholem, he described *Intellect as Antagonist of the Soul* (Klages's bombastic, well-nigh-unreadable magnum opus) as a "great philosophical work."[18]

Given Benjamin's fanciful theoretical indulgences, Adorno felt that the situation demanded unabashed forthrightness. "The collective consciousness is invoked," Adorno laments in response,

> but I fear that in its present form this concept cannot be distinguished from Jung's concept of the same. It is open to criticism from both sides: from the perspective of the social process because it hypostatizes archaic images, whereas in fact dialectical images are generated by the commodity character, not in some archaic collective ego but amongst alienated bourgeois individuals; and from the perspective of psychology because, as Horkheimer puts it, a mass ego only properly exists in earthquakes and catastrophes. (CC, 107)

Adorno would display little more tolerance for those Exposé passages that had been inspired by Benjamin's sympathetic reading of Klages. He continues: "if the crucial 'ambiguity' of the Golden Age is underemphasized … — that is, its relation to Hell — then the commodity as the substance of the age becomes Hell pure and simple, yet negated in a way that actually causes the primal state to appear as truth. Thus disenchantment of the dialectical image leads directly to purely mythical thinking, and Klages appears as a danger just as Jung did before" (CC, 107). In other words: By conceiving prehistory as a positive touchstone in the form of "classless society" or "Golden Age," Benjamin had lost contact with the nature of the historical present — above all, the way it was determined by the commodity form. Consequently, his vaunted *dialectical images* — the "wish images" and furtive "utopias" he described in the Arcades Exposé — had become indistinguishable from the *archaic images* that suffused Klages's flatulent and pompous tomes. As Adorno appropriately summed up the situation at the end of his letter: "The subjective side of the dialectic vanishes before an undialectically mythical gaze, the gaze of the Medusa" (CC, 110).

Remarkably, Benjamin seemed relatively unfazed by Adorno's sweeping and meticulous critical indictment. Notorious for his "Chinese politeness," he spoke instead of the "joy" that "it gives me to see our friendship so confirmed and so many friendly conversations renewed through this letter of yours." "All of your reflections," he continued, "go precisely to the productive heart of the issue, and hardly a single one fails to do so" (CC, 117).

It is doubtful that such professions of solidarity placated Adorno. In fact, later on in the letter, Benjamin responded to Adorno's challenges in a way that could only have heightened his concerns. After denying that the 1935 Exposé in any way constituted a betrayal of the *Arcades'* intentions, Benjamin conceded that it indeed lacked something essential: "the constructive moment," the principle of organization that would compel the welter of diffuse aperçus to coalesce into a meaningful whole. But it was Benjamin's ensuing analogical characterization of how that moment might be produced that likely caused Adorno's hair to stand on end: "one thing is quite certain: *what the constructive moment means for this book must be compared with what the philosopher's stone means for alchemy*" — certainly not the type of declaration that was likely to put Adorno's historical materialist concerns to rest (CC, 118).

In truth, Benjamin's unguarded allusion to the "philosopher's stone" and "alchemy" as positive methodological ideals for the *Arcades* was hardly a meaningless aside. Instead, it illustrates three matters of overwhelming importance for understanding his theoretical intentions for the project. First, it indicates his profound ambivalence concerning the sociological or "materialist" framework that Adorno and others were urging him to pursue. Second, it conveys how close his thinking about the *Arcades* remained during the mid-1930s to the more "phantasmagorical," "Dialectical Fairy Tale" approach of 1927–28. Lastly and most importantly, it illustrates the extent to which Benjamin's ideas, even at the height of his so-called materialist phase, remained profoundly marked by the theological categories of his youth. Thus, as he confessed in a letter to a friend during the early 1930s: "I have never been able to do research and think in any sense other than, if you will, *a theological one*: namely, in accord with the Talmudic teaching about the *forty-nine levels of meaning in every Torah passage*."[19] For all his talk about producing a new "materialist historiography" and the "primal history of the nineteenth century," it is remarks such as these that provide us with genuine insight as to what Benjamin hoped the *Arcades Project* would achieve.

History as a Site of Redemption

In the summer of 1940, as Western Europe succumbed to the fascist axe, Benjamin, his precious manuscripts in tow, abandoned his Paris apartment and sought refuge in the unoccupied zone, from which he hoped eventually to make his way across the Atlantic. Among his papers were the celebrated "Theses on the Philosophy of History," which he described as "theoretical accoutrements" for his "work on Baudelaire," and which stand in the closest proximity to his methodological plans for the *Arcades*. (It would be fair to say that virtually everything he wrote during the final decade of his life, including the outstanding essays on Kafka, Proust, and Nikolai Leskov, are related to themes that bear directly on the *Arcades*.)

In the "Theses" Benjamin takes aim at the delusions of "progress" — he observes at one point, "nothing has corrupted the German workers' movement so much as the delusion that it was moving with the current" — and meditates on the failures of the Popular Front era, as symbolized by the Hitler–Stalin pact. But, characteristically, his major concern at this exceedingly dark historical hour is the oblique relationship between history and redemption. And since experience has taught that so little can be expected from the immanent course of history — which Benjamin characterized starkly as "one single catastrophe that keeps piling ruin upon ruin" — "redemption" must instead be construed as a distinct *break* with the continuum of history.

In the "Theses" Benjamin describes the surreptitious nexus between history and redemption in the following manner: "The past carries with it a temporal index by which it is referred to redemption. There is a secret agreement between past generations and the present one. Our coming was expected on earth. Like every generation that preceded us, we have been endowed with a weak Messianic power, a power to which the past has a claim. That claim cannot be settled cheaply." And in the manner of an unconvincing afterthought, he hastily adds: "Historical materialists are aware of this."[20]

It is not hard to discern that, if one softens the theological undertones, this statement faithfully reflects Benjamin's theoretical intentions for the *Arcades Project*, above all, his concern with *the redemption of past experience*. Alternatively, he found the ideas of Proust, Baudelaire, and Marx serviceable for these intentions and thus duly incorporated their doctrines into his working notes and drafts. He fluctuated on the nature and degree of theology's role and involvement. But he never doubted its centrality for a moment.

What consequences might this redemption-centered paradigm have for the disciplines of philosophy and criticism? To begin with, it suggests that, for Benjamin, theology possessed privileged insight concerning the clandestine relationship between history and "fulfillment" (*Vollendung*; or, as he sometimes called it: "Messianic time") — insight distinctly superior to existing secular and scientific approaches, Marxism included. As he avows emphatically in the *Arcades*: "My thinking is related to theology as blotting pad is related to ink. *It is saturated with it*" (PW, 588). However, in order to achieve success in the profane realm of history, theology must rely extensively on the services of these ancillary secular approaches.

Undoubtedly, Benjamin's most lyrical and compelling depiction of the furtive relationship between theology and secular approaches to knowledge occurs in a parable worthy of Kafka. In Thesis I he tells the story of a chess-playing puppet constructed so that it would win every match, "answering each move of an opponent with a countermove." The secret of the puppet's success, Benjamin continues, lies in the fact that "actually, a little hunchback who was an expert chess player sat inside and guided the puppet's hand by means of strings." "One can imagine a philosophical counterpart to this device," suggests Benjamin. "The puppet called 'historical materialism' is to win all the time. It can easily be a match for anyone if it enlists the services of theology — which today, as we know, is wizened and has to keep out of sight."[21]

Nowhere does Benjamin indicate more forcefully than in this exquisite fable-in-miniature the imperative link between theology and the profane achievements of the human understanding. Each side of this equation, in lieu of its opposite number, risks losing its way: critique remains mired in the unredeemed "creaturely" world; and theology, for its part, overshoots the sphere of profane life that is so urgently in need of its unique resuscitative powers and capacities. Benjamin was convinced that a creative and vital cross-fertilization of these two poles, theology and materialist criticism, alone would produce a redeemed humanity. In Convolute "N" of the *Arcades*, he suggests how this approach might be fruitfully employed in the practice of cultural history:

> Modest methodological proposal for the cultural-historical dialectic. It is very easy to establish oppositions ... within the various "fields" of any epoch, such that on the one side lies the "productive," "forward-looking," "lively," "positive" part of the epoch, and on the other side the abortive, retrograde, and obsolescent .... It is therefore of decisive importance that a new partition be applied to the initially excluded, negative component so that, by a displacement of the angle of vision ... a positive element emerges anew in it too — something different

from that previously signified. And so on, ad infinitum, *until the entire past is brought into the present in a historical apocatastasis.* (PW, 573)

"Apocatastasis" is a term that derives from the Jewish apocalyptic tradition. It designates the restoration of an original paradisiacal state catalyzed by the coming of the Messiah. Thus restored, things would resume their proper relations to each other. The distortions caused by the "dream condition of the world" — the world's "falseness" — would be effaced. Scholem once felicitously described the redemptive dimension of Benjamin's work as follows: "The goal of Benjamin's 'dialectics of cultural history' is the abolition of the prevailing context of expression in favor of *the original context of Being* .... Benjamin transfers the catastrophic and redemptive elements coexistent in the apocalyptic doctrine of apocatastasis into the secular realm of history."[22]

Viewed in these terms, Benjamin's characterization of his methodological proposal as a "modest" one can only be understood as a gross understatement. He was of course deadly serious about his proposition, which in many respects constitutes the eschatological touchstone for the *Arcades Project*. He expressed an analogous insight in the "Theses on the Philosophy of History" when he declared that "*only a redeemed humanity receives the fullness of its past.*"[23] In light of such claims, it would not be far-fetched to suggest that Benjamin's intentions for the *Arcades Project* lay halfway between Proust and the *Zohar*.

A 1937 epistolary exchange with Max Horkheimer, faithfully recorded by Benjamin in his notes for the *Arcades Project*, well illustrates the strengths and limitations of his messianic approach to understanding history. Horkheimer, seeking to subdue Benjamin's strong redemptory aspirations, offered the following stern admonition: "Past injustice has occurred and is completed. The slain are really slain .... If one takes the lack of closure entirely seriously, one must believe in the Last Judgment" (PW, 588). Benjamin's response to Horkheimer's cautionary remarks — written but never sent (for reasons that are not hard to discern) — speaks volumes about his self-understanding as a philosopher and critic:

The corrective to this line of thinking [that is, Horkheimer's antitheological line] may be found in the consideration that history is not simply a science but also and not least a form of remembrance (*Eingedenken*). What science has "determined," remembrance can modify. Such mindfulness can make the incomplete (happiness) into something complete, and the complete (suffering) into something incomplete. That is theology; but in remembrance we have an experience that forbids us to conceive of history as fundamentally atheological, little as it may be granted us to try to write it with immediately theological concepts. (PW, 589)

Benjamin refused to accept Horkheimer's proposition that "the slain are really slain." Nor could he accept the idea of historical "closure" as something final or permanent. Instead, it fell due to the faculty of remembrance to keep the flame of hope alive until past injustice could be made good — bathed in the "now time" of messianic light, as it were. In Benjamin's view, approaches to history that fell short of these eschatological aspirations were indigent and deficient. They remained in league with the forces of corruption that had turned history into Hegel's proverbial "slaughterbench."[24] Theology alone could provide the conceptual and spiritual leverage needed to extricate the historical continuum from the sequence of perennial ruination that, in Benjamin's opinion, constituted its essence.

The problem with Benjamin's position is that it confuses "justice" with "happiness" and thus openly courts the dangers of political messianism. Justice refers to considerations of equity or fairness that are in principle applicable to all members of a given polity or society. Historically, political liberalism, owing to its capacity to protect individuals from the arbitrary depredations of state authority, has proved the most successful (though far from flawless) mechanism of achieving justice. Happiness, conversely, concerns questions of "human fulfillment" or the "good life." Unlike considerations of justice, such issues rarely admit of universal validity. Instead, they vary from context to context, according to the particular structure and needs of a given historical community.

If there is anything that twentieth-century history has taught us, it is that considerations of happiness must be carefully circumscribed by questions of justice. Without such fundamental guarantees, what Freud called the "narcissism of small differences" gains the upper hand, and communities become inflexible, self-aggrandizing entities. For Benjamin, who systematically mistrusted political gradualism and viewed apocalyptic political change as the only variety worth pursuing, profane considerations of "justice" would be deservedly swept away with the advent of the Messianic Age.

In many respects, Benjamin's fascination with political messianism is the "red thread" that underlies and unites the various phases of his work: literary-romantic, theological, and materialist. He explores this position in a 1921 text inspired by the work of Georges Sorel, "Towards a Critique of Violence." The conceptual opposition that structures the text is the distinction between "law-preserving" and "law-creating" violence. According to Benjamin, law-preserving violence is the type of violence that lies at the basis of the modern constitutional state. It is devoted exclusively to the — highly repressive — maintenance of the status quo. It bespeaks the harsh, prosaic, institutionalized violence that Max Weber had in mind when he developed his well-known definition of the modern state as disposing over a "monopoly of the legitimate physical violence within a certain territory." (Benjamin wrote "Critique of Violence" with the events of the German Revolution fresh in mind. Hence, in his view the historical incarnation of law-preserving violence would have been Gustav Noske's diabolical *Freikorps*.)

Law-creating violence, conversely, suggests the romantic ideal of a mystical, purifying violence. Instead of maintaining corrupt social institutions and practices, as does law-preserving violence, law-creating violence sweeps the latter away in one fell swoop. In keeping with the imagery of Jewish messianism Benjamin favored, law-creating violence represents a type of prelapsarian, divine violence: it is the violence one associates with the coming of the Messiah or the Last Judgment. As such, law-creating violence represents a pure, *noumenal* violence, a *violence of ends.* In *Spirit of Utopia,* a work that Benjamin greatly admired, Ernst Bloch captured the essence of law-creating violence when he described the ethical stance appropriate to the historical present as *"the categorical imperative with revolver in hand."* As Benjamin remarks in "Critique of Violence":

> The very task of destruction poses again ... the question of a pure immediate violence.... If mythical violence is law-preserving, divine violence is law-destroying; if mythical violence brings at once guilt and retribution, divine power expiates.... If the existence of violence outside the law, as pure immediate violence, is assured, this furnishes the proof that *revolutionary violence*, the highest manifestation of unalloyed violence by man, is possible, and by what means ... Divine violence ... may be called *sovereign violence.*[25]

There is an unspoken consensus among Benjamin scholars that his avowedly apocalyptic "diagnosis of the times" is an appropriate one;[26] that present history is indeed best described by the category of "incessant catastrophe"; that some form of political messianism — however indiscernible its contours may be — remains our best "hope"; and that "revolutionary violence," under appropriate circumstances and conditions, would be eminently justifiable.

Yet, Benjamin's supporters do his legacy no favor by indulging or passing over in silence the more far-flung and problematical aspects of

his thought: his embrace of political messianism or his apocalyptic
philosophy of history. However appropriate this messianic framework
may have been to the interwar generation of Central European Jews
that had all but abandoned prospects for gradual and progressive
historical change, it remains drastically out of step with the justly chas-
tened demands of the political and historical present. It is high time for
Benjamin enthusiasts the world over to permanently step out of their
time warp.

In March 1938 Gretel Adorno wrote Benjamin trying to lure him away
momentarily from the recesses of the Bibliothèque Nationale to visit the
Adornos in rain-soaked London. "You can probably hardly imagine
how much I would love to see you over here," she observes. "However,
I harbor the single fear that you are so at home amongst your Arcades
that you will never want to leave the splendid structure, and that it is
only when you have finally closed the door on it that any other subject
will catch your interest" (CC, 242). During the late 1930s, as the political world around him rapidly disintegrated, the Convolutes for the
Arcades Project took on a near-talismanic importance for him. One
might even say that, in certain respects, he tried to remedy this external
chaos through an immense, esoteric labor of scholarly "apocatastasis."
In the end, of course, his efforts, while daring and prodigious, remained
unconsummated — a "ruin," one might say. The beauty of ruins was of
course a common trope among the surrealists, one that Benjamin had
made his own as early as the 1925 habilitation study on *Trauerspiel*.
"Allegories are, in the realm of thoughts, what ruins are in the realm of
things," he once declared.[27]

Yet, it would be improper for us, his heirs, to romanticize or monu-
mentalize his failure. Instead, the reception of Benjamin's *Arcades
Project* would be better served by one of his own axioms: "To cultivate
fields where, until now, only madness has reigned. Forge ahead with the
whetted axe of reason ... Every ground must at some point have been
made arable by reason, must have been cleared of the undergrowth of
delusion and myth. This is to be accomplished here for the terrain of the
nineteenth century" (PW, 570–71).

One of the major problems of the *Arcades Project* as Benjamin
conceived it is that the foregoing prescription was too often honored in
the breach rather than in the observance. In the end, Benjamin, who
believed in the possibility of reading history and nature as "text,"
remained mesmerized and seduced by the Arcades qua "phantasmagoria": as repositories of quasi-mythological "wish" and "dream
images." As one leafs through his suggestive and voluptuous pages, one
soon realizes that far too few traces of the "whetted axe of reason" are
to be found.

2

The Adorno Centennial: The Apotheosis of Negative Dialectics

Venerating Negativity

In 2003 something remarkable happened in Germany. It was the year of the Adorno centennial. The entire nation reached out to embrace this renegade Marxist philosopher in ways that were truly surprising. Throughout the country, Adorno "festivals" took place — apotheoses reminiscent of Rousseauian "civil religion." In Frankfurt, there is now an Adorno-Platz cum bust. The Adorno family vacation home in neighboring Amorsbach has become a quasi-official pilgrimage site. A plethora of public exhibitions tracing his life and thought were staged. Public concerts featuring his compositions — most of which resemble Vienna School pastiches — were held. For those who could not get enough, his music was, in addition, released on affordable CDs. Documentaries examining his eventful intellectual itinerary aired on German television. Radio programs took note of his immense influence on postwar German politics and society. And, of course, there was the obligatory postage stamp bearing his likeness. Ponderous academic conferences took place at major universities, where German professors parsed Adorno conundrums such as: "Philosophy is there to redeem what lies in an animal's gaze." ("True thoughts are those alone which do not understand themselves," he once remarked.)[1] Volumes of previously unpublished correspondence also appeared, and transcribed lecture courses, as well as a number of compendious biographies.[2]

Why was it so remarkable that Germany — which, after all, prides itself on being a nation of *Dichter und Denker* (poets and thinkers) — took to its bosom a left-leaning, émigré philosopher who had been dead for some thirty-four years? Because, since his return to Germany from American exile circa 1951 until his untimely demise in 1969, Adorno specialized in telling Germans truths about themselves that they did not want to hear. The high point of these efforts was his 1959 address, "What Does It Mean to Work through the Past?" — a discourse that, upon rereading today, remains a model of deft and unflinching political insight. Moreover, the lecture's timing was crucial, insofar as the Federal Republic was in the painful throes of a neo-Nazi upsurge, the worst since the war's end. That year, across the nation right-wing thugs desecrated Jewish cemeteries with swastikas. A small but tenacious far-right political party, the NDP (National Democratic Party), began a disturbing political comeback.

As Adorno observed at the time, he was more concerned with anti-democratic tendencies *within* the Federal Republic — that is, the conti-nuity of personnel and *mentalité* dating from the Nazi era — than with antidemocratic forces acting *against* it (the NDP's recent electoral gains). In timely fashion, his lecture took up the gauntlet, seizing on the Freudian trope of "working through the past" — an unsubtle reference to the German catastrophe of 1933–45. It was a labor that, until then, Adorno's countrymen and women had pointedly refused to undertake, preferring instead to rest content with a series of specious half-truths and rationalizations: the Germans, too, were Hitler's victims; Allied war crimes were on a par with Germany's; the postwar threat posed by "World Communism" proved that, as far as the war in the East was concerned, Hitler had been right after all. From here it was but a short step to the conclusion that perhaps he had been right on other scores as well …

Adorno would stand for none of it. He claimed that when it came to the nation's past misdeeds, his fellow Germans had succumbed to a debilitating form of collective repression (*Verdrängung*). To facilitate the Freudian process of "working through" (*Aufarbeitung*), Adorno sought to transpose psychoanalytic concepts from the individual plane to the sociopsychological level — a methodological approach that, since the 1930s, had been one of the Frankfurt School's methodological hall-marks.[3] The philosopher showed how Germany's notorious "inability to mourn" — the title of a breakthrough book by Alexander and Margarete Mitscherlich — resulted in an acute and persistent mass psychic immobilism.[4] For a nation that systematically refuses to address the misdeeds of its historical past remains unable to transcend them.

The past persists unmastered as "trauma"; national consciousness is prevented from advancing. It was in a similar vein that Günter Grass, in a memorable passage in the novel *The Tin Drum,* mocked his countrymen's postwar emotional blockage by having them engage in compulsory onion-cutting ceremonies in order to shed tears.

For his efforts, Adorno was mocked and scorned. Having bravely punctured Germany's collective self-rationalizations, he was roundly accused of befouling his own nest. Since, following the war, Adorno had failed to receive a permanent teaching post, fellow Germans derided his position at the University of Frankfurt as the "Wiedergutmachung Stuhl" — the "restitution chair," thereby insinuating that it was essentially unmerited. Here, the irony is that during the 1950s he was unfairly derided for precisely the same reasons that, during the centennial year, he was fulsomely praised.

If during the 1950s Adorno was unfairly vilified by the German Right, during the 1960s he caught it from the opposite direction — namely the student Left. The German SDS (*Sozialistischer Studentenbund*), brandishing, to Adorno's and Horkheimer's voluble dismay, pirated reprints of classic Frankfurt School texts, seized the political stage. German politics became overheated. Buying into the (now disproven) Marxist "line" about the correspondences between capitalism and fascism, the student radicals adopted an antifascist credo ("antifa") and viewed themselves as part of a new "resistance" movement. This time, in a classical instance of "repetition compulsion," they would win the civil war that their forefathers on the German Left had ignominiously lost during the early 1930s.

Faced with a left-wing threat, the German Right could comfortably regress to its standard, fallback, authoritarian political mode. Politicians and opinion leaders roundly accused the Frankfurt School thinkers of having fostered an intellectual climate conducive to terrorism — an allusion to the murderous antics of the Baader-Meinhof group. Their sin? By encouraging "critical thinking," they had undermined the authority of family, church, and state, and thereby invited anarchy. Recycling classic (if woefully stale) arguments of the European Counter-Enlightenment, German conservatives argued that the Critical Theorists openly practiced a form of "cultural terrorism" that threatened to destabilize the foundations of the Christian West. The fact that Adorno and others had explicitly disowned the mindless activism of the APO, or antiauthoritarian student Left, mattered little. In the eyes of the German Right, the Frankfurt School represented a dangerous coven of "free thinkers." As such, they were "objectively" guilty.

A similar hysteria gripped the nation during the storied "German Autumn" of 1977, following the kidnapping and execution of Employers Association head Hans-Martin Schleyer by Red Army Faction terrorists.

Once again, the charge of "intellectual parentage" was laid at the Frankfurt School's doorstep, despite the fact that, by this point, nearly all its
original members — including Adorno, who died in 1969 — had passed
from the scene. In light of highly fraught controversies and polemics
surrounding the Frankfurt School's role in postwar Germany, Adorno's
2003 canonization seems doubly remarkable.

First Stirrings of Genius

Theodor Adorno was the progeny of a Frankfurt businessman and the
Italian opera singer Maria Calvelli-Adorno, from whom he acquired his
prodigious musical aptitude. In *The Story of a Novel*, Thomas Mann,
who understatedly described Adorno as "a man of remarkable intellect," quoted an American singer who observed: "It's simply incredible!
He [Adorno] knows every note in the world!"[5]

As a youth, Adorno — "Teddie" as he was known among intimates
— was precocity incarnate. At the age of fifteen, he developed an intense
friendship with the essayist and film scholar Siegfried Kracauer, his
senior by fourteen years, best known for his classic study of Weimar era
cinema, *From Caligari to Hitler*. In 1918, the pair engaged in a mutual,
line-by-line study of Kant's *Critique of Pure Reason*. They also
frequently vacationed together. Their friendship contained a profound
homoerotic component, reminiscent of the Stefan George *Kreis* antics.
(The George *Kreis* was of course a *Männerbund* (men's club), noted for
the authoritarian behavior of its talented and charismatic leader). These
revelations provoked a frisson of scandal when they were revealed
following the 2002 publication of Kracauer's letters to sociologist Leo
Lowenthal. As Kracauer avowed in a 1924 letter: "Do you know, I
think I feel an unnatural passion for this man [Adorno], which I can
only explain by the fact that on a non-physical level I'm homosexual,
after all. Otherwise, could I think of him in these terms and suffer
because of him like a lover pining for a beloved?"[6]

In 1924, Adorno witnessed a stunning performance of Alban Berg's
opera, *Wozzeck*, which confirmed his predilection for the "New" or
"Modern" Music of the Vienna School. The production inspired him to
move to the Austrian capital, where he could study directly with the
New Music maestros. Adorno would later attain renown as an interpreter of Schoenberg — a difficult man, whose insatiable desire for
dictatorial power purportedly exceeded that of Stefan George.[7]

For Adorno, the integrity of Schoenberg's music — above all, middle-
period Schoenberg, the master of "dissonance" — lay in its staunch
refusal to provide ideological window dressing for an inverted social
world: one in which social relations among persons are increasingly

dominated by relations among things or commodities. Atonal composition steadfastly resisted the idea of music as "consolation": sugarcoating for a "totally administered world." In Adorno's view, the rejection of harmony in favor of dissonance allowed New Music to unflinchingly articulate the language of social suffering. Under late capitalism, music, like all art, had become the flaccid blandishment of an all-encompassing consumer society. It had degenerated into *Gebrauchsmusik*: a "decorative" accompaniment to department store shopping. As Adorno observes: "If music is privileged above all other [art] forms by the absence of visual imagery ... then it nonetheless has participated energetically in the illusory character of the bourgeois work of art ... Schoenberg declared his independence from this type of art .... His music denies the claim that the universal and the particular have been reconciled."[8]

But in order to outwit the apparently seamless net of "total administration," New Music was forced to pay a high price. By steadfastly renouncing the enticements of consumer capitalism, it had become increasingly esoteric and inaccessible — to the point where it could only be understood and appreciated by "experts." As a result, it forfeited valuable communicative potentials and risked becoming stranded in a ghetto of self-imposed insularity.

Many of Adorno's insights about New Music were formed during the era of Germany's disastrous hyperinflation, circa 1923, which explains his at times strained efforts to view musical developments as expressions of capitalist developments or "social facts." Yet, so profound and thoroughgoing was Adorno's knowledge of musical matters that he could bring off such comparisons in a way that made lesser spirits look foolish.

In *Philosophy of Modern Music* (1949), Adorno contrasted Schoenberg favorably with Stravinsky, whose efforts to assimilate traditional folk motifs he viewed as "regressive": an attempt to provide a semblance of brotherliness and community amid a reified society in which large-scale organizations — corporations and state bureaucracies — continually marginalized potentials for social freedom. As Adorno bluntly observed apropos of the Russian composer: "The seemingly positive return to the outmoded reveals itself as a more fundamental conspiracy with the *destructive tendencies of the age*" — thereby insinuating a direct link between Stravinsky's compositional practices and European fascism ("the destructive tendencies of the age").[9]

Schoenberg distanced himself sharply from Adorno's imaginative interpretive forays. He held Adorno — an unlikely candidate for a "Miss Congeniality" award, in any event — personally in low esteem. As he bluntly observed on one occasion: "I could never really stand him."[10] Although Schoenberg was no fan of Stravinsky's compositions, after reading Adorno's unremitting indictment, he was momentarily tempted to leap to the composer's defense: "It is disgusting how [Adorno] treats Stravinsky. I am certainly no admirer of Stravinsky, although I like a piece here and there very much — but one should not write like that."[11]

The Redemptive Balm of Art

It was in Frankfurt during the 1920s that Adorno became acquainted with Walter Benjamin and Max Horkheimer, both of whom became decisive intellectual influences. Benjamin possessed a truly rare philosophical and literary acumen that, in many ways, established the parameters for Adorno's future development. In the 1920s, he already recognized the virtuosity of the French literary avant-garde — Baudelaire, Proust (both of whom he translated), and the surrealists — years before they became fashionable and grist for the mill of academic "seminar literature." Benjamin believed that their literary efforts hinged on a conception of "experience" that bore affinities with Henri Bergson's notion of "lived time" (*temps vecu*). With this approach, the French philosopher sought to contrast the debased, "industrial" approach to temporality projected by Western science with the nonquantifiable, temporal flux proper to human subjectivity. Similar concerns were at issue in German *Lebensphilosophie* as represented by Dilthey, Spengler, and Ludwig Klages. Yet, *comme les allemands*, their formulations were unserviceably couched in a reactionary and antidemocratic (not to mention anti-Semitic) idiom.

Benjamin's contradictory and risky lifelong project was to rescue vitalism's emancipatory potentials for the ends of the political Left. In his landmark essay on surrealism (1928), he provided a felicitous summary of these intentions when he proclaimed his goal was "*to win the energies of intoxication for the Revolution.*" His fragmentary opus on the Paris Arcades — the so-called *Passagenwerk* — represented the consummation of these efforts.[12]

Adorno's collected literary criticism, published as *Notes to Literature*, is unthinkable apart from these indispensable Benjaminian precedents.[13] In a world where, in his judgment, the dominant philosophical approaches, positivism and *Lebensphilosophie*, had abnegated their critical mission, works of art alone possessed the quasi-theological capacity to tell the truth — or, in one of Adorno's preferred formulations, "to call things by their proper names."

In 1925 Benjamin, Adorno's senior by eleven years, submitted *The Origins of German Tragic Drama* as a habilitation study, or second doctorate, to the Frankfurt University philosophy department. It was roundly rejected by his examiners, who viewed its submission as a provocation. One said he couldn't understand a word of it. Another declared with irony and pith: "Geist kann man nicht habilitieren" — "One can't habilitate Spirit." Thus ended Benjamin's academic career, a vocation he scorned in any event.

Still, the work's hermetic and convoluted "Epistemo-Critical Prologue" contained the germ of a revolutionary approach to philosophy that, in many respects, became programmatic for Adorno's future development. There, Benjamin lamented the experiential impoverishment of systematic philosophy and proposed his own "imagistic" approach — thinking in "constellations" — as an alternative. "Ideas are to objects as constellations are to stars," remarks Benjamin poetically. They are "timeless constellations, and by virtue of the elements' being seen as points in such constellations, phenomena are ... at the same time redeemed." The idea was that, by assembling a montagelike configuration of insights, one could circumvent the positivist rejection of philosophy's original mission and scope: to grasp the Absolute. By invoking "constellations" Benjamin gestured toward the ontotheological aspirations of Platonic metaphysics: the theory of Ideas.

Adorno's preference for a paratactic approach to philosophy, as evidenced by later masterpieces such as *Minima Moralia* and *Negative Dialectics*, were directly inspired by these passages. By the same token, he repeatedly voiced his reservations about Benjamin's profound and inspired theological longings, which he viewed as incompatible with a genuine materialist approach. Accordingly, Adorno's version of constellations approximated "negative theology." The state of redemption or "reconciliation" (*Versöhnung*) toward which Benjamin's thought inclined could only be deduced *ex negativo*: it would be the antithesis of the current degraded state. For this reason, Adorno was fond of quoting the philosopher F. H. Bradley's aperçu: "Where everything is bad, it must be good to know the worst."[14]

Adorno's "negative dialectics" was conceived as an antidote to the Hegelian variant, which justly stood accused of conflating the "real" and the "rational," and thereby glorifying the historical present in all its indigence. The Frankfurt School philosopher possessed an endemic aversion to the Hegelian moment of "synthesis." But at a certain point such resolute insistence on the "negative" seemed theoretically self-defeating. After all, if all attempts to transform the "totally administered world" merely reinforced its omnipotence, then all attempts to practically intervene — all *praxis* — seemed pointless. During the 1960s, Adorno was forced to respond to charges of "resignation." He did so with all the elegance and brio one had come to expect.

It was around the same time that the auspicious first encounter between Adorno and Max Horkheimer transpired. During the 1940s, from their exilic perch in Pacific Palisades, California, the two would collaborate on *Dialectic of Enlightenment*: a wholesale reinterpretation of Western cultural development in light of the unprecedented civilizational regression of National Socialist barbarism. One of the paradoxes of the Frankfurt School's reception history is that such a manifestly unrepresentative work would, willy nilly, become its signature theoretical achievement.

In light of this curious fact, it is important to point out that, despite a number of marked biographical affinities — both men were left-leaning, assimilated German Jews who shared a philosophical mentor (the neo-Kantian Hans Cornelius — ironically, the man responsible for disallowing Benjamin's habilitation study) — their intellectual partnership was hardly a case of preestablished harmony. The early Horkheimer was profoundly influenced by "philosophical materialism": an approach that derived from High Enlightenment thought (Julien Ofray de La Mettrie, Baron d'Holbach, Helvétius), Ludwig Feuerbach, and Marx. (His lectures on these figures, which make for fascinating reading and speak volumes about the early development of the Frankfurt School, are now available in his *Collected Works*).[15] According to materialists like Feuerbach and Marx, the doctrines of German idealism — Kant, Fichte, Hegel, and Schelling — sanctioned and glorified German authoritarian social relations. Hegel's *Lectures on the Philosophy of History* famously conclude with an apotheosis of the Prussian State as the apogee of "Reason in History." As such, their philosophies merited demystification: intellectual and political unmasking through the solvent of ideology critique.

Although Adorno periodically invoked materialist ideas, such references often seemed insincere and perfunctory. Given his background in aesthetics and music — not to mention his proximity to Benjamin, who was avowedly fascinated by the mysteries of kabbalistic numerology — his approach bore affinities with the Idealist delusions that Horkheimer rejected. One of the standard tropes in German idealism is the notion that, where profane knowledge falls short, art steps in to fill the void. This dynamic is evident in the philosophies of Schiller (*Letters on the Aesthetic Education of Mankind*), Kant (*Critique of Judgment*), and Schelling (*Philosophy of Art*). In *The World as Will and Representation* (1819), Schopenhauer follows suit, claiming that music possesses the soteriological ability to express the In-itself or noumenal truth — a capacity denied to human cognition.

Adorno's philosophical development, which culminated in the post-humously issued *Aesthetic Theory,* traverses an analogous route. He believed that philosophy, in its twentieth-century incarnation as positivism, relinquished its critical role and was reduced to the status of a servile handmaiden to the forces of science and industry. In his view, the baton of social criticism had passed to a select canon of "difficult" modernist artists: Schoenberg, Proust, Kafka, and Beckett. In Adorno's view, they alone maintained the capacity to unmask social oppression by virtue of a quasi-theological capacity to "call things by their proper names." Increasingly, Adorno mistrusted the wiles of discursive reason, which, following Nietzsche, he associated with a will to domination and control. As he pithily observed in *Negative Dialectics*: "The original sin of philosophy is its attempt to grasp the non-conceptual via conceptual means."[16] In other words: for Adorno the act of cognition itself had become an expression of social control. Only art and aesthetics — art's philosophical complement — retained the capacity to undo the damage wrought by science and knowledge qua manifestations of "instrumental reason." Yet, clearly, once one cedes "knowledge" to the terrain of the enemy — the forces of domination — outlets for critical thought remain negligible or few. Consequently, Adorno's philosophy risks becoming a quirky profession of intellectual impotence. It is as though philosophy's raison d'être were reduced to a series of mea culpas for its previous misdeeds.

Lifting Taboos

European liberals thought that the Jewish question could be solved by assimilation. However, once it became apparent that this approach was succeeding beyond anyone's wildest dreams — indeed, in the late 1800s, Jews who adopted German habitudes and mores flourished both professionally and culturally — detractors rapidly made their objections heard. Anti-Semites claimed that no matter how hard they tried Jews could never become *real* Germans — a reproach one finds already in Wagner's eerily prophetic essay "The Jews in Music" (1850), which concludes with a bone-chilling appeal for their "downfall" (*Untergang*) from German life. Racial anti-Semitism was one of the poisonous legacies of this mentality. Thereby, even converted Jews could be denied acceptance. Paradoxically, in certain cases, Jews themselves recoiled in horror at their own prodigious social acceptance. After all, what was the point of "success" if, in the end, it meant abandoning a dearly held, time-honored belief system?

Among contemporary German Jews there is a provocative saying: *Germans will never forgive the Jews for the Holocaust.* For decades, anti-Semites complained about excessive Jewish influence on German life. Perversely, in the Holocaust's aftermath, their deepest fears have seemingly been realized. In the sphere of German–Jewish relations, Auschwitz has become a talisman of lost innocence. Now, when Jewish matters are at issue, Germans must be on their best behavior. After the war, under Konrad Adenauer's stewardship, reparations to the Jewish people became one of the essential preconditions for Germany's readmittance to the community of nations. For Germans, one of the Holocaust's burdensome legacies is that the slightest scintilla of Judeophobia semantically intersects with the Final Solution.

Extreme historical and psychological indebtedness inevitably breeds resentment. In Germany the situation is aggravated by the fact that those to whom the nation is morally and economically beholden — the Jews — it once tried to efface from the planet. It would be naïve to deny that, in the German "collective unconscious," there are many who secretly wish Hitler had succeeded.

This extreme discomfort with moral indebtedness takes the form of "acting out," in the Freudian sense. Recent German cultural life is brimming with crude outbursts of anti-Semitic paranoia — attempts to "balance out" the psychologically burdensome and officially mandated philo-Semitism. During the mid-1980s the historian Ernst Nolte proposed that Hitler's Jewish persecutions were justified insofar as the Jewish Agency had suggested that, in the event of world war, Jews should cast their lot with the Western democracies.[17] A few years later, the filmmaker Hans-Jürgen Syberberg published a dyspeptic tract, *On the Fortune and Misfortune of Art in Germany after the War*, claiming that postwar German cultural life had been despoiled by the pervasive influence of Jewish émigrés like Horkheimer, Adorno, and Walter Benjamin. Thereby, Syberberg crudely recycled Wagner's canard that Jews could never be *real* Germans.

Following German reunification during the 1990s, the ante was raised. Books and articles began surfacing that urged Germans to take into consideration Nazism's "positive" side — as though one could somehow compartmentalize the millions of deaths the regime had wrought. Opinion leaders and cultural potentates like *Merkur* editor Karl-Heinz Bohrer accused their countrymen of *lacking the courage to be German* — however one might define it. (In fairness, during the postwar decades, there existed an unspoken taboo about exploring, in Nazism's wake, questions of German identity.) Soon the taboos were lifted and the floodgates opened. In 1999, the German novelist Martin Walser created a furor by claming that Germans had been beaten into submission by Jews who brandished the Holocaust like a "moral cudgel." Two years later, Walser demonstrated that his earlier eruption was in no way a fluke by writing a novel in which he fantasized about murdering Germany's leading Jewish literary critic, Marcel Reich-Ranicki.

One of the chief offenders was the *Frankfurter Allgemeine Zeitung*, the nation's leading conservative daily. Since reunification, the FAZ has moved increasingly to the right: belittling the legacy of the sixties, pandering to the claims of historical revisionism, glorifying the virtues of national homogeneity, celebrating tainted literati such as Ernst Jünger, and pontificating about geopolitical imperatives of the German *Mittellage*. The FAZ has published — unremarked — lavish death notices for former Hitler deputy Rudolf Hess and irredentist letters from Sudeten Germans, declaring that they, too, should have a say in determining the future of the Czech Republic. FAZ editorial writers fantasize about Germany's "geopolitical mission" in the East — a notion redolent of the proverbial "Drang nach Osten" (drive to the East), an ideal that fittingly came to grief in 1943 with the surrender of Field Marshal Paulus's Sixth Army amid the ruins of Stalingrad.

In his recently translated *Adorno: A Political Biography*, FAZ journalist Lorenz Jäger frequently employs a rhetorical tactic favored by the German Far Right. He cites anti-Jewish canards first floated by others as a clever way of simultaneously distancing himself from them as well as according them a semblance of plausibility. It is as if he were saying: "I don't partake of this view, but others do, and here's what they have to say." By the time one has finished the paragraph in question, for better or worse, the canard has been aired, and the damage has been done.

A case in point concerns the Nazi epithet "Judeo-Bolshevism." It was this figure that, during the final years of the war, managed to propagandistically "twin" the regime's two main adversaries, Communists and Jews.[18] As is well known, the Nazis embraced a delusional, "redemptive anti-Semitism," in which Jews became stand-ins for everything they claimed to oppose: capitalism, communism, monotheism, modernism, industrialism, and so forth. Whatever impeded the Third Reich's path, there was a Jew behind it.[19] In a 1943 speech, Goebbels, attempting to rally domestic support for the Eastern Front in the face of staggering losses, claimed that *the Jews* were the only group who had profited from the war — despite knowledge that the Final Solution was well on its way to completion.

At a pivotal juncture in his narrative, Jäger strategically invokes Judeo-Bolshevism. In his view, despite its "excesses," it is a concept that retains considerable explanatory value. The conclusion toward which readers are inexorably driven is: "Well, perhaps in their Judeophobia Hitler and company weren't so crazy after all." Thereby, Jäger turns rhetorical sleight-of-hand into a high art.

Initially, as a type of preemptive self-immunization, Jäger readily concedes that Judeo-Bolshevism was a warrant for genocide. But then, in a clever outflanking maneuver, the left hand removes what the right hand had granted. As Jäger avows in the very next sentence: "In spite of its terrible demagogic exaggeration *it contains a grain of truth.*"[20] What at first seemed like a classical case of Nazi paranoia now merits serious scrutiny.

The evidence? Jews like Trotsky and Zinoviev, Gustav Landauer and Kurt Eisner, Béla Kun and Georg Lukács, Rosa Luxemburg and Paul Levi, played a prominent role in the international communist movement. In other words, if one searches hard enough, one can find a Jewish communist under almost every bed. But the doctrinal differences among this rogues' gallery of Judeocommunists were significant and immense. Rosa Luxemburg was a trenchant and unrelenting critic of Bolshevik authoritarianism.[21] And the "direct democracy" ethos of council communism, as embraced by Landauer and Eisner, was singled out for praise by none other than Hannah Arendt — the twentieth century's leading critic of totalitarianism.

Jäger downplays or ignores all of these differences. Moreover, as we have seen, circa World War I European Jews succeeded in almost *all* walks of life. Was the attraction toward communism really so out of the ordinary, especially in the nations of Central and Eastern Europe where, as a result of a venomous backlash against the remarkable successes of Jewish assimilation, anti-Semitism had gained a new lease on life — another relevant tidbit that Jäger selectively omits? Nearly all French communists were Catholic. Is there also a special affinity between communism and Catholicism? On almost all of these questions, Jäger is resoundingly silent.

Jäger's other questionable practice is to opportunistically cite disparaging remarks about Frankfurt School members made by observers whom, for ideological reasons, he would otherwise shun. The most egregious instance is his extensive reliance on Bertolt Brecht. Since the communist playwright wrote an entire book — the so-called *Tui* novel — mocking Frankfurt School behavioral foibles, he is an especially fecund source. Here, for example, is one of Brecht's mordant diary entries following a 1941 émigré soirée:

At a garden party at Rolf Nürnberg's I met the two clowns Horkheimer and [Friedrich] Pollock, the two Tuis from the Frankfurt Sociological Institute. Horkheimer is a millionaire. Pollock merely from a good home, so that only Horkheimer can afford to buy a professorship wherever he happens to be staying "to provide a front for the Institute's revolutionary activities." This time it's at Columbia ....

With the help of their money they keep around a dozen intellectuals afloat, and in return the latter have to supply them with all their work without any guarantee that the journal will ever publish them. And so one could claim that "their main revolutionary duty throughout all these years has been to save the Institute money."[22]

Brecht's characterizations are witty and amusing. Still, one can't help but wonder about Jäger's underlying motives in incorporating this episode, which has little to do with his protagonist, Adorno. At one point, Jäger suggestively adverts to the "real reasons" behind German anti-Semitism — reasons, he insinuates, the Frankfurt School would never dare mention. Why? Because they demonstrate that anti-Semitism was, at least in part, historically justified. Thereby, Jäger flirts with another canard popular among German far-right circles: *the Jews themselves are responsible for anti-Semitism.* Hence, among the Germans, anti-Semitism is a type of understandable *défense légitime.*

Jäger's subtitle, a "political biography," is curious. For, among members of the Frankfurt School, Adorno was probably the most politically unsophisticated. In certain respects, he was a left-wing version of Thomas Mann's stereotypical "unpolitical German." During the early 1930s, as the Nazis consolidated their political stranglehold, Adorno was loath to leave Germany. In 1934, he published a fawning review of a song cycle of Hitler Youth leader Baldur von Schirach's poetry in the hopes of enhancing his publishing prospects. When the compromise was exposed after the war, it was a major embarrassment. Adorno reacted defensively, lashing out at his archenemy, Heidegger, whose philosophy was, unlike his own, "fascist to its innermost core."[23]

It would seem that to write a "political biography" of Adorno is a losing proposition. The only sense in which Jäger's study can be construed as "political" is that it provides the author himself with an opportunity to settle political scores against a familiar litany of enemies: communists, Jews, and ex-68ers.

"Education after Auschwitz"

Anyone who tries to make sense of Adorno's philosophical legacy must confront a paradox. On the one hand, he was the philosophical inspiration behind *Dialectic of Enlightenment* — a work that, counterintuitively, sought out the origins of Nazi barbarism in the age of Enlightenment. Little wonder that, in a culture where Enlightenment bashing has become an academic blood sport, the book has gained such a following.[24] The book's thesis is woefully wrongheaded. Nazism's rise represents a case of *failed Enlightenment* rather than a surfeit thereof. As Goebbels avowed just months following Hitler's seizure of power: "The year 1789 is hereby effaced from history."[25] The Third Reich was the *antithesis* of everything the Enlightenment represented.

Had Adorno followed the strictures of his own philosophy — above all, the tendency to equate "reason" with "domination" — he would have been intellectually paralyzed. Similarly, had he acquiesced to his own diagnosis of the age, which, employing a Spenglerian idiom, he often described as a "totally administered world," the idea of enlightening his countrymen concerning the virtues of democratic citizenship following twelve years of Nazi ideological hegemony would have seemed pointless.

To his credit, when questions of democratic education were at issue, Adorno acted the part of a German Voltaire. He even took to the mass media — above all, German radio — to make his case concerning the necessity of a postwar German Enlightenment. In pathbreaking addresses such as "Education toward Maturity and Responsibility" and "Education after Auschwitz," he repeatedly harped on the Kantian theme of moral autonomy. For Adorno knew that only by nurturing the values of autonomous citizenship could one guard against the dangers of a totalitarian relapse. As he remarks in "Education After Auschwitz": "Every debate about the ideals of education is trivial and inconsequential compared to this single ideal: *never again Auschwitz*. It is the barbarism all education strives against .... The single genuine power standing against the principle of Auschwitz is *autonomy*, if I might use the Kantian expression: the power of reflection, of self-determination, of not playing along."[26] In his conduct and activities as a critical intellectual, Adorno clearly realized that Nazism's success in Germany was the result of failed, rather than excessive Enlightenment.

In conclusion, let us return momentarily to the 2003 scene of Adorno's unlikely canonization. Needless to say, it was hardly a result the Frankfurt School would have welcomed. It was inimical to all that it stood for — especially in the case of Adorno, whose "negative dialectics," as a species of negative theology, revered the biblical taboo against graven images.

The Adorno centennial hysteria is eerily reminiscent of the conclusion of Michael Verhoeven's magnificent 1991 film *The Nasty Girl*, based on the life of Anna Rosmus. The protagonist, a young woman from Passau, Bavaria, exposes the collaborationist misdeeds of local notables during the Third Reich. The townspeople will do anything to thwart her. They curse her, break windows in her home, threaten her life as well as the lives of her children. Finally, when it becomes clear that acts of violence will not deter her, they arrive at an ingenious solution: they decide to shower her with accolades in the hope that, by embracing her, they will defuse her critical animus.

It seems that something similar happened in the case of Adorno's beatification. Let us hope that for his sake, as well as for Germany's, these efforts will have failed.

3

What Is Heideggerian Marxism?

The relatively late and then very rapid reception of Marcuse's work has allowed a historically inaccurate image of him to emerge: the older strata of his development remain unrecognizable. Marcuse's 1932 book on *Hegel's Ontology* remains essentially unknown. I suppose that one would find few among Marcuse's contemporary readers who would not be completely surprised by the Introduction's concluding sentence: "*Any contribution this work may make to the development and clarification of problems is indebted to the philosophical work of Martin Heidegger.*" I don't know what Marcuse thinks about this sentence today; we have never spoken about it. But I think that phase of his development was not simply a whim. Indeed, I believe that it is impossible to correctly understand the Marcuse of today without reference to this earlier Marcuse. Whoever fails to detect the persistence of categories from *Being and Time* in the concepts of Freudian drive-theory out of which Marcuse [in *Eros and Civilization*] develops a Marxian historical construct runs the risk of serious misunderstandings.[1]

Jürgen Habermas (1968)

Since Habermas first wrote these words some thirty-five years ago, more information concerning Marcuse's youthful Heideggerian allegiances has come to light. But confusions and misunderstandings persist. By reevaluating the philosopher's early, proto-Heideggerian writings, I hope to shed additional light on what remains a fascinating

and underresearched chapter of twentieth-century intellectual life:
an encounter between two schools of thought — philosophical
Marxism and fundamental ontology — that soon proceeded in opposite
directions.

In retrospect it is clear that Marcuse's political worldview was
shaped by the key events of his youth: the traumas of world war and,
above all, the failure of the German Revolution of 1918–19. At the
age of twenty Marcuse was elected as a Social Democratic deputy
to one of the Soldier's and Worker's Councils that mushroomed
throughout Germany during the climax of World War I. He resigned,
he later claimed, when he noticed that former officers were being
elected to the same bodies. He bid an unsentimental farewell to Social
Democratic politics following the vicious murders of Spartakus Bund
leaders Rosa Luxemburg and Karl Liebknecht by Freikorps troops
acting at the behest of the newly installed Social Democratic government in January 1919.[2]

During the early years of the Weimar Republic Marcuse underwent a
type of self-imposed "inner emigration." After writing a 1922 dissertation on *The German Artist Novel* heavily influenced by the early
aesthetics of Georg Lukács, he returned to his native Berlin to work in
an antiquarian bookshop.[3] During this time, he compiled a detailed
Schiller bibliography, steeped himself in the early Marx, and read two
classic texts of Hegelian Marxism that would have a profound influence
on his future philosophical development: Lukács's *History and Class
Consciousness* and Karl Korsch's *Marxism and Philosophy*, both of
which had appeared in 1923.

Later in the decade there occurred a publication "event" that lured
Marcuse back to the university: the 1927 appearance of Heidegger's
Being and Time. At the time Germany's philosophy seminars were still
dominated by staid and familiar prewar approaches: neo-Kantianism,
neo-Hegelianism, and positivism. For the younger generation, however,
the horrors of World War I represented a point of no return: the worldviews and perspectives that had predominated prior to 1914 seemed
entirely delegitimated. As Marcuse noted time and again, Heidegger's
thought seemed to offer something that the conventional academic
"school philosophies" lacked: a "philosophy of the *concrete.*"
Reflecting some fifty years later on the excitement generated by the
publication of *Being and Time*, Marcuse observed:

Heidegger's work appeared to me and my friends as a new beginning:
we experienced his book [*Being and Time*] (and his lectures, of which
we possessed transcripts) as, finally, a *concrete* philosophy: here was
talk of Existence, of *our* existence, of anxiety, care, boredom, etc.

And we also experienced an "academic" emancipation: Heidegger's interpretation of Greek philosophy and German idealism gave us new insight into lifeless texts.[4]

Marcuse's testimony concerning Heidegger's pedagogical prowess conforms with that of the philosopher's other prominent students during the 1920s: Hannah Arendt, Hans-Georg Gadamer, Hans Jonas, and Karl Löwith.[5] All five affirmed that what they found unique in Heidegger's approach was his capacity to revivify antiquated philosophical texts in light of present historical needs and concerns. In Heidegger's courses, doing philosophy ceased to be an exercise in disembodied, scholarly exegesis. Instead, their leitmotif seemed to be the Augustinian theme of *mea res agitur*: "my life is at stake." At issue was a momentous, hermeneutical encounter between the historical past and contemporary Being-in-the-world. By proceeding thusly, Heidegger was only being self-consistent: He was merely applying the principles of his own philosophy of *Existenz* to the subject matter of his lectures and seminars. Two of the central categories of *Being and Time*'s "existential analytic" were "temporality" and "historicity." Both notions addressed the way that we situate ourselves in time and history. In Heidegger's view, one of the hallmarks of "authentic" Being-in-the-world was a capacity to *actualize* the past in light of essential future possibilities. Conversely, inauthentic Dasein (called *das Man*) displayed a conformist willingness to adapt passively to circumstances — an existential lassitude that bore marked resemblances to the inert being of "things." Although at the time *Lebensphilosophie,* or "philosophy of life," flourished among popular writers (for example, Oswald Spengler and Ludwig Klages), Heidegger's genius lay in his ability to fuse the discourse of "everydayness" with the demands of "rigorous science" he had imbibed during his youthful apprenticeship with the founder of the phenomenological movement, Edmund Husserl. Thus, in view of the conservative approaches to scholarship that predominated among the German mandarin professorate during the 1920s, one can readily imagine the genuine excitement Heidegger's philosophical radicalism must have generated, especially among the "lost generation" of the postwar period.[6]

In a colorful 1929 letter, Marcuse described his initial impressions of Heidegger (whom he recalled from his previous stay in Freiburg as a PhD student in the early 1920s) as follows:

Concerning Heidegger: it is hard to imagine a greater difference between the shy and obstinate *Privatdozent* who eight years ago spoke from the window of a small lecture hall and the successor of

Husserl who lectures in an overflowing auditorium with at least six hundred listeners (mostly women) in brilliant lectures with unshakeable certainty, talking with that pleasant tremor in his voice which so excites the women, dressed in a sports outfit that almost looks like a chauffeur's uniform, darkly tanned, with the pathos of a teacher who feels himself completely to be an educator, a prophet and pathfinder and whom one indeed believes to be so. The ethical tendencies found in *Being and Time* — which aim at philosophy becoming practical — really seem to achieve a breakthrough in Heidegger himself, although, to be sure, in a way that is somewhat alienating. He is all in all too rhetorical, too preachy, too primitive ... In the large lecture on German Idealism and the philosophical problems of the present he has so far treated the dominant tendencies of contemporary philosophy as anthropological tendencies and metaphysics.[7]

Part of Marcuse's attraction to Heidegger's brand of *Existenzphilosophie* was spurred by the so-called crisis of Marxism. For Marcuse's generation hopes for a radical regeneration of the existing political order — one which seemed responsible for so much pointless social suffering and injustice — were rudely dashed with the collapse of the short-lived Council Republics (*Räterepubliken*) in Bavaria and Hungary following World War I. In his eyes, by brutally crushing the German Revolution, Social Democracy had merely compounded its sins of August 1914, when, by voting for war credits, it had forsaken the ideals of international socialism in favor of jingoistic militarism. Moreover, it is safe to assume that the Bolshevik Revolution of 1917 harbored few attractions for him. Marcuse undoubtedly accepted Rosa Luxemburg's trenchant critique of the authoritarian implications of Lenin's vanguardism.[8] In fact, most European socialists viewed Lenin's voluntarism as inappropriate for Western and Central Europe, where a more advanced and experienced proletariat existed.

Yet, concomitant with the *political* crisis of Marxism, there existed an *epistemological* crisis; in Marcuse's view, the two were necessarily linked. For under the tutelage of Engels and Karl Kautsky, the Second International had espoused a resolutely antiphilosophical, mechanistic interpretation of Marxism. This approach was predicated on an unreflective scientism (compare Engels's *The Dialectics of Nature*) as well as an antiquated theory of capitalism's automatic collapse.[9] Correspondingly, its leading theoreticians displayed a willful indifference to the "subjective" factor of working-class consciousness. Conversely, a willingness to address such questions directly and unapologetically made Lukács's *History and Class Consciousness* seem so refreshing — a beacon of illumination in the midst of a bleak intellectual and political landscape.

Thus, Marcuse believed that Heidegger's *Being and Time* represented a potentially valuable ally in the struggle against the reified social continuum of advanced industrial society. He conjectured that Heidegger's philosophy of existence possessed the conceptual means required to counteract an inverted social world in which, according to Marx, "social relations between men assume ... *the fantastic form of a relation between things*"?[10] In part, Marcuse read Heidegger's philosophy as an ontologically veiled *critique of reification*: an indictment of the way in which oppressive social circumstances militate against the possibility of human self-realization. It seemed that, like the critical Marxists Lukács and Korsch, Heidegger strove to surmount the fetishization of appearances that characterized the shadow world of bourgeois immediacy. Like Lukács and Korsch, in *Being and Time* Heidegger strove concertedly to break with the deterministic worldview of bourgeois science, in which human being or Dasein was degraded to the status of a "thing among things." After all, this was the main point behind Heidegger's critique of *Vorhandenheit* or Being present-at-hand as a mode of inauthenticity.[11] In Marcuse's view, the critique of "Everydayness" in *Being and Time*, Division I, in which Heidegger delivers a powerful indictment of inauthentic Being-in-the-world by recourse to concepts such as "Falling," "Idle Talk," "Publicness," and "the They," represents a welcome ontological complement to the discussions of reification in *Capital* and *History and Class Consciousness*. As Marcuse formulates this insight in "Concrete Philosophy":

> The world in which Dasein lives is also evolving to an ever greater degree into "busy-ness" [*Betrieb*]. The things encountered in it are viewed from the outset as "goods," as things that one must use, but not in the sense of using them to meet the needs of Dasein. Instead, they are used to occupy or to fill an otherwise aimless existence, until they actually do become "necessities." In this way more and more existences are consumed simply in order to keep the "busy-ness" operational. The form of existence of all classes had to hollow itself out in such a way that it has become necessary to place existence itself on a new foundation.[12]

In Marcuse's eyes, in *Being and Time* Heidegger, like the Hegelian Marxists, strove concertedly to break with the deterministic worldview of modern science, in which human being or Dasein was degraded to the status of a "thing among things." By proceeding positivistically, contemporary social science fetishized the standpoint of the "object" or "things." Methodologically speaking, it treated "persons" like "things" — as objects of administrative manipulation and control. The breakthrough entailed by Heidegger's philosophy of existence was that, proceeding from the standpoint of Dasein, it placed human reality rather than "objectivity" or "thinghood" at the center of its phenomenological perspective. It was this practice that provided it with the conceptual leverage to overcome the reifying orientation of traditional science.[13] As Marcuse explains:

> It becomes clear in this context why the ontological historicity of Dasein must also assume decisive significance for the methodology of the "social sciences." Social arrangements, economic orders, and political formations together constitute the happening of Dasein and must be viewed from the perspective of this existence (*Existenz*). If they are investigated from the outset as "things," with an eye towards their structure, their relationships and the laws of their development, the observations — most likely undertaken with the model of the natural sciences as their mistaken ideal — that result will be such that the meaning of these constructs cannot even appear. (HM, 39)

In the "Theses on Feuerbach" (1845) Marx had praised Hegel for having developed the "active side" of the dialectic, a dimension unknown both to the materialism of the High Enlightenment and to nineteenth-century positivism.[14] "The chief defect of all hitherto existing materialism — that of Feuerbach included — is that the thing, reality, sensuousness, is conceived only in the form of the object or of *contemplation*, but not as human sensuous activity, practice, not subjectively. Hence it happened that the active side, in contradistinction to materialism, was developed by idealism (but only abstractly, since, of course, idealism does not know real, sensuous activity as such)."[15] Could Heidegger, whose existential ontology seemed to be motivated by an analogous antiscientific animus, then be enlisted as fellow traveler in the Hegelian Marxist cause? This was the wager that Marcuse laid in 1928 when, as a twenty-nine year old, he followed Heidegger to Freiburg. At the time, Marcuse optimistically described the potential of Heidegger's 1927 masterwork as follows: "*Being and Time ...* seems to represent a *turning point in the history of philosophy*: the point at which bourgeois philosophy unmakes itself from the inside and clears the way for a new 'concrete' science" (HM, 10–11).

Marcuse was also favorably impressed by the Freiburg sage's efforts to break with the paradigm of German Idealism. The "transcendence of German Idealism": here was a project that seemed to unite Heidegger's existentialism and Marxism in a common cause. In the second half of the nineteenth century, neo-Kantianism, in keeping with the spirit of the age, had been transformed into a epistemological vindication of philosophy of science or positivism.[16] The noumenal dimension of Kant's ethics — for example, the regulative idea of humanity as a "kingdom of ends" — had been banished as an atavistic, metaphysical excrescence. From this standpoint it seemed impossible to redeem Kant as a genuine critic of the historical present. A similar fate of terminal irrelevance had apparently befallen Hegel's system. For it seemed that, with the exception of Dilthey's work, Hegel scholarship had degenerated into a type of neoscholasticism — an incessant, abstract clarification of the Master's impressive conceptual edifice as propounded in the *Science of Logic* and other works.[17] Since a critical thematization of "lived experience" played such a prominent role in Heidegger's fundamental ontology, at the time Marcuse surmised that it might provide the philosophical stimulus necessary to revivify an orthodox Marxist discourse that had lapsed into advanced senescence.

Marxism tried to diagnose the "objective," economic preconditions of capitalism's collapse, but it seemed to neglect the "subjective" side of the equation, working-class consciousness. Conversely, whereas Heidegger's philosophy excelled at describing the phenomenological structure of Being-in-the-world, its weakness lay in its incapacity to address those aspects of the contemporary crisis that were *social* and *historical* as opposed to *timeless* and *ontological.* A careful perusal of Marcuse's writings from 1928 to 1932 shows that his major reservation about Heidegger's thought concerned its capacity to descend from the rarefied heights of fundamental ontology in order to address matters of contemporary social and historical relevance. In other words: did the *Existenzialien* or basic concepts of *Being and Time* facilitate the tasks of concrete social analysis or were they, conversely, an ontological subterfuge?

In the "Theses on Feuerbach" Marx famously observed: "The question whether objective truth can be attributed to human thinking is not a question of theory but is a *practical* question. Man must prove the truth, that is, the reality and power, the this-sidedness of his thinking in practice. The dispute over the reality or nonreality of thinking which is isolated from practice is a purely *scholastic* question."[18] In a parallel vein, *Being and Time*'s existential analytic commenced with Dasein immersed in a series of practical involvements: everydayness, tools, concern, moods, Being-with-others, and, lastly, historicity. At the time Marcuse imagined, far from implausibly, that the two methodological approaches, both of which sought to transcend the ethereal claims of German idealism in a worldly and practical direction, could be viewed as mutual complements. In his 1929 essay, "Concrete Philosophy," Marcuse makes it quite clear why he believed *Existenzphilosophie* was uniquely relevant to the practical crises confronting humanity:

If the meaning of philosophizing is the making visible of truth, and if this truth has a fundamentally existential character, then not only is philosophizing a mode of human existing, but philosophy itself is, according to its very meaning, existential .... Authentic philosophizing refuses to remain at the stage of knowledge; rather, in driving this knowledge on to truth it strives for the concrete appropriation of that truth through human Dasein. Care [*Sorge*] for human existence and its truth makes philosophy a "practical science" in the deepest sense, and it also leads philosophy — and this is the crucial point — into the concrete distress [*Bedrängnis*] of human existence. (HM, 36)

In Marcuse's eyes, Heidegger's orientational breakthrough derived from the fact that in his thought, "philosophy is once again seen from the standpoint of concrete human existence and is interrogated with concrete human existence as its end" (HM, 37).

Part of Marcuse's attraction to Heidegger stemmed from his frustrations with the limitations of bourgeois "inwardness" (*Innerlichkeit*) — so pronounced in the tradition of German idealism — and his corresponding sympathies for the concepts of "action" and "life" that were so current during the 1920s. In this respect, Marcuse harbored a certain admiration for the "activist" components of existential ontology, in which "decisiveness" or "resolve" (*Entschlossenheit*) was one of the hallmarks of authenticity.

Similarly, in the 1930 habilitation study that Marcuse wrote under Heidegger's supervision, published two years later as *Hegel's Ontology and the Theory of Historicity*, the concept of "life" plays a key role. "Life" refers to the dimension of practical-experiential immediacy that, as a rule, is shunned by the contemplative and intellectualized orientation of bourgeois thought.[19] As Marcuse observes: "The 'we-like' process of Life, the confrontation through which reciprocal 'recognition' is actualized, is thus characterized by an 'act' [*Tun*]. Life fulfills its ontological meaning as well as its universal substantiality, that is, the bringing-to-truth and letting-be of all beings, only through the accomplishment of an *act*, through the concrete actual confrontation with itself and the world."[20] Undoubtedly, Marcuse felt that an infusion of "actionist" sentiment might awaken the proletariat from its narcoleptic torpor. Hence, in the passages from these early texts in which Marxian and existentialist notions are most intimately fused, Marcuse treats the proletariat both as the answer to the inequities of capitalism and as the solution to the (Heideggerian) problem of "authenticity":

Knowledge of authentic historicity and consciously historical existence is possible only when existence shatters reification ... Reified objectivities become historical by the very fact that living existence has become concerned with them .... Bourgeois philosophy, whenever it dealt with the world constituted by existence, had to relegate it to the immanence of consciousness ... [But] there is an existence whose thrownness consists precisely in overcoming its own thrownness. *Today, historical action is possible only as action of the proletariat, because the proletariat constitutes that existence which necessarily contains this action.* (HM, 32)

But undoubtedly the Heideggerian concept that most appealed to Marcuse during the late 1920s was "Historicity." As Marcuse observes in "Contributions to a Phenomenology of Historical Materialism": "It is precisely in knowledge of historicity that the most momentous decision leads to the decision either to struggle for the recognized necessity, even against Dasein's inherited existence" (HM, 23). In Division II of *Being and Time*, Heidegger abruptly shifted from the standpoint of a highly individualized, Kierkegaardian Dasein, reminiscent of *Fear and Trembling*'s Knight of Faith, to the perspective of a *historical collectivity*. Under Dilthey's influence, the categorial framework of Division I was drastically altered through the employment of concepts such as "destiny," "community," "generation," and "the historical life of a people" (*Volk*).[21] In Marcuse's view it seemed clear that "historicity" represented the essential link between existentialism and historical materialism.

In *Construction of the Historical World*, Dilthey had stressed the importance of *Erlebnis* — "lived experience" — as a response to the "crisis of historicism": the nineteenth-century understanding of history qua positive science. For if in the guise of historicism history writing strove to capture the past "the way it really was" (Ranke), it remained incapable of providing orientation or directives for the historical present. According to Dilthey, "Historicity" meant not only that all life was historically determined, but that it was in essence "meaningfully" structured in a way that facilitated hermeneutic understanding across generations. Thus, history qua "Historicity" represented a reservoir of interpretive meaning that transcended the soulless, positivist accumulation of data by traditional history writing (*Historie*).

But it was left to Heidegger in *Being and Time* to take the final step in the development of the concept. Whereas Dilthey stressed the fact that life, qua historicity, was *in* history, Heidegger emphasized that *existence was itself historical*: the past yielded traditions on which peoples and individuals could *act* in view of future possibilities. As such "futurity" (*Zukunftigkeit*) became Historicity's distinguishing feature. In this way, Heidegger imparted an *activist* component to historicity — historicity as a mode of authentic collective becoming — that remained occluded in Dilthey's formulations. As Heidegger remarks, "History as *Geschichte* signifies a happening [*Geschehen*] that we ourselves are, where we are there present.... We are history, that is, our own past. Our future lives out of its past."[22] Thus, in Heidegger's optic, Historicity ceased to be a category of contemplative, scholarly understanding. Instead, it became a virtual call to arms, a summons to authentic ontological engagement.

At the same time it is clear that Marcuse never identified with *Existenzphilosophie* uncritically or naïvely. In the essays that follow, time and again, he openly ponders whether Heidegger's ontological standpoint can be reconciled with the genuinely historical concerns of critical Marxism. As he demonstratively opines in "Contributions to a Phenomenology of Historical Materialism": "We therefore demand that ... the phenomenology of human Dasein initiated by Heidegger forge onward, coming to completion in a phenomenology of concrete Dasein and the concrete historical action demanded by history in each historical situation" (HM, 20). In the back of his mind there seemed constantly to lurk a troubling question: were Heidegger's efforts to produce a "philosophy of the concrete" genuine or did they merely culminate in an alluring yet deceptive "pseudoconcreteness"? For if the state of "alienation" (or "inauthentic Dasein") described by existential ontology were perceived as a timeless and unalterable *condition humaine*, there would be no real incentive to practically redress this condition. Instead, it would represent an inevitable destiny we would be powerless to emend. As Marcuse observes:

Now in order to be able to approach Dasein, in order to be able to take hold of it in its existence, concrete philosophy must *become historical*, it must insert itself into the concrete historical situation. The becoming historical of philosophy means, firstly, that concrete philosophy has to investigate contemporaneous Dasein in its historical situation, with an eye towards which possibilities for the appropriation of truths are available.... Concrete philosophy can thus only approach existence if it seeks out Dasein in the sphere in which its existence is based: as it *acts* in its world in accordance with its historical situation. (HM, 44, 47)

Marcuse's early essays make it unmistakably clear that *capitalism* — imperialism, finance capital, monopolies, cartels, and so forth — was the social formation that determined the nature of contemporary politics and society. In his view, in order to become "concrete," at some point philosophy would need to address these problems and themes.

After a prolonged philosophical apprenticeship under Heidegger's tutelage (1928–32), including the aforementioned postdoctoral study, Marcuse felt that Heidegger's approach was incapable of making the transition from the "ontological" to the "ontic" (or historical) plane of analysis. In other words, fundamental ontology's original existential promise remained unfulfilled: it provided only a "pseudoconcreteness." In a 1974 interview, Marcuse reflects on the reasons underlying his ultimate disillusionment with Heideggerianism:

> I first, like all the others, believed there could be some combination between existentialism and Marxism, precisely because of their insistence on concrete analysis of the actual human existence, human beings, and their world. But I soon realized that Heidegger's concreteness was to a great extent a phony, a false concreteness, and that in fact his philosophy was just as abstract and just as removed from reality, even avoiding reality, as the philosophies which at that time had dominated German universities, namely a rather dry brand of neo-Kantianism, neo-Hegelianism, neo-Idealism, but also positivism. (HM, 166)

One aspect of Heidegger's philosophy that, early on, raised suspicions in Marcuse's eyes was the metaphysical orientation his thought assumed following the appearance of *Being and Time*. In Heidegger's subsequent writings — "What Is Metaphysics?" *Kant and the Problem of Metaphysics*, and *The Essence of Reasons* — it seemed that instead of turning toward problems of lived experience, his thought became increasingly ethereal and unworldly. What differentiated his thought from the traditional contemplative ideal of *philosophia perennis* became difficult to specify. Indeed, circa 1930, with the celebrated "Turn" (*Kehre*) in his thinking, Heidegger's philosophy seemed to abandon the existential concerns that had occupied center stage in *Being and Time*. He increasingly gravitated toward a more hermetic, self-referential, ontological focus in which the "history of Being" (*Seinsgeschichte*) took precedence over the paltry pursuits of Dasein. Ironically, as his philosophy became more attuned to the primordial "sendings of Being" (*Seinsgeschick*), Heidegger personally became embroiled in a series of compromising political involvements on behalf of the twentieth century's most murderous political dictatorship: Hitler's Third Reich.[23]

The circumstances surrounding Marcuse's failure to habilitate under Heidegger with his study of *Hegel's Ontology* are still ambiguous. Moreover, it seems that, later on, Marcuse himself provided conflicting accounts of what actually transpired. To some, he claimed that

Heidegger had never read the work; to others, he maintained that Heidegger had refused to accept it.[24] The most likely scenario suggests that upon finishing the work in the fall of 1930, Marcuse, apprised of the fact that Heidegger would not accept it, refrained from submitting it in order to avoid the ignominy of having it formally rejected. During the 1980s Frankfurt School historian Rolf Wiggershaus found a 1932 letter from Edmund Husserl to University of Frankfurt Rector Kurt Riezler confirming that, for reasons that are still unclear, Heidegger "blocked" Marcuse's attempt to habilitate.[25] The ill-starred habilitation study was published in 1932. A year earlier, Marcuse had apparently felt no qualms about asking Heidegger for a letter of recommendation to the eventual publisher, Klostermann Verlag.[26]

Despite his failure to habilitate in 1930, Marcuse's fascination with the prospects of a Heidegger–Marx synthesis remained keen, as one can discern from a close reading of his important 1933 essay, "On the Foundations of the Philosophical Concept of Labor in Economics." Like his earlier forays, this text, too, tries to enrich the traditional Marxist understanding of labor by recourse to an analysis of labor's main ontological features.

    But one of the most surprising aspects of the 1933 essay is Marcuse's distinctly un-Marxian denigration of labor. In the Paris Manuscripts Marx had opposed the predominant Lockean-Puritan understanding of labor ("the sweat of our brow, the blood of our hands"), which is integrally tied to the notion of original sin, by viewing labor as an essential manifestation of human self-fulfillment. Under the influence of romantic doctrines of self-cultivation (*Bildung*), Marx argues that, through labor, humanity simultaneously humanizes the natural world and realizes its own innate potential. Conversely, in "On the Concept of Labor," Marcuse's operative idea is the "burdensome character of labor" (*Lastcharakter der Arbeit*). Contra Marx, he suggests that one is never free when one labors insofar as praxis remains subordinate to the contours and dictates of the "object" or "thing." As Marcuse contends:

> Whether explicitly or not, willingly or not, labor is always concerned with *the thing itself*. In laboring, the laborer is always "with the thing": whether one stands by a machine, draws technical plans, is concerned with organizational measures, researches scientific problems, instructs people, etc. In his activity he allows himself to be directed by the thing, subjects himself and obeys its laws, even when he dominates his object, directs it, guides it, and lets it go its own way. In each case he is not "with himself," does not passively stand by his own existence. (HM, 138)[27]

The philosophical sources for Marcuse's skepticism about the emancipatory potential of labor are various. In part, he relies on the Aristotelian (and scholastic) concepts of *scholē* or "leisure" as a sphere existing beyond the realm of material necessity. He also seems to embrace the Hegelian-German idealist elevation of "subjective spirit" (philosophy, culture, religion) over "objective spirit" (politics, economics, social institutions). Lastly, he seems to have been influenced by Marx's claim in Volume 2 of *Capital* that the "realm of freedom" exists "beyond the realm of necessity" — that is, beyond the sphere of labor.

The other notable feature of "On the Concept of Labor" is Marcuse's enthusiastic endorsement of Schiller's notion of the "play impulse" as a salutary contrast to the drudgery and toil of labor. (After he completed his dissertation on the *German Artist Novel* in 1922, one of the tasks to which Marcuse turned his energies was the compilation of a comprehensive Schiller bibliography, which he completed in 1925.)[28] In *Letters on the Aesthetic Education of Man* (1795), Schiller defined the "play impulse" as the activity capable of reconciling the "rational" and "sensuous" dimensions of human nature, which, in the modern age seem irreconcilably opposed. In Letter XV, Schiller set forth his radical proposition: "Man plays only when he is in the full sense of the word a man, and *he is only wholly Man when he is playing.*"[29] In "On the Concept of Labor" Marcuse emphatically agrees with Schiller, remarking that when one plays, one no longer gives oneself body and soul to "objects" or "things." Instead, "For once, one does entirely as one pleases with objects; one places oneself beyond them and becomes 'free' from them." "In the single toss of a ball," Marcuse continues, "the player achieves an infinitely greater triumph of human freedom over objectification than in the most powerful accomplishment of technical labor" (HM, 128).

As Marcuse admits in a later interview, given Germany's deteriorating political climate, as of 1932 he had abandoned his dream of becoming a university professor.[30] Through the mediation of Husserl and Riezler, he established contact with the Frankfurt-based Institute for Social Research, whose director, Max Horkheimer, had already made plans to transfer the Institute's administrative facilities to Geneva. Marcuse oversaw operations of the Geneva branch during 1933, before emigrating, along with other Institute members, to New York the following year.

But in 1932 a publishing event occurred that functioned as a watershed in Marcuse's intellectual development: the publication of Marx's *Economic and Philosophical Manuscripts of 1844* in volume three of the *Marx–Engels Gesamtausgabe* (MEGA). Marcuse wrote a long review essay that appeared in the Social Democratic journal, *Die*

Gesellschaft, in which he hailed the Manuscripts' appearance as "a crucial event in the history of Marxist studies." It would only be a slight exaggeration to say that, suddenly, what for four years Marcuse had been seeking in Heidegger he found in Marx: a philosophical grounding for historical materialism. As Marcuse observes in retrospect: in 1932 "the *Economic and Philosophical Manuscripts of 1844* appeared. That was probably the turning point. This was, in a certain sense, a new practical and theoretical Marxism. After that, Heidegger versus Marx was no longer a problem for me."[31] In this way, Marcuse brought to completion a philosophical odyssey that led "from Heidegger to Horkheimer."[32]

In Marcuse's eyes, the 1844 Manuscripts confirmed his suspicions (based on close readings of early texts such as *The Holy Family, The German Ideology*, and the "Theses on Feuerbach," as read through the prism of Lukács) that Marx's project had been formulated in dialogue with classical German philosophy. Moreover, it became increasingly clear that Marxism's philosophical origins, far from being a youthful excrescence, were absolutely central to its status as a program of social and political transformation. As Marcuse remarks, "A rough formula which could be used as a starting point would be that the revolutionary critique of political economy itself has a philosophical foundation, just as, conversely, the philosophy underlying it already contains revolutionary praxis" (HM, 87).

The Paris Manuscripts meant that the Second International's scientific understanding of Marxism qua "socialist economics" was based on a potentially fatal interpretive misunderstanding. Instead, Marxism was centrally concerned with problems of human self-realization — with humanity's "species being" (*Gattungswesen*) — that had preoccupied German idealism, albeit with an important methodological difference: Marx was interested in solving these problems "practically" rather than merely "theoretically." Moreover, in poring over the Manuscripts, Marcuse discovered that the "existential" concerns that, four years earlier, had attracted him to Heidegger were fundamentally shared by Marx. For their leitmotif was the concept of "alienation." Thus, they confirmed the reading of Marx that Marcuse had heretofore found most persuasive — Lukács's understanding of Marxism as a critique of "reification," the unwarranted transformation of human society into a world dominated by economic categories or "things." Moreover, Marx's discussion was tied to a vivid, quasi-phenomenological, sociohistorical portrayal of alienation's genesis and development — precisely the dimension of "concreteness" that Marcuse found lacking in Heidegger's ontological account.

Marcuse's momentous encounter with the early Marx is also fascinating for historical reasons. It foreshadows the rediscovery of the "philosophical Marx" by the Central European dissident movement during the 1960s (Leszek Kolakowski in Poland, Karel Kosik in Czechoslovakia, Agnes Heller in Hungary, and the Belgrade Praxis circle), which provided impetus for the reforms embodied in the slogan, "socialism with a human face" (of course, these hopes for internal reform were brutally crushed by the 1968 Soviet invasion of Prague).[33] Moreover, it anticipates the "phenomenological Marxist" vogue of the 1950s and 1960s, whose leading representatives were Jean-Paul Sartre, Maurice Merleau-Ponty, Tran Duc Thao, Kosik, and Enzo Paci.[34] Like Marcuse, the phenomenological Marxists (who often borrowed as much from Husserl's philosophy as they did from Heidegger) believed that phenomenology represented an important philosophical counterweight to the positivist domination of the human sciences — and thus a potential methodological stimulus toward the creation of a humane social world.

Shortly after Marcuse joined the Institute for Social Research, Germany's political landscape underwent a radical transformation: on January 30, 1933, Hitler was named chancellor. The end of the Weimar Republic was a foregone conclusion. On March 23, following the Reichstag fire a month earlier, German legislators (minus the Communists) voted emergency powers that facilitated dictatorial rule. Weeks earlier the Gestapo commandeered the Institute's facilities in Frankfurt, confiscating its library. On April 1, the Nazis implemented the anti-Semitic law for the Reconstruction of the German Civil Service, which effectively banned Jews from university life.

It was under these circumstances that, on May 1, with great fanfare, Heidegger officially joined the Nazi Party. A few weeks earlier, he had been elected rector of Freiburg University by an academic senate that had already been purged of Jews and political undesirables. In his new position of authority, Heidegger oversaw changes in the university system that accorded with the Nazis' *Führerprinzip*. In June he sent an urgent telegram to Hitler recommending that an upcoming conference of German university rectors be postponed until *Gleichschaltung* — the Nazi euphemism for the elimination of political opposition — could be completed. In the fall, he went on the stump on behalf of the Nazi referendum on Germany's withdrawal from the League of Nations, claiming "Let not ideas and doctrines be your guide. The Führer is Germany's only reality and its law."

One of the most troubling aspects of Heidegger's political conversion was the facility with which he was able to justify his Nazi allegiances based on concepts seamlessly culled from *Being and Time*. For example, he invoked the notion of existential "decisiveness" (*Entschlossenheit*) as a justification for collective engagement on behalf of the National

Socialist *Volksgemeinschaft*. In a stroke, Heidegger reconfigured the ontological framework of *Being and Time* Division II, which stressed concepts such as "destiny," "historicity," "*Volk*," and "choosing one's hero," to provide philosophical window dressing for Germany's "National Revolution." As Karl Löwith remarked perceptively: "One need only ... apply authentic 'existence' [in *Being and Time*] ... to specifically German existence and its historical destiny in order thereby ... to proceed from 'destruction' [*Destruktion*] now on the terrain of politics."[35] Marcuse claimed that, although at the time he and his fellow students had never suspected Heidegger's right-radical political allegiances, in retrospect, the philosopher's engagement on behalf of National Socialism made sense:

> If you look at his view of human existence, of Being-in-the-world, you will find a highly repressive, highly oppressive interpretation ... : "idle talk, curiosity, ambiguity, fall and Being-thrown-into, concern, Being-towards-death, anxiety, dread, boredom," and so on. Now this gives a picture which plays well on the fears and frustrations of men and women in a repressive society: a joyless existence; overshadowed by death and anxiety; human material for the authoritarian personality. (HM, 169)

To the shock of Heidegger's students and disciples, many of whom happened to be Jewish, it seemed that the philosopher had "chosen" Hitler as his "hero." It turned out to be a fateful decision that would dog Heidegger's reputation until the end of his life. Marcuse, for his part, having recently joined the Institute for Social Research — a milieu that was extremely unsympathetic to Heidegger's thought — had already distanced himself from the Master's framework and influence.[36] In his eyes, the philosopher's Nazism represented a point of no return.

As time progressed, Marcuse seemed able to separate Heidegger's philosophical genius from his ill-fated political alliance with Nazism. In "German Philosophy in the Twentieth Century," he avows that during the 1920s, "What Heidegger proposed as a concrete analysis of human existence and its modes of being constitutes one of the most fertile avenues of modern philosophy" (HM, 160). With the war's end, Marcuse returned to Germany in his capacity as OSS operative and met with Heidegger. By his own admission, the encounter was unproductive. There followed an impassioned exchange of letters, in which Marcuse implored his mentor to distance himself publicly from the evils of the regime he had briefly served.[37] Philosophers are allowed to err, remarked Marcuse. But in this case, the "error" — which involved unqualified allegiance to a fundamentally racist and genocidal regime — signified the negation of the Western tradition and all it represented. True to form, Heidegger remained unrepentant. In his eyes, the Allies had committed atrocities equal to those perpetrated by the Nazis. And certain Nazi goals — for example, a deliverance of the West from the ills of communism — in his view remained admirable. At this point, there seemed little more to say, and communication between them broke off.

Marcuse's renown during the 1960s was totally unexpected. As much as any other works of postwar cultural criticism, his *Eros and Civilization* and *One-Dimensional Man* anticipated the decade's libidinal-political strivings. Like Tocqueville a century earlier, Marcuse's political influence spread rapidly across two continents. He counseled both the American and German New Lefts that, at best, their actions could serve as a catalyst to heighten awareness about the injustices of imperialism and social inequality. However, should the students delude themselves into behaving as bona fide revolutionary actors, they were destined to run aground.[38]

One of the challenging interpretive questions that has beset Marcuse scholarship concerns the extent to which Heideggerian themes play a role in his later writings. Did Marcuse, in some meaningful sense, remain a *left-wing Heideggerian?* Did he in fact transpose a "diagnosis of the age" (*Zeitdiagnose*) formulated by Heidegger and others during the interwar period to the advanced industrial societies of the postwar era? As we have already seen, for a time Marcuse was highly intrigued by the prospects for "concrete philosophy" presented by Heidegger's existential interpretive framework. Did the later Marcuse then attempt to refunction the withering critique of mass society contained in Heidegger's treatment of "everydayness" for the ends of the political Left?

In order to answer these questions properly, one must take into account the historical situation with which Marcuse found himself confronted during the postwar period. Fascism had been defeated. Yet, monopoly capitalism — the economic system responsible for its original triumph — remained firmly entrenched. The cold war era, dominated by the apocalyptical prospect of nuclear annihilation, fomented a sinister atmosphere of international stalemate in which radical political demands could find no outlet. Moreover, unprecedented economic affluence lent Western societies a distinctly Huxleyan quality — as though the West had responded to *1984* by creating its own *Brave New World*. A ceaseless proliferation of superfluous commodities seemed to obliterate the distinction between true and false needs. Prodded by Madison Avenue, a narcissistic libidinal cathexis developed between consumers and their commodities: they seemed to be literally in love with their own affluence. In *One-Dimensional Man*, Marcuse proffered a memorable analysis of this strange social-psychological conjuncture in his discussion of "repressive desublimation." Whereas for Freud, sublimation bespoke the rechanneling of libidinal impulses into higher creative pursuits, the ethos of postwar capitalism, conversely, demanded a diversion of Eros towards the regressive ends of "consumption for consumption's sake." The entire system, lamented Marcuse, seemed impervious to rational critique. Its implicit rationality — its flawless capacity to "deliver the goods" — masked a greater irrationality: the fact that life's higher purposes were sacrificed to a never-ending cycle of "production for production's sake." Under these circumstances the later Heidegger's quasi-phobic concern about "technology" qua "Enframing" — the thoughtless expenditure of Being under the sign of "standing reserve" — seemed fundamentally confirmed. At a strategic juncture of *One-Dimensional Man*, Marcuse quotes Heidegger's argument in "The Question Concerning Technology" to drive home his point: "Modern man takes the entirety of Being as raw material for production and subjects the entirety of the object-world to the sweep and order of production .... The use of machinery and the production of machines is not technics itself but merely an adequate instrument for the realization of the essence of technics in its objective raw material."[39]

In "Some Social Implications of Modern Technology," written during the late 1940s, Marcuse hewed to the Marxist view that technology was socially neutral.[40] Its employment under a given set of social relations determined whether it was put to emancipatory or reactionary uses. However, in Marcuse's eyes, qualitatively new forms of domination that had been introduced by late capitalism had fundamentally altered this verdict. Instead, given the seductive blandishments of a new form of socially administered hedonism that classical Marxism had never anticipated, science and technology now appeared as *autonomous sources of domination*. In *Capital*, Marx foresaw capitalism's collapse based on a theory of social immiseration. But the "New Industrial State" (J. K. Galbraith) of late capitalism had forced critical Marxists to confront an unforeseen situation in which the basic needs of the working classes had been satisfied within the confines of the existing system. In essence, the consumer society had succeeded in rendering the emancipatory aims of social revolution superfluous.

Given the system's unprecedented capacity to sublimate and defuse social conflict, Marcuse had begun to search for heretofore untapped repositories of contestation. One well-known source was the "Great Refusal" of modern poetry and literature, whose foremost representative was surrealism. Marcuse perceived the surrealists' love of scandal and provocation — their open renunciation of the predominant universe of social signification — as a direct challenge to the reigning social order's raison d'être. But just as in *Being and Time* Heidegger had explored the ontological bases of social being, during the 1950s Marcuse began investigating whether new incentives to social rebellion could be discovered in Freud's theory of the instincts. Thus, in *Eros and Civilization*, departing from Freud's notion of the pleasure principle, Marcuse postulated a biological drive towards uninhibited libidinal gratification that had been blocked by the "performance principle" of late capitalism. Could there exist, mused Marcuse, an *instinctual basis for socialism*, one capable of undermining from within the contemporary continuum of domination? Certainly these late reflections on matters of philosophical anthropology bore a distinct resemblance to the mode of ontological questioning Heidegger had developed in *Being and Time*. As Marcuse speculates in *An Essay on Liberation*:

Prior to all ethical behavior in accordance with specific social standards, prior to all ideological expression, *morality is a disposition of the organism*, perhaps rooted in the erotic drive to counter aggressiveness, to create and preserve "ever greater unities of life." We would then have, this side of all "values," *an instinctual foundation for solidarity among human beings* — a solidarity which has been effectively repressed in line with the requirements of a class society but which now appears as a precondition for liberation.[41]

From these remarks, one can readily discern the extent to which German thought of the 1920s remained a determinate influence on Marcuse's later worldview. Without much effort, one can trace his powerful critique of social technocracy in *One-Dimensional Man* and other later works to the intellectual framework he developed under Heidegger's tutelage in the late 1920s and early 1930s. For it was under the Freiburg sage's influence that Marcuse first cultivated a sensitivity to the manifestations of societal reification, phenomena that, in *Being and Time,* Heidegger treated under the rubric of "inauthenticity."

If Marcuse's writings still speak to us today — and on this score there can be little doubt — it is because of his talents as an *unorthodox* Marxist. For in an era where official Marxism had degenerated into a repressive "science of legitimation" (Oskar Negt), the Frankfurt School philosopher proceeded to reinvigorate dialectical thought by drawing freely on a plethora of complementary critical approaches: Hegelianism, psychoanalysis, and the aesthetic dimension. In retrospect, however, it is clear that during the late 1920s he took an important first step in the spirit of left-wing heterodoxy when he experimented with the iconoclastic idea of fusing Heidegger with Marx. It is one of the true ironies of twentieth-century intellectual history that during the 1930s Marcuse went on to refine this paradigm under the auspices of the Institute for Social Research, where matters Heideggerian were viewed as heresy and anathema.

4

Critical Reflections on Marcuse's Theory of Revolution

From Berlin to Berkeley

Herbert Marcuse was an unlikely candidate for the role of spiritual godfather of the New Left. Born in Berlin in 1898, Marcuse witnessed the German Revolution of 1918–19 first hand, and these events would leave an indelible mark on his subsequent political formation. He was drafted into the German army at the age of eighteen, and his early political sympathies lay with the moderate Social Democrats. In 1918 Marcuse was elected as a deputy to one of the revolutionary soldiers councils that emerged throughout the country during the war's later stages. Like many leftists of his generation, his alienation from Social Democratic politics followed from the brutal murders of Spartacus League members Rosa Luxemburg and Karl Liebknecht in January 1919 at the hands of the ruling Social Democratic government.

Thereafter Marcuse embarked on a fascinating intellectual and political odyssey. In 1928 he moved to Freiburg where for four years he studied philosophy with Martin Heidegger. At the time he was convinced that Heidegger's existentialism offered a dimension of "concreteness" that was missing from the reigning scientific currents of Marxism. But soon he came to view the potentials of Heideggerian Marxism as illusory. In 1930 he submitted a habilitation study on Hegel that Heidegger rejected. In any event the political winds of Germany's moribund Weimar Republic were rapidly shifting. Heidegger himself would soon go over to the Nazis. As a Marxist and a Jew, Marcuse realized his future as a German academic was hopeless. Through the mediation of Edmund Husserl, he established contact with the Frankfurt-based Institute for Social Research, whose new director, Max Horkheimer, was already anticipating the rigors of political exile. Marcuse's association with the Frankfurt tradition of critical Marxism would prove a defining intellectual influence.

Marcuse recognized the 1932 publication of Marx's *Economic and Philosophical Manuscripts of 1844* as "a crucial event in the history of Marxist studies."[1] For these texts revealed a romantic, philosophical Marx, still under Hegel's thrall, for whom the alienation of human essence — man's "species being" — was the central issue. At odds with the narrowly determinist, economic approach to Marx that had been decreed by the Second International, the Paris Manuscripts unveiled a humanist Marx for whom "communism" represented a solution to the fundamental existential dilemmas of mankind.

The Paris Manuscripts confirmed Marcuse's antipathy to the reigning forms of institutionalized Marxism. In his mind Marx's humanistic message became fused with the ideals of German romanticism: the emancipation of human sensuality, a new harmony between man and nature, overcoming the antithesis between work and play. In Schiller's *Letters on the Aesthetic Education of Mankind* — a text that Marcuse revered — the German poet had celebrated the "play impulse" as the reconciliation between reason and feeling, two faculties that had become fatally dissociated in the modern age. In Marcuse's view, socialism would be utopian or it would not be at all. Any version of socialism that neglected the *aesthetic* dimension of human emancipation (in the Paris Manuscripts, Marx, in the romantic spirit, went so far as to associate socialism with the "emancipation of the human senses") remained chained to the realm of necessity. It was essentially bourgeois.

The relationship between Marcuse and the New Left was never entirely harmonious. Its anti-intellectual, mindlessly activist currents had little patience for Marcuse's brand of philosophical rigor, not to mention his strong allegiances to European cultural traditions. The New Left wanted to view itself as a new revolutionary subject. Marcuse, though sympathetic to its aims and objectives, time and again proclaimed the movement's historical limitations. In his view, the students at best could function as a catalyst for a broader alliance of marginalized social forces — minorities, the unemployed, women, third world activists — which, when united, might seriously challenge first world power and affluence. Still, the author of *One-Dimensional Man* was never overly sanguine about such prospects. He had lived too long and witnessed too many failed revolutions.

Perhaps the epitome of the ill-fated alliance between Marcuse and his youthful admirers occurred at the 1966 Socialist Scholars Conference in New York. Marcuse, along with Isaac Deutscher, was listed as a featured speaker for the inaugural panel "On Socialist Man." At the last minute, it was announced that Marcuse would not be able to attend. When word leaked out that he had shunned the New York gathering in order to attend a Hegel conference in Prague, it seemed there could be no doubt that his first allegiance lay with esoteric philosophy rather than with the political aims of the movement.

Still, in 1968 a contemporary observer could describe Marcuse as "the most widely discussed thinker within the American Left today."[2] A year earlier the *New York Times* cited Marcuse's 1965 essay, "Repressive Tolerance," as the document most often mentioned by student radicals in their discussions of tactics. To be sure, Marcuse's influence on the New Left was relatively late in coming. The impact of 1950s social critics such as David Riesman, C. Wright Mills, and Paul Goodman was of much greater importance during the student movement's crucial formative years. Nevertheless, the visceral radicalism of a book such as *One-Dimensional Man* (1964) — where Marcuse, invoking surrealism and Freud, spoke of the Great Refusal and the perils of "repressive desublimation" — found deep resonances among a generation of student rebels.[3]

After all, the rebellion's uniqueness lay in its ability to fuse existential concerns with more traditional political themes. By the early 1960s, the irreconcilable tensions between ideal and reality in American life could no longer be camouflaged or disguised. The ethos of total revolt embraced by Marcuse, his sensitivity to the Dionysian and poetic dimensions of contemporary political rebellion (epitomized by works such as *An Essay on Liberation*), outfitted him well for the unanticipated role of elder statesman of the student revolution. While his Frankfurt School cohorts, Horkheimer and Adorno, desperately sought refuge from the era's political turbulence, Marcuse eagerly confronted the intellectual and political challenges of the day. As his friend Jürgen Habermas once remarked: "Although a rather shy person, Marcuse was never afraid of being outspoken and taking the risk of oversimplification, if there seemed to be no other way to address an important issue."[4]

"A Biological Foundation for Socialism?"

Prior to all ethical behavior in accordance with specific, social standards, prior to all ideological expression, morality is a "disposition" of

the organism, perhaps rooted in the erotic drive to counter aggressiveness, to create and preserve "ever greater unities" of life. We would
then have *an instinctual foundation for solidarity among human beings*
— a solidarity which has been effectively repressed in line with the
requirements of class society but which now appears as a precondition
for liberation.

Marcuse, An Essay on Liberation

Habermas has referred to *Eros and Civilization* (1955) as "the most
Marcusian" of Marcuse's books.[5] It has often been hailed as a classical
example of the "Freud–Marx synthesis" that would become fashionable
during the 1960s. Remarkably, though, upon perusing the index, one
finds that Marx's name appears nowhere in the book's pages. By
employing this Trojan horse strategy, Marcuse managed to turn sleight-
of-hand into a tour de force: in McCarthyism's aftermath, and at the
height of the cold war, he presented an impassioned indictment of the
spiritual and libidinal deprivations of modern capitalism. In an era of
resounding political quietism and lockstep cultural conformity aptly
characterized by a series of memorable metaphors — "the lonely
crowd," "the power elite," and "the affluent society" — Marcuse
discovered a source of potential opposition where few had thought to
look: in the instinctual depths of the individual psyche. Whereas, previously, Freud's theories had been viewed as an unambiguous profession
of cultural pessimism (Freud once famously remarked that the goal of
psychoanalysis was to turn "hysterical human misery into normal
human unhappiness"), Marcuse reread them against the grain as
providing nothing less than an *anthropology of liberation*.

What was it that motivated Marcuse to turn to Freud in the 1950s?
Under the influence of Lukács and Hegelian Marxism, Marcuse had
always been interested in the problem of "consciousness." In his view,
objective conditions alone — a remarkable degree of economic
prosperity, for example — could never account for the co-optation of
the working class as a potentially revolutionary force. For, following
World War I and again in the 1930s, objective conditions for progressive social change seemed ripe; on both occasions, a full-scale crisis
existed, yet the working class succumbed to crushing defeats. Orthodox
Marxism, with its narrowly materialist epistemology, had essentially
dismissed the problem of consciousness as a pseudoproblem. But
Marcuse was convinced that the key to capitalism's staying power
resided in its formidable capacities to integrate its potential opponents
psychologically and ideologically. In his understanding, the reigning
structures of domination had been "internalized" to such an extent that
they preformed the psychic makeup of individuals. He conceived of

Eros and Civilization as a latter-day "discourse on voluntary servitude." Nor were his conclusions as entirely speculative as they might at first seem. Rather, they were based on empirical studies of working-class attitudes conducted by the Frankfurt School in the 1930s and 1940s.

As anyone familiar with his views knows well, Freud was anything but a libertine. Although his "libido theory" held that all neurosis possesses a sexual origin, Freud in no way subscribed to the converse proposition: that untrammeled sexual gratification would be a panacea. Freud's hard-nosed conception of the "reality principle" sought to put an end to all such potential misappropriations. In works such as *Civilization and Its Discontents*, he argued that human society was predicated on massive instinctual repression. Such repression was necessary for human cooperation upon which the self-preservation of the species depended. To think otherwise was utopian. Should humanity abandon itself to the "pleasure principle" — to the lures of instantaneous libidinal satisfaction — the fragile edifice of civilization would come tumbling down. In stolid Viennese fashion, Freud hailed the virtues of sublimation: the intellectually gifted should turn their unsatisfied cravings into great art or science. For the hoi polloi, conversely, there was presumably little to do other than to resign themselves to the rigors of manual labor — and take frequent cold showers.

In the opening chapters of *Eros and Civilization*, Marcuse claimed to have discovered a "hidden trend in psychoanalysis" that was profoundly at odds with Freud's vaunted cultural pessimism. Following Freud, Marcuse claimed that, for both the individual and the species, "the replacement of the pleasure principle by the reality principle is the great traumatic event in the development of man."[6] Taken by itself, the pleasure principle or Eros inclines toward immediate gratification. As Freud once put it: "the unconscious knows no 'no.'" Yet, owing to the imperatives of survival, these profound instinctual longings must be kept at bay by the psychic emissaries of the reality principle, the ego and superego. Freud's account of the pleasure principle's elemental libidinal yearnings suggested to Marcuse its fundamental emancipatory potential. Consequently, he would endow the unconscious — the site where the libido's repressed erotic longings have been stored — with a type of antediluvian utopian status: it represented the ultimate repository of humanity's desire for unlimited happiness and fulfillment. As Marcuse explains:

> The unconscious, the deepest and oldest layer of the mental personality, *is* the drive for integral gratification, which is absence of want and repression. As such it is the immediate identity of necessity and freedom. According to Freud's conception the equation of freedom and happiness tabooed by the conscious is upheld by the unconscious.

Its truth, although repelled by consciousness, continues to haunt the mind; it preserves the memory of past stages of individual development at which integral gratification is obtained.[7]

Whereas psychoanalysis stimulated memory in order to make what was unconscious conscious, thereby to effectuate a "cure," Marcuse endowed unconscious memories themselves with a social revolutionary function. In this sense he could go so far as to claim in a highly problematical, anti-Freudian vein, that *"Regression assumes a progressive function."*

Freud contended that the basic antagonism between the ego and the id — between reality and pleasure principles — was insurmountable. Marcuse responded to Freud's tendential misanthropy in Marxian fashion by *historicizing* the instincts or drives. He sought to show that the opposition between civilization and happiness that Freud assumed to be unalterable was in fact a product of specific historical conditions: economic or material "scarcity." Under conditions of material abundance, argued Marcuse, there was no reason why the instinctual antagonism identified by Freud could not be overcome or effaced entirely. Under such conditions, the utopian longings sedimented in the unconscious might for the first time truly come into their own.

In essence, Freud had made the same mistake that the political economists criticized by Marx had made: he assumed that capitalist social relations were immutable. By showing that Freud's basic concepts corresponded to a historically changeable reality, Marcuse sought to demonstrate that utopian tendencies were objectively rooted in the historical present.

According to Marcuse, under conditions of contemporary capitalism the reality principle assumes the form of the "performance principle." The performance principle corresponds to social conditions in which production is determined by *alienated labor*. As Marcuse explains:

Society is stratified according to the competitive economic performances of its members ... Their labor is work for an apparatus which they do not control, which operates as an independent power to which individuals must submit if they want to live. And it becomes the more alien the more specialized the division of labor becomes. Men do not live their own lives but perform pre-established functions while they work, they do not fulfill their own needs and faculties but work in *alienation* hope.... Libido is diverted for socially useful performances in which the individual works for himself only in so far as he works for the apparatus, engaged in activities that mostly do not coincide with his own faculties.[8]

The performance principle ensures the perpetuation of what Marcuse, taking his cue from the Marxian concept of "surplus value," would call "surplus repression." Given the prospects for material abundance that had been set in motion by capitalism, there was no longer any need for people to engage in senseless, unrewarding toil for the sake of an economic apparatus that undermined the ends of human happiness. Instead, the objective conquest of scarcity (a point Marcuse never bothered to prove, but merely assumed) had rendered alienated labor superfluous. Borrowing an argument Marx had briefly entertained in the *Grundrisse*, Marcuse suggested that technological progress made surplus repression obsolete: "Technology operates against the repressive utilization of energy insofar as it minimizes the time necessary for the production of the necessities of life, thus saving time for the development of needs *beyond* the realm of necessity."[9] Thus, in Marcuse's view, the sheer technological proficiency of modern industrial society indicated that the "realm of freedom" was at hand. With the vast release of instinctual energies that would accompany the anticipated change in social relations, individuals could devote themselves primarily to the tasks of self-realization and the beautification of life. Of course, civilization would always require some measure of social restraint or "basic repression." But the amount would differ radically from the extensive degree of repression — social, psychological, and sexual — demanded by the performance principle. Once surplus repression was eliminated, the entirety of human life could be infused with the values of the pleasure principle or Eros.

Here was Marcuse at his most outlandishly speculative. The senses of smell and taste, once liberated from the paradigm of repression, would "eroticize the entire organism," he claimed, thereby counteracting the "desexualization of the organism required by its social utilization as an instrument of labor." In its original state human sexuality was "polymorphous-perverse," argued Marcuse, echoing Freud. The imperatives of civilization demanded that these energies be genitally rechanneled, with all deviations from this "normal" path outlawed as "perversions." However, in Marcuse's view, the perversions contained a "promise of happiness": "Freud emphasized the 'exclusive' character of the deviations from normality, their rejection of the procreative sex act. The perversions thus express rebellion against subjugation of sexuality under the order of procreation, and against the institutions which guarantee this order."[10]

Finally, Marcuse suggested that, under the reign of a new, libidinally charged reality principle, the concept of death would itself be transformed. In a society predicated on gratification rather than deprivation, the death instinct would be deprived of its object: release from a life of humiliation, pain, and suffering. As Marcuse remarks: "Eros would, as it were, absorb the objective of the death instinct." Moreover, under utopian conditions, "Death can become a token of freedom," he observes. "Men can die without anxiety if they know that what they love is protected from misery and oblivion. After a fulfilled life, they may take it upon themselves to die — at a moment of their own choosing."[11]

Marcuse's partisanship for a society predicated on Eros rather than the "performance principle" of 1950s America was inspiring. The more closely one examined the particular elements of his argument, however, the more his position seemed on the verge of collapsing like a house of cards in a hurricane.

For in his rush toward utopia, Marcuse glibly jettisoned or discounted aspects of psychoanalytic doctrine he found uncongenial to his ends. The unconscious, which Marcuse celebrated uncritically, is not merely a reservoir of repressed utopian longings. It is also the repository of frustration, anxiety, trauma, and suffering — of memories too disturbing for the conscious mind to bear. Similarly, individual unhappiness cannot be palmed off on the libidinal injustices of an unfree society. For Freud, the process of individuation is replete with risks, uncertainties, and potential deformations regardless of social context. To be sure, the parameters of symptom formation might vary with historical circumstances, as Marcuse implies. Thus, for example, today the hysterical illnesses that were so prevalent during Freud's time have largely given way to a series of more diffuse, narcissistic disturbances. But to imply that the personality disorders and instinctual conflicts identified by Freud might one day disappear entirely is little more than wishful thinking. Such speculation promotes "delusion" rather than the "objective fantasy" that Marcuse cherished. Even his most sympathetic commentators were forced to avow that "Marcuse makes rather extreme — and, in the view of some critics, unsubstantiated — claims for Eros, the liberation of which will [allegedly] create a new reality, human and social."[12]

Erich Fromm expressed the misgivings of many in the analytic camp when he accused Marcuse of having misappropriated Freud for the sake of a political radicalism that was fundamentally incompatible with the Master's teachings: "It is obvious that from Freud's standpoint, there is no hope for any fundamental improvement of society, since no social order can transcend the necessary and unavoidable conflict between the claims of human nature and happiness on the one side, and the claims of society and civilization on the other."[13]

But Fromm and the psychoanalytic community in general misunderstood the fact that Marcuse was less interested in a literal reading of Freud than he was in reassessing Freud's political use-value for the historical present. While orthodox Freudians and their revisionist allies refused to budge from the letter of Freud's texts (though the revisionist allegiance to Freud itself proved highly selective), Marcuse was more concerned with the emancipatory implications of their spirit. Should we distance ourselves too quickly from Marcuse's unfashionable utopianism, we risk succumbing to the reigning mood of neoliberal cynicism — and thereby capitulating wholesale to a complacent, fin de siècle, antiemancipatory sobriety.

Hegel and Revolution

Marcuse was an Hegelian. From this fact one may glean both the strengths and the weaknesses of his approach to social theory. Not only were his first two books on Hegel. Marcuse believed that reality (*die Wirklichkeit*) actually moved in a Hegelian fashion. And if it temporarily failed to do so, so much the worse for reality.

When Marcuse came of age during the 1920s, Hegelian Marxism was a renegade current. The dominant understanding of Marx, shared by both European social democracy and the Third International, viewed him as an economic determinist, who had more in common with Darwin than with Hegel. Following the lead of Lukács in *History and Class Consciousness*, the Hegelian Marxists believed that Hegel's dialectical understanding of historical development was philosophically true but empirically false: in the lexicon of the early Marx, the world had not yet become philosophical. Marx had portrayed the proletariat as the heir to German classical philosophy. A successful proletarian revolution alone could bring the sublime truths of German idealism down to earth. Marx's writings merely gave philosophical expression to this standpoint. For the Hegelian Marxists, Marxism embodied a dialectical supersession of Hegel rather than a qualitatively new departure. One can only begin to imagine the sense of enthusiasm Marcuse must have felt when, in 1932, Marx's youthful Paris Manuscripts were first published, confirming the essential ties between Marxist thought and the heritage of German idealism.

Marxism's ineradicable debt to Hegel was the leitmotif of *Reason and Revolution* (1941). This philosophical approach to Marx was a slap in the face to all official versions of Marxism, especially to the "diamat" version that had been proclaimed by the doctrinaire guardians of Soviet orthodoxy. In the eyes of Hegelian Marxism, the proponents of orthodoxy, by forcibly divesting Marxism of its philosophical vigor and originality, had transformed it into an oppressive "science of legitimation." If one adhered rigidly to a scientized view of Marxism, one ended up with Pavlov and a society of conditioned reflexes — a critical standpoint that Marcuse would develop at length in *Soviet Marxism* (1958).

For Marcuse, Marxism was not only the heir of German idealism. It was the inheritor of the noblest promises of Western culture in general: Reason, Freedom, and Happiness. When in the Paris Manuscripts Marx famously described communism — in good Hegelian fashion — as the "resolution of the strife between existence and essence, between objectification and self-confirmation, between freedom and necessity, between the individual and the species," Marcuse believed every word.[14]

The problem, however, was that the gap between philosophy and reality had become nearly unbridgeable. In the 1930s prospects for revolutionary change were threatened with total eclipse. Fascism had become the political sign of the times. The Soviet Union plummeted into the dark night of Stalinism. Marx's prognostications concerning a nonalienated future seemed increasingly utopian. Hegel's *Philosophy of History* had been optimistically subtitled "Reason in History." To judge by current circumstances, however, the forces of Unreason had triumphed.

This was the historical situation Marcuse sought to confront in his philosophical and political studies. One can imagine his sense of betrayal. He had studied Hegel and Marx. He and a few fellow philosophers knew what the "solution to the riddle of history" entailed. Yet virtually no one else in the world did. The totalitarian era would soon be superseded by the cold war — not much of an improvement from the standpoint of utopian political prospects. How should a Hegelian Marxist respond?

In point of fact, Marcuse's responses were not always temperate or to the point. His oeuvre combines philosophical brilliance with political myopia. As a Hegelian Marxist, Marcuse always set his political sights high. And if political reality failed to conform to the sublimity of such heights, so much the worse for reality.

Repressive Tolerance and Educational Dictatorship

Marcuse's controversial essay "Repressive Tolerance" is a good example of the aforementioned myopic dimension. It would be unfair to judge Marcuse exclusively on the basis of some of his more questionable claims and statements. At the same time, should such claims be representative of deeper tendencies of his thought, it would also be dishonest to pass over them in silence. "Repressive Tolerance" demonstrates the peril of excessive revolutionary faith that has yielded to despair. It also illustrates the pitfalls of a theoretical approach that is convinced of its own privileged insight into the course of history.

When "Repressive Tolerance" appeared in 1965, Marcuse was despondent over the prospects of radical historical change. The United

States had drastically escalated its involvement in Vietnam: whereas in 1963 there were thirty thousand American military advisers, by the end of 1965 there were nearly two hundred thousand ground troops. Major protests against the war remained sporadic and isolated.

The United States was a nation that prided itself on the preservation of civil liberties and a tradition of tolerance. According to the Marxist catechism, however, these were bourgeois freedoms. At best they signified a partial and imperfect realization of "reason in history." In any event, they were not viewed as ends in themselves. Orthodox Marxism had always been progressivist: it assumed that the achievements of bourgeois society — both material and moral — would be incorporated in a future Marxist society. But owing to the historical setbacks of the 1930s, Marcuse, like his Frankfurt School colleagues, had abandoned all ties to this progressivist strain. One need look no further than the conclusion to *One-Dimensional Man*, where Marcuse cites Walter Benjamin's despairing maxim: "Only for the sake of those without hope is hope given to us."

In the early 1930s Marcuse had witnessed the collapse of the Weimar Republic. When confronted with the political challenge of the Nazi behemoth, the civil libertarian bulwarks of bourgeois liberalism had disintegrated ignominiously. Moreover, the Nazis had essentially come to power through normal electoral and political channels. As a result of these deeply ingrained historical experiences, Marcuse's faith in the virtues of political liberalism was minimal. By the early 1960s he had begun characterizing the United States as an essentially totalitarian society. He felt such characterizations to be justified in consequence of the near total eclipse of prospects for qualitative social change. He concluded that it would be foolish to respond to a latently fascist threat — the war in Vietnam, combined with widespread political coercion cum persecution at home — by traditional democratic procedures and means.

Moreover, Marcuse was writing in an era in which third world liberation movements had begun systematically challenging first world political hegemony. These movements necessarily resorted to violence in pursuit of their goals. Their actions had been philosophically consecrated by Sartre in his incendiary preface to Frantz Fanon's *The Wretched of the Earth*. It would be absurd, Marcuse believed, to condemn the third world revolutionaries on civil libertarian grounds. Echoing the sentiments of the German right-wing political philosopher Carl Schmitt, who believed that politics was best defined in terms of the friend–enemy dichotomy, Marcuse believed that drastic political situations called for drastic means.

This is the background to the political position Marcuse develops in "Repressive Tolerance." According to Marcuse, history demonstrates that violence is an indispensable concomitant of revolutionary historical change. He cites not only the English and French revolutions but also the "people's revolutions" of China and Cuba as cases in point. Had not Marx, moreover, defined revolution as the "locomotive of history"? It would be hypocritical, Marcuse argued, to hold the oppressed classes accountable to purportedly "universal" moral and ethical standards that essentially benefit the ruling classes. For Marcuse, therefore, the "decisive question" is not whether or not violence should be used, but rather on whose behalf and "in the interest of which groups and institutions such violence is released."[15] If one must use repugnant or immoral means to quash a despised political adversary, so be it. At times, there may be no other mechanism available to advance the cause of historical progress, to bring Reason to bear on the otherwise intractable forces of history. In an "emergency situation" — a locution also popularized by Carl Schmitt — extraordinary measures, such as the "suspension of the right of free speech and free assembly" for "regressive" historical persons and groups, must be enforced. "I maintain," Marcuse continues, "that our society is in such an emergency situation, and that it has become the normal state of affairs." In a proclamation worthy of a Bolshevik commissar, Marcuse suggests:

> Liberating tolerance, then, would mean intolerance against movements from the Right, and toleration of movements from the Left .... Withdrawal of tolerance from regressive movements before they can become active; intolerance even toward thought, opinion, and word, and finally, intolerance in the opposite direction, that is, toward the self-styled conservatives, to the political Right — these anti-democratic notions respond to the actual development of the democratic society which has destroyed the basis for universal tolerance.

Marcuse's Orwellian vision of "liberating tolerance" finds support in his account of one-dimensional society. In such a society individuals have become "cultural dopes," they are incapable of distinguishing true from false needs. On such grounds, too, drastic measures seem merited. Since, in advanced industrial society, tolerance has merely become a cover for the ideological hegemony of reigning social interests, it too must be abrogated: "When tolerance mainly serves the protection and preservation of a repressive society, ... when this perversion starts in the mind of the individual, in his consciousness, his needs, when heteronomous interests occupy him before he can experience his servitude, then the efforts to counteract his dehumanization ... must begin with stopping the words and images which feed this consciousness." As Marcuse acknowledges: "To be sure, this is censorship, even precensorship, but

openly directed against the more or less hidden censorship that pe
ates the free media."[16]

To justify such restrictions on speech, Marcuse has recourse to
Rousseau's theory of the general will — which, in the words of the
French philosopher, "can never err." According to Marcuse, the general
will always trumps the will of the majority insofar as, "in its very structure this majority is 'closed,' petrified; it repels 'a priori' any change
other than changes within the system."[17]

Marcuse's problem is one familiar to intellectuals schooled in the
tradition of Plato and Rousseau. As a philosopher, one possesses privileged access to ultimate truth or the logic of history. Yet, an ontological
abyss separates such philosophical insight from the unwashed masses,
the cave dwellers who perennially fail to perceive the light that could
lead to their own salvation. The philosopher is faced with two choices:
she can either sit back and watch them suffer or she can force them to be
free. Here, too, Marcuse remains faithful to his muse and strikingly
consistent, even at the cost of endorsing a remarkably unpalatable political course: the idea of educational dictatorship. "If the choice were
between genuine democracy and dictatorship," ruminates Marcuse,
"democracy would certainly be preferable. But democracy" — which
has been effectively colonized by political and business elites — "does
not prevail." Hence, Marcuse sees no reason why a "dictatorship of
intellectuals," who, in good Platonic fashion, have seen the light about
Reason and Happiness, would not be more just than "representative
government by a non-intellectual minority of politicians, generals, and
businessmen."[18]

Ten years earlier, in *Eros and Civilization*, Marcuse had explored a
similar option: "How can civilization freely generate freedom, when
unfreedom has become part and parcel of the mental apparatus? ...
From Plato to Rousseau, the only honest answer is the idea of an *educational dictatorship*, exercised by those who are supposed to have
acquired knowledge of the real Good."[19] And in the postscript to
"Repressive Tolerance," Marcuse unconvincingly appends a long cita-
tion from John Stuart Mill (who in *On Liberty* had proposed a system
of preferential voting that would reflect superior educational training)
concerning the need to preserve the political preeminence of educated
elites vis-à-vis the masses in an era of universal suffrage.

Like all revolutionaries, Marcuse began as a populist and ended up
flirting with despotism.

5

The Lion in Winter: Leo Lowenthal and the Integrity of the Intellectual

My friendship with Leo Lowenthal began relatively late in his life and relatively early in mine. We met in Berkeley in 1981, thanks to our mutual friend Martin Jay. Leo had recently entered his ninth decade; I was still in my third. Our friendship would prosper for twelve years. At the time I was finishing a PhD dissertation on Walter Benjamin. Leo was one of two people I have met who actually knew Benjamin, the other being Leo's close friend Herbert Marcuse. Their paths had frequently crossed in Frankfurt during the late 1920s. Later, of course, they had professional dealings in Leo's capacity as managing editor of the *Zeitschrift für Sozialforschung*.

When we met, Leo had just been invited to give a lecture at an international conference in Frankfurt in honor of the long-awaited publication of Benjamin's *Arcades Project*. Hence, our mutual interest in Benjamin formed the basis of a natural alliance. During our first meeting in Leo's book-lined study, we spoke for hours about Benjamin's brilliant reviews during the 1920s for the *Frankfurter Zeitung* — many of which Leo had undoubtedly read upon their initial publication — as well as Benjamin's uncanny oscillation during the 1930s between messianic and Marxist leitmotifs.

There are a number of themes that arose during these initial conversations that left a deep impression on me. For, despite our considerable differences in age, background, and intellectual training — after all,

Leo's mentors had been illustrious philosophers such as Paul Natorp and Heinrich Rickert — we discovered nevertheless a number of developmental similarities. Both of us had come of age in the aftermath of failed revolutionary situations — in Leo's case, the German Revolution of 1918; in mine, the student revolt of the 1960s. Unsurprisingly, we found that we were attracted to many of the same ideas and texts. In his autobiography Leo recounts how, like many members of his generation, he was alienated from the reigning school-philosophy, neo-Kantianism, which seemed conformist and unimaginative. The tools of analytic reason seemed patently inadequate in order to counteract an increasingly irrational political situation. The realization of utopia demanded more robust intellectual methods.

Similar observations apply to my generation's rejection of the predominant academic methodologies, positivism and analytic philosophy. Our disillusionment with these approaches accounted for our intoxication with the utopian promise of German philosophy in general and the Frankfurt School in particular. German classical philosophy was predicated on a potentially subversive dialectic of "essence" and "appearance." It argued against an uncritical reverence for the current state of things, which it denigrated as "immediacy." It remained resolutely skeptical vis-à-vis narrowly empirical approaches to truth that took their bearings from what was historically "given." It demanded that the present age be subjected to the rigors of dialectical reasoning. Instead of being revered, social reality stood in need of legitimation before the higher tribunal of the "Concept" (*der Begriff*). Its metaphysical encumbrances notwithstanding, Hegel's philosophy defended the idea of an emphatic concept of truth. It thereby retained a capacity for strong normative evaluation — one that was noticeably lacking among the reigning empiricist schools. Indigenous American intellectual traditions — endless permutations of the pragmatism–scientism nexus — offered nothing comparable.

This Hegelian element remained a prominent component of the Frankfurt School's methodological approach, "interdisciplinary materialism." Simply put, this approach required that empirical enquiries be guided by general theoretical or normative insights. Particular aspects of social life — the family, the individual, work, mass culture — needed to be viewed in light of broader historical or theoretical concerns: an orientation toward "totality." In the Frankfurt School's empirical and theoretical work, these insights came to fruition in the claim that Critical Theory was guided by an interest in emancipation. For a generation like mine that was desperately seeking theoretical leverage to counteract the depredations of the "Welfare and Warfare State," such ideas found great resonance. In the Frankfurt School's negative dialectics, many of us felt we had discovered the meaning of the critical spirit.

Upon emigrating to America in the mid-1930s, Leo was struck by the reigning ntellectual provincialism. Many works by major French and German authors remained untranslated. American cultural life seemed unworldly and complacent. But that situation changed radically by the mid-1970s, at least in part owing to the intellectual ambitions of New Left scholars. In his autobiography, Leo recounted these developments as follows:

> A sense of disappointment, disillusion, and outrage over what had happened in America after the Second World War slowly spread among the more enlightened young people.... Leftist intellectual circles reacted to this disappointment with a strong interest in political philosophy. And in this context the Frankfurt School was discovered. Most likely the new interest derived largely from the great popularity Herbert Marcuse enjoyed in this country ... This is the context in which we find a fairly broad reception for many of the ideas of the Frankfurt School, as well as ... a good number of French thinkers. Intellectual curiosity is great and nearly unquenchable.[1]

To the astonishment of many, the *Flaschenpost*, or "message in a bottle," launched by Horkheimer and others during the 1930s had washed up on American shores.

In the course of our conversations, Leo singled out the two books that had had the greatest impact upon him as a youth: Lukács's *Theory of the Novel* and Bloch's *Spirit of Utopia*. Both works offered a panoply of speculative directives for transcending bourgeois society qua continuum of reification. Lukács's *Jugendschrift* ends with a messianic appeal to Dostoyevsky as the prophet of a utopian literary form heralding the abolition of the bourgeois era of "absolute sinfulness" (Fichte) and the restoration of the "integrated totality" of classical Greece. *Spirit of Utopia* was the work of a confirmed unorthodox Marxist. Bloch employed an expressionistic literary style, reconceived Marxism as variety of political messianism, and, in a play on Kant, praised Bolshevism as the "categorical imperative with revolver in hand." The turning point of my own youthful intellectual development had been joining a Lukács reading circle as an undergraduate in Portland, Oregon. In *History and Class Consciousness* — our bible — Lukács, writing in a neo-Hegelian idiom, apotheosized the proletariat as the identical subject-object of history. My peers and I took him at his word.

Leo's Frankfurt talk, "Walter Benjamin: The Integrity of the Intellectual," which I had the good fortune to attend, was a resounding success.

For the qualities of intellectual integrity Leo generously attributed to Benjamin very much apply to him, too. After all, Leo and Benjamin were contemporaries. Both evinced a fascination with the conservative philosopher of religion Franz von Baader, on whom Leo wrote his dissertation in 1923. On a less sanguine note, both Benjamin and Leo had their habilitation efforts blocked by the same University of Frankfurt philology professor, Franz Schultz, during the mid-1920s. Unlike Leo, Benjamin's itinerary seemed haunted by the mischievous upsets of the "little hunchback" of German fairy tale lore who figured prominently in the "Theses on the Philosophy of History." Paradoxically, Benjamin's lack of worldly success during his lifetime stands in inverse proportion to the international renown he enjoys today.

By "integrity of the intellectual," Leo sought to highlight Benjamin's unshakeable faith in the power of ideas to change the world. However, unlike his Frankfurt School comrades, Benjamin set little store by Hegel. He believed Kierkegaard's "leap of faith" offered more possibilities for radical change than did the successful outcome of a dialectical syllogism. In this respect, his unorthodox Marxism bears comparison with that of his friend and *compagnon de route*, Ernst Bloch.

Benjamin's theoretical fecundity derived from sources that, according to the dogmas of the orthodox Marxist canon, were strictly taboo. Hence, his manifest fascination with representatives of the Counter-Enlightenment tradition — figures such as Johann Jacob Bachofen, Nietzsche, Ludwig Klages, C. G. Jung — whose ideas he sought to appropriate for the ends of the political left, often to the dismay of his Marxist colleagues at the Institute for Social Research. As Benjamin remarked in a letter from the early 1920s: "A philosophy of experience that does not include the possibility of soothsaying from coffee grounds cannot be a true philosophy."[2] Paradoxically, the only groups who shared the same concerns — who, like Benjamin, viewed cultural history as a potential repository of *profane illuminations* — were the leading lights of the "conservative revolution."

From its earliest inception, Benjamin's program was to make such concerns serviceable for the left. As he explained in his 1929 surrealism essay, his goal was: "to win the energies of intoxication [*Rausch*] for the revolution."[3] As early as 1918, Benjamin forcefully rejected the Newtonian-Kantian conception of experience, one that was predicated on the mechanical worldview of the natural sciences, in favor of a conception that was indebted to the tenets of animism, mysticism, and theology.[4] His experimentation with mescalin and hashish (following a time-honored literary tradition established by Thomas de Quincey and Baudelaire) must be understood along similar lines: these were attempts to decenter the Kantian "transcendental unity of apperception" in the direction of profane illuminations. When, in the *Arcades Project*,

Benjamin remarks that, "My thinking is related to theology as blotting pad is related to ink. *It is saturated with it*," he was deadly serious.[5]

Whereas orthodox Marxists spoke confidently of the laws of historical development and glorified science with Saint-Simonian zeal, Benjamin believed that to divorce revolution from theological concerns was a recipe for failure. It was tantamount to making peace with the profane continuum of history and, hence, to sell short revolution's redemptive potential. His conception of revolution bore greater affinities with the eschatological notion of the "Last Judgment" than it did with the traditional Marxist goal of socializing the means of production. In Convolute "N" of the Arcades Project ("On the Theory of Knowledge, Theory of Progress"), he associates revolution with the concept of *apocatastasis*: a term from the Jewish apocalyptical tradition that designates the restoration of an original paradisiacal state catalyzed by the coming of the Messiah.[6] As Scholem once observed concerning the redemptive dimension of Benjamin's theoretical program: "The goal of Benjamin's 'dialectics of cultural history' [was] the abolition of the prevailing context of expression in favor of the original context of Being."

This fascination with the redemptive promise of Jewish messianism also held its attractions for Leo. Following the twin debacles of the Great War and the German Revolution, Leo, like Benjamin, concluded that there could be no going back to the compromises and half measures of the bourgeois world. Hence, as a student in Heidelberg, he frequented left-wing Zionist circles. He had a long and fruitful association with the Freies Jüdisches Lehrhaus, a legendary center for Jewish learning founded by Martin Buber and Franz Rosenzweig. Prior to his work for the Institute in 1926, Leo, like Benjamin, was convinced that the idea of socialism could be enhanced by an infusion of a messianic dimension culled from the tradition of secular Judaism: "I believed that Jewish philosophy of religion ... contains a progressive rationalism with strong secular tendencies, which, though garbed in religious symbolism, also connote the idea of a paradise on earth ... I believed strongly in Judaism's messianic mission, its utopian political task."[7] However, during his long association with the Institute, these inclinations remained muted.

In view of his pioneering work on the sociology of literature, much of it done in the 1930s, it would be inaccurate to refer to Leo as a late bloomer. But it would also be unfair to underestimate the roll he played as a champion of Critical Theory's claims later in life as the Frankfurt School's last surviving member. Here, too, Leo expressed something of the integrity of the intellectual: helping to keep the flame of Critical Theory alive at a point when politicians and scholars had accused it of the Socratic sins of leading youth astray and worshipping gods other than those sanctioned by the city.

During the German Autumn — the events surrounding the kidnapping and murder of the head of the German Employers Association, Hans-Martin Schleyer, by Red Army Faction terrorists in 1977 — right-wing politicians Alfred Dregger and Hans Filbinger suggested that the Frankfurt School had been intellectually responsible for Red Army Faction (RAF) terrorism. Conservative academics jumped on the bandwagon, arguing that Horkheimer, Adorno, and others practiced a form of "cultural terrorism" that destabilized the foundations of the Christian West.[8] They adopted the cynical position that critical thought, rather than strengthening the virtues of civic consciousness, undermined them. Paradoxically, antidemocratic sentiments espoused by German conservatives during the waning years of the Weimar Republic suddenly gained a new lease on life.

By making such arguments Critical Theory's antagonists sought to rehabilitate a cornerstone of the Counter-Enlightenment worldview: the idea that unfettered employment of reason undermines credulity in inherited institutions. In *Reflections on the Revolution in France* Edmund Burke criticized the "fallible and feeble contrivances of [human] reason" which he claimed must be offset by the influences of habit, custom, and tradition.[9] Burke's critique of philosophy found many admirers across the continent among apostles of counterrevolution. During the 1950s and 1960s German conservatives such as Hans Freyer and Arnold Gehlen embraced a protechnocracy standpoint that was inspired by the "end of ideology" debate. They claimed that the idea of "popular sovereignty" was a dangerous, Rousseauian atavism, and that the imperatives of "social control" trumped normative concerns or considerations of "right." They viewed substantive justifications of democracy — as one finds, for example, in the tradition of modern natural law — as politically risky and epistemologically undemonstrable.[10]

That Horkheimer and Adorno had been outspoken critics of German student movement excesses seemed to matter little amid the hysteria generated by Critical Theory's growing chorus of right-wing detractors. Upon their return to Germany circa 1950, the Institute had championed two central components of the Enlightenment program: the Kantian paradigm of "autonomy" and the Freudian concept of "working through the past."[11] In "Answer to the Question: What is Enlightenment?" Kant had famously defined "autonomy" as humanity's emergence from "self-incurred tutelage." Autonomy was predicated on the unfettered employment of reason: a willingness to think without the guidance of experts or authorities. The autonomy and maturity of citizens would offset the need for dogmatic political authority — unenlightened despotism. This Kantian standpoint posed a direct challenge to conservative thinkers like Gehlen, Freyer, and Niklas Luhmann who used arguments about social complexity to proclaim the advent of *posthistoire*. By appealing to the "end of ideology," they reached an eminently ideological conclusion: the emancipatory project had ended. Questions of technical efficiency alone remained. "Man" was a dangerous and untrustworthy animal whose impulses must be closely monitored by institutional mechanisms of social control.[12]

In the autumn of his years, Leo played an indispensable role in keeping the torch of Critical Theory alive in the face of the neoconservative ideological shift that swept across Europe and North America during the 1980s. In interviews he regularly commented on current events and provided, in good Frankfurt School fashion, an ideology-critical perspective on the reigning intellectual fashion, postmodernism. As an octogenarian, he turned into an eloquent memoirist, penning moving reminiscences of Frankfurt School comrades Benjamin and Adorno. Far from being exercises in nostalgia, these essays were models of political-philosophical concision. What alarmed Leo most was that neoconservatives and postmodernists seemed to agree on the death of subjectivity and the end of history. He viewed such declarations as both premature and ideologically suspect.

From the Frankfurt School standpoint, the "death of the subject" was a politically sensitive topos. During the 1940s Horkheimer and Adorno feared that, given the realities of totalitarianism, this concept threatened to become an all-consuming reality. In "The End of Reason" (1941), Horkheimer described the elements of psychological regression that accompanied the emergence of "totally integrated societies." According to this optic, the distinctions between communism, fascism, and administered capitalism were differences in degree rather than in kind: the eclipse of the individual was characteristic of all three. Pollock's studies in political economy had chronicled the transition from laissez-faire to state-managed capitalism. In its empirical work, the Institute had documented the transformation of bourgeois character structure from the rugged individuals of classical capitalism to the pliable and conformist "authoritarian personalities" of monopoly capitalism.

In "Triumph of the Mass Idols" (1943), Leo provided additional documentation for this momentous social psychological transformation. He undertook a content analysis of popular magazines such as *Colliers* and *Saturday Evening Post*, showing how over the course of a forty-year period biographical profiles had changed from a focus on successful entrepreneurs to "personalities" drawn from the sphere of consumption. Instead of Horatio Alger types — that is, personifications of the bourgeois "achievement ethic" — the new "mass idols" were baseball players, boxers, radio crooners, and movie stars. The popular biographies Leo analyzed exhibited an unabashed, voyeuristic preoccupation with the idiosyncrasies of "leisure time," thereby suggesting a false intimacy between media stars and the person on the street, who purportedly shared the same after-hours pursuits. In Leo's opinion, beneath the veneer of harmless "diversion" lay insidious mechanisms of domination and social control:

> The distance between what an average individual may do and the forces and powers that determine his life and death has become so unbridgeable that identification with normalcy, even with Philistine boredom becomes a readily grasped empire of refuge and escape. It is some comfort for the little man who has become expelled from the Horatio Alger dream, who despairs of penetrating the thicket of grand strategy in politics and business, to see his heroes as a lot of guys who like or dislike highballs, cigarettes, tomato juice, golf, and social gatherings — just like himself. He knows how to converse in the sphere of consumption and ... he can experience the gratification of being confirmed in his own pleasures and discomforts by participating in the pleasures and discomforts of the great.[13]

In a witticism for which he has been justly celebrated, Leo once described mass culture as "psychoanalysis in reverse." Whereas Freud's goal had been to emancipate the subject from the grip of unconscious instinctual influences for the sake of human autonomy, the culture industry mesmerized individuals with distractions and infantile blandishments. Hence, in keeping with Leo's metaphor, socialization through mass culture could be accurately described as an un-*Bildungsprozess* or a *Bildungsprozess* in reverse. Instead of abetting the development of critical consciousness — the capacity for refusal or *Verneinung* that the Critical Theorists prized — it facilitated a condition of *immaturity*, adapting individuals to the value orientations and imagery of the reigning social totality.

It is at this point that the disagreement between the Frankfurt School and the champions of postmodernism emerges with unmistakable clarity. Whereas the Critical Theorists viewed the "death of the subject" as an manifestation of sociopsychological regression, postmodernists, faithful to a Nietzschean ethos of self-overcoming, greeted it with unbridled enthusiasm. Yet, as critics have pointed out, there remain a number of affinities between postmodern thought and the Frankfurt School approach. Adorno's animus against the identitarian strivings of "first philosophy" in *Negative Dialectics,* in which he argues that the "original sin" of philosophy is its attempt to grasp the nonconceptual by conceptual means, bears marked similarities to Derrida's critique of logocentrism — the notion that the history of the West is distinguished by the "tyranny of reason": the priority of unity, sameness, and totality at the expense of particularity, otherness, and difference. Since Leo's final intellectual project was a critique of postmodern thought — he researched this problem while he was a guest at the Wissenschaftskolleg zu Berlin in 1985 (a partial record of his conclusions may be gleaned from his interview with Emilio Zugaro published under the title "Against Postmodernism"), I would like to review some of the reasons he felt compelled to address these concerns.

One reason that comparisons between the Frankfurt School and postmodernism are overdrawn is that, throughout its various developmental phases, Critical Theory's focal point remained the link between reason and emancipation. This is one of the reasons why attempts to view the Frankfurt School and postmodernism as kindred spirits ultimately break down. Were the link between insight and emancipation severed, Critical Theory's raison d'être would cease to exist.

Conversely, one of the distinguishing features of postmodernism has been a disavowal of the dialectic of Enlightenment qua discourse of liberation. Whether one peruses the texts of Derrida, Lyotard, or Foucault, one encounters the argument that reason, instead of being a tool of emancipation, represents little more than a reprehensible mechanism of social control. This conclusion follows from Derrida's critique of logocentrism as well as Foucault's contention that knowledge is irremediably enmeshed in the corruptions of power. In this regard, all three thinkers echo Heidegger's controversial and potentially self-defeating maxim that "reason is the most stiff-necked adversary of thought."[14] In this respect it is imperative to distinguish the self-criticism of reason — which is necessary and indispensable — from the debilities of a standpoint that bids farewell to reason in the name of a new series of unfathomable, transcendental significeds: Being, *différance*, will to power, sovereignty, nomadic thinking.

Hence, despite the many interesting insights the aforementioned paradigms may have to offer, one cannot help but wonder whether the radical critique of reason risks depriving us of the means of our emancipation. After all, the social movements of the 1960s relied extensively on the eminently "logocentric" vocabulary of modern natural right to argue that the egalitarian promises of modern society had not been redeemed. To proclaim that the dialectic of emancipation is obsolete risks trivializing the democratic aspirations of peoples around the world who, in recent years, have employed the discourse of popular sovereignty to cast off the chains of authoritarian rule. (Here, I am thinking of the "velvet revolutions" in Eastern Europe, South Africa, and South America.) In many respects, despite the fashionable allusions to *posthistoire*, the democratic revolutions we have witnessed over the course of the last two decades confirm an old-fashioned Hegelian insight: contemporary history may be understood as "progress in the consciousness of freedom." Lyotard's celebrated proclamation of the "end of metanarratives" may have been premature. If these suspicions are correct, then today's cant concerning the "death of the subject" might best be understood as a profession of intellectual impotence. For if the subject is "dead," the idea of emancipation cannot be far behind.[15]

Leo interpreted the postmodernist vogue as a consequence of the failure of the New Left's political hopes. As he observed in an interview: "After the complete internal and external psychological collapse of [the New Left project], there arose a colossal need for the vacuum to be filled. Since other credible tools and ideologies were not available, a large part of the intelligentsia slowly sank into this irrational and mythological behavior, into this dangerous swamp."[16] Leo believed that integrity lay in refusing to follow the whims of academic fashion and a willingness to hazard strong judgments in the face of a rising tide of relativist vacillation. Thus, the Frankfurt School resisted the lures of "undecidability" and "power-knowledge" in favor of the legacy of immanent criticism. It was in this vein that thinkers like Horkheimer and Marcuse argued, following Marx, that the ideals of Western metaphysics should be "realized" rather than "deconstructed." They believed that idealism harbored a utopian potential which it was Critical Theory's duty to preserve and transmit. As Marcuse remarks in "Philosophy and Critical Theory" (1937):

Reason is the fundamental category of philosophical thought, the only one by means of which it has bound itself to human destiny. Philosophy wanted to discover the ultimate and most general grounds of Being. Under the name of reason it conceived the idea of an authentic Being in which all significant antitheses (of subject and object, essence and appearance, thought and being) were reconciled. Connected with this idea was the conviction that what exists is not immediately and already rational but must rather be brought to reason. Reason represents the hightest potentiality of man and of existence; the two belong together. For when reason is accorded the status of substance, this means that at its highest level, as authentic reality, the world no longer stands opposed to the rational thought of men as mere material objectivity. Rather, it is now comprehended by thought and defined as a concept ... In this form philosophy is idealism; it subsumes being under thought. But through this first thesis that made philosophy into rationalism and idealism it became critical philosophy as well. As the given world was bound up with rational thought and, indeed, ontologically dependent on it, all that contradicted reason or was not rational was posited as something that had to be overcome.[17]

One of the mainstays of the Frankfurt School's intellectual legacy concerns its innovations in the domain of cultural theory. Traditionally, cultural criticism has been one of the weak points of Marxist thought. In this area, Leo's role was central. His contributions to the sociology of literature are achievements that rank with those of other pioneers in the field, such as Arnold Hauser and Lucien Goldmann. Challenging the predominant formalist and textual approaches, Leo deciphered literary meaning as a repository of social knowledge. He believed that literature offered privileged insight into the dynamics of bourgeois intimacy: the crucible in which the modern self was forged.[18] For Leo, the bourgeois self could not be written off as a locus of heteronomy; it was not merely, as Foucault insisted, a site of domination operating at the behest of disciplinary society. The process of "subjectification" was not a total loss. Instead, Leo discerned a dialectical tension between the repressive and emancipatory aspects of bourgeois character structure. In this respect, he sought to do justice to the moment of autonomy that is an indispensable component of active citizenship. He thereby anticipated one of Habermas's key arguments in *Structural Transformation of the Public Sphere*: in democratic societies, private and public autonomy are mutually complementary.

Another component of the Frankfurt School program that Leo refused to surrender was the normative distinction between art and mass culture. This opposition had been central to the pathbreaking essays in *Kulturkritik* that appeared in the *Zeitschrift* during the 1930s: Adorno's "Fetish Character of Music and the Regression of Listening," Marcuse's "Affirmative Character of Culture," Horkheimer's "Art and Mass Culture," as well as Leo's own article on the "Sociology of Literature." These essays celebrated the utopian function of art: its capacity for "transcendence" vis-à-vis utilitarian constraints of workaday existence. Stendhal famously described beauty as a "promesse de bonheur." Autonomous art held out the prospect of a better life: one in which the deprivations and antagonisms of the current social order might be superseded. As Leo argued in "The Sociology of Literature in Retrospect":

> The most important thing to stress is that art and consumer goods must be held strictly apart. I cannot accept any of the current radical attempts ... to do away with this distinction ... To put it in even stronger terms: art teaches, and mass culture is learned; therefore, a sociological analysis of mass culture must be all-inclusive, for its products are nothing more than the phenomena and symptoms of the process of the individual's self-resignation in a wholly administered society.[19]

In later years, as Critical Theory's hopes for utopian political change faded, its proponents accorded a central role to modernist works of art, which they claimed harbored a unique capacity to resist the enticements and seductions of the "totally administered world": the "context of total blindness" that Adorno criticized in *Negative Dialectics* and other works. Art represented a negation of false consciousness. As Adorno once remarked: art's greatness lies in "[letting] speak what ideology conceals."[20] Even Marcuse, who had been most sympathetic to the political cause of the international student revolt, in *The Aesthetic Dimension* fell back on autonomous art's capacities for negation during the 1970s as the New Left's political star began to wane and a new period of normalization began to take hold.

Yet, in many respects, the traditional dichotomy between art and mass culture is unsustainable. During the 1960s the phoenix of "modernism" was consumed by flames and has yet to be reborn. Benjamin referred to art for art's sake as the "secular religion of art." Thereby he sought to highlight art's status as a supramundane repository of value and meaning: a sphere that contrasts with the demands of theoretical and practical rationalism that predominate in everyday life. The redemptory mission of high art was forcefully challenged by the twentieth-century avant-garde — in particular, surrealism — which contested modernism's trademark separation of art from life. By midcentury modernism's inability to neutralize or deflect the realities of political evil — total war, genocide, and nuclear annihilation — disqualified it in the minds of many. The aesthetic sphere seemed tantamount to a realm of unconscionable self-indulgence: a form of high-brow recreation tailored to the interests and pocketbooks of cultural and political elites.

Postmodernism emerged to fill the void that was left with the demise of the modernist program, whose last gasp may have been Abstract Expressionism. In the visual arts postmodernism picked up where dadaism and surrealism left off. It apotheosized an element that, in the case of surrealism, had represented merely a passing flirtation: *the anti-aesthetic moment.* In certain respects, it took the surrealist program of fusing the domains of art-and-life praxis much more seriously than surrealism itself.

By exploring the relationship between art and nonart, postmodernism continued the legacy of aesthetic democratization that had been initiated by the twentieth-century avant-garde: no subject matter or theme was too trivial to qualify as "artistic." But the end result was far from unproblematic, and one confronted an insurmountable paradox: postmodernism was an approach to art that was profoundly uncomfortable with its own status as art. It would only be a slight exaggeration to say that it was a form of art that wanted to be anything but art: shock, provocation, manifesto, document, found object, political intervention. The postmodernist de-differentiation of art and life bore strong affinities with the dadaist *objet trouvé*. The critic Harold Rosenberg coined the phrase the "de-definition of art" to describe this crisis of art's raison d'être.

In the 1820s Hegel had formulated the thesis of "the end of art." With the 1960s New York scene, this concept became a reality. Pop, op, minimalism, happenings, conceptual art, all aggressively favored the process Walter Benjamin had described as the "loss of the aura": the desacralization of autonomous art, art's fusion of purpose with the realm of everyday life. It was in this spirit that one of the leading interpreters of postmodern art, Arthur Danto, could plausibly title a recent collection of essays on post-1960s art, *After the End of Art*.

High modernism, for its part, was hardly blameless in these developments. It had become increasingly self-referential and esoteric: in essence, art produced for and consumed by other artists. By turning inward and becoming increasingly formalistic, modernism had surrendered the communicative dimension that for centuries had been one of art's sine qua non. Moreover, by midcentury modernist works seemed to have lost their revolutionary edge. They had become "masterpieces" and "classics," canonical works. They had degenerated to the status of "seminar literature": objects of scholarly veneration and reverence that had forfeited their critical thrust.

When Leo expressed his concerns about collapsing the distinction between "art and consumer goods," he had something very specific in mind. Towards the late 1970s, proponents of the academic left, basking in the afterglow 1960s populism, began to embrace the products of mass culture with unprecedented zeal. Under the influence of postmodernism, it became fashionable to decrypt B movies, comic strips, situation comedies, as well as all manner of Hollywood pap as repositories of utopian desire. As Fredric Jameson proclaimed circa 1980: there exists "utopian or transcendental potential [in] even the most degraded type of mass culture which remains implicitly, and no matter how faintly, negative and critical of the social order from which, as a product and a commodity, it springs."[21] Douglas Kellner, taking stock of innovations in network television programming during the late 1970s declared that, "Whereas the culture industries were once instruments of ideological conformity and cultural homogenization, they are now increasingly theaters for social conflict and instruments of cultural diversity."[22] In the *Cultural Studies Reader*, editor Simon During views the "Culture Industry" chapter of *Dialectic of Enlightenment* as a negative totem: it epitomizes how *not* to do cultural studies. As During explains: "Adorno and Horkheimer neglect what was to become central to cultural studies: the ways in which the culture industry, while in the service of organized capital, also provides the opportunities for all kinds of individual and collective creativity."[23] A greater contrast with Adorno's celebrated maxim from *Minima Moralia* — "Every visit to the cinema leaves me, against all my vigilance, stupider and worse" — could hardly be imagined.[24]

Leo diagnosed this trend as a lamentable instance of social sublimation: the once-robust political energies of the 1960s had been rechanneled along the more acceptable lines of academic *Kulturkritik*. It seemed that an entire generation had renounced the hazards of praxis for the less perilous pursuit of "textual strategies." The post-Frankfurt School approach was shored up by references to Gramsci ("counterhegemony") as well as the methodological innovations of reader response theory, which demonstrated that the way texts are read can be just as important as they way they are written.

The cultural studies approach blossomed during the 1980s. Under Foucault's growing influence as well as that of Stuart Hall and the Birmingham School, popular culture was viewed as a site of "resistance" to power. As decoded by its recipients, MTV fare was perceived as a locus of struggle that facilitated individual "empowerment." It was in this vein that "Madonna studies" blossomed into an academic cottage industry. Innovative critics could find instances of "oppositional practice" and "subversion" in the most unsuspecting places: youth in video arcades, hanging out on the beach, loitering in malls, pornography, soap operas, outlet mall shopping, even male rampage films like the *Die Hard* series.

On the one hand, the idea of clinging to the traditional left-wing goal of "socialization" would have been foolish. The political spectrum has been irretrievably pluralized. Class society, on which so much of traditional Marxist thought depended, has been irreversibly stratified — a fact that Madison Avenue and cable television marketing strategies have duly noted: hence the new ethos of consumer sovereignty and the market niche. This new reality was expressed in the orientation of new social movements that are often more concerned with questions of cultural identity than with the traditional left-wing goals of workers' control, democratization, or expanding the social safety net of the welfare state.

Critics of "cultural studies" have bridled at the idea of defining resistance down. The cultural Left, it seemed, was content to remain satisfied with "identity politics" and little more. Transgression and contestational practice have been virtualized; for the most part, they remained comfortably ensconced within the parameters of the dominant universe of discourse — within the confines of the affluent or consumer society. Transgression, too, has become a lifestyle niche. Marcuse's "great refusal" has shrunk to alternative strategies of consumption. After all:

how meaningful was it to identify Madonna worshippers — so-called wanna-bes — as the new vanguard of cultural political struggle? Did they not instead display the virtues of a socially respectable hedonism — thereby, from the standpoint of Madison avenue, fulfilling the demands of a well-defined marketing niche? Even Kellner raises serious reservations about his own conclusions concerning the potential for contestation embodied in the mass media: "when television portrays social change or oppositional movements, it often blunts the radical edge of new social forces, values, or change and tries to absorb, coopt, and defuse any challenges to the existing power structure."[25]

Moreover, during the unprecedented wave of corporate mergers during the 1990s, media giants such as Time-Warner, Fox, and Disney were featured prominently. Deregulation has allowed these corporate giants to monopolize entire media markets. Today they approach an Orwellian threshold of global domination. In light of these developments, the rejection of political economy in favor of "culturalist" approaches would seem to demand another look.[26] The Frankfurt School perspective, too, demands renewed attention.

The traditional Left had always tried to build on the achievements of democratic society. It advanced by expanding the definition of natural right: from civil rights, to political rights, to social rights. With the cultural turn, however, it seems that traditional left-wing goals, as well as the sphere of mainstream politics in general, have been prematurely abandoned. By narrowing the focus of social change to the realm of "culture," the academic Left has, to its own detriment, allowed the right to fill the political vacuum.

It has become a virtual commonplace to acknowledge the fact that, had it not been for Leo's efforts as managing director of the *Zeitschrift für Sozialforschung*, the Frankfurt School as we now know it would probably not exist. Leafing through its pages today, it reads like a who's who of the international scholarly intelligentsia. For, in no small measure owing to Leo's diligence, the Institute secured the collaboration of the likes of: Alexandre Koyré, Maurice Halbwachs, Raymond Aron, Georges Friedmann, T. H. Marshall, Charles Beard, Margaret Mead, and Harold Laswell. Moreover, we now know what a crucial role the review section of the journal, for which Leo was in the main responsible, played in funneling financial support to a generation of near-penniless German intellectual émigrés.

In the Festschrift commemorating Leo's eightieth birthday, Habermas paid tribute to his approach by observing: "While Marcuse relegated reason's historically darkened claim below the threshold of culture by a theory of instincts, Adorno set his empty hope on the solitary exercise of a self-negating philosophy. Lowenthal, who was overshadowed by the two others, represented a third possibility: one can object to the accusatory thesis of the end of reason without having to choose between metaphysics on the one hand and one of the fashionable or scientifically promoted forms of the liquidation of reason on the other."[27] Leo's contributions were selfless and made in an admirable spirit of intellectual fraternity. Unlike Horkheimer, Adorno, and Marcuse, he occupied a position that was always a step removed from the limelight. For this reason it is all the more appropriate to do justice to his legacy.

6

Levinas and Heidegger: The Anxiety of Influence

Influence is simply a transference of personality, a mode of giving away what is most precious to one's self, and its exercise produces a sense, and, it may be a reality of loss. Every disciple takes away something from his master.

Oscar Wilde, *The Portrait of Mr. W. H.*

Prologue: The "Little Lord of Being"

The later Heidegger, whom Gadamer once accused of having lapsed into unintelligible Being-mysticism (*Seinsmystik*) offers rich material for tongue-in-cheek treatment.[1] After all, a philosopher who in *Contributions to Philosophy* wrote that "Being is the trembling of the Godding" — a phrase that makes about as much sense in German as it does in English — would seem to represent an ideal target.[2] In *Philosophical Apprenticeships*, Gadamer relates how, during their Marburg years, Heidegger had a penchant for showing up for class bedecked in his native Schwarzwald ski attire, which students proceeded to dub the "existential outfit." During one lecture that began spiraling headlong into unintelligibility, Heidegger reputedly broke off in midsentence, lamenting, "This is all Chinese!"[3]

In the genre of literary parody, one of the most impressive achievements is the play *Todtnauberg*, by the Austrian writer Elfride Jellinek, who, in 2004, was awarded the Nobel Prize for literature. In Jellinek's play, one finds, among other gems, the almost untranslatable characterization of Heidegger, whose stature was notoriously diminutive, as the "Herrchen des Seins." Perhaps "little lord of Being" would be a rough English equivalent.

Crossing the Atlantic, we find that, in *Herzog*, Saul Bellow's down-on-his-luck, eponymous protagonist occupies himself by sending letters to philosophers, living and dead: Kierkegaard, Nietzsche, as well as the Freiburg sage. "Dear Doktor Professor Heidegger, I should like to know what you mean by the expression the 'fall into the quotidian.' When did this fall occur? Where were we standing when it happened?"

Like Jellinek, Bellow was a Nobel Prize winner. He won largely on the strength of this 1965 novel. The plot revolves around the fortunes of a recently divorced humanities professor. By the novel's end, Herzog arrives at the following *prise de conscience*: when it came to navigating the emotional hardships of his recent personal crisis, his surfeit of learned erudition was meaningless. Worse still, it proved an obstacle to self-understanding. Perhaps there are parallels between Herzog's situation and the delusions of grandeur that, in 1933, seduced Heidegger into believing he could play philosopher-king to Hitler's Dionysios.[4]

In *Dog Years* Günter Grass — a Nobel Prize winner-to-be — repeatedly mocks Heidegger's overblown linguistic pomposity: the philosopher's efforts to endow colloquial speech with a mystifying and inflated substantiality. But Grass had a higher end in view than ridicule for ridicule's sake — to wit, a distinctly political aim. Through parody he sought to indict Heidegger's philosophy for its complicity in postwar Germany's attempts to mask and repress the nation's egregious political misdeeds.

Grass's novel is set during the *Götterdämmerung* of Nazi Germany's final days. At one point, the Führer's dog goes missing. The remaining Nazi faithful launch "Operation Wolftrap" in an all-out effort to retrieve the errant "Führerdog," whom some heretically suspect of desertion. In order to outfox the rapidly advancing Soviets, the intrepid search team develops a foolproof linguistic code: Heideggerianese. "The Führerdog attuned to distantiality is acknowledged as the Nothing," they announce. The General Staff responds in kind: "The Nothing … discloses dread in every sector of the front." And so on. At the novel's end, the wayward *Führerhund* swims westward across the Elbe in search of — what else? — a new Master.

But perhaps the most devastating Heidegger parody ever written is "Remembering Needleman," Woody Allen's immortal lampoon of Heidegger obituaries:

As always, at the time of Needleman's death he was at work on several things. He was creating an Ethics, based on his theory that "good and just behavior is not only more moral but could be done by phone." Also, he was halfway through a new study of semantics, proving ... that sentence structure is innate but that whining is acquired. Finally, yet another book on the Holocaust. This one with cut-outs .... His own flirtation with National Socialism caused a scandal in academic circles, though despite everything from gymnastics to dance lessons, he could not master the goose step.

It is easy to criticize his position on Hitler at first, but one must take into account his own philosophical writings. He had rejected contemporary ontology and insisted that man existed prior to infinity though not with too many options. He differentiated between existence and Existence, and knew one was preferable, but could never remember which. Human freedom for Needleman consisted of being aware of the absurdity of life. "God is silent," he was fond of saying, "now if we can only get Man to shut up."[5]

Heideggerians are a notoriously humorless lot. Card-carrying guild members will no doubt take offense at the incorporation of Allen's remarks in a scholarly context. Yet, the thematic of "Heidegger and Satire" deserves a hearing.[6] Even Allen's light-hearted remarks deserve a place at the table, especially when Heidegger's relationship to Jewish matters is a topos. One should recall satire's paramount function as a literary device: a technique capable of unmasking grandiosity and deflating pomposity. After all, Heidegger viewed himself as the greatest philosopher since Heraclitus, who was active in the sixth century BCE. Exposing the pretensions of *l'esprit de sérieux* helps foster an atmosphere of intellectual openness. In cases where critical reflection has been stifled by dogma and unwarranted self-importance, satire, as practiced by the likes of Aristophanes, Juvenal, Chaucer, Pope, Swift, Voltaire, and Ionesco, opens up a space where it is possible not just to think, but to think freely. By dispensing insight under the camouflage of humor, satire makes distasteful revelations palatable. It is a courageous and exemplary literary practice that enables us to "speak truth to power."

Grass's anti-Heideggerian barbs foreshadowed Adorno's critique in the *Jargon of Authenticity*, which was published shortly after Grass's novel appeared. An exponent of negative dialectics, Adorno abhorred all premature claims to "reconciliation" or harmonious closure. Such attempts, he argued, served merely to sugarcoat the lacerated state of the post-Holocaust world. Negative dialectics' immediate target was

Hegelianism: in Adorno's view, a species of philosophical "positivism" which guaranteed that conceptual antagonisms would be surmounted by means of ever-greater feats of rational synthesis.

Like Grass, Adorno viewed the rhetorical portentousness of *Being and Time* and other Heidegger texts as far from innocent. Instead, he perceived them as complicitous with a widespread, mass psychological "strategy of avoidance" practiced in Germany during the postwar years.[7] For Heidegger, the world war and its attendant disasters were due to the "reign" of "Western metaphysics": the "will to will," the "devastation of the earth," the transposition of all existents into "standing reserve" (*das Bestand*).[8] In Adorno's view, the postwar German Heidegger vogue was part and parcel of a *mechanism of exculpation:* a manner of deflecting responsibility for the German catastrophe onto nameless, higher impersonal forces and powers.[9] It was in this vein that the later Heidegger honed the pseudohistorical concept of *Seinsgeschick* — the "destining of Being" — to suggest that neither particular individuals nor specific peoples bore direct responsibility for the so-called German catastrophe. Instead, the origins of Europe's descent into barbarism were to be found in the inscrutable and enigmatic "sendings of being" (*Schickungen des Seins*). As Adorno remarks insightfully:

> [With the jargon], the authority of the absolute is overthrown by absolutized authority .... The jargon has at its disposal a modest number of words that are received promptly as signals .... [It] sees to it that what it wants is on the whole felt and accepted through its mere delivery, without regards to the content of the words used .... This [rhetorical] element favors demagogic ends. Whoever is versed in the jargon does not have to say what he or she thinks, does not even have to think it properly. The jargon takes over the task and devalues thought.

Thereby, the Frankfurt School philosopher captured an essential component of Heidegger's distinctive philosophical idiom: its authoritarian *gestus*, its pseudosacral aversion to rhetorical give and take, its persistent denigration of the claims and counterclaims of rational argumentation. After all, in Heidegger we have a thinker who once openly declared that "Reason ... is *the most stiff-necked adversary of thought* [*Denken*]."[10]

Delusions of Assimilation

One of the paradoxes of Heidegger's reception history is that, during the 1920s, his most talented students were Jews. In certain respects, this fact should not be as surprising as it may appear on first view. After all, the Weimar Republic — Germany's first — was a paragon of Jewish upward social mobility. The subtitle of *Weimar Culture,* Peter Gay's standard work on the subject, felicitously describes the situation: Weimar Germany was a setting in which those who had previously been *outsiders,* became *insiders.*[11]

Still, as we now know, German–Jewish relations during this time were something of a time bomb, a conclusion that is not only valid in hindsight. Many contemporary witnesses — here, Victor Klemperer's memoirs are a good place to start — confirm the fact that the vituperative anti-Semitism of the pre–World War I years had in no way dissipated.[12] Instead, it enjoyed a vigorous subterranean afterlife in the German collective unconscious. This fact was recognized by figures like Martin Buber, Franz Rosenzweig, Gershom Scholem, and other participants in the so-called postwar Jewish Renaissance. All had grave doubts as to whether the German–Jewish symbiosis would fulfill its lavish promissory note of wholesale acceptance. "Cultural Zionism" was an expression of German–Jewish ambivalence. It was a mechanism whereby Jews hedged their bets vis-à-vis the so-called German–Jewish symbiosis, which, as we know, ended in tragedy.[13]

What this situation requires in retrospect is a critique not of Jewish assimilation per se, but of the *delusions* of assimilation: the belief that the logic of assimilation had rendered anti-Semitism in Central Europe permanently obsolete. This situation expresses a lack of Jewish self-knowledge: a deficiency in political awareness characteristic of Jewish identity. Thus, Heidegger's Jewish students were proverbial "non-Jewish Jews" who first discovered their Jewishness through the acid bath of anti-Semitism.[14]

In this respect, Hannah Arendt's autobiographical reflections are typical. In a 1964 interview she recalls the biases and omissions of her own assimilated upbringing as follows: "As a child I did not know that I was Jewish.... The word 'Jew' was never mentioned at home when I was a child. I first met up with it through anti-Semitic remarks ... from children on the street. After that I was, so to speak, 'enlightened.'"[15]

Arendt avowed that what shocked her was not the anti-Semitism of average Germans, which she expected, but that of fellow intellectuals. Her disappointment was so severe, the sense of betrayal so acute, that for a period of twenty-five years she renounced philosophy and insisted on being referred to as a "political thinker." As she explains in the aforementioned interview:

> The problem ... was not what our enemies did but what our friends did.... I lived in an intellectual milieu, but I also knew other people. And among intellectuals *Gleichschaltung* was the rule, so to speak....

I never forgot that. I left Germany dominated by the idea ... [that] I shall never again get involved in any kind of intellectual business. I want nothing to do with that lot.[16]

From the Pragmatics of Dasein to "Being-Mysticism"

As Heidegger progressively retreated from the worldly, pragmatic orientation of *Being and Time* — the approach that had stimulated so much interest in his thought initially — and accorded center stage to fanciful conceptions such as the "Fourfold" (*das Geviert*) of gods, humans, heaven, and earth, he abandoned the terrain of practical philosophy for the fatalism of or the "history of Being" (*Seinsgeschichte*). The concept of Being increasingly assumed the character of a quasi-Aristotelian, first unmoved mover, whose emanations it was humanity's duty passively to receive. As he states in "Recollection in Metaphysics": "The history of Being is neither the history of man and of humanity, nor the history of the human relation to beings and to Being. The history of Being is *Being itself and only Being.*"[17] But what could this declaration possibly mean? How could the "history of Being" acquire intelligibility apart from our interpretive efforts to decipher its modalities and shapes? Little wonder, then, that when Heidegger was asked in the celebrated 1966 *Spiegel* interview what counsel his philosophy might hold for contemporaries, he could do little more than proclaim in despair: "Only a god can save us."[18]

Heidegger always insisted that his philosophical standpoint was influenced by the "factical" character of "everydayness" or the *Zeitgeist*. How could it have been otherwise? After all, in *Being and Time,* by employing the modalities of Being-in-the-world or human finitude as his point of departure, Heidegger sought to counter the transcendental delusions of those who, from Plato to Husserl, sought to philosophize sub specie aeternitatis. Yet, careful attention to the early Heidegger demonstrates the extent to which the existential analytic of *Being and Time* was indebted to the regnant, conservative revolutionary diagnosis of the times. Circa World War I, a critique of mass society that during the nineteenth century had been honed by Kierkegaard, Nietzsche, and others was recast in a feverish ideological pitch. Now that the lecture courses from the early 1920s have been published, along with many revealing letters, we realize the extent to which Heidegger, willy nilly, wrote under the sway of the Zeitgeist. Many categories of *Being and Time* (or "Existentials") only become fully intelligible if one takes into account the depth of contemporary historical and intellectual influences: "Being-toward-death," "destiny" and "fate," "generation," "Volk," "resolve," and so forth. Who would deny that, in 1933, when Heidegger proudly traded in his lederhosen for a brown shirt and the so-called Hitler-Grüss, this was a way of "choosing his hero" (see *Being and Time*, paragraph 74) in the person of the Führer. As Heidegger opined at the time: the philosophical basis of his partisanship for Nazism was the concept of "historicity" as developed in *Being and Time*.[19] One could hardly ask for a more unequivocal declaration of intent. It was Karl Löwith, one of Heidegger's most illustrious PhD students, who has offered indispensable firsthand testimony concerning the link between politics and philosophy in Heidegger's work:

> Given the significant attachment of the philosopher to the mood and intellectual habitus of National Socialism, it would be inappropriate to criticize or exonerate his political decision in isolation from the very principles of Heideggerian philosophy itself .... A Swiss lecturer regretted that Heidegger consented to compromise himself with daily affairs, as if a philosophy that explains Being from the standpoint of time and the everyday would not stand in relation to the daily affairs in which it makes its influence felt and originates. The possibility of a Heideggerian political philosophy was not born as a result of a regrettable miscue, but from the very conception of existence that simultaneously combats and absorbs the "spirit of the age."[20]

Heidegger placed his philosophy at the disposal of a regime whose very raison d'être was a genocidal racial imperialism. The war it unleashed during the 1930s resulted in some fifty million deaths. From the outset, the Nazis never made a secret of their intentions to reshuffle the peoples of Europe according to the precepts of racial hierarchy. Nor did Heidegger ever unambiguously renounce the Third Reich and its practices. Instead, till the end, in keeping with the precepts of "essential thinking" (*wesentliches Denken*), he adhered to an "essentialized" definition of Nazism. As late as the 1950s, he spoke glowingly of the "inner truth and greatness of National Socialism," thereby implying that the regime had never lived up to its genuine, world-historical potential. Moreover, after the war he insisted that with the Allied victory nothing "essential" had been resolved. Among the political alternatives of communism, Nazism, and democracy, Heidegger insisted there was little to choose from. In his view, liberalism was "despotic" insofar as it left individuals subject to the tyranny of opinion.

Such extreme judgmental myopia gives pause. It demands that scholars who wish to avoid the apologetic mode so common among the Heideggerian faithful shun facile rationalizations and instead carefully reexamine Heidegger's legacy in light of its manifest ideological distortions. One of the ironies of the postwar Heidegger reception is that a quasi-Spenglerian, anticivilizational discourse honed by the German

Right during the 1920s became a major point of reference among the post-1960s Cultural Left. In this way, the legacy of Heidegger's "critique of reason" (*Vernunftkritik*), as promoted by French poststructuralists such as Derrida, Lyotard, and Foucault, was passed on unsuspectingly to the North American academic Left. There it served as one of the linchpins of "postmodernism" cum "identity politics." For the reverse side of postmodernism's condemnation of reason qua "universalism" was a celebration of the virtues of naked particularism. Thus, at a certain point, the logics of transmission came full circle. As a perceptive European observer once quipped: "'Identity politics': that's what they had in Germany between 1933 and 1945."

One of the lessons of the so-called Heidegger Affair concerns the pitfalls of narrow textual readings. Philosophers the world over who immersed themselves in texts with ahistorical blinders — Derrida's followers, to take one prominent guild — were caught off guard by the revelations concerning Heidegger's deep-seated involvement with Nazism. (Derrida's own response was infamously counterintuitive: he conjectured that Heidegger had succumbed to Nazism's lures due a surfeit of "metaphysical humanism.") Ironically, had they heeded Heidegger's own hermeneutic precepts, which, following the lead of Dilthey and Graf Yorck, stressed the centrality of historicity, they would have been better off. Those who read the texts of *Existenzphilosophie* antihistorically do so only at their own peril.

Discovering Being with Heidegger

According to several autobiographical avowals, the young Levinas originally thought of himself as a Heideggerian. During the 1928–29 academic year, he attended Heidegger's lectures in Freiburg. As Levinas himself phrased it: "I had gone to Freiburg to [study with] Husserl, and I found Heidegger."[21] He was also notably present during the legendary Heidegger–Cassirer confrontation later that year in Davos, Switzerland. In German philosophical lore, this event signified the passing of the baton from a staid and traditional neo-Kantian rationalism, as represented by Cassirer, to the new horizons that had been opened up by Heidegger's radical brand of *Existenzphilosophie*. In Levinas's words, the Davos summit represented *"the end of a certain humanism."*[22]

In conversation, Levinas revealed that the two most powerful prephilosophical influences on his development were the ethical injunctions of the Hebrew Bible and Russian literature — above all, the novels of Dostoyevsky. From these influences, one may discern the origins of his own unique contribution to the history of philosophy, which is epitomized by the maxim: *"ethics (not ontology) as first philosophy."*

For Levinas, two Old Testament parables stood out. First, the story of the Ten Commandments bestowed upon Moses at Mount Sinai. The Ten Commandments represented a historical (and moral) watershed insofar as they presented humanity with a series of theistically mandated, inviolable ethical precepts. As divinely ordained, these injunctions betray the trait of "transcendence": they have a status that is superior to beings or entities — the "worldhood of the world" (Heidegger) — and in this respect, to speak in a Levinasian idiom, they transcend "ontology" in the direction of "infinity." In Levinas's postwar ethics, the originary encounter with the "face of the other," which forms the basis of all sociality and world-relations in general, formally parallels the encounter with divine transcendence. For the Other's absolute alterity — the fact that the Other resists appropriation or assimilation by the Same or the Ego — is patterned after the Almighty's absolute alterity.

The other tale that Levinas revered was the Abraham parable — paradoxically, insofar as at issue is a potential violation of the Fifth Commandment, "Thou Shalt Not Kill." Yet in this case, too, transcendence materializes, insofar as Abraham rises above both worldly concerns as well as ethical convention by virtue of his unshakeable faith. Levinas's appreciation of Abraham was undoubtedly fueled by Kierkegaard's sublime commentary, *Fear and Trembling* — a fact that is confirmed by an important review essay Levinas wrote during the mid-1930s of Lev Shestov's *Kierkegaard and Existential Philosophy*.[23] In Kierkegaard's lexicon, Abraham enacts a "teleological suspension of the ethical." For Levinas, Abraham's actions — a classical case of *credo, quia absurdum* — and the parable in general paradigmatically exemplify the logic of transcendence. For Abraham must surmount the "finite" customs and morality of the creaturely world in the direction of the "infinity" of Revelation, whose transcendent prescriptions remain unintelligible to human intellection.

Levinas always made a point of strictly separating his copious religious musings from his narrowly philosophical writings.[24] As an heir to the phenomenological tradition, he knew his ethical doctrines must bring demonstrable evidence to bear on their subject matter. For all that, when one steps back to survey his philosophical project at a distance, there can be no doubt that one of its central leitmotifs concerns the attempt to play off "Athens versus Jerusalem" — a contrast that, in his work, by far redounds to Jerusalem's credit. Brusquely put: the fact that in the contemporary world "ontology" has supplanted "theology" — a process that had already begun with Plato and Aristotle — accounts for modernity's profound and widespread sense of moral paralysis cum disorientation. Correspondingly, in the aforementioned review of Shestov's Kierkegaard study, Levinas concludes by praising existentialism for "*[exploding] the synthesis of the Greek spirit and the Judeo-Christian which the Middle Ages believed to have accomplished.*"[25]

The forlornness of the human condition once it forsakes the redemptive balm of *caritas* in favor of modernity's secular intellectual blandishments is the topos of Dostoyevsky's novels. Immortal literary antiheroes such as Raskolnikov and the disoriented and perplexed "Underground Man" offer moving testimony to the pitfalls of modernity's God-forsakenness. In works like *Crime and Punishment* and *Notes from Underground*, Dostoyevsky reacted critically to Russia's attempt to imitate Western patterns of cultural development. He passionately rejected Enlightenment shibboleths concerning the Empire of Reason and the "infinite perfectibility of man." In his view, they represented soulless and idolatrous panaceas. Instead, in his novels he celebrated an ethic of Goodness, as personified by characters such as Alyosha Karamazov and Prince Myshkin: the sublime capacity for human warmth that stands at cross-purposes with the objectivating powers of ratiocination; in the lexicon of early Christianity, *caritas*. These youthful literary encounters had a profound and lasting effect on Levinas's ethical doctrines. He was especially fond of citing a maxim from *The Brothers Karamazov*: "We are all guilty of everything and everyone, towards everyone — and I more than all the others."[26] This ineradicable dimension of "guilt," which is related to Original Sin, betrays our irremediable indebtedness to the Other (*l'Autrui*) — an infinite debt that we can never repay and that, consequently, requires perennial vigilance.

By the phrase "ethics as first philosophy" Levinas suggests that the entire course of Western thought has been a false path. Since the pre-Socratics, philosophy's mission has been defined by ontology: the sober and objective study of Being. Consequently, ethics has occupied a derivative and subaltern role — almost as an afterthought or hiccup of "theoretical reason." Echoing Heidegger, Levinas holds that reason aims at "comprehension" for purposes of a predatory and objectifying world-mastery. By reversing the traditional hierarchy and according primacy to ethics, Levinas seeks to counter our intellectual tradition's grave imbalances. For Levinas, ethics derives from the claims of the Other, *l'Autrui*. The originary and indubitable phenomenological-ethical "evidence" (*Evidenz*) is *the face of the other*.[27] The face of the Other makes an infinite, prepredicative moral claim on us — one that is anterior to all theoretical judgments or syntheses. Levinas uses a series of dramatic metaphors — he frequently speaks of the Other's nakedness and destitution — to drive home the point that he or she stands totally at our mercy.[28] Since, given the limitations of creaturely existence, we can never entirely satisfy the Other's claims, at issue is a relationship of "infinity" or "transcendence." Theoretical reason, conversely, aims at a type of totalizing comprehension — an essay at finite closure — that Levinas belittles as "totality." Thus the animating antithesis of his work: "totality" versus "infinity."

In 1929, when Levinas first encountered *Being and Time,* he thought he had discovered a fraternal philosophical spirit. In his view, Husserl's notion of "philosophy as rigorous science" remained indebted to the misguided and fateful scientistic prejudices of Western thought — from Plato's theory of the numbers in the *Thaeatetus* to Auguste Comte's conclusion that evolution of Western reason culminated in nineteenth-century positivism.[29] Conversely, Heidegger's forte as a philosopher lay in his radical abandonment of "theoretical reason" or "thinking substance" as the alpha and omega of Western metaphysics. Casting off the prejudices and misconceptions of transcendental philosophy from Descartes through Husserl, Heidegger's "fundamental ontology" favored a pluralistic and multifaceted articulation of human Being-in-the-world. In Levinas's view Heidegger's démarche, which emphasized the primacy of human situatedness, opened up horizons and possibilities that left traditional modes of doing philosophy in the dust.[30]

Levinas perceived Heidegger's philosophy as a well-nigh providential response to the civilizational crisis that had been precipitated by World War I. This fact accounts for the fascination both thinkers displayed for Kierkegaard's doctrines, which stressed reason's ultimate bankruptcy (was it not, after all, a group of statesmen functioning as "rational actors" who had pushed Europe over the brink?) and the necessity of the "leap of faith." As Levinas plaintively argues in a 1930s text: "The moral crisis opened by the War of 1914 has given men a pointed feeling of the impotence of reason: *of the profound discord between rationalist civilization and the exigencies of the individual soul lost in the anonymity of the general.*"[31] For Levinas and many others, *Existenzphilosophie,* which relativized the primacy of "thinking substance," or the Cartesian "I think," in favor of other, more emotive human capacities and aptitudes, seemed to be a serendipitous philosophical antidote to the West's misguided stress on the powers of intellection.

We now know that Levinas was so taken with the early Heidegger's radical existential framework that he intended to write a book on his philosophy — a project that never came to fruition. Nevertheless, one can gain a sense of Levinas's lofty philosophical expectations if we examine his Heidegger-related articles from the early 1930s — above all, the 1934 essay "Martin Heidegger and Ontology," which appeared in *Esprit,* and which was one of the first articles on Heidegger's work to appear outside of Germany.

Under the guise of a nonpartisan exposition, the article is, clearly, the work of a "disciple." Levinas's Heideggerian partisanship is betrayed in an effusive passage that the philosopher chose to elide from the essay when it was later republished: "*No one who has ever done philosophy can keep himself from declaring, before the Heideggerian corpus, that the originality and power of his effort, born of genius, have allied themselves with a conscientious, meticulous, and solid elaboration.*"[32] In essence, Levinas offers the reader a post hoc vindication of the Davos confrontation: Heidegger is cast in the guise of "David" who has slain the antiquated "Goliath" of neo-Kantianism. However, thereby, Levinas uncritically imbibes Heidegger's smug view of the history of philosophy, which portrays Heidegger's own contributions as a watershed and caesura: the sine qua non for philosophy's ontological self-renewal.

Yet, as Levinas himself would later recognize, Heidegger's perspective on Western thought, in addition to being self-serving, is often reductive and one-dimensional. In articles such as "Plato's Doctrine of Truth," he treats the history of philosophy as purely and simply a story of decline. Since Plato's theory of ideas, the concept of "representation" — as perpetrated by the epistemological "subject" — has supplanted the more "original" notion of truth qua the "unconcealment of beings" (*Unverborgenheit*). As far back as Plato, alleges Heidegger, Western Dasein has been on a fast track toward *das Gestell*: the subjective "enframing" of all Being qua "standing reserve." In this way Heidegger advances the claim that Western reason is a project of domination, aiming at the manipulation and control of objects or things. But, thereby, he underplays reason's (in Greek: *nous*) theological component, which aspires to an intuitive, quasi-mystical grasp of the All. More seriously, perhaps, his account neglects the dimension of morality or "practical reason," which in Kant (to take one obvious counterinstance) admirably urges us to treat human natures as ends-in-themselves. Surely, Kant's moral philosophy transcends Heidegger's cynical understanding of reason as mechanism of technological mastery *simpliciter*.

As usual, Heidegger's claims tell us more about his own ideological biases than about the trends he is criticizing. To highlight only one major flaw: Heidegger never explains how it would be possible to accede to the promised land of "unconcealment" without relying on language qua faculty of "representation." For to speak of a truth wholly beyond "representation" would be meaningless. Such a truth could neither be expressed linguistically nor communicated to others. Even "poetic revealing," which the later Heidegger viewed as a praiseworthy alternative to the depredations of Western philosophy qua "onto-theology," in no way subsists beyond or apart from representation. From the rarefied standpoint of Heideggerian *Seinsgeschichte* (the history of Being), social evolutionary breakthroughs in moral development — what Hegel, in his lectures on the philosophy of history, aptly termed "progress in the consciousness of freedom" — remain imperceptible. They are written off as existentially retrograde: part of the rise of modern democracy, which Heidegger views as an ontological threat to the "teleology of Greco-German Dasein."[33] Since Heidegger, following Nietzsche, opts for an all-encompassing "total critique" of modernity, his criticisms assume the character of an unqualified, global indictment, in the manner of Spenglerian *Zivilisationskritik*. They are devoid of nuanced and specific ameliorative potential.

Philosophy and Betrayal

Following Heidegger's demonstrative embrace of Nazism in 1933, Levinas's sense of disillusionment was acute. In interviews, he remarks how he was later consumed with self-reproach for having, at Davos, cast his lot with Heidegger rather than Cassirer — who, as a Jew, was banned from teaching in 1933, despite his stature as a world-renowned Kant interpreter. For Levinas, Heidegger's Nazism was not an adventitious biographical fact but a philosophical problem of the highest order and magnitude. In his eyes, the issue was not that Heidegger the contingent individual had, circa 1933, joined the NSDAP. Instead, the problem was twofold: (1) the Freiburg philosopher explicitly justified his partisanship for the movement with the language of *Existenzphilosophie*; (2) the painful realization that fundamental ontology itself contained no effective theoretical or ethical bulwarks against the lure of Nazism's "radical evil."[35]

A 1934 article, "Some Reflections on the Philosophy of Hitlerism," represented Levinas's initial attempt to grapple with the Nazi behemoth as a "philosophical problem." Levinas observes that, insofar as Nazi racism constitutes the negation of humanity, it threatens the future course of Western development. He concludes (unremarkably) that one of the reasons Nazism poses a threat to occidental humanity in its entirety is that it represents a "new paganism": a frontal assault against the totality of the West's Judeo-Christian heritage. It is at this point in his analysis that the eerie parallels between the "philosophy of Hitlerism" (that is, Nazism) and Heidegger's avowedly pagan brand of *Existenzphilosophie* — in which, following Nietzsche, the loss of metaphysical assurances and guarantees opens up an "abyss" (*Abgrund*) of nihilism— undoubtedly hit home. Both the Nazis and Heidegger join forces in their assault on "transcendence" as an ultimate value. Both proceed to flirt with a type of "body politics" — in the Nazi case, the doctrine of "race" — although certainly, with Heidegger, the end result (at least as far as *Being and Time* is concerned) stops short of full-blown racism. Thereafter, Levinas's could never identify naïvely with Heidegger's philosophy as had been the case heretofore.

Levinas began a painstaking and concerted process of self-criticism. The way stations of his remarkable philosophical odyssey — from Kovno, Lithuania, by way of Freiburg and Strasbourg, to the Sorbonne in the heart of the Latin Quarter — have been recounted on numerous occasions. This itinerary culminated in a novel philosophical approach that stressed the primacy of ethics over ontology — one that, deservedly, has had worldwide repercussions and influence. Conversely, when queried shortly after the war by the French philosopher Jean Beaufret as to whether it was time to remedy fundamental ontology's ethical deficits by reviving "humanism," Heidegger reacted derisively: "I wonder whether that is necessary. Or is the damage caused by all such terms still not sufficiently obvious?"[35] As critics have pointed out, in Heidegger's thought, the problem of intersubjectivity is not successfully addressed or resolved. In his later philosophy man is deemed the "neighbor of Being," but never the neighbor of his fellow man. Levinas's conception of "Ethics as First Philosophy" was a response both to the radical evil of Nazism and to Heidegger's act of intellectual betrayal.

But what was it exactly that Heidegger betrayed? It is at this juncture that a central question arises, a question with which Levinas grappled throughout his mature years. According to another one of Heidegger's "children," Herbert Marcuse, the answer to this question was relatively straightforward: by casting his lot with the Nazis, Heidegger had betrayed everything that Western philosophy has stood for since time immemorial. For Nazism represented the denegation and antithesis of that tradition.

For Levinas, conversely, the answer to this question was decidedly more complicated. Unlike Marcuse, Levinas entertained the risky and hyperbolic conclusion that Nazism, rather than representing the *negation* of the Western tradition, constituted its *fulfillment*. The conclusion is "risky" for two reasons: (1) by conceiving of Nazism as the culmination of Western development, it potentially awards Hitler an undeserved, posthumous victory; (2) by insinuating that "first philosophy" or "theoretical reason" is itself directly implicated in the German catastrophe, Levinas risks depriving us of valuable resources by which we might attempt to think and work through the horrific experiences in question.

"Ethics as First Philosophy"

One of the dilemmas resulting from Levinas's conception of "Ethics as First Philosophy" is its denigration of cognition or knowledge. Here the ultimate irony is that, in trying to extricate himself from the clutches of Heidegger's fundamental ontology, Levinas ensconces himself more thoroughly in the Freiburg philosopher's grasp. Thereby, Levinas succumbs to the "anxiety of influence," to employ Harold Bloom's felicitous expression. Wittingly or unwittingly, the critique of Western metaphysics that Levinas purveys in *Totality and Infinity* and other works is, in essence, a Heideggerian critique. In "Overcoming Metaphysics" Heidegger indicts Western thought for reducing the totality of Being to mere stuff of domination. It is on this basis that he argues for the importance of a "new beginning" (*neues Anfang*) signaled by his own brand of "essential thinking." Methodologically speaking, Heidegger relies on the standpoint of a "totalizing" rather than "immanent" critique. In his view, when all is said and done, there is nothing about this tradition inherently worth saving — aside, perhaps, from a poem or two by Hölderlin and Trakl. Little wonder that, having ruled out the method of immanent criticism, time and again he has recourse to religious metaphors as a potential redemptive balm: the "saving power" (Hölderlin), the "Fourfold" (gods and mortals, heavens and earth), or the absent "god" who alone might "save us."

When Levinas, for his part, writes about the excrescences and misdeeds of "totality," he employs a similar idiom. In his thought totality becomes a figure for the "will to domination" which he identifies as the animating impetus of Western philosophy. Reason's raison d'être, as it were, is the subjugation of beings. Rather than "letting beings be," it destroys their inherent multifariousness by perennially reducing them to "sameness." Reason must be reconceptualized, Levinas argues, as hostility to "difference." It is incapable of appreciating the Other (*l'Autrui*) in his or her otherness. Instead, it functions as a universal solvent, employing its imperious theoretical "gaze" (the Greek word for reason, *nous*, is etymologically related to the verb "to see") to reduce otherness to ipseity or identity. In Levinas's optic, "ontology" becomes a code word for a type of pandemic, originary violence — the signature of Western cultural development in toto. As the Lithuanian-born philosopher asserts:

> The visage of being that shows itself in war is fixed in the concept of Totality that dominates Western philosophy.... The ontological event that takes form in this black light is ... a mobilization of absolutes by an objective order from which there is no escape ... But violence does not consist so much in injuring and annihilating persons as in interrupting their continuity [and] making them play roles in which they no longer recognize themselves.[36]

Here, we are but a short step from Foucault's famous dictum: "*Raison, c'est la torture.*" Little wonder that Levinas — the proto-typical *juif errant* — has been canonized as one of postmodernism's founding saints. The modish postmodern inclination to deduce "totali-tarianism" ideationally from the concept of "totality" is a Levinasian inheritance. The affinities between reason and totalitarianism are even clearer in Levinas's explicitly political essays such as "Beyond the State Within the State," where he associates "rationality" with "*ideology ... [or] the abstractions of totalitarianism.*"[37] Yet, this association remains glib in the sense that all attempts to explain immanent historical events on the basis of "metapolitics" (for example, Heidegger's notion of the "history of Being") remain glib.

In the programmatic text "Ethics as First Philosophy" we find a complementary censure cum rejection of theoretical knowing. Levinas understands knowledge as a species of "techne": a procedure that aims at domination and control. There we encounter the sweeping assertion that "Even before any technical application of knowledge, it expresses the principle ... of the future technological and industrial order." Like Heidegger, Levinas seems incapable of distinguishing between the life-enhancing and destructive uses of technology — a conclusion that cannot help but strike anyone who has recently viewed a neonatalogy ward, where "scientific miracles" are performed every day. His stand-point also peremptorily dismisses "hermeneutic reason," whose goal is "understanding" (*Verstehen*) rather than subjugation and mastery. As Levinas continues:

> In knowledge there ... appears the notion of an intellectual activity or of a reasoning will [:] seizing something and making it one's own, of reducing to presence ... an activity which *appropriates* and *grasps* the otherness of the known.... The metaphor should be taken literally: it expresses the principle ... of the future technological and industrial order.... Modernity will subsequently be distinguished by the attempt to develop from the identification and appropriation of being *by* knowledge.

> The Wisdom of First Philosophy is reduced to self consciousness. Identical and non-identical are identified. The labor of thought wins out over the otherness of things and men ... My being-in-the-world or my "place in the sun," my being at home, have these not also been the usurpation of spaces belonging to other men whom I have already oppressed or starved, or driven out into a third world; are they not acts of repulsing, excluding, exiling, stripping, killing.[38]

The foregoing observations help to highlight one of the major deficiencies of Levinas's theoretical framework. When, in a type of inverted Hegelianism, Auschwitz becomes the West's implicit historical telos, ethical breakthroughs such as the expansion of egalitarian normative consciousness (for example, the democratic revolutions of the eighteenth century) become imperceptible.[39] Only from this standpoint can Levinas, following Heidegger, reductively equate modernity with the triumph of "identifying reason" (ipseity) — as exemplified by the foregoing remarks.

Postmodernism, inspired by the "critique of reason" (*Vernunftkritik*) developed by Heidegger and Levinas, seeks to promote a permanent break with Hegelian metanarratives. But Levinas's philosophy of history essentially provides us with an *inverted metanarrative*: "progress in domination" supplants Hegel's "progress in the consciousness of freedom." But a metanarrative of decline is no less of a metanarrative than a metanarrative of progress.

Like much of postmodernism, Levinas's thought betrays a telltale performative contradiction. On the one hand, reason is unmasked and excoriated as a "will to domination." On the other hand, we have no other means at our disposal to advance arguments, articulate truth claims, or attain intersubjective understanding than through the "logos": the uniquely human capacity to provide rational accounts. According to Aristotle, it is the faculty of language that makes us distinctively human.[40] The radical critique of "logocentrism," an orientation that Levinas shares with Derrida, risks needlessly belittling — and thus squandering — these invaluable communicative potentials and capacities. It is at this point that the critique of logocentrism risks devolving into a "Logosvergessenheit" — a forgetting of the logos. Logocentrism did not cause Auschwitz. In point of fact, the ideology that was responsible — a fanatical, "redemptive anti-Semitism" — was a self-proclaimed *misology*: a hatred of reason.[41]

Like Heidegger and Derrida, fraternal spirits in the realm of *Vernunftkritik*, Levinas was hardly unaware of this problem. Increasingly, he came to view the language of metaphysics as misleading and unserviceable. Hence, in later works such as *Otherwise than Being, or Beyond Essence*, he self-consciously abandoned the lexicon of "first philosophy" in favor of a strategy of radical conceptual innovation. Thereby, however, his attempts to philosophize increasingly ran up against the "bounds of sense." Levinas seeks to address philosophical topics — God, the Self, transcendence, Otherness, the Infinite, and so forth — "otherwise": that is, in a *different* mode and idiom, one that is "beyond ontology" or "Being." The problem is that by emphatically rejecting the terminology of "representation" or denotative reason, Levinas deprives himself of the lexical means to articulate his positions.

The ineffable may be a topic of veneration. But, by definition, it is resistant to sense and syntax. The end result of his philosophical strivings is, paradoxically, that "philosophical language becomes almost, if not wholly, impossible."[42]

Levinas inexplicably defines the history of ontology as an egocentric, uniquely Hobbesian universe: a *bellum omnium contra omnes*. In Hobbes, however, the passage to the "civil state" nullifies the state of nature's unchecked bestiality. With Levinas, conversely, one finds the reverse: society, under the guise of civil peace, merely perpetuates the licentiousness and cruelty of the presocial state. Take the following representative passage from *Otherwise Than Being*: "Being's interestedness takes the dramatic form of egoisms struggling with one other, each against all, in the *multiplicity of allergic egoisms which are at war with one another* .... War is the chronicle or drama of Essence's interestedness."[43] But one of the risks of this perspective is that it highlights the *predatory* side of social life while totally neglecting *solidarity*: "mutuality" as an essential dimension of human intersubjectivity. Given Levinas's rather arbitrary Hobbesian point of departure, it is hard to imagine "community" as a viable human reality or value at all.

For this standpoint is much too cynical. The characterization of Being as a realm of possessive individualism gone haywire seems philosophically self-serving — to the point of bad faith. Philosophers of ordinary language have convincingly demonstrated that elements of a consensus-formation and mutual understanding inhere in the "lifeworld" of human interaction. The participants' self-understanding, as verified by third-person observers, remains meaningful. It is not reducible to the delusions of "false consciousness." "Objectification" is not all there is. It is misleading to equate "the force of the better argument," which predominates in logics of discourse, with force as such. To "convince" is not to "subdue." Instead, argumentation entails the capacity to expand the Other's — as well as one's own — conceptual and experiential horizons. Communicative reason does not aim simply at the *subjugation* of the Other. It also has a restorative capacity. It acts as a balm that is capable of healing prior wounds. It possesses the salutary ability to redress prior misunderstandings and injustices. The lifeworld of human intersubjectivity is much richer than the pessimistic, *homo homini lupus* attitude perceived by Levinas.

Levinas sweeps everything he finds philosophically distasteful under the rug of "ontology" or "Being." Thereby — and, here, too, Levinas follows Heidegger's bad lead — he fails to differentiate sufficiently between "ontology" and "epistemology," or classical and modern philosophy. Whereas ontology assumes that Being is prior to "cognition" — and consequently subsumes the latter under the former — epistemology is self-consciously nonontological. It realizes that an approach to cognition that fails to examine the faculty of knowledge itself risks becoming dogmatic. This axiom was conveyed felicitously by Kant in the concluding paragraph of the *Critique of Pure Reason*, where he observes: "*The critical path alone is open to us.*" Modern theories of knowledge contain a dimension of reflexivity and self-awareness not found in classical ontology. Levinas's philosophy fails to do justice to this important distinction. Kant's claim, which occurs at the end of the "Transcendental Dialectic," suggests that an approach to knowledge that wantonly flaunts the "limits of experience" risks regressing to those dogmatic intellectual habitudes that transcendental philosophy sought to hold in check. One must inquire whether an approach like Levinas's, that denegates the history of philosophy as a history of error, and thus insists on the need to re-create philosophy ab ovo, runs precisely such risks.

Levinas's prejudices against "discourse" are clearly in evidence in his elevation of "the Saying" over the "the Said" in *Otherwise than Being* and other works. "The Saying" connotes the prepredicative act of speaking per se — "that" we speak in abstraction from "what" is said. "The Said," conversely, indicates the cognitive or denotative aspects of speech: the (prosaic) role of language in conveying meaning.

With this distinction, Levinas evinces a well-nigh phobic distrust of communication processes and the exchange of validity claims they entail. Here, too, his Hobbesian understanding of social action leads him astray. It is as though all language, by virtue of its logical and denominative capacities, contained the seeds of yet another Holocaust. As soon as they leave the mouths of the speaker, words must be mistrusted. Their effects can only be *instrumental*, resulting in enhanced domination. Ultimately, Levinas's devaluation of practical reason — which he consigns to the woodshed of "ontology" — is self-defeating. It dismisses out of hand prospects of progressive social change. The binary opposition between "totality" and "infinity" that governs his work makes it nearly impossible to conceptualize meaningful intersubjectivity. As soon as one leaves the terrain of "ethics" as defined by the "face of the Other," one succumbs to the inescapable sway of "totality": the "sauve qui peut" or "every man for himself" ethos of human self-preservation run amok.

During the last sixty years, the most significant development in international politics has been the cultivation of a global consensus on human rights. Concomitantly, there has also been a reappraisal of the meaning and necessity of humanitarian intervention. In international affairs the "realist" paradigm — as epitomized by Hans Morgenthau's classic study *Politics Among Nations* — has yielded to a Kantian approach that seeks to reconceive international politics in terms of considerations of "right."

Levinas's "ethics as first philosophy" approach is distinctly uncomfortable with such developments. Human rights — the warrant for the modern notion of individual freedom — evolved from the eminently "logocentric" doctrine of modern natural law as developed by Hobbes, Locke, and Rousseau. In other words, it derives from the tradition of theoretical reason that Levinas opposes. In the few essays where Levinas addresses such questions directly — "The Prohibition Against Representation and the Rights of Man" and "The Rights of Man and the Rights of the Other" — he is palpably ill at ease. In his view, human rights are an instance of "totality-thinking" *simpliciter*. They derive from the generalizing spirit of Plato and Kant, the tradition of "ontology." They express the modern ethos of self-assertion, with all its attendant dangers and risks. Their point of departure is not the "otherness of the Other," to which we are "hostage," but the realm of identity or the self-same. In Levinas's view, the same "rights of man" that are the purported guarantor of modern liberty also provide a warrant for a *"totally industrialized society or a ... totalitarian society."*[44] This argument seems dubious, since, historically, the political employment of human rights — for example, freedom of speech and assembly — has helped to allay the adverse effects of industrial capitalism. Moreover, as we know from the experiences of 1989, it played a key role in undermining and delegitimating totalitarianism.

To be sure, universal rights do not address the specificity of the Other. Instead they treat abstract considerations of formal equality. For Levinas, the prerogatives of universality, such as human rights, are merely a way of "treating the person as an object by submitting him or her (the unique and incomparable) to comparison, to thought, to being placed on the scales of justice, and thus to calculation."[45] In Levinas's view, the deficiency of human rights is that they fail to do justice to "the trace of God in man": "the [oneness] of Adam marks individuals of incomparable uniqueness in which the common species disappears and [where] they affirm themselves to be, each one, the sole purpose of the world."[46]

Here, Levinas confuses questions of "the Good" or "forms of life" (*Lebensformen*), which pertain to the content and scope of individual and collective self-realization, with the formal parameters of *justice*. What Levinas fails to consider is that, as John Rawls has argued, a political system predicated on considerations of abstract right, in which basic liberties are assured, provides the optimal terrain on which a plurality of "forms of life" might flourish. The priority of the "Right" over the "Good" is an essential inheritance of political modernity. By belittling this conception, and by relying on theological criteria — "the trace of God in man" — to advance his argument, Levinas misapprehends the worth of this legacy and risks regressing behind it.

Moreover, Levinas's view of ethics is so narrowly tied to the experience of the "Face of the Other" qua "infinity" or "height" that it resists being generalized. The problem is that it seems all but impossible to translate this ethical vision, often described in terms of a quasi-mystical metaphorics of "transcendence," into meaningful political terms. One way of expressing this problem would be to say that an "epiphany" cannot be made an *object of legislation* in the customary sense. In Levinas's conception, indebtedness to the Other becomes a relationship of exclusivity to the point where it becomes physically and emotionally impossible to assume loyalty or allegiance to multiple others in precisely the same way. For this reason, the idea of responsibility for the Other, when generalized, assumes the quality of an unsatisfiable or impossible demand.

By the same token, the experience of the Other, as he describes it, is so overwhelming that it entails a virtual dissolution of the Self. According to Levinas, this experience produces a relationship of "heteronomy" — wholesale indebtedness to the Other — rather than "reciprocity" or "autonomy" in the Kantian sense. It would seem, therefore, virtually impossible to reconcile Levinas's ethical doctrine with the modern conception of freedom. Freedom is reconceptualized as being beholden to the Other.

Thus, with Levinas, as soon as one breeches the face-to-face relationship, one enters the predatory dimension of "the Third" or the group, where the ethical relation disintegrates.[47] One finds oneself, *nolens volens*, in the inauthentic and reified sphere of "totality" where reason and communication, qua mechanisms of "objectification," predominate. Levinas himself testifies to the impossibility of translating ethics into politics when, toward the end of *Totality and Infinity*, he avows that "Politics left to itself bears a tyranny within itself."[48] Predictably, if one surveys the secondary literature on Levinas's oeuvre, commentators have had fits trying to derive a viable political philosophy from Levinas's rarified and self-enclosed conception of ethics. One observer has even gone so far as to speculate that "In Levinas's world there is really no place for politics period, and it is precisely this that makes his account *dangerous*."[49] Hence, in his work, it seems that a well-nigh unbridgeable chasm opens up between ethics and justice.

Undoubtedly, Levinas's conception of "ethics as first philosophy" has helped sensitize us to the instrumentalizing perils and excesses of theoretical reason. These are perils that, in a post-Holocaust universe, should not be taken lightly. By the same token, his caveats concerning reason's excesses and his concomitant glorification of "otherness" denigrate intersubjective communication in a way that threatens to deprive us of something invaluable and essential: the resources of human solidarity. For speech — in Levinas's idiom, "the Said" — is not reducible to the pernicious intentions of "totality." It is also a means of reassurance, affection, care, thoughtfulness, and brotherliness. In sum, it is an indispensable means of ensuring that the bonds of mutuality are forged and perpetuated. Thus arises the imperative to think with Levinas beyond Levinas.

7

Karl Jaspers: The Paradoxes of Mandarin Humanism

I

According to a well-known witticism: a Frenchman, an Englishman, and a German each undertook a study of the camel. The Frenchman went to the Jardin des Plantes, spent half an hour there, questioned the guard, threw bread to the camel, poked it with the point of his umbrella, and, returning home, wrote an article for his paper full of sharp and witty observations.

The Englishman, taking his tea basket and a good deal of camping equipment, went to set up camp in the Orient, returning after a sojourn of two or three years with a fat volume, full of raw, disorganized, and inconclusive facts which, nevertheless, had real documentary value.

As for the German, filled with disdain for the Frenchman's frivolity and the Englishman's lack of general ideas, he locked himself in his room, and there he drafted a multivolume work entitled: *The Idea of the Camel Derived from the Concept of the Ego.*

The saying well captures the debilities of the German intelligentsia. Although during the nineteenth century the German university system — the quintessence of scholarly rigor — was, rightly, a model to the world, ultimately its mandarin biases proved its undoing. The German professorate prided itself on a stance of Olympian distance vis-à-vis worldly affairs — the compromises and corruptions of politics in particular. The attitude was well encapsulated by Nietzsche's self-characterization as the "last antipolitical German." Thereby, Zarathustra's ventriloquist distanced himself from the pettiness and folly of Bismarck-era domestic political horse-trading. But this maxim in no way meant that Nietzsche had bid adieu to politics *simpliciter*. Instead, as those who have read him carefully know, one of the dominant leitmotifs of his later work was the idea of *die grosse Politik* — "Great Politics." By that he meant a politics of conquest, subjugation, and empire as practiced by ruthless titans such as Alexander the Great, Caesar, Cesare Borgia, and Napoleon. "A dominant race can grow up only out of terrible and violent beginnings," proclaimed Nietzsche in his later years. "*Where are the barbarians of the twentieth century?*"[1] Fifty years hence, Heinrich Himmler's Death's Head Brigades would provide a more than rhetorical response.

Antipolitical should not be equated with *unpolitical*. As World War I broke out, foreign scholars rushed to defend Germany's hallowed spiritual traditions against detractors' accusations that these traditions constituted the basis of German militarism. This defense elicited a demonstrative and combative response from a prestigious coterie of German scholars — among them, Ernst Troeltsch, Friedrich Meinecke, and Max Scheler, author of a virulent tract, *The Genius of War and the German War*.[2] In a bellicose 1915 anthology, *Spiritual Mobilization*, German academics proudly claimed, *au contraire*, that the war effort was in effect the *consummation* of German *Geist* rather than its antithesis.[3] Similarly, we now know that, under the auspices of the Orwellian-sounding "Humanities War-Enlistment Program," during World War II a preponderance of notable German humanists — philosophers, historians, classicists, and literary scholars — clambered aboard the Nazi bandwagon.[4] They were not about to be outdone by technical specialists in fields such as engineering, jurisprudence, and "race-science," whose practical expertise proved logistically invaluable for the regime's drive toward European hegemony.

It would be consoling to think that, at some level, German cultural ideals remained immune from the war delirium that, over the course of the twentieth century, twice convulsed Europe. Sadly, this expectation remains at odds with the available evidence. As Thomas Mann astutely noted in 1945: "There are not two Germanys, an evil and a good, but only one, which, through devil's cunning, transformed its best into evil."[5] And while there was certainly nothing endemic to those ideals that predisposed German elites to succumb to the fanatical delusions of Nazism, the fact that they put up such little resistance and, for the most part, "played along," beseeches an explanation.

Undoubtedly, the resolutely "antipolitical" bent of the *Bildungsbürgertum*, or educated elites — an attitude famously codified in

Mann's 1918 tract, *Reflections of an Unpolitical Man* — represents an important part of the equation. (To his credit, upon witnessing Hitler's implacable rise to power, Mann radically altered his views about the virtues of "antipolitics.") *Bildung* was the defining ideal of German classicism, an age that produced poets and thinkers such as Goethe, Schiller, Hölderlin, Hegel, and von Humboldt. But from the outset, its political ambivalences were readily apparent. *Bildung*'s stress on the supremacy of cultural excellence was noble and high-minded. Yet, the ideal harbored a self-undermining, antidemocratic bias — a legacy of the romantic notion of genius — that permanently alienated Germany's elites from the virtues of political liberalism.

Thus, among the mandarin caste it had become a truism that *Bildung*'s treasures were the prerogative of a gifted few, forever inaccessible to the hoi polloi or unwashed masses. That democracy and cultural excellence were mutually exclusive was treated as a truism. Swiss classicist Jacob Burckhardt's conviction that democracy's rise was responsible for the downfall of the classical polis became a generally accepted commonplace. In the *Genealogy of Morals* Nietzsche expressed the prophetic, if potentially genocidal opinion that "Mankind in the mass sacrificed to the prosperity of a single stronger species of man — *that* would be an advance."[6]

Such attitudes enjoyed widespread acceptance among educated, middle and upper class Germans. Yet, the political downside of this illiberal temperament became painfully clear as the Weimar Republic began to unravel circa 1930. For, by this point, few notables or opinion leaders were motivated to come to its defense. Often, the allergy to democratic liberalism was buttressed by an impassioned antipathy to Reason that flourished in reaction both to the Napoleonic conquest (1806) and Hegelianism's demise. Nietzsche aptly summarized this attitude by observing, with admirable pith, that what could be known by reason was of little worth. In a similar vein, Germany's major twentieth-century thinker, Martin Heidegger, famously declared that *"reason is the most stiff-necked adversary thought"* — thereby in essence consigning to irrelevance two thousand five hundred years of Western philosophy.[7] In surveying the cultural landscape of modern Germany, it becomes almost impossible to separate intellectual politics from actual politics.

II

The case of the philosopher Karl Jaspers is a fascinating one for a number of reasons. In many respects, the pre-1933 Jaspers epitomized the ethos of antipolitical mandarinism represented by Thomas Mann's

1918 polemical tract, *Reflections of an Unpolitical Man*: a condescending (and remarkably "unchristian") disdain for "the masses" and their capacities; an overestimation of the civilizing potentials of *Kultur*; open contempt for politics as an inferior manifestation of life; and, finally, a naïve belief in charismatic personalities as the unique "bearers of civilization." Nevertheless, one should also note that, following the National Socialist debacle Jaspers's standpoint underwent a commendable learning process. To his credit, he exchanged the perspective of mandarin cultural elitism for a more open and democratic sensibility that stressed the criterion of "publicness" as the hallmark of genuine politics.

From an early age, he was afflicted with a chronic and debilitating lung ailment. As a young adult, he was diagnosed as suffering from "bronchiectasis." Medical experts concurred that the patient would not live much beyond his thirty-fifth birthday. As it turned out, their prognosis was off by fifty years: born in 1883, Jaspers died in 1969, a few days after celebrating his eighty-sixth birthday. In 1910, following a three-year courtship, Jaspers married Gertrud Mayer, who came from a prominent Jewish family in Berlin. Twenty-five years hence, as the Nazis promulgated the Nuremburg race laws, this fact would impact Jaspers' future in ways they could only dimly have imagined.

Jaspers's path to philosophical renown was, by any stretch of the imagination, circuitous. Jaspers came to philosophy relatively late in life. His university training was in medicine, with a specialization in psychiatry. In 1913, the thirty-year-old Jaspers wrote a well-received treatise on *General Psychopathology*. He interned at the prestigious Heidelberg Clinic of Psychiatry. Upon his arrival in Heidelberg in 1908, Jaspers immediately noted the impoverished state of "therapy." Psychiatric disorders were viewed in narrowly medical-physiological terms. As such, therapeutic methods focusing on the patient's life history or the doctor–patient relationship were virtually nonexistent.

Jaspers sought to redress this deficiency by relying on Heidelberg's rich, indigenous philosophical traditions. In Heidelberg, Jaspers had fortuitously landed in the mecca of the Southwest School of neo-Kantianism. The young physician was surrounded by luminaries such as Heinrich Rickert, Wilhelm Windelband, and Max Weber. These thinkers had pioneered a new "interpretive" methodological approach that stressed the gulf separating the natural and human sciences. They conceded that the natural sciences' goal was a positivist-inspired, causal explanation of phenomena. The human sciences, conversely, focused on the *intentionality of actors*. As a manifestation of conscious life, intentionality was a phenomenon that resisted physicalist methods of elucidation. Only a noncausal, interpretive or "verstehende" approach would do justice to the expressive capacities of human cultural life.

Thus, whereas the natural sciences sought to "explain," the human sciences sought to "understand."

Jaspers' methodological breakthrough was to apply the hermeneutic or interpretive approach pioneered by Weber and others to the realm of psychopathology. As Suzanne Kirkbright notes in her recent biography of Japsers: "Jaspers' book on *General Psychopathology* was a revolutionary contribution .... [It] implied that the discipline of psychiatry was confronted with a responsibility to recognize its limitations and to respect the confidential nature of patient interviews."[8]

Conceivably, Jaspers could have derived many of the same insights concerning the value of "therapy as interpretation" from Freud. Yet, when it came to the claims of psychoanalysis, Jaspers was peculiarly tone-deaf. On several occasions, he bluntly dismissed Freud's views as a species of pseudoscience. He also felt that psychoanalysis's stress on the primacy of the unconscious risked depriving men and women of their dignity.

Heidelberg's intellectual climate stimulated Jaspers's growing interest in philosophical matters. He was heartily encouraged in these pursuits by the doyen of German sociology, Max Weber. (It was no small honor that, when Weber died in June 1920, Jaspers was invited by the students to present a memorial address.) Although Jaspers was allowed to teach philosophical subjects from time to time, the Philosophy Department, led by Rickert, proved fiercely territorial. For years it put up stiff resistance to the idea of granting Jaspers an official appointment.

In 1919 Jaspers published, to widespread acclaim, the *Psychology of Worldviews*. In this work, Jaspers creatively applied the lessons of hermeneutics to distill fundamental attitudes toward life: moral, religious, philosophical. One of Jaspers's key concepts was the notion of "limit-situation" (*Grenz-Zustand*), those rare and precarious moments in life — struggle, death, chance, and guilt — where we come face-to-face with the existential realities of our own finite being-in-the-world. Jaspers contends that it is in limit-situations that the most intense consciousness of existence flares up, a consciousness of something "absolute."[9] Here, one can discern the way that the pathos of the 1914–18 "War Experience" — the defining event of Jaspers's generation — came to permeate his own "worldview."

The basic conflict of our existence, observed Jaspers, concerns the predicament of a finite being — human Dasein — that constantly strives to reach out and grasp the infinite. The *Psychology of Worldviews*' flaw was that it partook of the value relativism subtending German historicism as practiced by Ranke, Dilthey, and others. According to this view, scholarship could at best lead to a clarification of various belief systems and attitudes. But its prescriptive value was negligible. The choice of values or ends was a matter of arbitrary "decision" rather than reasoned conviction. Jaspers was well aware of the limitations of this approach. Nevertheless, he accepted them unquestioningly. As he cautioned readers: "Whoever wants an answer to the question how he should live will, in this book, look for it in vain."[10]

Professionally speaking, *Psychology*'s publication changed everything. Overnight, Jaspers became a sought-after philosophical eminence. The philosophy departments of Kiel and Greifswald dangled the prestigious rank of "Ordinarius" before him. At long last, Heidelberg, too, was persuaded of Jaspers's worth. He received a regular appointment in 1921.

III

It was during this period that the philosophical friendship cum rivalry between Jaspers and Heidegger first blossomed. The "school philosophies" of the prewar era — neo-Kantianism, Hegelianism, and positivism — seemed stale and discredited. Jaspers and Heidegger believed that the life of the mind was in need of a new beginning. Both thinkers shared a marked aversion to the reigning academic dogmas. Instead, their approach was suffused with the renegade, existential doctrines of Kierkegaard and Nietzsche. In "Science as a Vocation," Weber had pointedly observed that "science" (here, a figure for "academic knowledge") was meaningless insofar as it failed to address the one question that really mattered: What should we do, how should we live our lives? For both philosophers, albeit in different ways, a philosophy of *Existenz* offered an antidote to the manifest sterility of tradition-bound, conventional scholarship. It foregrounded questions of *life* that, in the academic mainstream, had become matters of utter indifference. Idealist approaches to philosophy, such as Hegel's quest for "Absolute Spirit," typically smothered existential questioning amid all manner of abstract, speculative conceptualization. A philosophy of *Existenz*, conversely, sought to do justice to the ever-particular, individual quest for an authentic modality of being: *Selbstsein* (Selfhood) in Jaspers's philosophical lexicon.

The two philosophers were so enamored of one another that they immediately hatched plans for a new journal: *Philosophy of Our Time: Critical Journals by Karl Jaspers and Martin Heidegger*. During the heyday of their camaraderie, they referred to their friendship as a *Kampfgemeinschaft* or "community of struggle." Here, echoes of the "front experience" were unmistakable (a risible fact, considering that, given the precarious state of his health, Jaspers was unfit for military duty. Heidegger's war service, which he later exaggerated, was for the most part spent in a *Wehrmacht* post office.)

Jaspers was so obsessed with his fellow philosopher of *Existenz* that, from the time they met, he kept a detailed record of their encounters and conversations, later published as *Notes on Heidegger*. In one revealing exchange shortly after Hitler's seizure of power, Jaspers berated his fellow existentialist for having fallen under the sway of a leader as "uncultivated" (*ungebildet*) as Hitler. Heidegger's terse response: "It's not a question of culture. Look at his beautiful hands!"[10] In other words: Hitler's virtue as a politician lay in the ineffable, charismatic qualities of his leadership. To judge him by normal political criteria would be a category mistake. Such reasoning speaks volumes about the delusions and risks of using "existential" criteria as a basis for political judgment.

From the very beginning, it seemed impossible to immunize their friendship against the strains of intense philosophical rivalry. One example of this tendency was the lengthy and polemical 1921 review essay Heidegger penned of Jaspers's *Psychology of Worldviews*. An index of the seriousness with which Heidegger viewed Jaspers's opus may be found in a letter he wrote to Rickert: "This book must, in my opinion, be fought in the severest manner, precisely because it has so much to offer that Jaspers has learned from everywhere and because it appropriates a trace of the times."[11] In the review, Heidegger, who at this point had published very little, used Jaspers's text as a sounding board to develop his own ideas concerning "fundamental ontology." As such, the article, which remained unpublished until the late 1960s, provides valuable documentation concerning Heidegger's own evolution as a thinker.

Many of Heidegger's criticisms were similar to those he leveled against other contemporary philosophical approaches, the majority of which he held in low esteem. Jaspers's treatment of philosophical questions was not "fundamental" enough; it lacked a sense for the "primordial"; his attitude toward inherited philosophical paradigms was insufficiently "destructive." As such, Heidegger claimed that Jaspers's hermeneutical approach to understanding "worldviews" failed to transcend the faddish and diffuse tide of *Lebensphilosophie* (philosophy of life) that had emerged in the prewar period as an antidote to positivism. In Heidegger's disparaging view: "The characteristic feature of this intellectual situation is ... a muddled interplay of biological, psychological, social-scientific, aesthetic-ethical, and religious concepts of *life*."[12] Jaspers was clearly taken aback by the polemical directness of Heidegger's criticisms. He perceived the review as a "sly misappropriation of trust; thoughts were expressed in an aggressive manner that merely intensified Jaspers's suspicions of [Heidegger's] sincerity towards their joint aims."[13] Jaspers later complained that he found Heidegger's review "boring" and "untruthful." But, in view of the weighty stakes involved — philosophical preeminence in a nation renowned for its "poets and thinkers" — his objections seem distinctly understated. At the time, Heidegger, who was Jaspers's junior by six years, was a mere "lecturer" in Freiburg. Thus, Heidegger also seemed to be flaunting social roles vis-à-vis his better-established colleague.

In 1933 Heidegger, who fancied himself the most important philosopher since Heraclitus (active during the sixth century BCE), succumbed to the delusion that he could "lead the leader" — that is, Hitler. At this point, the "parallel lives" of Germany's two leading philosophers of *Existenz* diverged radically.

Heidegger foolishly sought to reenact Plato's ill-fated attempt to realize the precepts of philosopher-kingship with Syracusan tyrant Dionysios. Plato ended up fleeing for his life. When, in 1945, the Allies marched into southern Germany, Heidegger, too, beat a hasty retreat to a sanitarium in Switzerland, where, in a moment of despair, he tried to take his own life.

In 1937, Jaspers, who twenty-seven years earlier had entered into what the Nazis termed a *Mischehe* — a racially impure marriage — was deprived of the right to teach and publish. The couple's various plans to emigrate foundered. Rather than launch any efforts to oppose the regime (which would have placed Gertrud at particular risk), Jaspers buried himself in his work, writing books on *Existenz*, the philosophy of Descartes, and, as a way of offsetting the Nazis' Germanocentrism, a major study of world religions. As he wrote to his parents shortly after his forced retirement: "That I have my work, with quite definite plans and significant lines of thought [suggests] a new task: to work more intensely and quickly than is possible during lecture times."[14]

Jaspers's goal under the Nazis was to remain as inconspicuous as possible and, thereby, hopefully, to ride out the storm — the familiar "inner emigration" strategy. As he would observe in retrospect: "What we had to do was to act naively, to pretend no interest in the affairs of the world, to preserve a natural dignity ... and if need be to lie without scruples. For beasts in possession of an absolute power to destroy must be treated with cunning and not as ... rational beings."[15]

For her part, Gertrud endured a full range of Nazi-contrived, anti-Semitic persecution: she was disallowed entry to museums, theaters, concert halls, and other public places. The couple lived in constant fear of her being deported. They devised a suicide pact involving cyanide capsules in the event their worst fears came to pass. Only after the war did they learn how, in 1945, as the Third Reich teetered on the brink of collapse, Gertrud had come within a hair's breadth of being sent to a concentration camp. Providentially, friends in high places had forestalled this eventuality.

Certainly, there is no categorical imperative decreeing that, faced with persecution, one must become a "hero" — especially when one thereby risks jeopardizing loved ones as well. In retrospect, however, there seems to be something delusional about Jaspers's response to the Nazi behemoth — the stereotypical, mandarin retreat into "inwardness." After all, when confronted with a despotism as bloody and ruthless as any in human history, Jaspers's response was "*to work more intensely and quickly as possible.*" An index of how widespread this disorientation was among German philosophers is the curious fact that, shortly after Hitler's seizure of power, three of Germany's leading thinkers — Heidegger, Jaspers, and Karl Löwith — "responded" by writing hefty tomes on Nietzsche: a reaction that carries the notion of "misplaced concreteness" (Alfred North Whitehead) to new heights. Rather than trying to understand — let alone to combat — the existing political situation, all three repaired to their studies to immerse themselves in the texts of a nineteenth-century thinker who once declared that his ideas would only be understood fifty years hence.

In Jaspers's case a poignant irony arises from the fact that his post–World War II political thought centered on the concept of "publicness." This was Jaspers's rejoinder to the fact that a disreputable political clique had hijacked German politics in the name of a genocidal imperialism the likes of which had been previously unknown. Yet, notably, when the chips were down — even during the early 1930s when the Nazis had not yet consolidated their political stranglehold — Jaspers made no effort, by word or deed, to publicly oppose the regime.

After the war, Thomas Mann, who had chosen exile, aggressively castigated the so-called inner emigrants. He bluntly declared that nothing written in Germany between 1933 and 1945 was worth the paper it was printed on. Beyond the hyperbole, Mann's remarks were cogent and on target. For there is no getting around the fact that to "emigrate inwardly" during the Third Reich amounted to a de facto sanctification of the regime's genocidal policies. Jaspers in effect admitted as much when, in 1946, he analyzed the parameters of "political guilt":

[Political guilt], involving the deeds of statesmen and of the citizenry of a state, results in my having to bear the consequences of the deeds of the state whose power governs me and under whose order I live. Everybody is co-responsible for the way he is governed ... Every human being is fated to be enmeshed in the power relations he lives by ... Failure to collaborate in organizing power relations, in the struggle for power for the sake of serving the right, creates basic political guilt and moral guilt at the same time. Political guilt turns into moral guilt where power serves to destroy ... the achievement of what is right.[16]

It was as though Jaspers were directly challenging his own timorous quiescence during the Nazi years.

IV

Heidegger and Jaspers saw each other last in 1933. The author of *Being and Time* sought to provide the Nazi movement with philosophical leadership — to make Germany safe for the *Seinsfrage* (the question of Being), as it were. When charged with enforcing anti-Semitic legislation in his capacity as Freiburg University rector, he dutifully complied. Jaspers assumed that, after 1933, Heidegger had broken off contact because of Gertrud's Jewishness. But in a letter to Jaspers written after the war, the Freiburg philosopher provided a different explanation: he was simply ashamed of his own conduct. If this response is genuine, it represents his only avowal of contrition. Only Heidegger's own conscience can tell us whether he spoke the truth. On other occasions, he did not shy away from wholesale fabrications concerning the circumstances surrounding his compromised political past.

Yet, curiously, even after the war, the fates of Germany's two leading representatives of *Existenzphilosophie* remained inextricably interwined. When, in 1945, Heidegger's political future lay in the hands of a favorably disposed university denazification tribunal, the committee chairman turned to Jaspers to help resolve matters. After all, any decision concerning Heidegger's case would potentially have international repercussions. Jaspers rose to the occasion, interjecting a welcome Solomonic tone into the thorny deliberations:

> It is absolutely necessary that those who helped place National Socialism in the saddle be called to account. Heidegger is among the few professors to have done that.... In our situation [that is, after the war] the education of youth must be handled with the greatest responsibility.... Heidegger's manner of thinking, which to me seems in its essence *unfree, dictatorial*, and *incapable of communication*, would today be disastrous in its pedagogical effects .... His manner of speaking and his actions have a certain affinity with National Socialist characteristics, which makes his error comprehensible.[17]

The commission decided to accept Jaspers's recommendations verbatim. In the interests of political and moral reconstruction, Heidegger's *venia legenda*, or right to teach, was revoked for a period of five years. Yet, in view of his stature as an internationally acclaimed philosopher — a fact that Jaspers acknowledged forthrightly — a pension was granted in order that he might thereby continue pondering the condundrums and mysteries of "Being."

It is also instructive to contrast their respective responses to the cataclysms of world war. True to form, Heidegger deflected questions of German responsibility through recourse to a series of specious, metapolitical rationalizations. No individual or nation could be blamed for the European catastrophe since it was a product of the unfathomable "destiny of Being" (*Seinsgeschick*). In his eyes, there were no "essential" differences between Nazism, communism, and democracy. Since all three political formations were governed by the same soulless, technological frenzy — the logic of mindless, industrial "Gigantism" — they were merely birds of a feather.

In the aftermath of Germany's liberation by Allied forces, Jaspers, conversely, seized the occasion to call his countrymen to account. In 1946 he published *The Question of German Guilt*, a clarion call for German contrition that today remains something of a landmark in the political history of the Federal Republic. Jaspers posited four levels of guilt: criminal, political, moral, and metaphysical. He urged his fellow Germans to plumb the depths of their consciences. Relying on a thinly veiled Protestant idiom, Jaspers argued that heartfelt repentance, guided by an unflinching acknowledgement of Germany's egregious political and military misdeeds, represented an indispensable precondition for national renewal.[18]

Predictably, the public dialogue Jaspers hoped to provoke failed to materialize. Everyday Germans were still too busy licking their wounds, preoccupied with the onerous burdens of reconstruction, to commence the requisite labor of moral reckoning. Moreover, they preferred to think of themselves — delusively, albeit — as *victims*: of power-crazed Nazi cadres as well as Allied military excesses. Jaspers's efforts had backfired, and he soon became a target of widespread resentment. Ultimately, life in Germany became unlivable. In 1948, disgusted by his countrymen's self-centered moral numbness, he fled Germany for the relative tranquility of Basel, Switzerland.

Still, despite its admirable forthrightness, Jaspers treatise was far from unflawed. By employing the lexicon of Lutheran-Romantic spirituality, Jaspers once again sought refuge in the domain of German "inwardness" — as though atonement pertained solely to questions of conscience. As such, *The Question of German Guilt*'s major failing was that it both avoided and precluded all attempts to understand the Nazi dictatorship in concrete historical or political terms: for example, as one of the legacies of authoritarian patterns of socialization bequeathed by the Second Empire (1871–1918). As one contemporary observer — Hannah Arendt's husband, Heinrich Blücher — commented appropriately:

> Jaspers's guilt-monograph, despite all its beauty and noble-mindedness, is an anathematized and Hegelianized, Christian/pietistic/hypocritical nationalizing piece of twaddle ... Jaspers's whole ethical purification-babble leads him to solidarity with the German National Community ... instead of solidarity with those who have been degraded ... Wearing the thick spectacles of the Romantic *Volk*-concept, he seeks the nature of the true German ... In order to find this phantom, he accepts a truly Lutheran servitude in a Hegelian way ... Germany finally has the opportunity to make clear the fronts of the real civil war of our times: Republicans against Cossacks, in other words the battle of the *Citoyen* against the Barbarian ... Instead, Jaspers is calling for loving understanding and discussion, in order to establish the essence of the *real* German.[19]

V

Posterity has not treated Jaspers especially well. His philosophy, when it is discussed at all, is treated as either a historical curiosity or period piece. In philosophy seminars, it is taught sparingly, if at all. During the late 1920s, his approach to *Existenzphilosophie* was left in the dust by Heidegger's, and Jaspers never seems to have caught up. A North American Karl Jaspers Society exists. But its members could be safely crammed into the back of a Volkswagen. To be sure, following the precedent of *The Question of German Guilt*, Jaspers made a commendable name for himself as a public intellectual, writing thought-provoking books on the atom bomb, the failings of German political culture, and world politics. Yet, his brand of conservative liberalism, which relied on the authority of "notables" or "great men" to keep the degenerate risks of mass society at bay, remained at odds with the virtues of active citizenship. As a political thinker, Jaspers, despite all his insight, never successfully made the transition to becoming a "convinced democrat." Consequently, his doctrines were justly associated with the political and psychic immobilism of the Adenauer era (1949–62), whose discouraging watchword had been "No Experiments!"

During the1960s, as the allure of neo-Marxism gripped the European political imaginary, Jaspers's approach to philosophy and politics fell increasingly out of favor. In *The Destruction of Reason*, Georg Lukács, who in 1956 risked life and limb in his capacity as Minister of Culture with Imre Nagy's breakaway Hungarian Soviet Republic, condemned Jaspers as someone whose ideas were suffused with a "deadly hatred of the masses" and a "fear of democracy and socialism."[20] Despite its harshness (not to mention the fact that the text in question often reads like an intellectual "enemies list"), Lukács' verdict contains an important kernel of truth. In the *Jargon of Authenticity* (1964) Theodor Adorno's estimation of Jaspers proved hardly more favorable. The Frankfurt School philosopher alleged that Jaspers's mandarinic partiality to the values of "inwardness" translated into a studied neglect of the material basis of society and thereby encouraged political passivity.

In light of Jaspers's willingness during the postwar period to take controversial positions on the major political issues of the day, these criticisms seem distinctly uncharitable. Yet, if one closely examines Jaspers's political attitudes during the years immediately preceding the Nazi seizure of power, the portrait that emerges is indeed a disturbing one. It demonstrates the ease with which the ethos of "antipolitical" mandarinism could slide into an idiom of antirepublican, authoritarian bluster.

Jaspers's main offense — and the point of reference for Lukács's and Adorno's alarm — pertained to a volume he published in 1931 that was translated into English as *Man in the Modern Age*. It was at this point that Jaspers, who two years earlier had published his three-volume chef d'oeuvre, *Philosophy*, condescended to address the Zeitgeist. The results were, by all accounts, deeply troubling.

Man in the Modern Age was an essay at a German specialty: a *Zeitdiagnose*, or diagnosis, of the times. Perhaps the best-known precedent was Spengler's portentous *Decline of the West* (1918). Jaspers's book was written in a distinctly Spenglerian idiom. As such it contained many of the standard German lamentations against the ills of modern society: a loss of authority, the decline of ultimate values, a rising tide of conformity cum mediocrity, and so forth. Given the precedents that had been set by Nietzsche, Thomas Mann, Spengler, and Arthur Moeller van den Bruck, this oxymoronic, "conservative revolutionary" discourse had become a political lingua franca among educated German elites.

What was disturbing, however, was not just that the previously apolitical Jaspers adopted this paradigm, but that he openly embraced its most problematic and compromising features — at the very moment the National Socialists were in the process of toppling Germany's fledgling experiment in democratic government. For a long time scholarship on the Third Reich adhered to a comforting separation between "national conservatives," like Jaspers and Hans-Georg Gadamer, and "radical Nazis" such as Heidegger. Today, however, this dichotomy no longer seems tenable. Instead, we have become acutely aware of the malevolent role that so-called spiritual reactionaries played in undermining the Weimar Republic's tenuous legitimacy. For once Germany's educated elites rejected Weimar en masse, the fledgling republic's days were numbered.

Moreover, we now know that it was not only convinced Nazis who provided the regime with invaluable ideological cover. During the early 1930s a political alliance of traditional conservatives, German nationalists, and protofascists coalesced to significantly bolster the Third Reich's credibility and prestige during its precarious initial months. The national conservative Edgar Jung got to the heart of the matter when he observed that *the preconditions for National Socialism's triumph were created outside of National Socialism.*[21] Members of the nationalist alliance were united in the belief that, however uncouth Hitler and his minions might be, under their leadership the traditional aims of German nationalism would be well served.

In *Man in the Modern Age* Jaspers consistently belittled "society" as a mere *Daseinordung* — a sphere of individual self-preservation, inimical to all higher concerns ("The masses do not know what they really want. Masses relate to average-matters, capable of being expressed in the crudest terms.")[22] Aping Spengler, he openly defended the values of political authoritarianism as an acceptable bulwark against the risks and confusions of parliamentary democracy ("The State, in itself neither legitimate nor illegitimate, is not deducible from anything else, but is the self-establishing life of the will to which power has been allotted and which has assumed power for itself.")[23] In a spirit of militaristic bluster — somewhat laughable in Jaspers case, owing to his frail constitution — he celebrated the virtues of "war" and "manliness" as the best way to shake a nation out of the torpor of political normalcy and spur it to higher pursuits. As one insightful commentator has cautioned: "Jaspers's endorsement of war as a transcendent fate and end-in-itself … invites its own misuse … War and struggle become ends-in-themselves, vehicles for authentic Selfhood."[24]

Additionally troubling were the circumstantial aspects surrounding the publication of *Man in the Modern Age,* which was featured as the one thousandth volume of the prestigious Goschen publishing series. Jaspers had indeed put his finger directly on the Zeitgeist: the book proved so popular that, within its first year, it went through five extensive printings.

Had the publication of a politically compromising diatribe constituted Jaspers's worst offense, one could confidently move on to the next chapter of his storied legacy. However, we now know that, when the Nazis acceded to power in 1933, Jaspers made a determined effort to collaborate in the realm of National Socialist educational policy.

In July 1933, Jaspers drafted a detailed document delineating his ideas for university reform, a topic he had also addressed ten years earlier in *The Idea of the University*.[25] In part, Jaspers's motivations derived from the "anxiety of influence." His perennial rival and doppelgänger, Heidegger, had already jumped aboard the Nazi bandwagon. Belying its title, Heidegger's May 1933 Rectoral Address, "The Self-Assertion of the German University," focused extensively on the question of how German universities might be integrated with the Nazis' Brown Revolution. At the time, Jaspers showered fulsome praise upon Heidegger's speech, referring to it as "the only lasting document of today's academic will."[26] Not to be outdone, in "How Can the Universities Be Rejuvenated? Some Theses (1933)," Jaspers proceeded to develop his own ideas on the subject.

Jaspers's text is littered with the standard denunciations of the inadequacies and failings of the university system under Weimar, where "science degenerated into busy work" and "substantive and lively speech became information and cant."[27] He wears his elitism on his sleeve. It is the "aristocracy," rather than average men and women, that produces timeless "standards." In order to prevent further deterioration, he claims that the university needs to recapture a "reverential attitude" toward the "Great Man."

Although Jaspers seems to argue for a measure of university autonomy under Nazism, his convictions are expressed so evasively as to be virtually indiscernible. By the same token, his language and phraseology unabashedly bask in a narrow-minded Germanocentrism that, at times, remains only a hair's breadth removed from the official Nazi version. Jaspers's text is replete with references to the virtues of "German science," the "German desire to know," and superiority of the "Northern Mind."[28] He repeatedly avows that "knowledge is conditioned by Volk and State." The university, claims Jaspers, "grows out of the same root as the State" and "out of the roots of Peoplehood" (*Volkstum*).[29]

Let there be no mistake: to write in this idiom in 1933 is to acquiesce in the face of the Nazi revolution, including its predatory delusions of racial grandeur.

Was Jaspers myopic enough to think he could find a niche in a regime that was anti-Semitic through and through, and that never attempted for a moment to disguise this fact; a regime that, two months into office, initiated a nationwide anti-Jewish economic boycott and summarily banned Jews from civil service professions — university teaching included?

It seems that, given his disdain for parliamentary democracy, Jaspers shed few tears over the Weimar Republic's passing. Like many national conservatives, he readily welcomed Weimar's demise. He seems to have objected more to Hitler's plebeian background and orientation than to his authoritarian political practices.

As part of the *Gleichschaltung* process (the National Socialist euphemism for the elimination of political opposition), one of the Nazis' most heinous educational reforms was to eliminate long-standing traditions of university self-governance in favor of an authoritarian regimen overseen by party loyalists. As one scholar has observed: "Self-government … was not only a fundamental part of the specifically 'German' university tradition that predated the liberal era but also one that had roots in ancient Germanic tribal voting practices."[30] Such traditions, one might note, were especially revered in the relatively liberal milieu of Heidelberg. Incredibly, in "Theses on University Reform," Jaspers voluntarily signed off on many of these repugnant measures, declaring that, "Instead of majority decision there should develop a tradition … of an administration by chancellor and deans."[31] At the time, it was common knowledge that, in keeping with the *Führerprinzip*, or "leadership principle," the university chancellor was directly appointed by Nazi party officials.

Another distasteful Nazi measure used to undermine academic freedom was to mandate student participation in unremunerated "labor service" as well as "military sports." Both programs expressed the Nazis' contempt for the autonomous "life of the mind." Since these programs were administered by trusted party members, they also served as important vehicles of National Socialist ideological indoctrination. Although Jaspers gave voice to one or two minor reservations about these measures, on the whole, he wholeheartedly endorsed them. As he writes at the time: "Labor service and military sport serve as connection to actuality. Through them the student is in touch with *the ground of existence and the entire Volk.*"[32] One can only imagine how Gertrud Jaspers would have reacted to this document, had it ever been shown to her.

As it turns out, Jaspers's text never saw the light of print. Nevertheless, the reasons behind this failure are worth recounting. Because he had married a Jewish woman, for his ideas to be considered by the Nazis, Jaspers needed the backing of a party sponsor. As he rues at the time: "I cannot do anything unless I am asked, since I am told that, as I do not belong to the Party and am married to a Jewish woman, I am merely tolerated and cannot be trusted."[33] To whom, then, did he turn for political assistance? To none other than Heidegger — although, as it turned out, Jaspers's appeal for support fell on deaf ears. At the time, Heidegger was engaged in an attempt to lead the Nazi charge at German universities and wanted no additional competition. Moreover, from his correspondence at the time, we know that he held Jaspers's political judgments in particularly low esteem. As he observes derisively in

March 1933, describing his impressions of a recent stay with Jaspers: "I saw that one can write about 'the spiritual situation of the age' without being touched by actual events — or even knowing about them."[34]

Thinking politically in a narrowly mandarin-aristocratic mode, Jaspers conceptualized European decline in terms of the disappearance of "eminent personalities." But, thereby, he merely reiterated the ideological delusions of German genius: the one who, because of his superior character and insight, is licensed to break the law — which, in any event, was only promulgated to keep inferior natures in line. So beholden was Jaspers to the elitist prejudices of his milieu that he never stopped to consider that an egalitarian society, governed by the idea of "careers open to talent," might well provide the optimal terrain for human excellence to flourish. Moreover, when the hour of decision struck in 1933, most of Germany's "eminent personalities," in whom Jaspers placed his trust (Heidegger's case is merely the tip of the iceberg), gave themselves over freely to Nazism's visions of racial predominance. After all, Hitler, too, was a German genius of sorts.

Part II
Exiting Revolution

8

What We Can Learn from the Revolutions of 1989

I

Amid the annals of modern European history there are telltale dates, whose very mention evokes major turning points — 1789, 1848, 1914, and 1945. All of these years represent either years of revolutionary upheaval or the commencement or conclusion of major European conflicts.

I'd like to suggest an analogous status for the year 1989 — the year of the revolutions of Eastern Europe as well as the bicentennial of the French Revolution. Indeed, certain analogies with 1789 are far from inappropriate. Both revolutions came seemingly out of nowhere; their unprecedented nature left virtually all major commentators temporarily at a loss for words. Both events sounded the death knell for ancien régimes that had pointedly failed to alter their forms of political rule in keeping with portentous economic and technological transformations. In the case of both regimes, it soon became clear that it was no longer a question of instituting this or that reform from above; instead, the entire autocratic structure of political domination needed to be swept away. Thus, both Louis XVI and Mikhail Gorbachev regarded themselves as "progressives," as enlightened autocrats. In both cases, however, the process of reform, once unleashed, rapidly began to take on a life of its own, outstripping the capacity of the officials in charge to determine the pace of social change. The results soon catapulted the major actors onto uncharted historical terrain where all precedents and analogies ceased to hold. Instead, the historical stage became a great improvisational laboratory: invention and experimentation became the order of the day; the exceptional had become the norm and the norm the exception.

There exists, nevertheless, a fundamental difference between the revolutions of 1789 and 1989, one whose importance must not be lost sight of. The revolutionaries of 1789 soon became intoxicated with the very idea of revolution. In the years 1793–94, this spirit of revolutionary intoxication became synonymous with political extremism: a lust for revolutionary government, a hatred of everything moderate or temperate, and an infatuation with the purgative attributes of revolutionary terror. The ideology of Jacobin radicalism was aptly embodied in Robespierre's celebrated equation of "virtue" with "terror." Or, as his faithful ally Saint-Just once remarked: "Great revolutions demand great crimes." In a way that would in many respects foreshadow the ideology of Bolshevism as codified by Lenin, the French revolutionaries scorned mechanisms of formal justice and due process, which were too measured and timorous when set against the dramatic unfolding of the glorious revolutionary tableau. Instead, they displayed a distinct preference for the "great crimes" advocated by Saint-Just. Allow me to add that, as a child of the 1960s, not a few members of my generation succumbed to a similar sort of ideological fascination (to wit: the obligatory posters of Che Guevera that adorned the dormitory walls of middle-class students circa 1970).

In stark contrast, the historical actors of 1989 viewed themselves as *victims* of the revolutionary ideology of 1789, as updated and revised by Lenin in 1917.[1] Having experienced the historical and political effects of this ideology firsthand, they self-consciously sought to initiate a revolution of a novel type: a regime change that would at long last bring to a definitive end to revolutions of the Jacobin-Bolshevik variety, whereby, under the cover of human emancipation, a historically unique species of despotism was spawned. Their aversion to the concept of total revolution can be sensed from the adjectives used to describe their aims: the *velvet* revolution in Czechoslovakia, the *self-limiting* revolution in Poland. Thus, in a felicitous turn of phrase, Andrew Arato has spoken of "the historical novelty of revolutions that reject the idea of modern revolutions."[2] At the same time, the unprecedented nature of these revolutions lies not merely in their choice of nonviolent means. Instead, their success is attributable to the fact that they were able to invent *a new conception of politics* — an "antipolitical politics" as it has sometimes been dubbed — which succeeded in reconceptualizing the relationship between the state, civil society, and the political sphere. In sum, the Robespierres and Lenins of yesteryear have been supplanted by the Adam Michniks and Vaclav Havels of the 1970s and 1980s. They have bequeathed to us a "new political science" (Tocqueville): a conception of politics sensitive to the existential requirements of humanity in today's hyperindustrialized societies, where the traditional geopolitical differences between North and South, East and West, have begun to pale in the face of a logics of technological globalism that has succeeded in rendering the furthest reaches of our planet increasingly homogeneous. More and more we are confronted with the hyperrealities of a postindustrial global consumer society, in which the nearest McDonald's is but a block away and CNN accessible to anyone with cable TV or a satellite dish.[3]

Of course, such innovations are far from an unmitigated advantage. Instead, they dramatically alter traditional modes of human perception and interaction. At a fundamental level, they threaten to negate the engaged, participatory bases of modern republican government, thereby transforming the idea of active citizenship — the crux of any functional democratic society — into merely another passive, spectator sport. In all of the foregoing respects, citizens of the West have yet to take to heart the important political lessons 1989.

II

To begin with I would like to turn to the way in which the revolutions of 1989 have been systematically misread by commentators in the West. Such misreadings, one might say, are the result of one part misapprehension, one part condescension. Fundamentally, it has been difficult for most Western observers to acknowledge the fact that there could be lessons concerning modern political life that one might be able to draw from the comparatively "backward "societies" of Eastern Europe. Thus, one of the fascinating aspects of the reception of 1989 under Western eyes has been the relative unanimity of the verdict. No matter what side of the political spectrum one turns to — be it neoconservative, liberal, or leftist — the received wisdom concerning these tumultuous events and their implications has been remarkably uniform. In the phrase of the German left-wing political philosopher Jürgen Habermas, the revolutions of 1989 represent little more than "catch-up revolutions" (*nachholende Revolutionen*). As Habermas explains, "The revolutionary collapse of bureaucratic socialism seems ... to indicate that modernity is extending its borders — the spirit of the West is *catching up* with the East not simply as a technological civilization, but also as a democratic tradition."[4] Of course, if the revolutionary overthrow of communism

amounted to little more than a belated arrival at Western democratic
and economic standards, we in the West would stand to learn little
indeed from them. It is on this basis that Habermas has claimed —
wrongly in my estimation — that in 1989 one detects a "total lack of
ideas that are either innovative or oriented toward the future."[5]

If one turns to one of the standard liberal accounts of 1989, that of
the German Anglophile Ralf Dahrendorf, one finds a remarkably
similar conclusion. For Dahrendorf the revolutions of 1989 represent an
important affirmation of what he calls (with reference to Karl Popper)
the values of the "open society." Like Habermas's, Dahrendorf's
account is relatively enlightened, insofar as he refuses to limit the significance of this momentous transformation to its crude economic repercussions: the belated arrival of the free market system. Thus, for
Dahrendorf, the meaning of 1989 cannot be captured solely through the
transition from a planned economy to one that is market-based and
laissez-faire. The triumph was not simply one for the "supply-side"
economic doctrines of Ronald Reagan and Margaret Thatcher. In truth,
many of the leading dissidents and political theorists of the revolutionary movements remained volubly wary concerning the prospect of
turning their societies into mirror images of the consumption-oriented,
spiritually impoverished West a (point which is confirmed by the recent
electoral successes of the former communist parties in Hungary, Poland,
eastern Germany, and, more recently, the former Soviet Union).[6] They
had little interest in exchanging the political chains of bureaucratic
socialism for the existential uncertainties of Western-style, market-
driven capitalism (even if they harbored few illusions as to which form
of domination was more bearable). Instead, as Dahrendorf observes, the
revolutions of 1989 were in the first instance *political* revolutions. They
aimed at preserving the inviolability of the private sphere vis-à-vis arbitrary and unwarranted state encroachments. Here, too, parallels with
the French Revolution — at least in its initial antiabsolutist, liberal-
constitutionalist phase — are entirely apt. Nevertheless, Dahrendorf
continues, such fundamental political lessons had been set forth and
internalized by Western nations as far back as 1688 with England's
Glorious Revolution.

Thus, in Dahrendorf's view, if there are any lessons to be gleaned
from the revolutionary upheavals of six years ago, they are ones with
which jaded Western political analysts have been long familiar. To be
sure, the category of civil society — so crucial for the antitotalitarian
strategy of the Eastern European revolutionaries — plays a role in his
analysis, but it is largely a negative one. It has very little to do with the
values of political reconstruction or active citizenship. Instead, it merely
connotes a sphere of private autonomy cum pluralism that is separable
from the realm of the state. Yet as Arato has remarked in his important

review essay, "Interpreting the Revolutions of 1989," Dahrendorf's proliberal account suffers from a "democracy deficit": he "does not tell us nor does he attempt to justify why the ground rules of democracy are any less important from a normative point of view than those of liberalism."[7] Dahrendorf appropriately cites the definition of pluralism provided by James Madison: "Whilst all authority will be derived from and dependent on the society, the society itself will be broken into so many parts, interests and classes of citizens, that the rights of individuals or of the minority, will be in little danger from the interested combinations of the majority." According to this definition, civil society possesses an essentially negative role: it guards against tyrannical trespasses both from below — the tyranny of the majority — as well as from above — on the part of the state. As Dahrendorf himself glosses Madison's remarks: "In other words, a multiplicity of groups and organizations and associations provides sufficient checks and balances against any usurpation of power."[8] Thus, the indispensable positive role played by the *democratic reconstruction of society from below* — in lieu of which the epochal efforts at constitution-making lauded by Dahrendorf would likely never have come to pass — fall wholly out of account in his interpretation.

If we now veer toward the right side of the political spectrum, we find a range of opinion that possesses few significant differences from the representative social democratic (Habermas) or liberal (Dahrendorf) positions previously discussed.

Here, of course, the locus classicus is Francis Fukuyama's *The End of History and the Last Man.* As is by now well known, the author concludes that, with the collapse of communism, liberalism has for the first time been left without a major ideological competitor. To be sure, on the margins of Europe a certain ethnopolitical, fratricidal tribalism has acquired a new life. And from the steppes of the former Soviet Union to the shores of the Maghreb, an assertive Islamic fundamentalism has been reborn. In seeking to challenge the infringements of the modern West, it has raised the specter of a new confrontation between civilizations; a confrontation to which, in the eyes of some, the Bosnian civil war represents a prelude. Nevertheless, in Fukuyama's view, none of these developments constitutes a threat to his thesis concerning the ultimate demise of any substantive challenges to the spirit of Western liberalism. Hence, his much-maligned conclusion that history, in the neo-Hegelian sense he has elected to define it (that is, a conflict among competing ideological *Weltanschauungen* or worldviews), has essentially come to an end.[9]

Unfortunately, few commentators have paid much attention to the more provocative and less uplifting side of Fukuyama's thesis, which he took pains to incorporate into the book version of his argument: his claim that now that history is at an end, our current struggles and commitments are destined to become pedestrian and unexalted. In this regard, we are doomed to dwell in a civilization inhabited by Nietzsche's proverbial, unheroic "last men": men who, in their self-satisfied mediocrity, represent the antithesis of the Nietzschean superman:

"We have invented happiness," say the last men, and they blink. They have left the regions where it was hard to live, for one needs warmth. One still loves one's neighbor and rubs against him, for one needs warmth....

One still works, for work is a form of entertainment. But one is careful lest the entertainment be too harrowing. One no longer becomes poor or rich: both require too much exertion.

Alas, the time of the most despicable man is coming, he that is no longer able to despise himself. Behold, I show you the *last man*. "What is love? What is creation? What is longing? What is a star?" thus asks the last man, and he blinks ....

No shepherd and one herd! Everybody wants the same, everybody is the same: whoever feels different goes voluntarily into a madhouse.[10]

There is one final interpretation of the revolutions of 1989 that merits scrutiny: constitutional theorist Bruce Ackerman's *The Future of Liberal Revolution*. In a slender, yet perspicacious study, Ackerman, unlike the other critics treated thus far, recognizes that the political significance of 1989 cannot be reduced to a type of skeletal liberalism — that is, to the values of the "open society" or a certification of "negative freedom." To be sure, Ackerman does not belittle such achievements, which, taken by themselves, are monumental. Rather, he is interested in showing that upon closer examination the political stakes involved in this regime change were even more profound. In his view, at issue was a type of "constitutional politics" that aimed at reestablishing the very terms of political sovereignty. The events of 1989 were revolutionary not by virtue of their results — the elimination of the old regime and the establishment of a new social contract. The means, too, were revolutionary in the best sense of the word: a series of peaceful popular uprisings succeeded not only in disrupting the fragile political legitimacy of the old regime; they also represented an instance of "constitutional" or "higher lawmaking" which provided a radical new basis for political society. Ackerman presents his doctrine of "revolutionary liberalism" in the following terms:

> The higher [or constitutional] lawmaking track ... is designed with would-be revolutionaries in mind. It employs special procedures for determining whether a mobilized majority of the citizenry give their considered support to the principles of one or another revolutionary movement that would pronounce in the people's name. Although many small movements feel called to the tasks of revolutionary renewal, dualists emphasize that few are chosen by a mobilized majority of a nation's citizens. Hence, the higher lawmaking system imposes a rigorous set of institutional tests before allowing a revolutionary movement to transform fundamental political principles .... Before a revolutionary change is adopted, it should have the sustained support of a substantial majority, not just support at a single moment.[11]

In the American context, Ackerman cites three such instances of "higher lawmaking," all of which resulted in significant constitutional renewal: (1) the social consensus against slavery, culminating in the Civil War and the Fourteenth Amendment; (2) the restructuring of the relationship between private and public sectors in the aftermath of the Great Depression, resulting in legislation attendant to the New Deal; and (3) the civil rights movement of the 1950s and 1960s, spurred by the landmark Supreme Court ruling in *Brown v. Board of Education of Topeka*, which culminated in the Civil Rights Act of 1964.

Ackerman identifies all three cases as examples of the way in which the democratic essence of modern liberal society must be periodically revitalized from below. In his view, each represents an instance of revolutionary renewal that in its own way is no less radical than the original act of political foundation as embodied in the Constitution. The European revolutions of 1989 also constitute an act of political foundation in the spirit of the radical democratic tradition Ackerman reveres. At the same time, their vigor and vitality present a cautionary tale for Western democracies which, having become conservative and self-complacent, run the risk of betraying their revolutionary heritage.

In his emphasis on the crucial interrelationship between popular pressure and "higher-lawmaking," Ackerman goes far toward capturing the political singularity of the revolutions of 1989. Yet, strangely, the concept of civil society remains virtually absent in his account. However, it is this concept alone which is able to highlight the real uniqueness of the momentous political transformations at issue. For only the concept of civil society is able to account for the astounding proliferation of mediating agencies and institutions — trade unions, political clubs, discussion groups, flying universities, citizen initiatives, human rights groups, and so forth — which make the extraordinary success of the movements in question comprehensible.

III

I would now like to turn to the "reinvention of politics" in Eastern Europe as it transpired over the course of the 1970s and 1980s.[12] For one can safely say that with the advent of totalitarian rule, "politics" in any meaningful sense of the word was pushed to the margins of these societies. Hannah Arendt once described the essence of politics as the creation of a public space in which men and women have the capacity to unveil and display their authentically political natures — that is their natures as a *zoon politikon* or political animal. It is a space, she adds, in which the virtues of human plurality are permitted to flourish.[13] The despotic communist regimes succeeded in closing off this space. The acute sense of existential claustrophobia that resulted has been brilliantly portrayed in the literature of the period — an unprecedented efflorescence of the novel form under oppressive conditions — in the works of Milan Kundera, Ivan Klima, George Konrad, and others.

The 1970s represented the wilderness years for reform-oriented members of Eastern European society. In the 1960s, the watchword among reformers had been "socialism with a human face." They adhered to the conviction that communist regimes could be reformed from within. In 1956 the temporary thaw produced by Khrushchev's speech at the Twentieth Party Congress denouncing the "crimes of the Stalin era" had spurred the Hungarian uprising, soon to be crushed by Soviet military power. Revolution from below, reasoned the 1960s reformers, risked too many instabilities and the threat of Soviet intervention. Thus, extremely high hopes were placed on the alternative strategy embodied by the Dubĉek government: the attempt to transform the regime by means of enlightened, incremental improvement from above. Yet, as we know, the hopes of the 1968 Prague Spring were also brutally quashed under the weight of Soviet tanks. That same year a wave of anti-Semitic purges swept Poland. Two years later, a protest movement in Poland's Gdansk shipyards — the home of the future Solidarity movement — was met with gunfire that left seventy workers dead.

Where were reform-minded Eastern Europeans to turn now? Had all conceivable strategies been exhausted? Had the Western powers abandoned them to the clutches of Soviet oppression with the 1945 Yalta agreement? Time, it seemed, was running short. Vital ties to precommunist cultural and democratic traditions were becoming irrevocably severed. The nations of Eastern Europe were in danger of becoming lands without history and without memory. Orwell's dystopian vision had been realized, it seemed, some fifteen years in advance.

Nevertheless, amid the despondency that seized the Eastern European intelligentsia following the suppression of the Prague Spring, a new approach emerged. Since both revolution from below as well as enlightened reform from above had been stifled by Soviet intervention, a different strategy was mandated. Dissidents in several Eastern European countries spontaneously began to fashion an inventive course of action. To all intents and purposes, they would respect the existing regime's de facto monopoly of political power. Nominally, their new social movements would seek to establish a modus vivendi with the political status quo. On a subpolitical level, however — that is, at the all-important level of civil society — they had a very different agenda in mind. Their avowed goal was to carve out as many regions of autonomous social action as possible in the spheres of culture, the economy, religion, and so forth. In this way, despite the self-proclaimed monopoly of political power enjoyed by the various communist parties, the dissidents sought to reconquer their own societies bit by bit — ultimately reaching a point where all that remained of communist rule was a brittle husk that could be cast off with the first loud sneeze.

In their wildest dreams the Eastern European reformers could not have realized how successful their new strategy for democratization would ultimately prove. In their refusal to challenge the constitutionally enshrined "leading role of the communist party," the dissidents technically agreed to play by the established rules of the game. They refrained from constituting themselves as an explicitly political grouping. Therein precisely lay the ingenious nature of their approach. For in a society in which one entity claims a monopoly of power, any competing claims to authority — even be they, strictly speaking, social rather than political claims — by definition serve to erode the monopolist's power base. The concept of "power-sharing" was not part of the lexicon of Communist Party politics. As one dissident observed: "In Soviet semantics the word *socialism* means the total domination of the Communist Party, whereas the word counterrevolution denotes all actions that subvert the totality of this domination."[14] The reformist strategy of reinventing civil society was thus predicated on an immense sleight-of-hand: under the guise of promoting a series of apolitical *social* reforms, the dissidents ultimately succeeded in effecting a wholesale political transformation of Soviet-type societies. A closer examination of the program pursued by the various Eastern European reformers will underline the novelty and inventiveness of their approach.

In 1976 KOR (Workers' Defense Committee) founder and dissident Adam Michnik penned an essay entitled "A New Evolutionism," in which he outlined what would become in retrospect a landmark strategy for Eastern European social renewal. With the 1960s strategy of political reform from above — an experiment in "enlightened socialist despotism" in the words of one observer — seemingly at a dead end, a new approach was called for. For the events of 1968 in both Poland and Czechoslovakia had put to rest the illusion that there might exist a democratic wing within the Communist Party that would have the courage to institute the necessary reforms. In the words of Michnik it was at this point that the myth of the need for a "Polish Dubĉek" came to naught. Instead, those who were interested in constructive social change began to put their hope and trust in social groups that were outside of and opposed to the traditional party hierarchy: students, workers, and oppositional cultural organizations. As Michnik explained in 1976:

> consistent revisionism as well as consistent neopositivism both inevitably lead to unity with the powers-that-be and the assumption of their point of view. To offer solidarity with striking workers, with students holding a mass meeting, or with protesting intellectuals is to challenge the intraparty strategy of the revisionist and neopositivist policies of compromise. Social solidarity undermines the fundamental component of both strategies: acceptance of the government as the basic point of reference.

> In my opinion, an unceasing struggle for reform and evolution that seeks an expansion of civil liberties and human rights is the only course East European dissidents can take.... To draw a parallel with events at the other end of our continent, one could say that the ideas of the Polish democratic opposition resemble the Spanish ... model. This is based on gradual and piecemeal change, not violent upheaval and forceful destruction of the existing system.[15]

This was the essence of Michnik's and KOR's theory of "the new evolutionism." It was a strategy that consciously renounced the ideology of "revolution" — indeed, these were societies that had had a surfeit of negative experiences with the European revolutionary tradition. Instead their approach concentrated on establishing a network of alternative public spheres, a type of grassroots associative democracy. In Michnik's words: "the democratic opposition must be constantly and incessantly visible in public life, must create political facts by organizing mass actions, must formulate alternative programs .... The intelligentsia's duty is to formulate alterative programs and defend the basic principles [of civil liberty]."[16]

The precepts of a new gradualist approach to evolutionary social change were thus formulated at the height of the dogmatism and inflexibility of the Brezhnev era. One can only admire the tenacity of the democratic opposition in its belief that, even at this bleak historical hour, inventive new avenues might be found for loosening the party apparatus's totalitarian hold on society. The results of this strategy are, at least in part, a matter of historical record. Out of the efforts of KOR, Solidarity was born, resulting in the historic Gdansk accords of August 1980. Solidarity's extraordinary success in constituting itself as an independent trade union with which the communist authorities were now forced to bargain represented a watershed in the history of Soviet-style societies. It stood as a model to be emulated for dissidents and critics in all of the Eastern European lands. As one critic has pointed out: "Solidarity opened a new chapter in the history of Eastern Europe by showing that possibilities existed for waking the long-dormant social trends and that the cracks in the apparently monolithic totalitarian edifice could be exploited in an imaginative way to restore civil society."[17]

While Michnik and KOR were formulating their scheme for social reform in Warsaw, parallel developments were taking place among leading members of the Prague-based Czech democratic opposition. A breakthrough of sorts came with the publication of Charter 77 in 1977. The occasion for the drafting of this historic document — a sort of dissident Declaration of Independence — was the fate of a popular rock group, the Plastic People of the Universe. Their arbitrary arrest early that year sent shock waves of uncertainty throughout the Czech society. Previously, it was believed that the ground rules for peaceful coexistence with the Soviet-backed Husak regime were relatively straightforward. A certain measure of freedom of expression would be tolerated as long as the regime's monopoly of political power remained unchallenged. The sudden arrest of the Plastic People demonstrated precisely how fragile was this unwritten agreement between the party and Czech society. The rock group had hardly posed a threat to Czech internal security. The arbitrariness of their incarceration merely illustrated the utter untrustworthiness and capriciousness of the regime. It drove home the point that, under current political conditions, no one was safe.[18]

The strategy of the Charter bore profound resemblances to that of Solidarity and KOR. Its signatories gainsaid all political aspirations and aims. Instead, they justified their efforts by appealing to the 1975 Helsinki accords on human rights, which had been signed by all the Warsaw Pact states. In the end, this narrowly legalistic approach proved to be astonishingly effective. For it allowed the Chartists to claim time and again that they were in no way seeking to challenge the political legitimacy of the Husak government. Instead, they were merely trying to compel it to live up to precepts and principles that the regime itself had already publicly avowed in a respected international forum. Of course, such pointed proclamations of apoliticism entailed a profound, hidden agenda. For the very act of compelling a totalitarian regime to recognize basic civil libertarian norms — fundamental rights to freedom of assembly, freedom of speech, due process, and so forth — would mean that their claims to political omnipotence had endured a devastating, insuperable blow. Thus, as the Chartists themselves proclaimed:

> Charter 77 is a loose, informal and open association of people of various shades of opinion, faiths, and professions united by the will to strive individually and collectively for the respecting of civil and human rights in our own country and throughout the world — rights accorded to all people by the ... Final Act of the Helsinki conference ... and which are laid down in the United Nations Universal Declaration of Human Rights.... Charter 77 is not an organization; it has no rules, permanent bodies or formal membership. It embraces everyone who agrees with its ideas and participates in its work. It does not form the basis for any oppositional political activity. Like many similar citizen initiatives in various countries, West and East, it seeks to promote the general public interest.[19]

The Charter's signatories were subject to persistent harassment and imprisonment. Havel's philosophical mentor, Jan Patocka, died during the course of a police interrogation. In 1979 Vaclav Havel himself was sentenced to prison for four and one-half years. Nevertheless, despite a number of short-term setbacks, Charter 77 became an indispensable rallying point both for other Eastern European dissidents and for world opinion in general. In many ways, the civil libertarian principles it advocated represented a time bomb for the nomenklatura of the various communist regimes. For a state cannot be both "pluralist" and "totalitarian" at the same time. From this point hence, party officials went to bed at night with many fewer certainties and assurances than before. Not until 1989 would the bomb explode in spectacular fashion.

Following publication of the Charter its members embarked on a strategy for social renewal that bore marked similarities with that of the democratic opposition in Poland. In the face of the state's monopolization of political power, the Czech dissidents strove to carve out spheres of social autonomy, thereby enlivening the contested median terrain of civil society. It was at this point that the philosopher Vaclav Benda developed his doctrine of the "parallel polis."[20] Since political society was wholly controlled by the party nomenklatura, it fell due to reform-minded activists and intellectuals to create a parallel network of non-party-dominated enclaves and institutions, which, once stabilized, would be relatively immune from the repressive tentacles of the state. In this way, the seeds of a future nonauthoritarian social structure would be permitted to germinate in the womb of the present political system. With the case of the Plastic People of the Universe in mind, Benda's conception of a nonofficial, parallel polis concentrated on the cultural sphere: alternative theaters, educational institutions, publishing houses, information services, and so forth.

It was at approximately the same time that Havel's landmark essay, "The Power of the Powerless" appeared — one of the most important documents in the annals of dissident literature. Havel offered an uncanny description of the everyday, subcutaneous workings of the totalitarian system: a society so thoroughly permeated by the duplicity and corruption of the reigning power structure that its very hypocrisy could no longer be recognized. It was a system in which deception had attained the status of an all-encompassing, metaphysical principle, becoming the alpha and omega of everday life. The genius of Havel's critique lay in his capacity to expose the inner workings of the communist system at its most rudimentary, corpuscular level. In so doing he was able to show that the system itself would not be able to function were it not for the unthinking complicity of millions of Eastern European citizens from all walks of life. To blame society's ills solely on the misdeeds of commissars and apparatchiks would be to take the easy way out. Instead, Havel seems to say: we have met the enemy and his face stares out at us each morning from the bathroom mirror. He is a relative, a friend, a coworker. Or, to take Havel's most celebrated example: he is the greengrocer down the street, who, though he has never been a party member and has long ago shed all illusions about the current regime, nevertheless takes the time and trouble each morning to place a sign in his shop window that reads, "Workers of the World, Unite!" If one multiplies the greengrocer's actions — which are carried out for the most part mechanically and unenthusiastically — by several hundred thousand, one begins to obtain a more precise idea of the implicit support structure that keeps the regime functioning on a day-to-day basis. The psychologically convenient distinction between perpetrators and victims begins to blur; now, everyone seems to be implicated in what Theodor Adorno called the *Verblendungszusammenhang* — the universal network of guilt. In a very different political context (that of postwar Germany) Hannah Arendt once remarked that, where everyone is guilty, no one can be punished.

For the sake of terminological precision, Havel referred to the former regime as a "post-totalitarian system." It was *post*-totalitarian insofar as mechanisms of physiological terror no longer needed to be employed in order to keep citizens in line. Instead, one finds a web of total social complicity. As Havel explains, in a post-totalitarian society,

> the line of complicity runs through each person, for everyone in his or her own way is both a victim and a supporter of the system. What we understand by the system is not, therefore, a social order imposed by one group upon another, but rather something which permeates the entire society and is a fact in shaping it.... The post-totalitarian system touches people at every step .... This is why life in the system is so thoroughly permeated with hypocrisy and lies: government by bureaucracy is called popular government; the working class is enslaved in the name of the working class; the complete degradation of the individual is presented as his or her ultimate liberation.[21]

In the former German Democratic Republic, it was the same all-encompassing system of officially codified discursive cynicism that referred to the Berlin Wall as the *Freiheitschützmauer* — "the wall that protects our freedom."

In Havel's view the entire decrepit system was predicated on a lie or on a series of lies: "a world of appearances, a mere ritual, a formalized language deprived of semantic contact with reality and transformed into a system of ritual signs" — as in the paradigmatic case of the aforementioned greengrocer — "that replace reality with a pseudo-reality."[22]

Havel's antidote to this "system of ritual signs," this "pseudo-reality," is the deceptively simple recommendation "to live within the truth." "To live within the truth" stands as an appeal to counter at every step the artificial tissue of lies that holds the system together, to reacquire the habit of calling things by their proper names, as it were. Thus, if perchance our hypothetical greengrocer would cease one morning to place his proregime sign in his shop window, and if one could then multiply this incipient act of refusal by thousands of other similar acts — then virtually overnight, the system would be deprived of its extremely tenuous social basis, it would be forced to confront the fragility of its own power. "The decision by an individual to break the enchanted circle of complicity with the powers-that-be and to utter his own truth is the premise for civil society to resurrect itself."[23] As Havel observes:

> In the post-totalitarian system, living within the truth has more than a mere existential dimension (returning humanity to its inherent nature), or a Gnostic dimension (revealing reality as it is), or a moral dimension (setting an example for others). It also has an unambiguous *political* dimension. If the main pillar of the system is living a lie, then

it is not surprising that the fundamental threat to it is living the truth. This is why it must be suppressed more severely than anything else.... If the suppression of the aims of life is a complex process, and if it is based on the multifaceted manipulation of all expressions of life then, by the same token, every free expression of life indirectly threatens the post-totalitarian system politically, including forms of expression to which, in other social systems, no one would attribute any political significance, not to mention explosive power.[24]

Havel's essay was written in 1979. Yet, I know of few more prophetic accounts of the situation in which the self-imploding communist regimes would find themselves some ten years later in the momentous, historical year of 1989.

The transitions to democracy in the countries of Eastern European have been fitful. Such adaptations have been most successful in Poland, Hungary, and the Czech Republic — unsurprisingly, nations that possessed the greatest cultural and historical ties to the West. But, in addition, these were the countries in which the democratization of civil society during the 1980s had advanced the farthest. Conversely, in those nations where the revival of civil society remained the least advanced — Rumania, Bulgaria, and Slovakia — the transitions to democratic rule have been fraught with difficulty. Predictably, these nations have inclined toward the nationalist and authoritarian traditions of the precommunist era.

IV

I began this meditation with a critique of interpretations of the revolutions of 1989 that attempted to view their achievements predominantly via the categories of Western liberalism. I have argued instead that there was a good measure of political novelty at stake: in the words of Vladimir Tismaneanu, a "reinvention of politics," from which our complacent Western democracies could stand to learn a good deal. At this point it is worth considering precisely what such a learning process might entail.

Belatedly, historians and political philosophers have rediscovered the "Radicalism of the American Revolution."[25] As it arose in the 1960s, this new understanding of the radical democratic origins of American political culture was intended to supplant the conventional wisdom according to which liberalism, rather than democratic radicalism, was the guiding thread of American political life.[26] Thus, in two key works of the period, J. A. Pocock's *The Machiavellian Moment* and Gordon Wood's *The Creation of the American Republic*, we are offered an inspired portrait of the elementary republics of revolutionary America — a community-based, model instance of grassroots, participatory politics.[27] To be sure, the portrait that emerges is a fairly idealized one, which — slavery and the disenfranchisement of women notwithstanding — tends to gloss over the markedly elitist, anti-democratic inclinations of the Federalists. Nevertheless, as Hannah Arendt observes in her classic study, *On Revolution*:

> the course of the American Revolution tells an unforgettable story and is apt to teach a unique lesson; for this revolution did not break out but was made by men in common deliberation and on the strength of mutual pledges. The principle which came to light during those fateful years when the foundations were laid ... was the interconnected principle of mutual promise and common deliberation; and the event itself decided indeed, as Hamilton had insisted, that men "are really capable ... of establishing good government from reflection and choice," that they are not "forever destined to depend for their political constitutions on accident and force."[28]

It is not so much the nostalgic hues used by Arendt and others to portray political life in the early days of the Republic that is of greatest interest in the context at hand. Instead what is worth noting is that in the revolutionary era one found a commitment to the ideas of public life and active political engagement that has few contemporary parallels. For example, in recent national elections as many as 50 percent of the registered electorate seldom turn out to pull a simple lever in a voting booth. Today's average American probably spends more time reading his or her daily horoscope than busying him or herself with public affairs.[29] To be sure, part of this unwillingness to vote very likely reflects a healthy cynicism on the part of an electorate justifiably disenchanted with the rituals and tergiversations of contemporary party politics.

Of course, the causes of America's current alienation from politics are complex and multifaceted. Nor do I wish to deny that in recent decades positive signs of a reemerging interest in politics have appeared on the horizon. Here, one would do well to keep in mind the astonishing transition from the stifling apoliticism of the 1950s to the political efflorescence of the 1960s — a decade that witnessed the birth of the civil rights movement, Students for a Democratic Society, the anti-war movement, the women's and ecology movements. Despite the reigning mood of political business as usual, it would be hard to imagine what our society would look like today were it not for the aforementioned protest movements, social struggles, and citizen's initiatives.

We have undeniably allowed the valuable space between electoral politics and the private sphere — viz., the interim realm of civil society — to lie fallow. It is waiting to be seized and exploited. But in our case, too, we have met the enemy and she is us. Today, our primary interests and orientations are far from public-spirited. Instead, they revolve around what one might call the values of familial-vocational privatism. We have internalized the achievement ethic of bourgeois society, to the point where success in crudest monetary and vocational terms has been enthroned as an end in itself. In private life we tend to fall back on the insularity of the nuclear family as a "haven in a heartless world." As private individuals we tend to submit passively to the reigning logic of commodification: we complacently identify ourselves as consumers, allowing ourselves to be defined by what we possess instead of by who we are — or, better still, by who we might become. We thereby permit ourselves to be co-opted by the other-directed conformism of David Riesman's "lonely crowd," instead of opting for value-ideals that would enhance the ends of autonomous self-development. When the ethos of bourgeois inwardness and self-seeking is allowed to reach the proportions of a new religion — a situation aptly described by the late Christopher Lasch as a "culture of narcissism" — then of necessity all larger public commitments that transcend the boundaries of the monadic self begin to atrophy.[30]

By a strange twist of fate, we find ourselves in a societal predicament remarkably similar to the one described by Havel in "The Power of the Powerless." We, too, live predominantly amid a milieu of social conformity that is buttressed by a network of ritualized signs. Like our brethren in pre-1989 Eastern Europe, by ceding to the prevailing logic of social illusion, we fail to live in truth. Though we are perhaps loathe to admit it, Havel's compelling description of "a world of appearances, a mere ritual, formalized language deprived of semantic contact with reality and transformed into a system of ritual signs that replace reality with a pseudo-reality," could, mutatis mutandis, easily be applied to our contemporary social situation too. In this respect we have become akin to Nietzsche's proverbial "last men": individuals who are incapable of recognizing the "heavens," "creation" and "longing." We content ourselves instead with nonharrowing tasks and cheap amusements, with an array of safe interactions in which elements of exertion and risk are studiously avoided. It was in this vein that Max Weber accurately characterized the classical bourgeois "type" as "Specialists without spirit, sensualists without heart; this nullity imagines it has attained a level of civilization never before achieved."[31]

In allowing the rich potentials of public life and civil society to wither, we have placed a burden on the private self which it is in truth unable to bear. History instructs us concerning what happens to great republics — Athens, Rome, and Florence — when the ethos of public-spiritedness atrophies and instead citizens turn their attention to personal enrichment and private pursuits: the *res publica* shrivels, corruption flourishes, and ultimately, the civic void is filled with authoritarian or tyrannical forms of rule. As Tocqueville observed some one-hundred and fifty years ago: "those who prize freedom only for the material benefits it offers never keep it long."[32]

In *Democracy in America* Tocqueville, one of the first great critics of American society, pointed out many of the aforementioned contradictions. He thus perceived, with an acuity few subsequent analysts have matched, many of the fundamental societal tensions that successive generations of Americans have sought to confront. On the one hand, he identified a forcible logic of social conformity that was part and parcel of an ingrained American mistrust of class and status differences. His characterization of this tendency as "the tyranny of the majority" has remained an important part of our lexicon of social criticism. On the other hand, and partially offsetting the aforementioned trend, he noticed among Americans a profound interest in establishing and joining voluntary associations. As Tocqueville explains:

> Americans of all ages, all stations in life, and all types of disposition are forever forming associations. There are not only commercial and industrial associations in which all take part, but others of a thousand different types — religious, moral, serious, futile, very general and very limited, immensely large and minute…. As soon as several Americans have conceived a sentiment or an idea that they want to produce before the world, they seek each other out, and when found, they unite. Thenceforth, they are no longer isolated individuals, but a power conspicuous from the distance whose actions serve as an example; when it speaks, men listen.

And he concludes with the following apposite observation: "democratic peoples … are independent and weak. They can do hardly anything for themselves, and none of them is in a position to force his fellows to help him. They would all therefore find themselves helpless if they did not learn to help each other voluntarily."[33]

As a remedy for the isolation in which democratic citizens otherwise find themselves, the associations of civil society represent essential vehicles of communication and common action. As such they constitute repositories of meaningful human solidarity which form an essential bulwark against the encroachments of both government and capital. By reanimating their logics of community and civic participation, we take the first step on the road to living within the truth.

9

From the "Death of Man" to Human Rights: The Paradigm Change in French Intellectual Life, 1968–86

In France, structuralism's death can be dated with a fair amount of precision: the evening of May 10–11, 1968 — the famous "night of the barricades" that was one of the highlights of the legendary "May Movement." Lucien Goldmann, author of *The Hidden God* and other works, conceived a memorable bon mot to describe this watershed. Ever since, it has served as structuralism's unofficial epitaph: "*structures do not go out into the street to make a revolution.*" Thereby, Goldmann served notice that structuralist proclamations concerning "the end of history" had been distinctly premature.

For nearly two decades, structuralism, borrowing a page from Alexandre Kojève's celebrated Hegel lectures, had dismissed the idea of progressive historical change as one of the primary delusions of modern consciousness. "Events" — in the sense of *événements* — ceased to exist. Change was a deception. It operated at the level of "appearance." It served to conceal long-term continuities that, in the last analysis, were determined by deep structures. Whether one examines Lévi-Strauss's theory of kinship, Lacan's view of the unconscious, Althusser's conception of "science," or Foucault's quasi-fatalistic notion of the episteme — which purportedly defines with algorithmic precision the limits of "discursivity" (the regime of the "sayable" and "unsayable") — viewed formally, the results were the same. (Thus, in a well-known passage in *The Order of Things*, Foucault claims that, from a structuralist point of view, the differences between Marx and David Ricardo are trivial. They are part and parcel of the same episteme). Attempts at conscious historical transformation were decreed an illusion. What counted — to use the expression made famous by Fernand Braudel — was the *longue durée*. Subjectivity and politics were the *écume* or foam predestined to be subsumed by the undertow of deep structures.

May '68 gave the lie to the truisms and pieties of two decades of French intellectual life. As one contemporary observer remarked: May '68 was not merely a student revolt; it was "the death warrant of structuralism."[1]

Latin Quarter students staged an unforgettable month of cultural revolution and political theater. Conversely, the Left Bank's so-called *maître penseurs* (master thinkers) — the progenitors of "French Theory" — had egg all over their faces. A year later, de Gaulle, whose imperial presidency dated from 1958, was out of office. Wheels of change had been set in motion that left the cultural and political landscape of modern France permanently transformed. For out of the ashes of May emerged a plethora of vibrant contestatory social movements: "Doctors without Borders," the Mouvement Libération des femmes (MLF), the prison reform movement (GIP), gay rights (FHAR, led by the charismatic Guy Hocquenghem), as well as the *autogestionnaire*-oriented "deuxième Gauche." As subsequent research has shown, many of these groups developed directly out of the prolific, militant-dominated "Action Committees" of May 1968. To borrow nomenclature developed by Nanterre sociologist Alain Touraine: the self-production of civil society had begun. As one observer has astutely noted: "The many Action Committees that flourished in 1968 may have thought they were overturning capitalism, but in fact they were generating participatory democracy."[2] For a time at least, a plethora of grassroots social movements and civic associations had effectively seized the reigns of "historicity" from the "state."

In *Democracy in America* Tocqueville famously observed that a vibrant and multilayered associational life is the surest safeguard against the risks of a despotic-authoritarian usurpation of "the political." "Democratic peoples … are independent and weak," claimed Tocqueville. "They can do hardly anything for themselves, and none of them is in a position to force his fellows to help him. They would all therefore find themselves helpless if they did not learn to help each other voluntarily."[3] One of the best-documented gains of May has been the effective burgeoning of French civic and associational life. As Pierre Rosanvallon has shown in a recent book, *Le Modèle politique français: La société civile contre jacobinisme de 1789 à nos jours*, since the May events participation in a wide range of engaged civic associations has expanded dramatically. During the 1950s around 5,000 associations were created each year; in the 1960s around 10,000; in the 1970s, 25,000; in the 1980s, 40,000; and in the 1990s, 60,000. Today approximately, 40 percent of the French adult population belong to an association. All told, there are around 700,000 associations in a country of 60,000,000.[4] Many of these gains are directly attributable to the new confidence in the value and effectiveness of participatory democracy that has proven to be one of May's most impressive and enduring legacies.

In sum, following years of stultifying Gaullist repression, with the student-worker insurrection France experienced an unprecedented explosion of *repressed subjectivity*.[5] Ironically, in philosophical terms, May was widely perceived as a vindication of Sartre's conception of the *pour-soi* or self-positing subjectivity. The May revolt was populist and democratic. Conversely, structuralism and poststructuralism were perceived as a resolutely *mandarinic idiom*: the very cant of hierarchy and privilege against which the students were rebelling. "*Althusser is useless!*" proclaimed one of the most visible banners to appear on the walls of the University of Nanterre. Whereas both structuralists and poststructuralists had written off change in favor of underlying glacial, impersonal constants, Sartre's theory of subjectivity contained a voluntaristic optimism about progressive historical change that, in the eyes of many, had come to the fore during the May events. Whereas structuralists and poststructuralists freely embraced the dour and pessimistic "death of man" thesis, in many respects May '68 appeared as a rousing vindication of Sartre's faith in the capacity of men and women to endow history with meaning. As François Dosse notes in *The History of Structuralism*: "Sartre's analysis of the alienation of individuals caught up in the practico-inert, and his insistence on the capacity of individuals to impose freedom by the actions of committed groups fused into a dialectic that made it possible to escape isolation and atomization, shed more light on May 1968 than did any structuralist position about structural chains, the subjected subject, or systems that reproduce or regulate themselves." Dosse appropriately titles his chapter devoted to the May revolt, "Jean-Paul Sartre's Revenge."[6] Similarly, in *Les Idées qui ont ébranlé la France* (*The Ideas That Shook France*), Didier Anzieu, alluding to Sartre's concept of the "group-in-fusion," writes: "[In essence,] the May student revolt tried out its own version of Sartre's formula, 'the group is the beginning of humanity.'" Thus, it is hardly an accident that, during May, Sartre was the only French intellectual permitted by student leaders to address the large rally at the Sorbonne.

In a perceptive article, François Furet identified the historical preconditions behind structuralism's rise. He suggested that the movement's endemic cynicism about historical change represented a theoretical corollary to the widely sensed impasse of Fifth Republic political culture. After all, following the brutal, 1956 Soviet invasion of Hungary, the French Communist Party suffered irreparable damage as a credible source of political opposition. The French Socialist Party's luster was also permanently tarnished. For it was largely as a result of its policies — the senseless war in Algeria, for example — that the Fourth Republic had run aground, allowing de Gaulle to assume the role of political savior. Lastly, under the General's eleven-year quasi-benign, authoritarian reign, until May at least, all sense of political possibility seemed brusquely foreclosed. Little wonder, then, that, among French intellectuals, structuralism's apocalyptical "death of the man" thesis found keen resonance.

One of the main ironies of poststructuralism's reception history, then, is that at the very moment its star began to fall precipitously in France, it gained a new lease on life across the Atlantic. Thus, as one oft-cited study of Derrida's work has shown, during the early 1980s, when articles devoted to his thought in France slowed to a trickle — at most, one or two a year — in North America, conversely, an academic cottage industry spawned translations of and commentaries on his texts.[7]

In sum and bluntly put: in the aftermath of May, a new generation of intellectuals perceived the structuralist/poststructuralist attack on the "subject" as counterproductive and self-defeating. For, according to the new consensus, the denegation of subjectivity manifestly stifled attempts to conceptualize problems of social change. Consequently, in May's wake there blossomed numerous, alternative competing theoretical paradigms that, unlike the structuralism/poststructuralism dyad, took the ideas of "practice" and "action" seriously. One fruitful approach was developed by University of Nanterre sociologist Alain Touraine. In books like *The Voice and the Eye* and *The Return of the Actor,* Touraine sought to do justice to the rebirth of a vibrant and oppositional associational life both in France and throughout Europe. At a later point, Touraine would extend this "action-oriented" framework to cover the development of antinuclear and environmentalist citizen initiatives, not to mention Solidarity, the independent trade union movement in Poland.

These developments have led observers to speak of a new actor-centered, "pragmatic turn" animating French social and political thought. It is in this vein that commentators have proclaimed "the birth of a new paradigm ... : a communicative action that could represent a real path of emancipation as a social project.... The pragmatic turn accords a central position to action endowed with meaning; it thereby rehabilitates intentionality."[8] Accordingly, the motivations and self-understanding of the actors themselves regain pride of place. Such considerations remained imperceptible from the standpoint of the previously dominant paradigm: a joyless and misanthropic "antihumanism." The new theoretical approaches, conversely, stress the creativity and open-endedness of social action. In a neo-Kantian spirit, they unite in recognizing *the primacy of practical reason*. Recoiling from structuralism's languorous positivism as well as poststructuralism's inability to theorize "the social" (in the eyes of most critics, owing to its "linguistic idealism" or inordinate focus on questions of "textuality"), the new methods portend what might be called a *rehumanization of the social sciences*. Thus, in the eyes of one acute observer: with the emergence of the new, action-oriented analytical frameworks, "The social is no longer conceived as a thing; it is no longer an object of reification .... [Instead], the social fact is perceived as a semantic fact bearing meaning. Habermas's theory of communicative action ... is mobilized to recapture social actions as facts at once psychological and physical."[9]

One of the major casualties of the new stress on the value of inter-subjectivity has been French Nietzscheanism: the intellectual lineage that extends from Georges Bataille and Pierre Klossowski in the 1930s to the postwar appropriations by Derrida, Deleuze, and Foucault. In the 1880s Nietzsche had famously proclaimed: "the one thing that counts is to give style to one's character.... He exercises it who surveys all that his nature presents ... and then moulds it to an artistic plan until everything appears as art and reason, and even the weaknesses delight the eye."[10] Ultimately, however, the aestheticist approach seemed suitable only to a socially indifferent elitism: an ethos conducive to hedonistically inclined *Übermenschen und -frauen*. At base, it seemed incompatible with the *esprit de sérieux* mandated by the imperatives of democratic self-transformation. May '68 had demonstrated that society was open and susceptible to the constructive influence of democratic participation. In May's aftermath a new interest emerged in what might be called "logics of justification." Men and women took stock of the fact that the virtues of "public reason" could be mobilized for purposes of constructive social change.

Even among former poststructuralists the spirit of May proved infectious. Many began revising their theories accordingly. Thus, during the late 1970s, the "rebirth of the subject" became an omnipresent topos.[11] Roland Barthes published a semiconfessional, well-received autobiography, *Roland Barthes par Roland Barthes*. Foucault abruptly abandoned *The History of Sexuality* project in order to investigate the ideas of aesthetic self-fashioning — an "aesthetics of existence" — in ancient Greece and Rome as well as among modernists such as Baudelaire. Led by Philippe Sollers and Julia Kristeva, the *Tel Quel* group belatedly jumped aboard the bandwagon of Eastern European "dissidence."

In 1978, to their disciples' chagrin, they announced — to anyone who was still listening — that in the upcoming parliamentary elections, they would be voting for Valéry Giscard d'Estaing's center-right Union de la Democratie Française.[12] Proclamations concerning the "death of the author," once so fashionable, now seemed rash and outdated.

The May movement had effectively unmasked Marxism — at least in its official, orthodox variants — as an ideology of domination. As is well known, the 1974 translation of Solzhenitsyn's pathbreaking exposé of the Soviet Gulag had a far-reaching impact in France. Chroniclers of French political life are fond of referring to the "Solzhenitsyn effect." Shamed by years of pro-Moscow fealty and embarrassed by a misguided *tier-mondisme*, in which the frustrated revolutionary expectations of first world intellectuals were paternalistically projected upon the third world, since the mid-1970s French thinkers had begun a long-term process of reassessing the forgotten virtues of democratic republicanism. Within a matter of years, among French opinion leaders, political loyalties were dramatically transformed. French intellectuals vowed that never again would they allow blind allegiance to a political cause to stifle considerations of conscience. After a long postwar hiatus, "morality" once again became a legitimate topic of political discussion.

Seemingly overnight, the posters of Mao, Fidel, and Che were removed from Latin Quarter dormitory walls. The new exemplars of *moral politics* were a generation of Eastern European dissidents who had staked life and limb on "speaking truth to power": figures like Russia's Andrei Sakharov, Czechoslovakia's Vaclav Havel, and Poland's Adam Michnik. Among French intellectuals, the ethos of *droits de l'homme* — human rights — had been reborn. As an insightful observer has remarked: "The modern French left's heightened sensibility to the issues of human rights and civil liberties ... and its tireless activism on behalf of these issues, is ... one of the most important legacies of [May]."[13] In 1977, during a lavish state visit to the Elysée Palace by Soviet President Leonid Brezhnev, a number of media-savvy French intellectuals — led by Foucault, Sartre, and New Philosopher André Glucksmann — decided to stage a high-profile, rival soirée in honor of Soviet dissidents. Foucault, with characteristic eloquence and understatement, commented as follows:

> This isn't a meeting ... and above all it isn't a reception symmetrical with the one that is taking place at this very moment. We simply thought that, on the evening when M. Brezhnev is being received with pomp at the Elysée by M. Giscard d'Estaing, other French people could receive other Russians who are their friends.[14]

Twenty years earlier, Sartre, oblivious to "really existing socialism's" appalling political track record, had claimed that Marxism was the "unsurpassable horizon of our time." Conversely, for a subsequent generation of engaged intellectuals, human rights had become the incontestable benchmark — the alpha and omega — of any future politics.

As is often the case in a country where politics and intellectual life are intimately intertwined, major developments on the international political stage played a key role in solidifying this transformation:

1. Unspeakable revelations concerning the scope and extent of Cambodia's so-called killing fields, where, within the space of a few years, approximately 1.5 million persons were brutally murdered; moreover, as is well known, during the 1950s Khmer Rouge luminaries such as Pol Pot, Ieng Sary, and Khieu Samphan received their training in Marxism at the finest Parisian universities. As Ieng Sary's deputy, Suong Sikoeun, observed: "The French Revolution influenced me very strongly, above all Robespierre ... Robespierre and Pol Pot: both men have the same quality of decisiveness and integrity."[15]

2. The perilous exodus, circa 1978, of Vietnamese "boat people," fleeing political persecution from a recently installed Marxist regime that, just a few years earlier, many left-leaning French intellectuals had cheered on to victory.

3. What in retrospect might be described as the coup de grâce for *marxisant* French intellectuals: the 1979 Soviet invasion of Afghanistan and ensuing nine-year brutal occupation.

Little wonder, then, that within a few years' time, the vote totals of the PCF, historically one of Western Europe's most successful communist parties, dwindled from over 20 percent to the low single digits.

Undoubtedly, in American academic culture the figure who has had the most far-ranging and pervasive influence on the development of "postmodernism" is Michel Foucault. It is therefore worth enquiring how the foregoing narrative — the retreat from structuralism's "end of history" / "death of man" hypothesis — affected Foucault's own intellectual and political development. For it is well known — and Foucault himself has avowed as much in interviews — that, for the author of *Discipline and Punish*, May '68 represented something of a methodological and political watershed — despite the fact that, since Foucault himself was teaching in Tunisia at the time, he had no first-hand contact with the May events. Nevertheless, ample evidence suggests that, during the 1970s, Foucault developed a new understanding of politics that closely paralleled the political evolution of the '68ers themselves. That evolution gradually abandoned the *gauchisme* or "leftism" that, in the post-May era, had become the dominant political credo and turned increasingly toward a politics of human rights.

We know that, for a time, Foucault worked closely with members of the post-May, Gauche Prolétarienne (GP) on questions of prison reform. His work for the Prison Information Group (GIP) coincided with his research on his most influential book, *Surveiller et Punir (Discipline and Punish)*. Should one desire a measure of Foucault's own, post-'68 flirtations with an uncompromising *gauchisme*, one would do well to examine his 1972 text, "On Popular Justice: Dialogue with the Maoists." In the course of a conversation with GP leader Pierre Victor (nom de guerre of the late Benny Lévy), Foucault famously praised the 1792 September massacres — an important prologue to the so-called Big Terror of the Year II — as an "*approximation of ... popular justice*; a response to oppression which was strategically useful and politically necessary."[16] He went on to observe that, by establishing revolutionary tribunals, the Committee of Public Safety, had erred on the side of "proceduralism." Instead, they should have allowed the thirst for popular vengeance — famously exemplified by the blood-soaked, revolutionary *journées* — to find a direct and unmediated outlet.

However, it is of interest to note that Foucault refrained from practicing what he preached. Later that same year, a working class girl was brutally murdered in the northern coal-mining village of Bruay-en-Artois. Frustrated by the authorities' unwillingness to prosecute a local notable, GP leaders tried to convene a popular tribunal to effect summary justice — that is, to try and execute the suspected culprit. (At the time, Pierre Victor condemned the separation of trial and sentencing as an atavistic bourgeois encumbrance.) In this case, however, Foucault exercised a cautionary influence on the young *gépistes* (the members of the GP), urging them to abandon their irresponsible revolutionary theatrics. In fact, Foucault was slowly coming to the conclusion that there was no hard and fast line separating the penchant for violence on the part of the revolutionary left from that of the revolutionary right. Later that same year in his introduction to Gilles Deleuze and Félix Guattari's *Anti-Oedipus* he expressed this realization as follows: "How does one keep from being fascist, even (especially) when one believes oneself to be a revolutionary militant? How do we rid our speech and our acts, our hearts and our pleasures, of fascism? How do we ferret out the fascism that is ingrained in our behavior."[17]

Foucault's partisanship for *droit de l'hommisme* first surfaced during the mid-1970s in his defense of so-called "New Philosophy." Writing in the pages of *le Nouvel observateur*, the philosopher penned a fulsome, three-page review essay of André Glucksmann's *Les Maîtres penseurs*. In retrospect, one might say that it was Foucault's review, rather than "new philosophy" itself, that enunciated a sea change in French intellectual politics: the movement away from Marxism and toward the paradigm of human rights. In many respects, New Philosophers like Glucksmann and Bernard-Henri Lévy were Foucault's bastard intellectual progeny. For Glucksmann's thesis in *Les Maîtres penseurs* overlapped with a Nietzschean standpoint that Foucault himself had helped to popularize: "la volonté de savoir" = "la volonté de pouvoir"; "the will to know" = "the will to power." Simply put: Western thought betrays a "will to domination" that culminates logically in the "totally administered world" of the Gulag.

> The whole of a certain left has attempted to explain the Gulag ... in terms of the theory of history, or at least the history of theory. Yes, yes, there were massacres; but that was a terrible error. Just reread Marx or Lenin, compare them with Stalin and you will see where the latter went wrong. It is obvious that all those deaths could only result from a misreading. It was predictable: Stalinism-error was one of the principal agents behind the return to Marxism-truth, to Marxism-text which we saw in the 1960s. If you want to be against Stalin, don't listen to the victims; they will only recount their tortures. Reread the theoreticians; they will tell you the truth about the true.[18]

Although Foucault's disciples have often criticized his endorsement of Glucksmann's arguments — as is well known, his actions precipitated a major break with Gilles Deleuze, whom he had hired in the philosophy department at the University of Vincennes — in many ways the philosopher acted with admirable uprightness and consistency. Heretofore, the French left had vehemently denounced the totalitarianisms of the Far Right. By what right should it ignore the equally murderous totalitarianisms that had been established by left-wing regimes? Moreover, in a crypto-Trotskyist spirit, the French left had historically exonerated Marx and Marxism from any responsibility for the Gulag. (One especially egregious example of this failing was Sartre's declaration, following the Warsaw Pact invasion of Hungary, that the Soviet Union was still "objectively" a worker's state.) Yet, at this historical juncture, such denials seemed morally untenable — a pure and simple act of bad faith. It was Foucault, marching shoulder to shoulder with the New Philosophers, who helped precipitate this breach.

During the late 1970s, Foucault worked closely with France's leading left-liberal trade union, the CFDT (*Confédération française et démocratique du travail*). It was this organ that, by stressing theories of worker self-management or *autogestion*, laid the groundwork for the so-called *deuxième Gauche* or "second Left." By encouraging ideals of worker autonomy and democratic self-governance, the CFDT represented the authentic heir to the spirit of May.

In 1979 Foucault, once again in the company of Sartre and New Philosopher André Glucksmann, played a key role in calling attention to the plight of Vietnamese refugees — the so-called boat people — fleeing in droves from an oppressive communist regime. Similarly, in December 1981, when Poland's General Jaruzelski declared martial law, thereby suppressing Soviet-dominated Eastern Europe's only independent trade union, Foucault was in the forefront of the protest against newly elected president François Mitterrand's de facto acquiescence in the face of this disheartening and tragic state of affairs. It was at this point, moreover, that a political friendship blossomed between Foucault and Bernard Kouchner, the founder of *Médecins sans Frontières* and France's most outspoken human rights advocate. During this period Foucault assembled a small group of journalists, activists, and intellectuals to closely monitor human rights abuses around the world.[19]

François Dosse has glossed Foucault's remarkable political metamorphosis as follows:

> In the late seventies and early eighties, Foucault embraced the cause of human rights .... Slowly, under the influence of the profound changes of the day, [he] once again began acting like a universal intellectual cum defender of democratic values. As his thinking and practice changed, he drew closer to Sartre, to whom he had been completely opposed until then.[20]

By helping to popularize and affirm a human rights agenda, Foucault inherited Sartre's coveted mantle as France's leading public intellectual. Ironically, the thinker who once articulated a theory of the "specific intellectual" established himself as an eloquent spokesman for what has become, since the dark days of Auschwitz, the world's most valuable universalistic moral and political credo. At the time of Foucault's death in 1984, prominent observers noted the irony that the ex-structuralist and "death-of-man" prophet had played a pivotal role in facilitating French acceptance of political liberalism. As one commentator has aptly noted: "As much as any figure of his generation, [Foucault] helped inspire a resurgent neo-liberalism in France in the 1980s."[21]

To be sure, there was always a tension between the later Foucault's theoretical pronouncements and his political practice. Having abandoned the démarche of *La Volonté de savoir*, according to which "power" was omnipresent and inescapable, in his later writings

Foucault flirted with the trope of an "aesthetics of existence." He displayed an intense fascination with Baudelaire's dandyism — as well as Nietzsche's famous maxim in *The Gay Science* concerning the paramountcy of "style." In a similar vein, in the final pages of *The History of Sexuality*, as an antidote to the false promises of sexual emancipation — "le roi sexe" — Foucault counsels us to seek out a "different economy of bodies and pleasures."

Yet, viewed according to another optic, these two antithetical political frames — "body politics" and "human rights" — prove complementary rather than mutually exclusive. As political thinkers from Kant to Rawls to Claude Lefort have suggested, liberal democracy provides an optimal framework for the ends of individual self-realization. Since, unlike communitarian approaches to politics, it is agnostic concerning the summum bonum, democracy is compatible with a dizzying plurality of *Lebensformen*, or "forms of life." In this sense, democracy provides the ideal terrain for a Foucauldian "aesthetics of existence" to flourish. This would seem to be one of the undeniable lessons of the modernist aesthetic — as embodied by Rimbaud's immortal maxim: "Il faut être absolument moderne" — with which the later Foucault so profoundly identified.

However, were this hypothesis concerning the complementarity of "body politics" and political liberalism to be borne out, Foucault's reductive equation of "modernity" with "carceralism" — the normalizing practices of a disciplinary society — would stand in need of drastic revision. I would therefore like to suggest that, in his political involvements, Foucault gave the lie to his philosophy of history or "metatheory," which misleadingly conflated "norms" with "normalization." In this respect, later in life Foucault seems to have come to a conclusion analogous to the leading representatives of the Frankfurt School: "rule of law" or *Rechtsstaat* provides a necessary and indispensable "magic wall" safeguarding civil society from the constant threat of authoritarian encroachments.[22]

The *gauchistes* of the 1960s and early 1970s equated Gaullism with fascism. By the same token, they viewed themselves — mistakenly, as it turns out — as a new "resistance." (One might point out that, viewed sociologically, the conflation of Gaullism with fascism helps to explain the preponderance of Jews in Gauche Prolétarienne leadership positions). But the 1970s taught the leftists — Foucault included — an important lesson: societies governed by "rule of law" contain internal prospects for progressive social change; and it is this fact that distinguishes them profoundly from political dictatorships. In the eyes of France's left-wing militants, the proliferation of new social movements that proceeded under the banner of "cultural revolution" — feminism, gay rights, environmentalism, citizen initiatives, and the so-called second Left — drove this point home indelibly and irretrievably. Along with his fellow leftists, Foucault realized that to deny this fundamental normative insight would be both hypocritical and politically self-defeating. The theory of "soft totalitarianism," according to which communist dictatorships and Western-type "disciplinary societies" are birds of a feather, was disingenuous. It masked the fact that the constitutional democracies remain open to the transformative potentials of "public reason" in a way that sets them apart qualitatively from authoritarian regimes.

There remains the issue of the widespread and influential American academic reception of French theory, much of which has proceeded under the banner of "postmodernism." This theme raises a number complex questions. The reception rhythms of French theory have differed from discipline to discipline. Initially, postmodernism seemed to harbor certain muted, redemptory expectations — for example, in influential works such as Lyotard's *The Postmodern Condition*, a book that first appeared twenty-five years ago. Suffice it to say that, at this point in time, these expectations have dimmed significantly. The "left Heidegger" take on modernity as an incessant technological nightmare — "the desolation of the earth," the reduction of all Being to "standing reserve"— has proved untenable.[23] It would seem that modernity's emancipatory potentials merit a second look.

In 1976 Christopher Lasch published *The Culture of Narcissism*, an important book on the demise of the 1960s as highpoint of public political engagement. According to Lasch, with the Vietnam War's end, the already-problematic counterculture maxim "the personal is the political" was elevated to the status of an idée fixe. A movement-oriented politics of active contestation had given way to a highly privatized lifestyle politics. While neoconservatives began to regroup effectively following the debacle of Nixon's presidency, ex-1960s radicals embarked on various New Age–inspired voyages of personal discovery.[24] Significantly, these were also the years when the French Theory vogue began to take root in North American universities. Viewed from the standpoint of "sociology of knowledge," there seems to be a strong correlation between an age of depoliticization and postmodernism's rise to academic prominence. One feels compelled to enquire whether, to borrow a phrase from Foucault, the postmodern "implantation" was not essentially an expression of political *displacement* in the Freudian sense: a sublimation of *public sphere politics* in the direction of *cultural politics*. In describing academic trends of the 1970s and 1980s, given the paramount role played by French thinkers who prided themselves on "difficulty" — to the point where *illisibilité*, or "unreadability," became a paradoxical virtue — it is common practice to refer to the "detour of theory." What is worrisome in retrospect is that, bluntly put, what began as a "detour" turned into a blind alley from which the devotees of postmodernism failed to emerge. For if one surveys postmodernism's reception history, one fact that stands out is its stark inability to make inroads beyond the bloodless and antiseptic corridors of academe.

As an academic phenomenon, one of postmodernism's hallmarks was an abiding obsession with things cultural. From a methodological standpoint, this meant a heady fusion of the Frankfurt School and Gramsci, along with the high priests of Left Bank structuralism/poststructuralism. There is little doubt that, compared with the pieties and clichés of orthodox Marxism, the "cultural turn" was a breath of fresh air. Yet, in the long run, it fell victim to its own reductive and dogmatic assumptions. The standard metaphors of poststructuralist discourse — "textuality," "episteme," and the seemingly omnipresent Lacanian "Symbolic" — were often stretched to the point of absurdity. We now know that attempts to understand domination from a strictly cultural standpoint can be severely limiting. Crushing poverty, "ethnic cleansing," and structural unemployment are not merely the by-products or effects of "discursivity." They contain an inexpungeable *empirical dimension* that culturalist paradigms have either overlooked or systematically downplayed. Paradoxically, the upshot of the academic Left's culturalist obsessions has been in a consequential neglect of traditional sources of power: political domination (for example, as practiced by the Republicans from 1980–92) and expanding economic injustice. When one surveys the preoccupations of the cultural Left, it seems that both of these concerns have fallen under the radar. Thus, it is far from happenstance that the 1990s, as an epoch of globalization, witnessed a timely return of the political economy paradigm.[25]

For some time now overseas observers of the American academic scene have reacted with bemusement at the idiosyncratic manner in which French ideas have been received across the Atlantic. One frequent target of criticism has been the appropriation of poststructuralist thought for the ends of "identity politics" — a concept that the French, educated in the rigidly assimilationist, civic republican tradition, have a difficult time comprehending. (Or, as a French friend remarked a few years back: "identity politics — that's what they had in Germany between 1933 and 1945"). In France, where, for generations, the "immigrants-into-Frenchmen" model of citizenship has predominated, the hyphenated ethnicities that are integral to American melting pot lore — Irish-American, African-American, Japanese-American — are essentially unknown.

One of the most common objections concerns the way that, across the Atlantic, European scholarly discourses have been refashioned to

suit the utilitarian needs of political groups in search of social advancement. French commentators have been taken aback at the way in which
demanding theories and concepts have provided a glib epistemological
warrant for the follies of American-style political correctness and multiculturalism. They are fond of pointing to the paradox that poststructuralist doctrines that are endemically suspicious of "meaning" and
"subjectivity" have become a rallying cry for the political activism of
"marginalized subjectivities." Thus, ironically, in North America
French philosophers whose stock-in-trade has been a deconstruction of
the "transcendental subject" have been turned into intellectual oracles
or gurus, provoking an adulation bordering on hero worship.

10

The Republican Revival: Reflections on French Singularity

Historically, French exceptionalism has been synonymous with its vaunted revolutionary heritage, epitomized by a series of legendary political dates: 1789, 1830, 1848, 1871, and 1968. After World War II its meaning was expanded to incorporate the immense prestige enjoyed by the French Communist Party (the *parti des fusillés*) — a situation that, with the exception of Italy, was unparalleled among Western democracies. Until quite recently, France's Jacobin-revolutionary traditions had been the source of enormous national pride. However, in recent decades the misdeeds of "really existing socialism," as amplified by the impact of Solzhenitsyn's influential book on the Gulag, made that heritage appear in an entirely new and extremely negative light. In his pathbreaking *New French Thought* anthology, Mark Lilla, taking cognizance of these developments, heralded the "legitimacy of the liberal age." For the first time since the early nineteenth century, the ideals of political liberalism enjoyed favor among French intellectuals. However, with ten years' hindsight, one cannot help but wonder whether Lilla's prognosis was significantly premature.

The astonishing results of the April 2002 presidential elections are a good case in point. This was the infamous date when the National Front candidate, Jean-Marie Le Pen, dumbfounded the French public by racking up an unprecedented 17 percent during the first round of voting. Le Pen thereby qualified for the runoff with incumbent Jacques

Chirac at the expense of Socialist Party standard-bearer Lionel Jospin. Jospin garnered an anemic 16.2 percent of the vote — the lowest score for a socialist presidential candidate since 1969. Equally disturbing is the fact that, if one factors in the totals of National Front renegade Bruno Mégret, one realizes that far-right, antiparliamentary candidates managed to attract approximately 20 percent of the vote.

Without irony, the French commonly refer to April 21, 2002, as their "11 Septembre." However, as it turned out, the Le Pen debacle was only the tip of the iceberg. Chirac's percentage, which dipped below the 20 percent mark, was the worst result for a presidential incumbent in the Fifth Republic's history. Two Trotskyist candidates, Olivier Besancenot and Arlette Laguiller, managed to attract 10 percent of the vote. If one adds to these figures the totals of two additional left-wing candidates, the PCF's Robert Hue and Christiane Taubira of the Parti Radicale de la Gauche, one realizes that parties to the left of the PS gained nearly 17 percent of votes cast — more than Socialist standard-bearer Jospin.

One of the upshots of these figures is that on April 21, 2002, the combined vote count of avowedly antirepublican candidates garnered approximately 39 percent of the votes, thereby surpassing the results of the two mainstays of France's political center, Chirac's Union pour une majorité présidentielle (UMP) and Jospin's Parti Socialiste (PS).[1]

It is hardly surprising that the next day lachrymose journalistic doomsayers prophesized — as one *Le Monde* headline blared — "La Mort de la Vième République."[2] Fortunately, this worst case scenario did not come to pass. Instead, French voters rallied solidly behind the republican candidate, Chirac, both in the second round of the "presidentials" and in the parliamentary elections two months later. Nevertheless, it would be foolish to minimize the portentous nature of the first-round electoral results — an expression of radical dissatisfaction with the "liberal" political mainstream. During the last twenty-five years both Gaullists and socialists have made a point of rejecting economic *dirigisme* in favor of laissez-faire economics. Mitterrand's stunning political volte-face took place in 1983. Dismissing his communist allies from the government, he brazenly declared in a nationally televised address: "the French are beginning to understand: it is *the firm* that creates wealth, it is *the firm* that creates employment, it is *the firm* that decides our standard of living and our place in the world hierarchy." Since then voters on the left have legitimately wondered: why cast my vote for a Socialist Party that has openly renounced socialism?[3]

If one turns to the heavenly city of French intellectual life, attitudes toward liberalism seem hardly more favorable. Instructive in this respect is the political evolution of Marcel Gauchet — one of the featured authors of the neoliberal turn celebrated in the aforementioned *New French Thought* anthology.

One is tempted to say that Gauchet is a figure who needs no introduction. He is a student of Claude Lefort, who, during the 1950s, as a founding member of *Socialisme ou Barbarie*, authored a series of pioneering critiques of Stalinism.[4] Following a series of flings with several post-'68, ultra-left philosophical journals (*Textures* and *Libre*), in 1980 Gauchet was named coeditor of *Le Débat*, the most influential French review of the last two decades. During the 1980s *Le Débat* introduced a new sobriety into French intellectual discourse. For by this point the dreams and illusions of May '68 had faded. Poststructuralism's antihumanism — as embodied in Foucault's celebrated maxim announcing the "death of man" — seemed radically out of step with the new political awareness that had been inspired by the Eastern European dissident movement. The shock waves from the "Solzhenitsyn effect" — the 1974 publication of *The Gulag Archipelago* — reverberated throughout the mid- to late 1970s. With the publication of Charter 77 in Czechoslovakia, a mere two years after the Helsinki Accords on human rights had been signed, French intellectuals developed a profound, symbiotic attachment to their persecuted Eastern European sisters and brethren.[5] As numerous commentators have pointed out, from a group psychological standpoint, much of this sentiment may be viewed as a labor of atonement on the part of left-leaning French intellectuals for having supported left-wing dictatorships in Europe and the Third World. Even the *Tel Quel* group, led by the inimitable Philippe Sollers, which had dogmatically embraced the PCF's Stalinism against the students during May '68 (and which, thereafter, belatedly jumped on the Maoist bandwagon — a sinking ship if there ever was one), proclaimed in 1978 that they had been "dissidents" all along.[6]

Gauchet has been typecast as one of the intellectual luminaries responsible for rehabilitating French liberalism.[7] In 1980 he wrote an insightful introduction to a new edition of Benjamin Constant's classic study on "Ancient and Modern Liberty."[8] There, he seconded Constant's view that what distinguishes the modern conception of liberty is its valorization of individual freedom. In classical republicanism, conversely, in which the notion of virtu figured prominently, individual freedom was typically sacrificed to the common good. The same year Gauchet published a magisterial essay on Tocqueville in the inaugural issue of *Le Débat*. In the spirit of *Democracy in America*, Gauchet highlighted the degenerative risks of democratic government: the perilous affinities between "equality of condition" and despotism that Tocqueville had famously diagnosed as one of political modernity's foremost ills.

However, in his more recent work Gauchet voiced, with alarming stridency, his profound disillusionment with the unfulfilled promises of political liberalism — a skepticism that remained muted in his earlier writings. For example, in *La Démocratie contre elle-même* he denounced the shortcomings of liberal democracy in an overheated, Spenglerian rhetorical idiom. As some critics have observed, Gauchet, who during the 1960s belonged to a far-left student milieu in Caen, seems to have been a victim of a post-May, generational Marxist superego.[9] Since Gauchet and his fellow *soixante-huitards* had set the bar of political utopia so high, it became nearly impossible to adapt to conditions of democratic normalcy, despite the fact that the Socialists dominated the landscape of French politics during the 1980s and 1990s.

In the introduction to the aforementioned book, Gauchet argues that although the ethos of human rights may have been serviceable for offsetting the excesses of totalitarianism, when it came to remedying the shortcomings and deficiencies of "really existing democracy," they failed miserably. Gauchet insinuated that members of the post-May generation had fallen victim to a political swindle. Having abandoned their former radicalism for "droit-de-l'hommisme," all they received in return were the decadent blandishments of consumer society. During the 1970s and 1980s, France succeeded in making the transition from Gaullist "authoritarian democracy" to the "era of the individual" (to employ Alain Renaut's phrase), but at a terrific cost: the socially administered hedonism accompanying third-wave, post-Fordist, "flexible response" capitalism. Gauchet, the disillusioned *gauchiste*, accepted at face value Gilles Lipovetsky's conclusions in *L'Ère du vide*, which, following Christopher Lasch, argued that a profligate and conformist "culture of narcissism" has replaced the autonomous individualism of the laissez-faire era.[10] As Lipovetsky contends:

> May '68 was a "soft" revolution, without deaths, traitors, orthodoxies, or purges. Indeed, it manifested the same gradual softening of social mores that Tocqueville first noticed in personal relations characteristic of an individualistic and democratic age ... The spirit of May recaptured what historically has been the central tenet of the consumer society: *hedonism*. By emphasizing permissiveness, humor, and fun, the spirit of May was largely molded by the very thing it denounced in politics ... : the euphoria of the consumer age.[11]

These remarks merely summarize Tocqueville's concerns about the absence of virtue and the general softening of mores under modern democracy. But it is also second-rate Tocqueville. Moreover, Lipovetsky's analysis represents a one-dimensional and simplistic analysis of May that blithely ignores the advances in participatory democracy and citizenship rights that emerged from the insurrection's ashes. Here, I am thinking of developments such as the so-called *deuxième Gauche* (led by Michel Rocard), the advances of women's and gay rights (Paris today has a gay mayor, Delanoe, a development that would have been unthinkable twenty years ago), Doctors Without Borders, an incipient ecological consciousness (*les Verts*), as well as a new awareness concerning the value of humanitarian intervention (the so-called *droit d'ingérance*), and so forth.

Gauchet's denunciations of contemporary French democracy were so harsh that, along with novelist Michel Houllebecq and neo-Straussian political philosopher Pierre Manent, he earned the sobriquet "nouveau réactionnaire" (new reactionary) in Daniel Lindenberg's 2002 polemic, *Le Rappel à l'ordre*. Lindenberg went so far as to compare Gauchet's views with the antidemocratic, "neither right nor left" antics of Georges Bataille's Collège de Sociologie in the 1930s.[12]

Gauchet's critique of contemporary democracy is based on a misleading conflation of economic and political categories: a confusion of economic and political liberalism. Contra Gauchet, the best way to offset the temptations of consumer hedonism and flaccid individualism is *the democratic self-organization of civil society*. The activation and expansion of existing civic and political freedoms, rather than being a symptom of cultural disequilibrium, is an essential part of the solution.

Other proclamations of the "end of French exceptionalism" (as a figure for France's constitutional allergy to a political moderation) predated the one found in *New French Thought*. However, whereas Lilla viewed French intellectuals' belated embrace of liberalism as fundamentally praiseworthy, within France itself a number of leading political analysts increasingly viewed the "liberal turn" with dismay and alarm.

Thus, following the 1988 presidential and legislative elections, which yielded the "high tide" of French socialism à la Mitterrand, three leading historians — François Furet, Jacques Julliard, and Pierre Rosanvallon — published *La République du centre*, bemoaning the drastic foreshortening of France's political spectrum. The authors lamented the swan song of the nation's major alternative political traditions: the "idea of the left" (*la gauche*), socialism, and, lastly, republicanism. The only worldview left standing was, seemingly, political liberalism, which the authors perceived as an immense ideological void. The 1989 bicentennial celebration — which in truth found very little to celebrate beyond August 26, 1789 (date of the Declaration of the Rights of Man and Citizen) — confirmed the authors' deepest fears: politically speaking, France had become afraid of its own shadow. Historically, the idea of French singularity had derived from the nation's celebrated revolutionary tradition. "This [combative] spirit of politics," remark the authors, "is what we are in the process of losing." They contend that fin de siècle France has experienced a wholesale and irreversible "*banalization of politics.*"[13]

Echoing Furet's extremely pessimistic introductory comments, Rosanvallon, in his chapter on "Malaise dans la représentation," regrets the "strange void" that has "hollowed out ... French politics." "France has become *soft* ... [its] political life *dull*." "French political life has been reconfigured in the idiom of an *ecumenical liberalism*, a vague celebration of '*rights*' and an *insistent apology for the market, supported by a slack and minimalist reading of Tocqueville and Benjamin Constant*," he continues. In French politics, nothing concrete is left. Instead all that remains is a "*consecration of [our own] impotence.*"[14]

Of course, Tocqueville prophesied these developments one hundred and fifty years ago. In modern democracies, "everything that was once great has shrunk ... moderation dominates in every respect, with the exception of *the taste for well-being* .... What's lacking is political life itself ... *languor, impotence, immobility, and boredom [predominate].*"[15] Like Furet, Rosanvallon views the end of French exceptionalism, as I have just defined it, as an unequivocal misfortune. The "normalization" of French political culture means that the hexagon has succumbed to the baser political and cultural tendencies of the modern age: that is, the traits that predominate among the "Anglo-Saxon" cultures. Echoing Gauchet, Rosanvallon's concludes that "There is much naïveté in trying to base politics on human rights. It is impossible to envisage the future of democratic societies from the standpoint of individual autonomy...."[16]

Yet, was it not François Furet himself who, as far back as 1978, had proclaimed the "revolution was over" and who used his influence at two powerful institutions (the Fondation Saint-Simon and Centre Raymond Aron) to extirpate the last traces of Revolutionism from French political and intellectual life?[17]

While Furet and company — colloquially known as the "galaxy" — were ruing the advent of *La République du centre*, they should have glanced over their shoulders at recent electoral results. They might have noticed that May 1988 — the twentieth anniversary of the legendary "Mai" — was the month of Le Pen's first presidential electoral breakthrough. The ex-paratrooper, indicted torturer, and former Poujadist deputy stunned the nation by garnering 15 percent in the first round (as the *Le Monde* headline put it: *Le Séisme Politique* — "The Political Earthquake").

Another major reason that political liberalism has failed to take hold in France has been the phoenixlike rebirth of French republicanism — a political paradigm that, during the 1970s and 1980s, had taken a back-seat due to the triumph of *droit de l'hommisme*.

During the 1990s France was confronted with a new set of regional and international economic demands that spurred many on the left to reevaluate the desirability of both the European Monetary Union (EMU) and globalization. Following the Maastricht agreement, the "entry ticket" to Europe became a rejection of deficit financing. In France the 3 percent deficit quotient required of EU members led to significant public sector layoffs, culminating in a massive, incapacitating strike by public employees in December 1995. Faced with insecurities resulting from American-driven globalization — the triumph of neoliberalism qua "la pensée unique" — prominent left-wing intellec-tuals began to reassess republicanism's promise.[18] The political corol-lary of these developments was the creation of renegade PS minister Jean-Pierre Chevènement's Pôle Républicain, which in the 2002 elec-tions ran on an avowedly anti-European, pro-Republican platform and garnered a surprising 5 percent.

Still another strong incentive for revisiting the republican model derived from the ethnic hostilities that exploded in Central Europe during the early 1990s: above all, the bloody, fratricidal wars in the former Yugoslavia. In the eyes of French intellectuals, one of republi-canism's strong points was a no-nonsense, secularizing and centralizing, *étatiste* approach to politics — summarized by the concept of *laïcisation* — an approach that effectively trumped considerations of religious, ethnic, and regional difference. In the eyes of many commentators, postcommunist global political instability — the omnipresence of "failed states" and genocidal civil wars — confronted Europe with a potential immigration tidal wave. Given these new geopolitical chal-lenges, French republicanism, which had always stressed an inflexible, assimilationist model of citizenship — the so-called immigrants into Frenchmen approach — acquired new currency.[19] It offered an alternative to the fashionable 1990s ethos of multiculturalism, which French thinkers equated with the evils of romantic nationalism and neotribalism.

Neorepublicanism was the French intellectual response to the polit-ical conundrum posed in Benjamin Barber's 1997 book *Jihad vs. McWorld*. French opinion leaders viewed republicanism as a potential via media, or third way, capable of staving off the twin evils of religious fundamentalism (Jihad) and American-style hyperconsumerism (McDonaldization). Its leading intellectual advocates have been Régis Debray, Luc Ferry, and Alain Touraine.

One analyst has aptly glossed the republican revival's theoretical agenda in the following terms:

> To fall back on *la République* means to preserve the gains of the progressive tradition while withdrawing, however reluctantly, from the more radical positions that the demise of Stalinism and the exhaustion of social democratic labor movements have rendered untenable. Many left-wing intellectuals are allergic to the postmodern ambience because of all that still keeps them within the orbit of the critical rationalism of the Enlightenment. They simply refuse to pack up and walk over to the camp of liberalism, radical individualism, and unadulterated free-market ideology. They see the defense of the republican ideal as the only way to combine a commitment to social justice with the defense of civic liberties and to reconcile the role of the state in the reduction of inequalities and redistribution of wealth with the critique of the kind of totalitarianism on which the communist utopia ran aground.[20]

Still, in an era where scores of articles have appeared heralding the "death of the intellectual" (that is, the "intellectual engagé" following the mold of Voltaire, Victor Hugo, and Sartre), it seems that the "republican revival" is in part an exercise in political nostalgia. It permits French thinkers to reconnect with a more glorious, idealized past: Valmy, Rouget de Lisle, and the Year II; Michelet's inspired histories; the early years of the Third Republic, when, under the leadership of Léon Gambetta and Jules Ferry, the Enlightenment "Cult of Reason" at long last conquered the bogies of dogma, superstition, and provincial ignorance.[21]

Republicanism's return signifies the final nail in the coffin of the structuralism/poststructuralist dyad. From a methodological standpoint, it represents the triumph of "philosophy" over the "social sciences." It reaffirms the *philosophe* project of human self-determination vis-à-vis the 1950s mood of Spenglerian *Kulturpessimismus*. In retrospect structuralism's rise — and the poststructuralist vogue that succeeded it — corresponded to the widely sensed political impasse under de Gaulle's authoritarian presidency. It purveyed a determinism that suited the mood of political despair that predominated during the pre-'68 era. Structuralism claimed that, in comparison with the *longue durée*, conscious, intentional political change was meaningless. The ideology of Western humanism duped men and women into thinking they were autonomous "subjects." Building on the interpretation of modernity qua "nihilism" that had been developed by Nietzsche and Heidegger, structuralism countered that the idea of self-positing subjectivity was an illusion. Thus, according to Lévi-Strauss, we are all prisoners of "cultural codes." We are captives of "regimes of significa-tion" that predefine our innermost ability to think, speak, and act. When in *Les Mots et les choses* Foucault proclaimed the "death of man" — going on to observe that his disappearance would somehow *make us better off* — he merely summarized structuralism's basic, anti-humanist credo.

In a recent essay Martin Jay claims that "there can be no doubt that the issue of human rights was neglected by the ... poststructuralists, as it was by many of their predecessors, such as Nietzsche."[22] But this failing seems less an oversight than a systematic blind spot. After all, only with the greatest of difficulty can a philosophy such as Derrida's, that is pred-icated on the dismantling of the "logocentric" biases of Western thought, be reconciled with a conception of "human rights" whose intellectual pedigree derives from the eminently metaphysical tradition of modern natural law. As numerous critics have pointed out, the problem is that the poststructuralists' Nietzschean-derived hermeneutic of suspicion knows no logical stopping point. As intellectual solvents, deconstruction and Foucauldian genealogy are *too effective for their own good*. By the time they are through working their magic and casting their spells, all trace of substantiality has been eliminated. By relegating the "subject" to the history of philosophy's dustbin, the post-structuralists effectively precluded the prospect of a meaningful or effi-cacious resistance to "power." In contrast with Habermasian discourse ethics, deconstruction's centerpiece is the well-known adage that all understanding is a species of misunderstanding — a veritable nonstarter when the question of meaningful political change is at issue. It is no accident, then, that during the late 1980s feminists began abandoning deconstruction in droves.[23] As the late Edward Said once remarked:

> The effect of [deconstructionist] logic (the *mise en abîme*) is to reduce everything that we think of as having some extratextual leverage in the text to a textual function.... Derrida's key words ... are unregen-erate signs: he says that they cannot be made more significant than signifiers are. In some quite urgent way, then, there is something friv-olous about them, as all words that cannot be accommodated to a philosophy of serious need or utility are futile or unserious.[24]

Still, neorepublicanism's historical memory has proved highly selec-tive. Its advocates have conveniently occluded republicanism's concep-tual weaknesses and egregious historical missteps. After all, well before the excesses of the Year II (the dictatorial rule by the "Committees"), the Republic was the scene of the September massacres and Louis XVI's

summary beheading. For all its admirable qualities, Michelet's patriotism bears discomfiting affinities with the anticosmopolitan, romantic
nationalism that, today, given the return of ethnonationalism, seems so
problematic. The Third Republic witnessed not only the commendable
triumph of the Dreyfusards and *laïcisation*. In Northwest Africa and
Indochina, under the cover of the "mission civilisatrice," it practiced a
ruthless "social imperialism" that, in its wanton brutality, left little to
the imagination.[25] Early on, the conservative republicans — the so-
called Opportunists — triumphed over the radicals, a development that
sapped much of the nascent republic's political élan. Thus, in the words
of one historian:

> The opportunists, supporters of economic liberalism, were developing
> an overall conception of progress in which resounded a sort of distant
> echo of Saint-Simonism: expansion, greater knowledge of one
> another's worlds, increased activity in trade, industry, overall wealth,
> the gradual spread of prosperity, 'openings' of all kinds ... It ... could
> be described as *very American*.[26]

The Third Republic's record on the "social question" — the
economic misery of France's toiling, urban masses — was abysmal,
opening the door to challenges from the left and challenges by anarcho-
syndicalism. Its historical legacy will forever be stained by the pointless
slaughter of some twenty thousand Communards — one of nineteenth-
century Europe's truly great massacres. As one critic of republicanism
has pointed out, the Third Republic was the embodiment of political
paternalism: a mechanism for distancing rank and file citizens from the
apparatus of government, a byword for the hauteur and condescension
of the *classe politique*.[27] "One should remember," declares Jacques
Julliard, "that, armed with the immortal principles of 1789, this scoun-
drel Third Republic treated its colonies worse than Brezhnev dared to
treat Bulgaria; that it treated the working classes worse than we treat
immigrants [today] ... Its professors and instructors ... constituted a
motley crew of schemers, bootlickers, and money-grubbers."[28]

Although, to its credit, the Third Republic persevered for seventy years,
as a parliamentary system it was beset by instability and endemic structural weakness. On more than one occasion, these conditions provided
fertile terrain for the claims of an authoritarian "savior": Général Boul-
anger in 1889; Colonel de la Rocque and his far-right allies in 1934;
and, lastly, Général de Gaulle, who ruled the Fifth Republic with an iron
hand during its first eleven years (1958–69). All three men were avowed
antiliberals, yet professed republicans. Nor should one harbor any illusions about the antidemocratic features of the constitution of 1875: an

autocratic presidency and an aristocratic Upper Assembly. As historian Claude Nicolet points out, only the eventual incorporation of "Anglo-American" liberties ("les grands principes libéraux déja enracinés en Angleterre et en Amérique") — separation of powers, individual rights, and popular sovereignty — prevented the Republic from turning into another instance of that recurrent French political deformation, *ministerial despotism.*[29]

Under the guise of "communitarianism," the ethos of republicanism has recently enjoyed a resurgence of interest among a talented international coterie of political philosophers. In North America its most vigorous advocates have been Michael Sandel, Charles Taylor, Sheldon Wolin, and Frank Michelman. In England its foremost champion has been the political theorist (and ex-Thatcherite) John Gray.

The main drawback of neorepublican political theory is that, in its aversion to the formal and procedural encumbrances of the *Rechtsstaat* or constitutional state, it overvalues the dimension of shared cultural traditions — what Hegel referred to as *Sittlichkeit* or "ethical life." Since contemporary democracies are afflicted by a surfeit of centrifugal tendencies coincident with the rise of modern individualism, the neorepublicans believe that an emphasis on shared "forms of life" (*Lebensformen*) will provide an element of desperately needed social cohesion. Yet, by pursuing this approach neorepublicans relativize democracy's core normative precepts: constitutionalism, rule of law, basic rights. Instead, they openly flirt with a communitarian orientation that prizes *ethnos* over *demos*: the ethical self-understanding of a given political community over the formal attributes of "public reason" (Rawls). Ultimately, this approach risks sacrificing considerations of principle to the contingent self-understanding of a determinate people or *Volk.* Viewed through the lens of the history of ideas, it is a credo that seeks to supplant *Kant* with *Herder*: the morally risky idea of the *Volksgeist* trumps the notion of universal moral legislation. The result is an ethical (in the Hegelian sense) foreshortening of political discourse. "Politics may not be assimilated to a hermeneutical process of self-explication of a shared form of life or collective identity. Political questions may not be reduced to the type of ethical questions where we, as members of a community, ask ourselves who we are and who we would like to be."[30] Once formal considerations of justice take a backseat to the values or belief system of a specific political community, we risk sacrificing general precepts to communal whim.

From a contemporary vantage point, republicanism's major failing has been its tone deafness to the demands of multicultural citizenship. Historically, this one-size-fits-all, "immigrants into Frenchmen" model of citizenship stands opposed to the American "melting pot" approach, which has typically celebrated ethnicity at the grassroots or neighborhood level. In the words of political scientist Dominique Schnapper: "The French political tradition has always refused to accept the American model of ethnicity. In the school, the factory, in the union, the 'ethnic' dimension has never been taken into account … The promotion of Frenchmen of foreign origin comes about *individually*, and not collectively through groups organized collectively."[31] There is perhaps no more striking illustration of this sentiment than Régis Debray's emphatic declaration in *Contretemps* that "A republic has no *black mayors, yellow senators, [or] Jewish ministers …*"[32] Thus, in stark contrast to the American conception, the goal of the French republican ideal has been a situation where, after several generations, nationality ceases to matter.

Yet whereas the assimilationist model may have worked for earlier generations of predominantly European immigrants, it seems patently inadequate to the immigration wave following decolonization. A casual stroll through the *bidonvilles* (slums) of Belleville or la Défense reveals more about the failure of the one-size-fits-all, republican model of citizenship than ten UNESCO conferences or one hundred memos by Nicholas Sarkozy (former Minister of the Interior and likely center-right 2007 presidential candidate).

France is home to five million Muslim immigrants. But until 2003 when President Jacques Chirac created a Central Islamic Council, French Muslims possessed no official representative organ or body — a step that Napoléon took for French Jewry in 1807, nearly two hundred years ago! Today, among the five hundred and seventy seven members of France's National Assembly, there are no Muslims. Nor are there any Muslim government ministers. Although France possesses nine thousand state-supported religious schools serving Catholics, Protestants, and Jews, there is currently only one Muslim lycée.[33]

In fact, until the 1980s, government policy toward North African immigrants was predicated on the expectation that, since many were recruited as laborers to remedy temporary manpower shortages, they would ultimately return voluntarily to their countries of origin. A late 1960s report published by France's Economic and Social Council presented the following striking conclusions: "It seems desirable … more and more to give to [immigrants] of non-European origin, principally [those] from the Maghreb, the character of *temporary immigration for work* … linked as much as possible to the need for labor … and in cooperation with the country of origin."[34] Strong evidence suggests that these policy recommendations were seriously pursued throughout the 1970s by the French authorities acting at both state and local levels.

In the late 1940s, the British sociologist T. H. Marshall formulated his famous theory of modern citizenship: an evolutionary progression from civic to political to social rights. One could make a plausible argument that the next stage in this sequence would be the recognition of cultural rights, which were the subject of a productive 1993 United Nations conference held in Vienna.

By the same token, it does not require a Solomon to realize that the debate over cultural rights demands a delicate balancing act. On the one hand, a basic sensitivity to cultural difference is imperative insofar as, for many individuals, cultural distinctiveness remains an indispensable source of meaning and fulfillment. Although vocational success might be viewed in terms of formal criteria, in many societies the terms of individual self-realization are still defined culturally. At the same time, multiculturalism's more ardent defenders often downplay the degree to which traditional cultures can be oppressive and limiting: especially, as has been widely documented, in the case of women.

Certainly, one cannot rule out the possibility that the republican model could be conceptually updated to accommodate the needs of difference. Yet, if one carefully examines the discourse of its contemporary exponents — Debray, Luc Ferry, and Pierre-André Taguieff — one finds a studied aversion to these questions and themes. Instead, the image of republicanism one encounters is a throwback to the 1870s. For example, in *Contretemps* Debray views "democracy," in stark contrast to republicanism, as a recipe for *multicultural anarchy*. It represents American-style "identity politics" gone haywire: the *sauve qui peut* (every man for himself) mentality of savage capitalism transposed to the sphere of culture. Thus, "neorepublican intellectuals frequently use the United States as an example of what life in France would be like if the nation continued to neglect the [unifying] features of the republican ideal. The United States is portrayed as a country ravaged by the selfish dictates of the marketplace and virtually 'Balkanized' by its racial, ethnic, and cultural divisions."[35] Of course, the practice of selectively highlighting American democracy's failings has the negative benefit of reinforcing the republican model's attractiveness.

Luc Ferry's spirited defense of republicanism takes on additional weight insofar as, until spring 2004, he was France's Minister of Education. As such, his ministry became the locus of France's fractious "culture wars" — the foulard affair and so forth. According to opinion polls, Ferry gained the dubious honor of being the most unpopular politician in the (Jean-Pierre) Raffarin ministry. Undoubtedly, this status was largely attributable to his striking inflexibility on the issue of *laïcité* — a term that connotes not only "secularism" but that has also become a byword for the utter tone deafness to "difference" of the imperious, radically assimilationist, "immigrants into Frenchmen" model of citizenship.

As one commentator has pointed out, "Perhaps the biggest contradiction of all resides in the fact that the republican ideal, once the inspiration for a veritable progressive cultural revolution, has become a much more conservative paradigm."[36] Worse still, in their open hostility to the

claims of cultural difference the neorepublicans seem to be openly
borrowing a page from the anti-immigrationist agenda of Le Pen's
National Front. It is at this point that the neorepublican veneration of
"Frenchness" risks transforming itself into something quite reactionary.
One could perhaps sympathize with the goals and intent of *laïcité* were
France's secular heritage at risk from a militantly antirepublican, ultra-
montane Catholicism. However, today the laicist agenda seems
woefully anachronistic — as though the French state and its defenders
were seeking to relaunch a battle it has already won.

Two years ago the world gazed on uncomprehendingly as the French
National Assembly vigorously reaffirmed the republican-assimilationist
credo by banning the Islamic headdress from public education.
The action was harshly criticized by leading intellectuals — the historian René Rémond and the sociologist Alain Touraine — who feared
that a blanket legal approach would only spawn new antagonisms
between French secularism and the nation's five million Muslim immigrants.[37] The reassertion of the assimilationist model contravenes the
broader European Union consensus that, in a global age, "multiculturalism" has become an indelible component of European identity, which,
in keeping with European traditions of tolerance, merits understanding
and acceptance. Equally disconcerting is the fact that the National
Assembly's recent decision regresses behind two earlier, more tolerant
Conseil d'Etat verdicts: a 1989 judgment that left enforcement of the
dress code up to local school authorities (the *circulaire Jospin*); and a
slightly more restrictive, 1994 ruling permitting the display of inconspicuous religious symbols, but forbidding more "ostentatious" displays
of religious affiliation should they, in the opinion of school authorities,
be worn with disruptive intent (the *circulaire Bayrou*). (A November
1995 Conseil d'Etat ruling had reaffirmed that the foulard itself was not
intrinsically "ostentatious.")

Nevertheless, in the interests of fairness, a word must be said on
behalf of the foulard's left-wing critics. Among French socialists, one
prominent concern — and hardly a misplaced one — is the subjugation
of women under fundamentalist Islam. As such, the French Left's objections to the Islamic headdress are related to the emancipatory goals of
Western feminism: above all, a fear that perpetuating the patriarchal
biases of traditional Islam means that women would be relegated to
second-class citizenship.

The socialists' major failing has been to omit a context-sensitive,
cultural reading of the foulard as a politicotheological symbol. When
second-generation Muslim girls comport the foulard in metropolitan
France, this act has a very different meaning than it does in societies
where traditional Islam is practiced. In a French context, it becomes
a gesture of cultural hybridity. Among Muslim women the foulard

represents a form of protest against what they perceive as republicanism's racist core: the patronizing demand that followers of Islam abandon their cultural identity in a nation where they are habitually regarded as second-class citizens.

At what point does French exceptionalism translate into French provincialism? Undeniably, "French philosophy of the 1980s" engaged in a productive dialogue with liberalism — something of a watershed in the history of French political thought. At the same time, if one carefully surveys the terms of debate, one cannot help but be struck by its discursive insularity. Inevitably, the points of reference are well-nigh exclusively *French* — Constant, Tocqueville, and Victor Cousin. Thus, despite the efflorescence of a global intellectual culture, to peruse the recent French debates, one would be tempted to conclude that liberalism was a French invention — *une affaire franco-française*, as it were. Surprisingly, the contributions of Locke, Kant, and Mill are rarely mentioned. As one insightful critic of liberalism à la *française* has observed:

Ultimately, the greater value of [Lilla's] collection is anthropological rather than philosophical; there is something rather compelling about watching a collection of French thinkers grapple with an idiom which is so completely alien to their discursive instincts and cultural traditions. But while this effort to broaden their intellectual horizons is laudable, parochialism dies hard in France. It is unfortunate that modern French liberals — at least most of the ones assembled here — do not seem to have thought seriously about the philosophical works of their colleagues in the Anglo-American tradition. After all, it is not impossible that men and women who have been thinking about liberalism for much longer than they could have something to contribute to French liberalism.[38]

Let me provide a concrete illustration of where recent trends in French political thought have gone amiss. The republican revival of the 1990s was meant to address the limitations of neoliberalism, which French thinkers associate with "marketization" qua "la pensée unique." Previously, I have reviewed republicanism's shortcomings. I would like to suggest that the missing term in contemporary debates over French political thought is "deliberative democracy" — a term that, during the 1990s, has had a rich career in both European and North American political thought. The deliberative democracy approach has a distinct advantage over "republicanism," insofar as it incorporates the two breakthroughs of modern politics: the complementary goals of private and public autonomy, individual rights and popular sovereignty. Republicanism's historical weakness lies in its tendency to sacrifice autonomy on the altar of patriotism. Moreover, by valuing *national* sovereignty over *popular* sovereignty it undervalues civil liberties and openly courts antidemocratic, *étatiste* biases. Deliberative democracy, conversely, strives to limit the risks of political technocracy — government by unresponsive, administrative elites — by expanding the bases of democratic will formation. It promotes the expansion of autonomous public spheres, thereby cultivating the development of public opinion at the grassroots level. It envisions the expansion and dissemination of the value of "public reason," in contrast to what John Rawls once referred to as "comprehensive worldviews." In this way, it seeks to promote an ethic of public responsibility vis-à-vis an ethic of ultimate ends — one of the primary sources of ethical and political intolerance. Deliberative democracy seeks to approximate the counterfactual ideal of basing political decisions on norms to which all parties could agree should they become participants in an actual dialogue.

Postscript
Hexagon Fever

In the fall of 2001 a slight book with a stern title, *Call to Order: Investigation concerning the New Reactionaries*, sent minor shock waves throughout Parisian intellectual circles. The book's author was Daniel Lindenberg, a historian and frequent contributor to the left-liberal monthly, *Esprit*.

The key to understanding this tempest is in the book's subtitle. Who are the purported "New Reactionaries"? Do they share a common ideology? And, if so, is it worth much time and energy to expose their alleged misdeeds?

Among Lindenberg's antagonists are:

- literary enfant terrible Michel Houllebecq. This novelist is the author of *The Elementary Particles*, a merciless indictment of the narcissistic excesses and unbridled hedonism supposedly practiced by the ex-68ers who have dominated French cultural and intellectual life for the past three decades. In a recent outburst, he has also referred to Islam as "the stupidest religion of all" ("La religion la plus con"), an offense for which he was sued for religious defamation by two of France's leading Islamic organizations;

- novelists Philippe Muray and Michel Dantec. Although they are less well known in the Anglo-Saxon world, Muray and Dantec, like Houllebecq, have expressed a similar revulsion against left-wing "political correctness," in various forms like antiracism and cultural populism. They also attack what they see as libidinal licentiousness bordering on social irresponsibility;

- Luc Ferry, a philosopher and now minister of education under the current Chirac-Raffarin regime. In *French Philosophy of the 1960s* (co-written with Alain Renaut) and other works, Ferry pointedly criticized hedonistic individualism as an unintended outcome of the May '68 student revolt. More recently, Ferry has been a noted champion of "republicanism," a political ethos that privileges the well-being of the nation over individual rights and liberties;
- Marcel Gauchet, co-editor of the influential quarterly *Le Débat* and the author of *Democracy against Itself*, a collection of essays criticizing the corrosive effects of democratic individualism;
- Pierre Manent, a noted political philosopher and disciple of Leo Strauss, who has written a number of books that criticize the insufficiencies of political liberalism.

Lindenberg thinks these figures are united in an unholy alliance against France's reigning democratic political consensus. They are, he believes, neo-Spenglerian prophets of decline, who reprise the lamentations of counterrevolutionary *Kulturkritik*, denouncing the failings of mass society in the mandarinesque idiom of the German 1920s.

Lindenberg complains that this antiliberal idiom has flourished not only among the anti-'68 literati, but also among leftists. He identifies a trio of former followers of the late communist philosopher Louis Althusser as the main offenders. In Lindenberg's view, Etienne Balibar, Alain Badiou, and Jacques Rancière are stridently dismissive of French socialism's genuine achievements: maintaining the minimal trappings of the welfare state despite formidable international pressures to "liberalize"; standing up to the xenophobic populism of Jean-Marie Le Pen's National Front; stressing "human rights" as the indispensable moral-political basis of the expanding European Union. The ex-Althusserians belittle these gains in stereotypically Marxist fashion as an ideological ruse that masks bourgeois interest, in this case, the globalization agenda. Lindenberg thinks that this sort of politics has deprived French socialists of badly needed support on the left. Now the socialists are in dire political straits — easy prey for the Gaullists whose grip on power seems, for the foreseeable future, unchallengeable.

Call to Order reads like a hastily conceived book. It weighs in at fewer than 100 pages. Still, it appears to have scored a direct hit against its targets. For several weeks, *Le Monde, Le Figaro,* and *Le Nouvel Observateur* opened their pages to Lindenberg's detractors and defenders. The fallout from the "Lindenberg debate" was dissected by journalists throughout Europe, in keeping with the (risky) maxim that Parisian intellectual strife is inherently newsworthy. At the same time, many French *maîtres-à-penser* (master thinkers) sought to belittle the controversy as much ado about nothing. And in January

2003 *Esprit* — Lindenberg's journalistic base — published a sizeable dossier harshly critical of his book's main tenets.

Nevertheless, this overheated debate attests to the fact that the book touched a raw nerve. It seems to have exposed the divisions that, in recent years, have rent the French intellectual left. In the eyes of many, these fissures were in part responsible for the Socialist Party's disastrous performance in the first round of the 2002 presidential elections, in which Lionel Jospin ran behind Le Pen (who, in the ensuing runoff, was handily bested by Jacques Chirac.)

Lindenberg doesn't propose that the "new reactionaries" actually conspired against the Fifth Republic's left-liberal political culture. He does maintain that, wittingly or unwittingly, they undermined the democratic-egalitarian political consensus that has been actively fostered during the two decades that the Socialist Party dominated French politics. Between 1981 and 2000, there were only two years — 1995–97 — during which the Socialists failed to hold the office of president or prime minister. One of Lindenberg's motivations in condemning the "new reactionaries" — both "right" and "left" — was to defend the honor of the last twenty years of Socialist governance.

Among "literary reactionaries" like Houllebecq, Muray, and Dantec, it is fashionable to question left-wing "political correctness." They have tried to show in a deliberately provocative manner that the "Other" is not always the loveable and well-intentioned soul he or she is made out to be according to antiracist pedagogy. All three authors tried to unsettle the commonplaces of French "antiracism," which, since the 1980s, have served as a left-liberal mainstay against the chauvinism of the National Front. Yet since the "antiantiracist" idiom in question transpires in a largely *literary* discourse, it is hard to know just how seriously to take the "offending" speech acts.

Lindenberg seems to have overplayed his hand by drawing parallels between contemporary antidemocratic disaffection and two previous epochs: the 1890s, which saw the emergence of a vituperative, anti-Republican and anti-Semitic right led by Action Française founder Charles Maurras; and the 1930s, in which "nonconformist" intellectuals and politicos crossed over from "left" to "right" in significant numbers, thereby preparing the ideological terrain for Vichy. One reason why Lindenberg's search for historical antecedents seems tenuous is that figures like Ferry, Gauchet, and ex-Guevarista Régis Debray (another of Lindenberg's *bêtes noires*) remain convinced republicans. Hence, although each has chastised Socialist Party orthodoxies — often from the left — to tar them with the "new reactionary" label as Lindenberg does defies common sense.

Few would deny that Lindenberg provoked an extremely confused debate. Nevertheless, the controversy reveals fault lines within the

French left and reflects the disorientation that arose following Le Pen's "April surprise" in the 2002 elections. (It is worth noting that the French press commonly compares the April 21 débâcle — without a trace of irony — to the September 11 terror attacks.) As Jospin's presidential aspirations collapsed, commentators proclaimed the end of the era that began with Mitterrand's 1971 Epinay-sur-Seine program and crested with his election to the presidency ten years later. Above all, the Lindenberg affair reveals the existence of overlapping crises: a crisis of the French left that overlaps with an intellectual crisis and a general crisis of European socialism.

Jospin's defeat left Mitterrand's Socialist Party (PS) in tatters. In 1993 legislative elections with Mitterrand president, the Gaullists won 500 National Assembly seats to a mere 50 for the Socialists. But, thanks to a magisterial political blunder by Chirac — a premature call for new legislative elections — the PS, now led by Jospin, recovered and became the majority party once again in 1997. Jospin moved to the Matignon (the prime minister's residence).

Following the 1993 setback, several outstanding, even charismatic, candidates positioned themselves to be Mitterrand's heir. These included ex-Prime Ministers Laurent Fabius and Michel Rocard, former European Commission president Jacques Delors (who eventually decided not to seek the party leadership), as well as Jospin. In the eighteen months since the 2002 defeat, however, no clear leader has emerged. Relatively bland figures such as François Hollande, Dominique Strauss-Kahn, and Pierre Moscovici, all of whom convey competence rather than charisma, have jockeyed for power. The reigning consensus suggests that none of them is "presidentiable." Last spring's party congress at Dijon seems to have resolved few issues. For a long time, Mitterrand's knack for electoral success allowed him to camouflage the PS's ideological confusion. But the party's 2002 thrashing left party stalwarts without cover. Mitterrand's political origins were one complicating factor. When he refashioned a moribund French socialist party at the Epinay Congress in 1971, marking the birth of the "modern" PS, Mitterrand opportunistically crossed over politically from a small center-republican party.

In his very early years — back in the 1930s — he flirted with far-right politics, attending meetings of the conspiratorial, antirepublican Cagoule ("monk's cowl"). Following a stint as a prisoner of war, he served as an administrator under Pétain before joining the Resistance circa 1942. Before his change, Mitterrand was personally rewarded by Pétain with Vichy's highest honor, the *francisque*. Many of these facts first came to light in 1994 when Pierre Péan's biography of Mitterrand, *Une Jeunesse française*, was published. Mitterand's PS comrades were shocked to learn that their leader had also maintained close personal ties with René Bousquet. This ex-Vichy police commissioner had been responsible for the infamous July 1942 deportation of French Jews. From a political standpoint, Péan's revelations were indispensable in understanding Mitterrand. They demonstrated that his "anticapitalist" sentiments derived not from socialist ideas but from the right-wing Catholic milieu he frequented as a youth.

These facts allow us to make more sense of Mitterrand's dizzying political opportunism. He ceaselessly reinvented himself. First he was a right-wing nationalist, then a Vichyite, then a *résistant*, then a unifier of the left, then an Olympian President, and finally an ardent Europeanist. When his two-term presidency finally ended in 1995, he seemed more of an enigma than ever. The man was once one of the Fifth Republic's leading critics (in 1964 he penned a scathing diatribe against the "presidential republic" called *The Permanent Coup D'etat*), ultimately turned its institutions to his own advantage. His fourteen year "reign" — an "imperial presidency" if ever there was one — lasted longer than any French head-of-state since the Second Empire of Louis Bonaparte. By the end it seemed that his sole passion was a desire for power.

What had he supported as a "Socialist"? The 1971 PS platform stressed a "rupture with capitalism." Mitterrand reoriented the French left around a neo-Keynesian program of radical, state-driven reforms (expansion of the public sector, widespread nationalizations, income redistribution). This allowed the PS to fashion its 1972 "Programme Commun," or alliance with the then powerful and ever Stalinist French Communist Party (PCF). Mitterrand realized that without the PCF — the Communists were still attracting close to 20 percent of the French vote — he would never win the presidency.

The political alliance with the communists failed to survive the first two years of Mitterrand's presidency (1981–83). The socialists learned that an individual nation-state could not isolate itself from global economic trends. The Mitterrand government paid dearly for its initial orgy of state spending and nationalizations. Indeed, by the end of 1981 inflation was rampant, reaching 14.1 percent. The franc was devalued three times in Mitterrand's first two years.

So he reversed policy, switching from Keynesianism to monetarism. A "modernization" drive aimed to "streamline" the public sector, despite the fact that civil servants represented the PS's leading electoral constituency. Although Mitterrand arrived in power with a platform that promised full employment and a break with capitalism, France soon underwent draconian austerity measures, a wave of privatizations, and a "break with socialism." The Epinay program had proclaimed that "socialist transformation" sought "not to manage a system *but to replace it with another.*"[1] Yet, in a January 1984 television appearance Mitterrand declared: "the French are beginning to understand: it is *the firm* that creates wealth, it is *the firm* that creates employment, it is *the firm* that decides our standard of living and our place in the world hierarchy."[2] In short, the PS now seemed to pursue a benign version of the marketization strategies that in Anglo-Saxon countries were associated with Thatcher and Reagan.

"Europe," or a push for greater European economic and political integration, was the cover under which Mitterrand pursued these reforms. In this way, political responsibility for unpopular economic measures could be blamed on Brussels (the seat of the European Commission). But French socialism's radical change of course was not accompanied by any serious philosophical or doctrinal adjustments. Party rhetoric continued to reflect the values represented by the heyday of European social democracy — the so-called thirty glorious years from 1945 to 1975 — despite the fact that socialism's traditional class basis had altered radically.

The collapse of communism finally undid socialist *dirigisme*. By the time of Mitterrand's exit from politics in 1995, the country suffered from a structural unemployment rate that hovered around 12 percent. As historian Serge Berstein has aptly remarked, "All that was left in the wreckage were liberal policies: market forces, free competition, monetary orthodoxy, a balanced budget without a balance of payments deficit, and an unregulated labor market. The left had completely lost its identity."[3] Those who sought to mount a fresh approach, such as the PS's Rocardian wing — advocates of workers' self-management and market socialism — remained marginalized (despite the fact that Michel Rocard served as prime minister from 1988 to 1991). The consequence was an identity crisis about the very meaning of "socialism." The contradictions of the Mitterrand era finally caught up with the PS in April 2002. Le Pen won 16.9 percent and the PS won 16.2 percent of the vote. Two Trotskyist candidates attracted 10 percent. The Communists registered an anemic 3.3 percent.

In part, the explanation is simple: voters on the left who wished to protest globalization or the tyranny of markets opted for one of the Trotskyists over Jospin. It was little consolation for the PS that Chirac's 19.88 total was the worst ever for an incumbent president. The Socialists had to cope with the depressing fact that only 14 percent of its active members were under 40 and adherents over 60 years old make up 40 percent of the party. The PS electoral base is rapidly reaching the age of retirement and new, younger militants are hard to find.

One irony of the PS's defeat was that Jospin had comported himself relatively well in office. After the 1993 electoral débâcle, he revived the party through a novel "gauche plurielle" ("plural left"), that is, a coalition of the PS with the Communists, Greens, and Jean-Pierre Chèvenement's anti-European Citizen's Movement. Jospin restored integrity to the socialist leadership (there were many scandals during the later Mitterrand years) and instituted a series of progressive economic reforms: the 35-hour work week (at no loss of pay) as well as an ambitious youth employment program. He pushed through tough new measures to ensure electoral parity for PS women. Above all, he reduced unemployment. Between 1997 and 2002, joblessness declined from 12.4 percent to 9.1 percent.

Jospin also kept his distance from the "third way" approach proclaimed by fellow European socialists like Britain's Tony Blair and Germany's Gerhard Schröder. He remained wedded rhetorically and ideologically to redistributive ideals and paid lip service to antiglobalization rhetoric. Still, he also pursued strategies designed to enhance France's global competitiveness and this may have proved crucial in his undoing.[4] Jospin was outflanked on the far left. Some commentators called it the revenge of French socialism's "Marxist superego." The French far left has few parallels elsewhere in Europe and it chastised the PS as "social liberal." In the meantime, Chèvenement, the Greens, and the Communists all ran hard against the PS in the first round of presidential voting, playing directly into the hands of the National Front.

This brings us back to Lindenberg's acrimonious book. Viewed in a political-intellectual optic, it appears as an attempt to settle scores with left-wing intellectuals who positioned themselves to the *left of the established left*. In Lindenberg's view, these figures were indirectly responsible for the 2002 embarrassment. More generally, however, the Lindenberg debate suggests a breakdown of the "antitotalitarian political consensus" that, for two decades, functioned as the reigning paradigm among French intellectuals.

In the post – World War II decades "French exceptionalism" signified the major role the PCF played in a national political life that markedly contrasted to other Western European democracies (excepting Italy). Marxism dominated left-leaning French intellectuals. But there was a volte-face in the 1970s. Revelations about Pol Pot's "killing fields" were interpreted against the background of the "Solzhenitsyn effect." The publication of *The Gulag Archipelago* in 1974 permanently undermined the French romance with communism. The Soviet invasion of Afghanistan in 1979, coupled with the 1981 declaration of martial law in Poland, and the crushing by Polish Communists of the budding Solidarity movement, appeared to tarnish irremediably Marxism's fate among French intellectuals. Havel, Sakharov, and Walesa replaced Marx, Lenin, and Mao in the left-wing intellectual pantheon of the 1980s.

But this antitotalitarian consensus began to unravel during the massive December 1995 public sector strikes protesting attempts to restructure France's generous pension system. Journals leaning to social liberalism like *Esprit* supported the conservative government's retrenchment policy, whereas *Marxisant* intellectuals such as the late Pierre Bourdieu cast their lot with striking workers and chastised globalization. In 1997 Jospin became prime minister under President Jacques Chirac. Yet it soon became clear that the Socialist response to EU-decreed, anti-inflationary austerity measures differed little from the strategies proposed by the Gaullists.

Left-leaning French intellectuals soon concluded that the antitotalitarian intellectual consensus failed to provide a program for the 1990s. A new leftist mantra was heard: *human rights is not a politics*. This may be true, but a slogan like this seriously underestimated the beneficial change that resulted from acceptance of the antitotalitarian ethos in the first place. In the 1970s it provided a badly needed exit strategy from all varieties of left-wing dogmatism. Today, some aging *gauchistes* appear to be suffering from political memory loss or they missed the point. The best way to combat the excesses of globalization is not via regression to the homilies of left-wing sectarianism but by extending logics of democratization that rely on human rights as an indispensable safeguard against the ever-present dangers of authoritarian political relapse.

Coda

During the summer of 2003, just when it appeared that things couldn't get any worse for the PS, another challenge arose from the antiglobalization movement led by José Bové, spokesman for the Confédération Paysanne (Farmers' Confederation). Bové achieved fame in 1999 when he was arrested for bulldozing a McDonald's restaurant under construction in the southern town of Millau. In June 2003 he was arrested again, this time for destroying stocks of genetically modified rice. After two months in prison, Bové was released last August and immediately staged a back-to-the-land, counter-globalization festival/protest in the Larzac region of southern France. Organizers had anticipated 100,000 protesters; according to reliable accounts, twice that many showed up. Flush with success, Bové, alluding to last summer's unprecedented heat wave (which, according to the latest statistics, was responsible for some 15,000 deaths), warned of a "red-hot" September (*un Septembre brulânt*). His revulsion for the PS — whose exhibit at the Larzac gathering was pointedly "dismantled" by antiglobalization activists — is well known. He disparages the PS as neoliberals and perceived the Jospin ministry as a little more than a Trojan Horse for the IMF and backers of the European Monetary Union (EMU).

Although the media-savvy Bové has gained considerable notoriety for his neo-Luddite antics, he has been reprimanded recently by fellow protesters for being too camera-friendly. After the McDonald's incident one of Bove's longtime allies, ex-Situationist René Riesel, demonstratively broke with him, claiming the Confédération Paysanne spokesman had succumbed to "bovémania." Nor did Bové do much to enhance his credibility as a left-wing advocate when, returning from a visit to the Middle East in spring 2002, he announced on French radio that the Mossad (the Israeli Secret Service) was behind the recent, nationwide attacks on French synagogues and other Jewish sites. Many savor the irony that Bové, the antiglobalization movement's poster child, has become an international media celebrity and thus one of global society's primary beneficiaries. Bové has also been criticized by Doctors Without Borders founder and former PS Minister of Health Bernard Kouchner — the PS's most popular and trusted political figure. According to Kouchner, Bové's knee-jerk populism and antiparliamentarism are more reminiscent of the tactics and orientation of the nativist political right than the left. Kouchner went so far as to compare Bové's antiglobalization orientation to that of Pierre Poujade, who during the 1950s led a short-lived smallholder's revolt against the Fourth Republic.

These criticisms seem to have taken their toll on Bové. He has now announced his intention to resign as spokesman for the Confédération Paysanne. For the moment, he represents more of a thorn in the side of the ailing PS as opposed to a serious political threat.

11

What Is Global Democracy?

The "Third Wave"

As denizens of the twenty-first century, we are the beneficiaries of the so-called Third Wave of democratization. As recently as 1975, authoritarian regimes presided over 68 percent of the world's nations. As of 2000, conversely, this figure had shrunk to 26 percent — a remarkable turnabout by any standard.

Democracy's most recent wave dates back to the democratic transitions in Portugal, Spain, and Greece during the mid-1970s. Ten years later, similar democratic enthusiasms seized hold of the nations of South America, putting an end to decades of brutal and oppressive authoritarian-military rule.

In 1989 — also the French Revolution's bicentennial year — Central Europe's Velvet Revolutions, precipitating the collapse of the political dictatorships of "really existing socialism," constituted a historical watershed. In May 2004 another breakthrough was attained as the Velvet Revolutions' progeny — the independent states of Poland, Latvia, the Czech Republic, Slovenia, and so forth — became full-fledged members of the European Union.

In retrospect, it is easy to take the outcome of these revolutions — the largely successful, if fitful, transition to democracy — for granted. Yet, much of their success may be attributed to the actors' emphatic rejection of the Jacobin-Bolshevik revolutionary model — historically, one of the leading paradigms of left-wing authoritarianism. Instead, the Eastern European dissidents self-consciously opted for an alternative conception of social change: the model of democratization from below, or so-called *self-limiting revolutions*. It was undoubtedly this conscious strategy of self-limitation — the democratic self-organization of civil society — that goes far to explaining their relatively positive outcomes.

How is it that the Central European opposition movement arrived at this particular recipe for political change? With the 1960s strategy of political reform from above — the Dubček experiment in "enlightened socialist despotism" — at a dead end following the 1968 Warsaw Pact invasion of Prague, the reformers sought a new approach. The military crushing of the Prague Spring put to rest the illusion that a democratic wing within the Communist Party might have the capacity to institute the necessary reforms. The dissident movement now placed its trust in social groups that were outside of and opposed to the traditional Communist Party hierarchy: students, workers, church groups, and oppositional cultural organizations. As Workers' Defense Committee (KOR) cofounder Adam Michnik explained in a 1976 essay, "The New Evolutionism" (written in the months following the historic Helsinki Accords legally obligating the nations of Eastern Europe to respect human rights):

> An unceasing struggle for reform and evolution that seeks an expansion of civil liberties and human rights is the only course East European dissidents can take.... To draw a parallel with events at the other end of our continent, one could say that the ideas of the Polish democratic opposition resemble the Spanish ... model. This is based on gradual and piecemeal change, not violent upheaval and forceful destruction of the existing system.[1]

Remarkably, creditable democratic transitions have also occurred in regions with little prior experience in democratic government: South Africa as well as Asian nations such as South Korea. Such instances of relatively successful democratization have given the lie to a claim that has been one of the staples of postmodernist cultural relativism: that government predicated on human rights and popular sovereignty might be suitable for various Western nations but is inappropriate elsewhere.

Instead, recent political developments have shown that, by underestimating the capacity of peoples around the globe for political self-determination, defenders of cultural relativism have succumbed to a different manner of prejudice. One of the lessons we have learned from democratization's Third Wave is that democracy and cultural difference, far from being incompatible, are complementary. One of democracy's distinct advantages is that it provides an open-ended, procedural framework for collective self-determination, a framework that is compatible with a wide variety of "forms of life" or particular cultural identities. Hence, one of the keys to successful democratization is that "comprehensive" or eschatological worldviews remain bracketed in favor of the temporizing balm of "public reason" (Rawls). Max Weber hinted at a similar conclusion when in "Politics as a Vocation" he distinguished between an "ethic of responsibility" and an "ethic of ultimate ends." Modern life's irreducible value pluralism makes it impossible to agree on ultimate value choices or the ideal path toward "salvation." Yet, we *can* agree on a system of political rules that allows us to pursue these ends in private and associational life.

Democracy's first wave — which would perhaps be more accurately described as a powerful ripple — coincided with the French and American revolutions. It is worth noting that when France proclaimed the birth of the Third Republic some eighty years later (1870), only *three* other republics existed in continental Europe at that time: Luxembourg, Switzerland, and Holland.

Democratization's second wave emerged following the collapse of the Central European monarchies in 1918. However, this wave was distinctly short-lived. The war itself — which claimed a staggering total of fifteen million lives and ruined countless others — was at best a pyrrhic victory for the Western powers. Its physical and moral toll unquestionably did more to *delegitimate* European cultural ideals than reinforce them. In nineteenth-century Europe, state formation oscillated between civic and ethnic conceptions of nationalism — between Rousseau and Herder, as it were.[2] Burgeoning nation-states alternated between competing definitions of citizenship: *jus soli*, which stressed its voluntarist and elective components, and *jus sanguinis*, which accorded priority to questions of ethnicity and descent. Woodrow Wilson's Fourteen Points famously emphasized the prerogatives of national self-determination. This formula sounded fine in principle but proved disastrous in practice. For in lieu of effective guarantees for minority rights, what resulted in the war's aftermath was a turbulent orgy of competing ethnicities — an extension of the same poisonous, ethnopopulist mentality that had engendered the war in the first place. Democracy had nominally triumphed, but often in an adulterated, retrograde version. In essence, the integral nationalism of Maurice Barrès, Heinrich Treitschke, and Mussolini had temporarily bested the liberal nationalism recommended by Rousseau, Kant, and Giuseppe Mazzini.

The Search for Authority

In the succeeding years, the fervor of integral nationalism would succeed in stifling the emancipatory promises of its civic-democratic counterpart. For a brief shining moment liberal democracy — the political legacy of the nineteenth century — seemed the norm. Following the Great Crash of 1929, however, the democratic wager seemed an entirely lost cause.

Dictatorship proved to be the next political wave. The new political reality was recognized by Carl Schmitt, who, during the 1920s, glorified dictatorship at the expense of parliamentary-democratic normalcy. The first sentence of Schmitt's 1922 book on *Political Theology* famously proclaimed: "Sovereign is he who decides in the state of exception" (*Ausnahmezustand*). In Schmitt's view, the authoritarian military cabal under Ludendorff and Hindenburg that ruled Germany during the last year of the war established an important precedent. Lenin's voluntarist recasting of orthodox Marxism, which presaged the October 1917 Bolshevik seizure of power, was certainly of equal importance. Thus, following the short-lived Hungarian Soviet Republic, Admiral Horthy established a dictatorial regime in Hungary. Primo de Rivera seized power in Spain, Antonio Salazar followed suit in Portugal, and Marshal Pilsudski established authoritarian rule in Poland.

But the most important precedent was set in 1922 by Mussolini's March on Rome, which inspired Hitler's unsuccessful Munich Putsch attempt the following year. In his Naples speech just prior to the October 1922 coup, Il Duce proclaimed: "We have created a myth; this myth is a belief, a noble enthusiasm; it does not need to be reality ... Our myth is *the nation*, the great nation which we want to make into a concrete reality." His contempt for liberal democracy set the tone for the refashioning of the European Right during the interwar years:

> Fascism rejects in Democracy the conventional lie of political equality, the spirit of collective irresponsibility and the myth of happiness and indefinite progress ... One should not exaggerate the importance of Liberalism in the last century and make of it a religion of humanity for all present and future times when in reality it was only one of the many doctrines of that century ... All political experiments of the contemporary world are *anti-liberal* ... The present century is the century of authority, a century of the Right, *a Fascist century*.[3]

Since the fin de siècle, talk of European decline had been rife. On the right, assertions of "political will" were valorized in quasi-eschatological terms. It was widely believed that dictatorship alone could redeem

Christian Europe from a rising tide of atheism, communism, and "decadence" — in sum, the ills of "mass society." In this way, the "revolt against reason" that dominated fin de siècle thought and culture — the profound intellectual influence of European thinkers such as Nietzsche, Dilthey, Bergson, and Georges Sorel — found a corresponding political outlet.[4]

In the 1930s the floodgates burst. Disdain for democracy reached new heights. Europe was inundated by a new wave of authoritarian political challenges. Although the Nazi seizure of power officially dates from 1933, in its waning years the Weimar Republic was already run by presidential decree, thanks to the antidemocratic provisions subtending the constitution's notorious Article 48.[5] In February 1934, the Austrian Right, bolstered by Chancellor Dollfus's dictatorship, "cleaned house" in Red Vienna as well as the provinces. In this way "Austria followed Portugal in pioneering the kind of self-consciously Christian nationalism that would later permeate Slovakia, Spain, Greece, Croatia, and Vichy France, as well as right-wing politics in Poland, Hungary, and Romania."[6] That same month, France endured an abortive right-wing coup attempt — an assault from which, in many respects, the Third Republic never recovered. In 1936 the republican cause began to founder in Spain under the weight of attacks by the Falange as well as Franco's legionnaires.

The growing consensus among European diplomatic circles was that democracy was not suitable for all nations, nor were all nations suited for democracy. Western statesmen harbored few ethical objections to dealing with the likes of Mussolini and Franco, both of whom, after all, had performed a "useful" ideological service in keeping communism at bay. As a young American diplomat, George Kennan, remarked at the time: "benevolent despotism has greater possibilities for the good" than democracy. He recommended that the United States, too, travel the "road which leads from constitutional change to the authoritarian state."[7]

Many observers agreed that liberalism promoted deleterious centrifugal social and economic tendencies. Hence, it was widely held that authoritarianism represented a desirable corrective to liberalism's manifold excesses. The ideology of clerico-fascism vigorously contested the Enlightenment shibboleth concerning the "infinite perfectibility of man." Seeking to draw political lessons from the doctrine of original sin, it viewed "man" as a fundamentally dangerous creature — motivated by base, animal instincts and, hence, inherently untrustworthy. Since human beings were constitutionally incapable of self-rule, authoritarian government was perceived as the logical mechanism to save humanity from its own degenerative tendencies.

Democracy and Discontent

In recent years political scientists have researched the preconditions and elements of successful democratic transitions. As we have seen, twentieth-century history is replete with lessons concerning the fragility of democratic rule. We possess no guarantees that democratization's Third Wave will not be subject to reversals analogous to those experienced by the nations of Central and Eastern Europe following World War I. In April 2004 news reports highlighted growing dissatisfaction with democracy in two of the world's major regions: Russia and South America. For months Russian human rights activists have been alarmed by the summary arrest and conviction of multimillionaire Mikhail Khodorovsky on unsubstantiated corruption charges. There is a growing consensus that if enhanced economic growth were to be achieved at the cost of a return to political authoritarianism, the price would be well worth paying. Although few fear that a return to the dark days of Stalinism is imminent, "the notable thing is the degree to which much of the public has accepted — even embraced — new limitations on [civil liberties]."[8]

Nor has democracy in Latin America proved an unmitigated blessing. Colombia, Venezuela, and Peru have been rife with social and political instability — whose causes in most cases predate the democratic transitions of the 1980s. South American economies are a testament to globalization's false promises: whereas since the 1990s first world affluence has risen steadily, third world nations, in order to qualify for desperately needed capital infusions from the World Bank and International Monetary Fund, have been subjected to draconian "belt-tightening" strictures. Consequently, throughout the Southern Hemisphere democratization has been accompanied by demoralizing economic stagnation instead of the widely pledged standard of living increases. According to a detailed report issued in April 2004 by the UN Development Program, "the first generation of Latin Americans to come of age under widespread democracy has experienced virtually no per capita income growth, and disparities in the distribution of income is widening."[9]

The South American case demonstrates that economic and social injustice, which have been in part ameliorated in many first world nations, remain widespread elsewhere. The danger is that following the precedent of interwar Europe, endemic economic hardship will translate into a disqualification of democracy *simpliciter* — a pressing concern in a region where, according to one recent poll, 55 percent claim they would enthusiastically support a return to authoritarian rule were it to prove economically advantageous.[10]

One of globalization's irreversible consequences is enhanced social and political interconnectedness. Thus, it would be unwise to view the loss of democratic self-confidence in Russia and Latin America as essentially localizable phenomena. Instead, like the Asian economic collapse of the late 1990s, these developments may have unanticipated ripple effects: massive unrepaid bank loans and substantial emigration waves. On both moral and pragmatic grounds it falls due to the Northern Hemisphere's affluent nations to address these problems.

Despite the European Union's considerable economic and political achievements, it would be erroneous to claim that, today, European democracy has become risk free. For during the last two decades right-wing authoritarian populist parties have made significant political and electoral inroads across the continent: France's Jean-Marie Le Pen, Austria's Jörg Haider, Belgium's Filip de Winter, and Italy's (somewhat mellowed) Gianfranco Fini. In the first round of France's 2002 presidential elections, Le Pen ousted Socialist Party candidate — and sitting Prime Minister — Lionel Jospin, precipitating a runoff with incumbent Jacques Chirac. In many respects, the Socialist Party, which, under François Mitterrand's guidance, dominated the landscape of French electoral politics during the 1980s and 1990s, has yet to recover politically from this unprecedented electoral debacle.

Although nowhere in Europe are these parties, which are dominated by a brazenly racist, anti-immigrant agenda, capable of acceding to power, they are likely to exert a baneful influence on the fabric of European political culture. Since their electoral totals have consistently ranged in the "respectable" vicinity of 10–15 percent, they have enjoyed a certain "kingmaker" status, often enticing mainstream parties to pander to their nativist, anti-European Union agendas. From an ideological standpoint, they represent an ominous throwback to the ethos of integral nationalism that, as we have seen, gained widespread favor during the interwar period. Their ethnocentric mentality is perhaps best captured by Le Pen's notorious "concentric circle" theory of politics: "I like my daughters better than my cousins, my cousins better than my neighbors, my neighbors better than strangers, and strangers better than foes."[11] In point of fact, today, most European countries have become, like the United States, de facto "immigration nations." France is home to five million Muslim immigrants. Among Germany's seven million immigrants are over three million Turks. The options seem clear: unless the virtues of civic nationalism are actively cultivated, Europe risks succumbing to neotribalism.

Democracy or Government by Elites?

Heretofore I have avoided the fraught issue of how best to define democracy. Until quite recently, in the annals of Western political thought democracy has been widely despised. After all, it was at the behest of a democratic government that, in 399 BCE, Socrates was forced to drink the cup of hemlock that solidified his reputation as a pre-Christian martyr. In the *Republic*, Plato, his star pupil, delivered a persuasive and unsparing critique of democratic rule that, over the years, has become canonical. Plato equated democracy with the "rule of the many," or the *hoi polloi*: citizens whose character was dominated by the appetitive faculty or base instinct. Their highest "aim" was either pleasure or the accumulation of wealth. In Plato's view, the relationship between democracy and tyranny was self-evident insofar as the anarchy of mob rule was predestined to be replaced by the rule of one.

Today Plato's cynicism about democracy has many influential adherents — among political theorists, for example, the Straussians, who are currently well represented in the Bush administration's Department of Defense.[12] Such cynicism figured prominently among political scientists who came of age in the World II era and who became advocates of political technocracy or government by elites. Having witnessed the horrors of death camps and world war, numerous Western opinion leaders drew the conclusion that one of the key causes of totalitarian regimes, right or left, had been popular mobilization from below: the involvement of the unwashed masses in politics. Consequently, they embraced a critique of mass society that metastasized into a condemnation of democratic government *simpliciter*.

In the lexicon of the political technocracy theorists, all forms of populism, be they right- or left-wing versions, are condemnable. They often draw on the work of prominent European conservatives — the Spanish philosopher Ortega y Gassett's 1927 classic, *The Revolt of the Masses*, for example — who usually opposed not only democracy but liberalism *tout court*. According to the classic conservative standpoint, both of these "risky" political formations, democracy and liberalism, are inextricably intertwined. After all, was there not a causal relation between freethinking, of which *liberalism* had, historically, been a major carrier, and *anarchy*? As Jacques Rivarol, a major exponent of the European Counter-Enlightenment, observed in defense of the ancien régime: "From the day when the [sovereign] consults his subjects, sovereignty is as though suspended ... When people cease to esteem, they cease to obey. A general rule: peoples whom the [sovereign] consults begin with vows and end with wills of their own."[13] Edmund Burke, who once declared, "*A perfect democracy therefore is the most shameless thing in the world*," offered a classic statement of Counter-Enlightenment cynicism, when he observed: "We are afraid to trust the stock of reasons in the common man, because we fear that stock is small."[14]

The popularity of elite theory raises one of the most important questions in contemporary democratic theory: how best to define democracy? Which is preferable, a "thick" or "thin" definition? A "thick" approach favors the idea of democratic inclusiveness or widespread participation. A "thin" approach sanctions the program of "political technocracy" advocates, who believe that increasing complexity demands government by trained experts rather than rank amateurs. They urge that one should rest content with a "minimal" definition of democracy as a mechanism for selecting political elites. As one of elite theory's most influential proponents, Seymour Martin Lipset, has claimed with breathtaking candor: "The distinctive and most valuable element of democracy is the formation of a political elite in the competitive struggle for the votes of a mainly passive electorate."[15] According to this model, what distinguishes democracy from other types of rule is regular and fair elections. Political participation should ideally be confined to pulling the lever in a closed election booth. Excessive "input" from below would only gum up sophisticated decision-making mechanisms on the part of wise and powerful "experts."

Elite theory gained plausibility in an era in which the notion of totalitarianism had won broad acceptance. Among political scientists and cold warriors, the idea of "totalitarianism," despite its conceptual imprecisions, functioned as a convenient ideological mechanism whereby the crusade against Nazism could be extended to the postwar political enemy, World Communism.

One may trace the origins of modern "elite theory" to early-twentieth-century studies in political sociology by Gabriel Mosca and Vilfredo Pareto. In 1911 former socialist Robert Michels wrote a classic study, *Political Parties*, in which he set forth the so-called iron law of oligarchy: the inevitable tendency of elites to rise to the top of social and political organizations. Michels, who became an ardent Mussolini supporter and accepted a university position under fascist rule in 1929, intended his theory as a direct refutation of political egalitarianism as represented by socialism and democracy.

Another influential exponent of elite theory was Michels's teacher, Max Weber.

It was Weber who coined the famous "iron cage" metaphor to describe the stultifying routinization of modern life owing to bureaucracy's omnipresent spread.[16] Weber was an ethical positivist who dismissed the moral content of modern democracy — that is, all normative claims concerning individual autonomy or self-determination — as so much undemonstrable ideological dross. Instead, he demonstrated a preference for what he called "leader democracy" — *Führerdemokratie*. He believed that, as a political form, democracy's major advantage was as a mechanism of selecting ruling elites. His hope was that a charismatic leader could elevate bureaucratic politics to great heights — in the manner of Nietzsche's appeal for "Great Politics." In light of the subsequent course of twentieth-century German history, this appeal cannot help but seem problematic.[17]

Weber was a major theoretical forebear of the "elite theory" that dominated North American political thought during the 1950s. The mediator between these two lineages of political sociology — German and American — was Joseph Schumpeter. In his classic 1942 study, *Capitalism, Socialism, and Democracy*, Schumpeter, following Weber, defined democracy as the best method of producing a strong, authoritarian government in an era of mass society. Schumpeter described democracy as "an institutional arrangement for arriving at political decisions in which individuals acquire the power to decide via competitive struggle for the people's vote." He described modern politics in the idiom of laissez-faire economics: politicians are "sellers" — hence, their programs are "commodities" or "wares" — who compete for the acclamation of voters, who act as "buyers" or "consumers." As one critic has aptly remarked, the problem with Schumpeter's model is that

> No ideals are attached to the definition of democracy. It does not imply any notions of civic responsibility or widespread political participation, or any ideas of the ends of man .... Liberty and equality, which have been part and parcel of past definitions of democracy, are regarded by Schumpeter as not being integral parts of such a definition, however worthy they might be as ideals.[18]

Under the pretense of "realism," Schumpeter's view of democracy raises anthropological cynicism to new heights. It anathematizes the egalitarian spirit stemming from the age of democratic revolutions — the idea that democratic politics might be related to the attainment of higher moral or substantive ends — insofar as such ends are allegedly contaminated with the bacillus of political utopianism. Technocracy theorists likewise disparage political participation insofar as it flirts with dangerous, unwieldy, and ultimately uncontrollable political passions. Lipset, one of Schumpeter's heirs, openly avows that one of elite theory's main goals is the suppression and containment of mass political movements. In his view, mass politics appeals primarily to social misfits: "to the disgruntled and the psychologically homeless, to the personal failures, the socially isolated, the economically insecure, the uneducated, unsophisticated, and authoritarian persons at every level of society."[19] It seems that, at this point, we have regressed to a Hobbesian-authoritarian social and political universe, one defined by the phrase *homo homini lupus* (man is a wolf to man). The highest goal to which politics might aspire is the merely negative end of avoiding "stasis" or civil war. For Hobbes, too — who, one might recall, coined the maxim "authority, not truth, makes the law" — politics is fundamentally a mechanism of preserving order. Beyond that, it is devoid of meaningful content.

Proponents of political technocracy argue further that in advanced industrial society conditions of increasing social complexity make democratic participation both superfluous and undesirable. They claim that social differentiation — the growing refinement and specialization of professional and vocational life — mandates that politics be administered by trained and reliable experts. Paradoxically, then, among an influential contingent of political thinkers, apathy — the devaluation of popular input — has become a highly valued desideratum.

By stripping democracy of any substantive content, elite theorists propose "saving" democracy by eviscerating its meaning. Their goal is to reduce politics to the Saint-Simonian ideal of educational dictatorship: rule by enlightened technocrats. Of course, were one to choose a different theoretical starting point — for example, Aristotle's spare, yet elegant, characterization of democracy as "ruling and being ruled in turn"; Thomas Jefferson's celebration of the joys and virtues of democratic citizenship — one would arrive at a very different set of conclusions. Here, one of the ironies is that advocates of political technocracy end up endorsing an authoritarian political logic they otherwise claim to oppose.

It may, then, come as no surprise to learn that amid the outpouring of literature on democratic transitions following communism's 1989 demise, elite theory was prominently on display. In fact, one of the most influential treatises on the post-1970s democratization mania, Samuel Huntington's *The Third Wave*, constituted a ringing endorsement of the political technocracy approach. The aspect of postcommunist transitions that Huntington singled out for praise was that "responsible elites" seized control of the transition process from the fickle and unpredictable "masses." But this observation conveniently overlooks the fact that had it not been for the eminently peaceable and self-restrained populist uprisings in Czechoslovakia, Poland, and the German Democratic Republic — where, atop the ruins of the Berlin Wall, the populist refrain "We are the people" (*Wir sind das Volk*) proudly rang out — it is unlikely these oppressive regimes would have fallen in the first place.

In *The Third Wave* Huntington pointedly warns readers about the dangers and risks of raising the bar of democratic expectations. With awe-inspiring condescension, he ridicules supporters of participatory democracy for their conceptual imprecision: "Fuzzy norms," he cautions, "do not yield useful analysis." He explicitly builds on Schumpeter's paternalistic, top-down model of politics, claiming that

> By the 1970s the debate was over, and Schumpeter had won. Theories increasingly drew distinctions between rationalistic, utopian, idealistic definitions of democracy, on the one hand, and empirical, descriptive, institutional, and procedural definitions, on the other. [Observers] concluded that only the latter type of definition provided the analytical precision and empirical referents that make the concept a useful one. Sweeping discussions of democracy in terms of normative theory sharply declined ... and were replaced by efforts to understand the nature of democratic institutions, how they function, and the reasons why they develop and collapse.

By the same token one could argue that had the political actors in Central Europe not been inspired by the ideals of strong democracy — Vaclav Havel's immortal phrase "Living in Truth" is only one example — they may have never taken to the streets at all. The major problem with Schumpeter's tepid procedural-empirical model is that it fails to inspire allegiance: from a motivational standpoint, it capitulates prematurely to the cynicism and suspicions of democracy's detractors and critics. Hence, should the beneficiaries of democracy's Third Wave suffer reversals — as has in part already happened in the cases of Russia and Latin America — one wonders if they will be able to summon the level of conviction required to uphold the democratic idea. Was not an analogous scenario largely responsible for the collapse of the Weimar Republic? For ultimately Germany's so-called *Vernunftrepublikaner* — republicans of the intellect rather than of the heart — failed to see democracy as an ideal worth defending. One of the consequences of "defining down" the definition of democracy is that, in times of crisis, it will prove difficult, if not impossible, to find a quorum of committed citizens willing to come to democracy's aid.

Borrowing from Schumpeter, Huntington's definition of democracy stresses the minimalist criteria of bona fide political pluralism coupled with regular and fair elections. But from historical experience we know that many democratic polities, despite a relatively healthy electoral track record, are suffused with powerful social interests that disfigure and usurp democracy's egalitarian normative claims. It is no secret that contemporary democracies operate with marked plutocratic biases. Certain political actors and interest groups — well-to-do campaign contributors, major corporations, other large-scale organizations — benefit handsomely from a disproportionate capacity for political influence. This syndrome unfairly perpetuates a social and political system that is marred by far-reaching political and economic inequalities. Huntington's technocratic-authoritarian model occludes the fact that, on numerous occasions, acts of "mobilization from below" have restored democracy to its nobler, egalitarian impulsions. To take the case of recent American history: the social movements of the 1950s, 1960s, 1970s — that is, the civil rights, free speech, antiwar, feminist, and gay liberation movements — invoked the universal, humanitarian moral precepts contained in the republic's founding documents (the Declaration of Independence, Constitution, and Bill of Rights) in order to secure a range of civic and political freedoms of which their constituents had been unjustly deprived. Had they relied on the intrinsic benevolence of the bureaucrats and experts in whom Huntington blindly trusts, it is doubtful whether these groups would have achieved their ends.

One of the keys to successful democratization means, as Tocqueville once put it, cultivating "habits of the heart." Hence, my conclusions are the *opposite* of Huntington's. Democratic habitudes are not something that can be perfunctorily activated every two years when elections roll around. They are convictions that must be deeply held. A passion for liberty is not a sentiment that can be unthinkingly entrusted to a benevolent elite for preservation and safekeeping. Instead, the best guarantee against the usurpation of democratic freedom by a self-interested vanguard is to promote the virtues of active citizenship. In this manner alone can one ensure that a haughty and self-serving political class abide by the constitutional *règles du jeu*. The objective of social movements emanating from civil society is to force unresponsive elites to live up to the basic precepts of democratic inclusion. Thus, if one studies the ebb and flow of democratization, one often finds a direct correlation between logics of popular contestation and progressive social reform.

"Controlled Globalization"

In the academy today, we are often subjected to jeremiads about the evils of globalization. But we rarely hear about this phenomenon's positive side. Globalization's vociferous detractors exhibit an anticapitalist, antigrowth animus. Were these prejudices allowed to hold sway, large swaths of the developing world would be consigned to crushing impoverishment for generations to come. Hence, the question is not: globalization vs. antiglobalization. Instead, it is one of anarchic vs. controlled globalization. Here, "controlled globalization" means that, instead of living in a world society where the IMF and World Bank treat the developing world like racially inferior fiefdoms, world markets are subjected to norms of occupational fairness that, in the postwar period, have more or less become common currency among the democracies of the Northern Hemisphere.[20] In other words, the same provisions for social insurance, a living wage, adequate health and safety standards, and the right to unionize and strike — stipulations and norms that the labor force of advanced industrial societies has acquired over the course of decades of social struggle — must be upheld in the developing world. The aforementioned "social rights" have been enumerated in the 1948 UN Universal Declaration of Human Rights as well as by numerous regional treaties. Companies operating in developing nations that violate these norms should be subject to harsh financial penalties and public censure. But, heretofore, IMF officials, who have been narrowly focused on the demands of marketization, have, like the international community in general, been content to look the other way.

One of the key issues the world will face in ensuing decades is the question whether logics of democratization, which in recent years have been so potent at the nation-state level, can be extended to the emerging global order. Some two hundred years ago, Immanuel Kant articulated an attractive vision of cosmopolitan governance in his treatise on "Perpetual Peace." Kant, who in a series of remarkable political essays had provided a compelling justification for enlightened republican government, conjectured that the precepts of liberty could be transposed from the nation-state to the international world order.

It is important to appreciate how heretical Kant's proposals were in his day. For in the eighteenth century the rules of international conduct had been established by the Treaty of Westphalia (1648), in the aftermath of Europe's sanguinary Thirty Years' War. The Westphalian system openly sanctioned a world order that resembled a Hobbesian state of nature: a *bellum omnium contra omnes* (a war of all against all), where individual states were viewed as autonomous political actors. Thereby, the precepts of "political realism" became the basis of international law. According to the Westphalian agreement, norms of international governance were kept to a bare minimum: for the most part they pertained to the laws of war. In keeping with the understanding of states as sovereign entities, one of the main provisions was the principle of domestic noninterference. Thus, the way a state acted toward its own indigenous population was deemed a strictly internal matter — in no way a matter for redress or adjudication on the part of the international community.

The Westphalian order remained more or less in place through World War I, whose unprecedented carnage revealed the system's egregious flaws. An incipient movement toward a more stable order of world governance emerged in the war's aftermath. But its centerpiece, the League of Nations, received a mortal blow in the early 1920s when the

U.S. Senate refused to ratify it. In the 1930s Europe's bellicose fascist dictatorships delivered the *caput mortem*. Hence, it was only following the atrocities of the Nazis and their allies that the idea of Crimes Against Humanity (Genocide Convention of 1948) as well as a conception of Human Rights that transcended the unpredictable flux of nation-state politics was born.

Yet, one could argue that, until recently, this system, too, remained stillborn. Following Nuremburg, the next international trials concerning crimes against humanity did not occur until the 1990s, when the genocides in the former Yugoslavia and Rwanda became objects of criminal investigation at the International Criminal Court in the Hague.

Nevertheless, commentators have pointed to dramatic developments in the realm of international governance that have occurred over the course of the last fifteen years. In the eyes of many observers, this trend has precipitated a *revolution in humane international governance*. As evidence they cite:

1. A new international consensus in favor of human rights (and against cultural relativism), that one may date from the 1975 Helsinki Accords; the Central European — and Soviet — "dissidence" movement; and, at a later stage, the "divestment" movement against South Africa's apartheid regime; thus, the international human rights consensus helped to facilitate movements of democratization.

   This new consensus, which upended the presuppositions of the Westphalian system, also places new pressures on more traditional, authoritarian regimes as human rights violators: witness the precarious situation of former Chilean dictator Augusto Pinochet, who, at the behest of a Spanish judge (Garza), was arrested and held in Great Britain for a period of several months. (On the American side, one might note that Henry Kissinger's international movements have been noticeably restricted.)

2. The new role played on the international stage by nonstate actors: NGOs or nongovernmental organizations such as Greenpeace, Human Rights Watch, Amnesty International, and Médecins sans Frontières. These actors place new "soft" or "moral" constraints upon nation-states that are now often compelled to justify their conduct on the international stage in terms of precepts of humane governance.

As one observer has aptly summarized these developments: "We have in recent years been passing through the zone of the 'impossible': the emancipation of the countries of Central and Eastern Europe from

Soviet rule, the abandonment of apartheid by the white elite in South Africa, the end of the cold war."[21] The new international consensus is predicated on the distinction between power that is based on relations of domination and force, and power that is legitimate because it is predicated on shared norms. Whether democratic international governance might prosper depends on whether the second half of this equation can maintain the upper hand.

12

Religion and Public Reason: A Contemporary Debate

As is well known, during the seventeenth century religious wars devastated the lands of Central Europe. In their aftermath the population of German cities was decimated by one-third. Devastation was even worse in the countryside, where two-fifths of the inhabitants were lost. All told, among the principalities of the Holy Roman Empire, the population declined from twenty million to sixteen million inhabitants. The 1631 siege of Magdeburg was an event unprecedented in its brutality, even judging by the standards of the day. The civilian population was brutally massacred by marauding Catholic troops. When the smoke cleared, a mere five thousand of the original thirty thousand inhabitants had survived. The effects of the terrible conflagration were felt for years to come. As one Swabian family, writing a year before the Peace of Westphalia, observed: "They say the terrible war is now over. But there is still no sign of peace. Everywhere there is envy, hatred and greed; that's what the war has taught us ... We live like animals, eating bark and grass."[1] In the words of one prominent historian, "Morally subversive, economically destructive, socially degrading, confused in its causes, devious in its course, futile in its result, [the Thirty Years' War] was *the outstanding example in European history of meaningless conflict.*"[2] For an analogue to these events, one must have recourse to the Armageddon-like ideological wars of the twentieth century.

The seventeenth-century wars of religion provide a perfect example of a *negative learning process*. In their aftermath, the nations of Europe moved fitfully in the direction of toleration. England took the lead following the Glorious Revolution of 1688, which, owing to James II's Roman leanings, possessed a profound religious undercurrent. It was John Locke who, more than anyone else, attempted to distill philosophical consequences from these developments in his 1689 "Letter Concerning Toleration." Here, we have for the first time a detailed moral argument concerning the imperative of separating secular and salvific ends. As Locke observes:

> I affirm that the magistrate's power extends not to the establishing of any articles of faith, or form of worship, by the force of his laws .... Any one may employ as many exhortations and arguments as he pleases, towards the promoting of another man's salvation. But all force and compulsion are to be forborne. Nothing is to be done imperiously. Nobody is obliged in that matter to yield obedience unto the admonitions or injunctions of another, further than he himself is persuaded. Every man in that has the supreme and absolute authority of judging for himself. And the reason is because nobody else is concerned in it.[3]

In the passage just quoted, Locke underlines the fact that questions of faith are, in the first instance, *matters of conscience*. Thereby, Locke sought to distill the ethical and political consequences of the antinomian spirit that had catalyzed the Protestant Reformation: the idea that salvation is a question of "faith," or inner conviction, rather than "works." In this respect, Locke, following Luther, realized that to prescribe politically what men and women should or should not believe concerning the ends of salvation is a *contradictio in adjecto*. Bluntly put: *matters of faith cannot be legislated*.[4]

With this insight Locke, who in his *Essay concerning Human Understanding* had set forth the terms of philosophical empiricism, took an important step toward defining the contours of public reason. He recognized that if religious belief was a matter of belief rather than knowledge, its ultimate bases were intellectually undemonstrable. To infuse politics with questions of salvation could therefore only prove divisive. It could only be a recipe for sowing dissension among the ranks of the body politic by appealing to reasons or grounds that transcended the limitations of the finite human understanding.

When Immanuel Kant, writing nearly a century later, declared in *The Critique of Pure Reason* that he "had to deny knowledge in order to make room for faith," he was following in Locke's footsteps.[5] In

Kant's view, to sully cognition with supersensible claims — with specious assertions that transcended the "bounds of sense" — would only encourage dogmatism and invite confusion. Following Friedrich Wilhelm II's accession to the throne in 1786, Kant's attempt to separate philosophical and religious concerns — "reason" and "faith" — ran afoul of the Prussian censors. For his part, Kant was far from what one might call a "free thinker." In works such as "Answer to the Question: What Is Enlightenment?" (1784), he was careful to stress that whereas citizens must exercise forbearance and circumspection in their capacity as private persons — when they are acting in the employ of others — conversely, in their public capacity as scholars, freedom of opinion must prevail.

Following the publication of *Religion within the Limits of Reason Alone* in 1793, Kant received the following censorial missive from Friedrich Wilhelm himself:

> Our most high person has for a long time observed with great displeasure how you misuse your philosophy to undermine and debase many of the most important and fundamental doctrines of the Holy Scriptures and Christianity; how, namely, you have done this in your book, *Religion innerhalb der Grenzen der blossen Vernunft*, as well as in other smaller works ... We ... expect that in the future ... you will give no such cause for offense, but rather, in accordance with your duty, employ your talents and authority so that our Paternal Purpose may be more and more attained. If you continue to resist, you may certainly expect unpleasant consequences to yourself.[6]

Kant responded by pledging no longer to write on religious subjects. Accordingly, critics have accused him of lacking *Zivilcourage*. After all, the central precept of Kant's philosophy is the "autonomy of reason": reason's principled refusal, in its public employment, to capitulate before unwarranted social authority. Kant's act of intellectual self-renunciation vis-à-vis Friedrich Wilhelm seemed to directly contravene reason's sovereignty. Apparently, Kant himself had some private reservations concerning his acquiescence to the king's demands. Among his posthumous jottings, one finds the following remarks: "Recantation and denial of one's inner convictions is base, but silence in a case like the present is a subject's duty. And if all that one says must be true, it does not follow that it is one's duty to tell publicly everything that is true."[7]

Kant's political timorousness, his willingness to place "duty" ahead of conviction, betrays the ambivalences of the "German conception of freedom." According to this conception, one places a higher value on the freedom of spiritual inwardness than on that of external, political freedom. As Marx observed in 1843, the Germans "have shared the restorations of modern nations without ever having shared their revolutions."[8] Whereas other nations, such as the French, valorize political freedom, since the Reformation the Germans have rested content with spiritual freedom or free interiority.

It would seem that today, with the possible exception of the lands of the European Union, around the globe religion is making a dramatic comeback. In the Middle East the resurgence of fundamentalist Islam in the aftermath of Arab nationalism's decline is perhaps the most visible and consequential manifestation of this tendency. In the United States evangelical Christianity has enjoyed a remarkable resurgence. As a voting bloc this group played a pivotal role in ensuring George Bush's reelection in November 2004.[9] As a result of these surprising developments, sociologists who monitor these trends have called into question the "secularization" thesis predicting religion's growing marginality. Instead, they have begun to speak boldly of the "desecularization of the world," thereby standing the secularization thesis on its head.[10]

To contrast today's global religious revival with the nineteenth-century critique of religion — which at the time became something of a full-fledged ideational obsession — demonstrates how significantly commonplace assumptions about spirituality and belief have changed. The nineteenth century was, of course, simultaneously the age of history and the age of positivism. Few epochs in human history can have been so antagonistically disposed toward the claims of religious truth. This was, after all, the era of Ludwig Feuerbach, Auguste Comte, Karl Marx, Friedrich Nietzsche, and Mikhail Bakunin. All of these thinkers perceived religion as little more than, to employ Marx's pet phrase, socially engendered "false consciousness." Religion was viewed as, in essence, an atavism of superstition — the vestige of an earlier era when men and women believed in spirits and demons. Social theorists and the educated classes agreed that extirpating religious consciousness was an indispensable prerequisite for human emancipation. In many ways Feuerbach's critical insights concerning religion in *The Essence of Christianity* set the tone for what was to come. For the German philosopher, theism was a perversion of consciousness. The more stock mankind placed in the Beyond, the more it devalued itself — *tertium non datur.* Theism and humanism stood in a relationship of irreconcilable, mutual exclusivity. As Feuerbach explains: "By negating God, I negate the negation of man. In place of the illusory, fantastic, and heavenly position of man, which in real life necessarily becomes the negation of man, I posit the sensuous, real, and, therefore, political and social position of man. The question of the Being or non-Being of God is really the question of the Being or Non-Being of man."[11]

We know, moreover, how influential Feuerbach's position was for the young Marx. It was through Feuerbach's "anthropological humanism" that Marx broke with the position held by the Young Hegelians. Whereas the Young Hegelians vehemently criticized state religion, following the precedents set by the French and American revolutions, they had few reservations about recasting faith as a matter of conscience. Conversely, Marx, following Feuerbach, suggested that the privatization of belief would amount to little more than the privatization of delusion and error.

Feuerbach's secular humanism also inspired Marx's break with Hegelian Idealism. It was in a Feuerbachian spirit that, in his "Contribution to a Critique of Hegel's *Philosophy of Right*," Marx declared that, "The abolition of religion as the *illusory* happiness of the people is the demand for their *real* happiness. To call on them to give up their illusions about their condition is to call on them to *give up a condition that requires illusions*."[12] There followed his oft-cited remark characterizing religious belief as a malign addiction: "*Religion is the opium of the people.*"

It seems that even when nineteenth-century thinkers sought to embrace religion, their efforts backfired. In the age of historicism religion, too, was subjected to the scrutiny of systematic historical study. Scholars reasoned that they might be able to validate religion's claims by employing the day's most advanced empirical methods. They believed that one could thereby bolster religion's authenticity. Successful historical studies of Jesus's life were written by David Friedrich Strauss and Ernst Renan. In the form of the *Wissenschaft des Judentums*, Judaism, too, gave itself over to the new empirical scholarly approach.

But once sacred themes are subjected to profane methods of investigation, they risk disenchantment. They rapidly lose their halo. In the words of Walter Benjamin, they become *de-auraticized*. They succumb to profanation and are reduced to the status of mere "facts among facts." Instead of mutually reinforcing one another, it would seem that Reason and Revelation operate at cross-purposes.

Apostles of the European Counter-Enlightenment realized that were Revelation to adopt the lexicon and methods of Reason, it would have already lost the game. In order to retain its sanctity and aura, religion depended on human credulity, as in Tertullian's maxim *credo quia absurdum est*. Once it sought to compete on Reason's terrain, by means of proofs and demonstrations, it might as well surrender. Kierkegaard's antinomianism, which developed in reaction to philosophy of religion's growing popularity, and, more generally, the Hegelian idea that religion and philosophy were ultimately reconcilable posed the problem cogently. If Revelation is in the first instance a question of belief, all attempts to reconcile it with the demands of rational cognition are self-defeating and pointless. As the Danish theologian knew well, the challenge of belief is that it transcends the comforting assurances and tautologies of formal logic.

In earlier epochs, when religion's claims enjoyed a manifest self-evidence, there was no need of philosophy of religion to provide it with an epistemological guarantee or warrant. In the modern world, conversely, religion's situation has changed drastically. The "sacred canopy" religion once provided — that is, religion qua theodicy, or a cushion against worldly suffering and the injustice of fate — has been permanently tattered.[13] In the age of science, insight increasingly triumphed over the claims of faith. Religion no longer functions as a self-evident, all-encompassing worldview. Ultimately, belief succumbed to the logic of social differentiation. Undeniably, religion continues to occupy a determinate cultural niche. Yet, increasingly, it has forfeited its former soteriological and cosmological centrality. Faced with the irredeemable "value pluralism" of the modern world, religion has shrunk to the status of *one standpoint among others*. Max Weber consummately articulated the stakes at issue when, discussing modernity's value pluralism, he spoke of an age of *"warring gods and demons."*

"The fate of our times is characterized by rationalization and intellectualization and, above all, by the 'disenchantment of the world,'" Weber famously observed in "Science as a Vocation."[14] Weber himself was ambivalent about these developments. Progress in technological world mastery or the domination of nature was accompanied by indubitable losses. A world dominated by instrumental reason was simultaneously a world divested of mystery and enchantment — hence, the thesis of *Sinnverlust*, or loss of meaning.[15] The spread of bureaucracy, for its part, threatened to turn life into an entirely predictable routine. In all likelihood, the end result would resemble something like Huxley's *Brave New World*, which seems to have been an important point of reference for Theodor Adorno's dystopian notion of a "totally administered world." The division of labor, whose superior efficiency remained unarguable, had triumphed at the expense of fulfillment and wholeness. Accordingly, narrow-minded specialists or *Fachmenschen* supplanted well-rounded Renaissance types. For these reasons, toward the end of his career, Weber began to place value on the idea of charisma: a prophetic leader type who might be capable of single-handedly providing the disenchanted landscape of modernity with meaning and direction. However, in a German context, this recommendation was fraught with obvious and profound moral difficulties.

Weber's French counterpart, Emile Durkheim, also viewed religiosity's decline with mixed emotions. On the one hand, Durkheim, a methodological positivist and anticlericalist, was wholly committed to the twin values of republicanism and individualism. As a convinced secularist and champion of social evolution, he denied that religion contained any intrinsic content or meaning. For Durkheim, like Freud, religious claims were nothing but a form of "illusion." However, viewed sociologically or in functional terms — that is, as a collective mind-set or *mentalité* — they were a form of *socially necessary* illusion: According to Durkheim, religion was a form of societal self-projection: a mechanism by which society worshipped itself. As a form of communal self-adoration or collective narcissism, among premodern societies religion played an essential role in ensuring social cohesion: it bound members ideationally to the community and thereby represented an indispensable source of affective solidarity. Its rites, rituals, and symbology were an indispensable means of preserving social cohesion. Thus, in Durkheim's view spirits and demons ultimately only made sense in worldly terms.

Yet, late in life, Durkheim displayed some surprising ambivalences about the developmental trajectory of modern individualistic societies. He recognized that the transition from *Gemeinschaft* to *Gesellschaft* had been achieved at a high social cost: a fateful diminution of social solidarity. For whereas religion provided the "social cement" — the cultural incentive "to belong" — among premodern societies, the modern world had found no reliable affective equivalent. Modern societies were threatened by a variety of centrifugal tendencies: exponential increases in divorce, criminality, suicide, and violence.

In *The Elementary Forms of Religious Life*, which appeared a few years before his death in 1918, Durkheim openly lamented the fact that modern societies had found no functional equivalent for religion. They suffer in extremis from a *paucity of higher ideals*. By allowing base motivations such as egocentrism and self-interest to subsume all other motivations and concerns, they ran the risk of extreme fragmentation. At times, Durkheim displayed a marked nostalgia for the dimension of collective enthusiasm that members of traditional societies felt in the presence of the sacred — a sentiment that had become virtually unknown among secularized societies of the modern type, in thrall to the prosaic idols of "progress" and the division of labor. As his nephew, Marcel Mauss, put it in *L'Année sociologique*: in premodern societies, "the dances performed, the songs and shows, the dramatic representations given between camps or partners, the objects made, used, decorated, polished, amassed and transmitted with affection, received with joy, given away in triumph, the feasts in which everyone participates — all these ...are the source of aesthetic emotions as well as emotions aroused by interest."[16]

It is doubtful whether the representatives of classical sociology would embrace "return of the sacred" in the contemporary world. Yet, as I have tried to show, nor would they be entirely surprised. Both Durkheim and Weber realized that in traditional societies religions of salvation provided indispensable stores of value and meaning, not the least of which being *theodicy*: a rationalization of life's multifarious injustices and inequities. Modernity, conversely, presents its denizens with a thoroughly disenchanted cosmos. Weber once despairingly characterized this normatively impoverished landscape as an "iron cage." Only with great difficulty can one today find functional equivalents for the profound existential consolation religion once provided.

Still, "the return of the sacred" presents inhabitants of the modern world with a serious dilemma — one that is embodied in the value conflict between sacred and profane. Bluntly put: in many cases, religious fundamentalism's resurgence poses a challenge to the ethos of toleration that emerged following the seventeenth century's religious wars. In a more general sense, religious fundamentalism's jeremiads against modernity's failings — none of which should be underestimated — engender a broader cynicism about the shortcomings of a secular-democratic political culture. No one described the nature of the contrasting valuations at issue better than Weber in the well-known contrast between an "ethic of responsibility" (*Verantwortungsethik*) and an "ethic of ultimate ends" (*Gesinnungsethik*) with which his essay on "Politics as a Vocation" concludes.

The two "ethics" described by Weber operate at cross-purposes. An ethic of "ultimate ends" brooks no compromises. The stakes it raises are those of salvation or redemption. (It should be remembered that forms of political messianism — communism, fascism, integral nationalism — also purvey a *Gesinnungsethik*). In comparison, worldly ends pale in significance. There can be no "talking down" someone who has seen the light of salvation and whose very being has been convulsed by its promises. Unlike the *Verantwortungsethik*, or ethic of responsibility, it is a standpoint that does not admit of half measures. It remains impervious to the give-and-take of rational argumentation. Therein lie its intoxications, its sublimity — but also its intractability from the standpoint of the methods and ends of public reason. At times, Weber uses the term "virtuoso" to describe the charismatic leadership abilities of the great religious prophets. Nevertheless, to those who march to a different drummer, their claims may seem portentous and devoid of sense. Thus, often it can be difficult to discriminate between genuinely inspired leadership, on the one hand,

and false prophets or demagogues, on the other, who worship tin idols. Moreover, conventional secular criteria seem patently unsuited to making such judgments.

Today we realize the potential for abuse when governments, assuming the role of a "tutelary state," employ "comprehensive doctrines"— be they religious, moral, or philosophical in nature — in order to proclaim a monopoly on truth and virtue.[17] The democratic antidote to such authoritarian practices and habitudes — from Kant to John Rawls — has been a commitment to the norms of "public reason." Since, as we have seen, modernity is inescapably an age of *value pluralism*, when debating considerations of justice we tacitly agree to put aside or bracket our "comprehensive doctrines" or conceptions of "the Good" for the sake of arriving at what one might call a lesser order, "political truth."[18] Given the entwinement of religious dogmatism and political absolutism in early modern Europe (prerevolutionary France representing the archetype), it is not difficult to fathom the rationale behind the emphatic affirmation of public reason by the most gifted representatives of the liberal political tradition. Toward the end of the First *Critique*, Kant discusses the cultivation of public reason as an indispensable political imperative for successful republican government:

> Reason must in all its undertakings subject itself to criticism; should it limit freedom of criticism by any prohibitions, it must harm itself, drawing upon itself a damaging suspicion. Nothing is so important through its usefulness, nothing so sacred, that it may be exempted from this searching examination, which knows no respect for persons. Reason depends on this freedom for its very existence. For reason has no dictatorial authority; its verdict is always simply the agreement of free citizens, of whom each one must be permitted to express, without let or hindrance, his objections or even his veto.[19]

The idea of public reason entails a number of controversial background assumptions concerning the nature of selfhood and morality. Most of these assumptions are at odds with traditional religious conceptions of personhood. For according to such conceptions, human fulfillment lies not in self-determination or autonomy, but instead in an act of self-sacrifice: *credo quia absurdum est*, or belief qua "leap of faith."

Public reason presupposes the complementarity of individual and collective self-legislation. Rephrased in political terms, this entails the reciprocity of basic rights and popular sovereignty. In *Between Facts and Norms*, Jürgen Habermas glosses the entwinement of individual and collective self-determination that is presupposed by modern democracy as follows:

The internal relation between the rule of law and democracy can be explained at a conceptual level by the fact that the individual liberties of the subjects of private law and the public autonomy of enfranchised citizens make each other possible.... Human rights do not compete with popular sovereignty; they are identical with the constitutive conditions of a self-limiting practice of publicly discursive will-formation.[20]

To accord primacy to either side of this equation would be to eviscerate democracy's substance and meaning. For to argue for the primacy of "rights" in the absence of a body politic capable of ratifying their existence would be to deprive rights of their political basis. Conversely, to endorse the primacy of popular sovereignty would be to sanction a classical republican doctrine of politics in which subjective liberties fail to receive their due — an insight that is reinforced historically by the French Revolution's Jacobin-republican phase.

The standpoint of public reason upholds the ideal of a society of free and equal persons. It is subtended by an (implicitly Kantian) ethical standpoint that holds that a life deprived of moral autonomy (*autonomia* = self-rule) is a life devoid of fulfillment. As such, it is diametrically opposed to the fundamental assumption of classical political theory — from Plato to Nietzsche to Leo Strauss — that the majority of men and women are incapable of self-rule and, hence, require the tutelary guardianship of a paternalistic elite, as in Plato's doctrine of "Philosopher-Kings." For Plato, not only did this doctrine pertain to persons whom the Greeks viewed as morally inferior — for example, women, slaves, and barbarians (non-Greeks) — but also for persons of dissolute character who were incapable of allowing reason, or *nous*, to triumph over their own appetites.

The tenets of public reason mandate that political reasons must be publicly accessible. This standpoint is merely consistent with basic ideals of equal citizenship and deliberative democracy. Such conceptions hold that, despite the time constraints and pragmatic limitations of the decision-making process, political will-formation should be open, public, and inclusive. Trust in public reason signifies a fundamental confidence in the reasoning capacities of average citizens. It means that we endow them with the ability to weigh evidence and evaluate reasons before arriving at intelligent political positions and conclusions.

Successful democratic polities have long realized that political reasoning capacities are not innate. Instead, they must be consciously cultivated, bred, and nurtured. For this reason, such polities place a premium on the value of democratic education.[21] As Adorno once observed, democratic education must aim at "Education toward

Autonomy": the cultivation of mature and self-reliant citizens. Historically, the encouragement of autonomous citizenship has been the most effective bulwark against the seductions of political authoritarianism.

Paradoxically, the parameters of democratic will-formation are always subject to self-imposed limitations. In other words: *citizens cannot will any decisions they choose*. Instead the scope of popular sovereignty is always bounded by basic rights: a catalogue of fundamental, inalienable liberties. The stipulations of self-limitation are one of the defining features of modern democracy as opposed to "the liberty of the ancients."[22] Under normal conditions, citizens of democratic polities cannot be sold into slavery; nor may they be denied the prerogatives of habeas corpus or due process. In many respects, this fundamental respect for the status of the individual is a secularized legacy of the Christian belief in the intrinsic worthiness of all persons. This same religious inheritance reverberates in the omnipresent traces of civil religion: our attempts to sanctify the body politic by appealing to the tenets of "deism." For in their founding documents modern democracies frequently claim that the social contract has been divinely sanctioned. (The Declaration of Independence, for example, speaks both of "Nature's God" and proposes that men have been endowed "by their Creator with certain unalienable Rights.") By the same token, these foundational texts almost always make it clear that this imprimatur is meant metaphorically rather than literally. Deist catchphrases such as "God-given" or "in God we trust" are a way of signaling that the social contract, as the guarantor of our freedom, possesses a peculiar sanctity.

One approach that has emerged in recent decades to challenge the credo of public reason is the paradigm of political technocracy.[23] According to this view, in the modern world the increased demands of social complexity have rendered the ideals of deliberative democracy patently obsolete. The social subsystems of economy and bureaucracy can no longer afford the luxury of the ideals of "communicative reason": dialogue oriented toward mutual understanding. Instead, they require expertise: prompt and efficient decisions. Proponents of political technocracy contend that the subsystems' technical intricacies surpass the understanding of the average citizen, thereby rendering the demands of democratic participation anachronistic. According to this Huxleyesque scenario, what contemporary democracy needs most is the rule of a knowledgeable technocratic elite. The outmoded ideals of participatory democracy must cede before the technical requirements of managerial science. The social complexity engendered by the post-industrial, information age economy suggest that political transparency and publicly accessible reasons are "indulgences" we can no longer afford.

The risks posed by this approach are unambiguous. Political technocracy threatens to annul the moral basis of modern democratic societies: a conception of self-determination predicated on the confluence of popular sovereignty and individual autonomy. One might well argue that, today, the greatest hindrance to progress in democratization lies in the scientization of knowledge practices and a corresponding fetishization of technological expertise. Such practices threaten to usurp the reasoning capacities of average citizens. "Privileged access to the sources of relevant knowledge makes possible an inconspicuous domination over the colonized public of citizens cut off from these sources and placated with symbolic politics."[24] The challenge of political technocracy is a primary example of what Habermas has felicitously described as the "administrative colonization of the lifeworld."

The ethos of public reason remains suspicious of political maxims that are explicitly couched in or justified by an all-encompassing *Gesinnungsethik*. The case of religion poses a special dilemma, insofar as, for a great many persons, religion remains the source of their most deeply held values and convictions. Why, it is argued, should one's most highly prized beliefs be extruded from the sphere of political decision making?[25]

In part, the problem is that a perspective grounded in an ethic of "ultimate ends" or "belief" transcends the Kantian "bounds of sense": it is neither publicly demonstrable nor may it be rendered transparent through the time-honored methods of empirical accounting or rational argumentation. Moreover, the standpoint of "ultimate ends" violates one of the norms that John Rawls has identified as integral to the discourse of public reason: the norm of *reciprocity*.

Reciprocity speaks to the dignity of our interlocutors or public partners-in-dialogue. It presupposes that the perspectives I advanced stand a plausible chance of acceptance among members of the reasoning public who may not partake of my particular comprehensive standpoint. As such, reciprocity embodies one of the crucial values of deliberative democracy — *civility*: treating the other as intrinsically worthy of respect even though he or she may not share the same comprehensive worldview. As Rawls puts it: "The criterion of reciprocity requires that when those terms are proposed as the most reasonable terms of fair cooperation, those proposing them must also think it at least reasonable for others to accept them, as free and equal citizens, and not as dominated or manipulated, or under the pressure of an inferior political or social position."[26]

On this basis, Rawls differentiates between "reasonable" and "unreasonable" comprehensive doctrines. *Reasonable comprehensive doctrines* admit of compromise with other such doctrines or standpoints with an eye toward achieving the ends of justice. Conversely, *unreasonable comprehensive doctrines* violate norms of tolerance by narcissistically refusing to countenance the validity of competing comprehensive views or claims. Fundamentalist religious creeds, theories of divine right of kingship, as well as modern dictatorships — both left and right — are examples of comprehensive doctrines that refuse to honor the criterion of reciprocity.

For these reasons, to merit political consideration religious perspectives must be capable of being "translated" into publicly accessible, secular forms of reasoning, a qualification that Rawls refers to as the "proviso." As he states in "The Idea of Public Reason Revisited": we are allowed "to introduce into political discussion at any time our comprehensive doctrine, religious or nonreligious, provided that, in due course, we give properly public reasons to support the principles and policies our comprehensive doctrine is said to support."[27]

By the same token, in most cases democratic polities welcome religious conviction as a crucial fount of ethical and political inspiration. After all, the strong conception of justice proper to redemption religions — for example, the theological idea of the "Last Judgment," according to which the righteous shall be saved and the wicked shall perish — stands as an important precursor of our modern secular doctrines of equity and fairness. In a recent interview, Habermas has glossed this legacy as follows: "For the normative self-understanding of modernity, Christianity has functioned as more than just a precursor or a catalyst. Universalistic egalitarianism, from which sprang the ideals of freedom and a collective life in solidarity, the autonomous conduct of life and emancipation, the individual morality of conscience, human rights and democracy, is the direct legacy of the Judaic ethic of justice and the Christian ethic of love."[28]

Moreover, viewed historically, religious conceptions have played an indispensable role in twentieth-century emancipatory social and political movements. Three examples lend emphatic support to this claim:

1. The American civil rights movement of the 1960s, led by the Reverend Martin Luther King, would have been unthinkable had it not been for the active participation of the southern churches.

2. The delegitimation of communist dictatorships in Eastern Europe was in many cases spearheaded by church-based resistance movements: the Catholic church in Poland and the Evangelical church in East Germany.

3. The poignant, 1986 American Catholic bishops' Pastoral Letter, "Economic Justice for All," a paradigmatic fusion of traditional Christian religious teachings about love and charity with a

contemporary concern for the gross economic injustices of laissez-faire capitalism.[29]

Nevertheless, religion's influence on public life has been far from unequivocally positive. Its deleterious aspects must also be highlighted. For redemption religions, by virtue of their focus on salvation or justice in the Hereafter, have typically turned a deaf ear to worldly justice. Gospel maxims such as "Render unto Caesar the things which are Caesar's" and "Should thy enemy smite thee, turn the other cheek" well express the nature of the dilemma at issue. Because of the dichotomy endemic to redemption religions between worldly existence, discounted as a "vale of tears," and the Hereafter, glorified as a state of "eternal bliss," they frequently devalue justice in the here and now as a matter of subaltern concern. In post-Reformation Europe, the effects of this worldly/otherworldly split was reflected in (1) the Lutheran/Protestant unquestioning obedience to secular authority; and (2) the Pietistic credo of "Inwardness" (*Innerlichkeit*), with its antinomian stress on the "Inner Self" and its correlative indifference to considerations of worldly success. In many respects, the deformations of German political culture, formerly described in terms of the *Sonderweg* (special path) problem, are directly traceable to the aforementioned religious legacy. Historical experience has shown that, in times of political crisis, the doctrine of "Inwardness" translates into a dearth of *Zivilcourage*.[30]

For these reasons, perhaps when all is said and done, the nineteenth-century critique of religion has retained some of its cogency and relevance. The problems at issue are endemic to the dialectic of religion and theodicy: the theological rationalization of injustice and social suffering. To be sure, in the West where the value spheres of science, morality, and art have been differentiated, religion must compete with other normative orientations. Hence, it is no longer hegemonic. Correspondingly, theodicy's seductions pose less of an immediate threat. In the developing world, conversely, where religion's influence remains preponderant, the situation is different. The "opiate character" of religion, against which the nineteenth-century materialists vehemently polemicized, remains an ideological force — a primary source of socially engendered "false consciousness."

Writing during the 1920s, Walter Benjamin, who knew something about theology's temptations, formulated the doctrine of "profane illumination" in order to remedy theodicy's enticements. He thereby sought to push the tension between theology and Enlightenment to the point of an immanent resolution. Benjamin firmly believed that the stars must be brought down to earth: in order to become meaningful, the epiphanies and visions formerly associated with religious experience must be alchemically transformed on a secular and immanent basis. His main point of reference was surrealism, which had sought to poetically trans-figure the detritus of everyday life into the "marvelous": an experiential passport to transcendence that could be found *within* the proverbial "bounds of sense." In Benjamin's eyes, Breton and his followers were proponents of an *immanent mysticism*: "No one before these visionaries and augurs [the surrealists] perceived how destitution — not only social but architectonic, the poverty of interiors, enslaved and enslaving objects — can be suddenly transformed into *revolutionary nihilism*."[31] Thereby, surrealism sought to produce illuminations that, unlike the religious variety, were *secular* and *exoteric*. By studying Benjamin's work, we realize that in the modern age religion's redemptory promises have suffused not only the claims of universalistic morality but also the *promesse de bonheur* of avant-garde art.

13

The Disoriented Left: A Critique of Left Schmittianism

Ever since the collapse of the 1960s antiwar coalition of students, civil rights activists, feminists, and liberals appalled by the atrocities their country had perpetrated in Vietnam, the Left, it seems, has been grasping at straws. Whereas pluralism is healthy, fragmentation is not. Too often, the Left's internecine schisms and disagreements have risked handing the political Right sweeping gains on a silver platter. There is a political novel waiting to be written on the years 1980–92 called "While the Left Slept."

During social democracy's so-called thirty glorious years — 1945–75 — in both Europe and the United States the Left recorded some impressive triumphs: above all, the realization of a creditable welfare state that succeeded in extending traditional claims of democratic equality from the political to the social sphere. Thereby, following decades of struggle, many traditional social democratic dreams were achieved. But during the late 1970s the realities of the business cycle and the welfare state's endemic inflationary biases spurred a reassessment of the social democratic project. With the decline of Fordism, the manufacturing sector, and the traditional industrial state, in Western societies working-class composition fell to approximately 30 percent.

Today there can be no doubt about the extent to which these developments precipitated disorientation on the Left. Among its key manifestations were a delusional Third Worldism, terrorism (Baader-Meinhof, the Weather

Underground), and rampant political sectarianism. Whereas during the 1960s, for a time at least, university-based intellectuals and movement activists forged an alliance, over the course of the last three decades this solidarity has progressively unraveled — to the point where, today, the gulf between what passes in the academy as "theory" and the political concerns of average men and women has become cavernous.

During the 1980s, under the banner of "difference," postmodernism became the academic fad du jour. Postmodernism's focus was resolutely "culturalist." Glib celebrations of "textuality" and "discourse" left little room for the Left's historical focus on questions of social inequality. Hence, in most cases, former 1960s activists kept their distance. Yet, by the 1970s the emergence of "new social movements" such as feminism, gay liberation, environmentalism, and antinuclearism had demonstrated that the spectrum of the political Left had become *irretrievably pluralized*. The orientation and goals of these new movements could no longer be comprehended by the classical left-wing framework of class struggle. A key question became: could new social movements be reconciled with the orientation and aims of the traditional Left, or had the Left entered entirely uncharted waters?

As beneficiaries of social democracy's "thirty glorious years," the new social movements no longer focused on questions of economic redistribution. Taking for granted the affluence of the so-called two-thirds society (two-thirds of the populace lead lives of relative privilege, while the other third is allowed to languish in poverty), the economic plight of the underclass fell beneath their political radar scope. Instead, at issue was what one might retrospectively term a "politics of recognition": women, gays, blacks, and ethnic minorities sought affirmations of their identities qua *other* in ways that transcended liberalism's traditional emphasis on formal equality. These groups advanced legitimate claims to group recognition or cultural legitimacy in ways that superseded the traditional "melting pot" metaphor.

One of the most provocative attempts to reconcile the demands of the pluralized left with the challenge of postmodernist theory was Chantal Mouffe and Ernesto Laclau's *Hegemony and Socialist Strategy* (1985). The authors foregrounded Gramsci's stress on questions of cultural domination, whose prominence was indisputable in an Italian context, where strong regional and ecclesiastical allegiances had impeded working-class solidarity. Mouffe and Laclau wagered that the "antifoundationalist" discourse of Derrida and other French thinkers might provide a new theoretical basis for understanding the altered dynamics of political struggle in a post-Fordist era, where the claims of class had lost their salience. It is in the same spirit that, in the "mission statement" for a recent publishing venture, "Phronesis," they declare: "We believe that the most important trends in contemporary theory — deconstruction, psychoanalysis, the philosophy of language as initiated by the later Wittgenstein and post-Heideggerian hermeneutics — are the necessary conditions for understanding the widening of social struggles characteristic of the present of democratic politics, and for formulating a new vision for the Left in terms of radical and plural democracy."

Although this approach harbored a certain plausibility, its limitations, too, seem evident. What, after all, was still "socialist" about the methodological approach of *Hegemony and Socialist Strategy*? Had the authors not abandoned the redistributionist program of traditional socialism at the moment of its greatest vulnerability: the triumph of the heartless "neoliberal" economic policies of Thatcher and Reagan? And what about the tendency of the new social movements the authors embraced to forsake public engagement in favor of a self-absorbed and narcissistic "lifestyle" politics — a development that, already in the 1970s, had been astutely diagnosed in pioneering books by Christopher Lasch and Richard Sennett?[1]

One of the major problems with "identity politics" — the academic left's favored terrain of struggle — is that it prematurely abandons the public sphere to the Left's traditional enemies, thereby leaving it ghettoized, weak, and disoriented. Moreover, by modishly inflating the values of "textuality" and "discourse," the cultural Left seriously neglected traditional sources of domination: political power and economic inequality. Critics of postmodernist "antipolitics" have pointed out that its sweeping critique of the "subject" (epistemological, moral, and political) — a debilitating Nietzschean inheritance — translated into a deprecation of human agency *simpliciter*, thereby effectively eliminating the prospect of constructive political contestation. Other critics on the Left, suspicious of deconstruction's well-nigh unintelligible jargon, accused its champions of having abandoned "public reason" for an esoteric discourse of "professional legitimation." To sum up: during the 1980s, while the Republicans were taking over the country, the academic left was busy storming the ramparts of the Modern Language Association, thereby substituting "textual" politics for actual politics.

Ironically, Mouffe and Laclau's celebration of "difference" occurred at a moment when French intellectuals had abandoned this paradigm in droves. For one, its political implications were profoundly relativistic, in keeping with a trademark Nietzschean scorn for "objective truth" (following his oft-cited maxim, "truth is an illusion without which a certain species could not live"). Thus, in France, the rejection of "difference" was tied to a new appreciation of human rights, whose origins derived from the eminently "metaphysical" standpoint of modern natural law (for example, Grotius, Locke, and, Kant).

During the 1990s a new fascination developed among the academic "theory" crowd: the doctrines of the controversial German right-wing political philosopher Carl Schmitt (1888–1985). During the 1920s Schmitt had written a series of provocative political studies: *Dictatorship* (1920), *Political Theology* (1922), *The Crisis of Parliamentary Democracy* (1923), and *The Concept of the Political* (1927). At the center of his work lay a fascination with dictatorship, which he perceived as a means of restoring "sovereignty" in an era where it had been eroded by mechanisms of political pluralism such as parliament and rule of law. Schmitt famously derided the bourgeoisie as the "chattering class" (*die diskuttierende Klasse*). He denigrated parliament — the bourgeois institution par excellence — as a political "debating society" and held it responsible for the depletion of modern political will. The trappings of bourgeois rule — separation of powers, rule of law, rational debate, judicial review — were, in his opinion, tantamount to an *abnegation of sovereignty*. Schmitt's antiliberalism culminated in "decisionism": a glorification of political will, without regard to its content or direction. In Schmitt's view — and on this point, he was unequivocal — "decision" (*Entscheidung*) is oriented toward "*dictatorship*, not *legitimacy*."[2]

Schmitt's partisans on the academic left feign surprise that, when Hitler seized power in 1933, their man enthusiastically jumped on the Nazi bandwagon. Yet, given his glorification of dictatorship throughout the 1920s, what else should one have expected? During the regime's initial months, Schmitt coauthored *Gleichschaltung* legislation justifying the exclusion of political "enemies." He defended the lawlessness of the June 30, 1934, Röhm purge (the Night of the Long Knives) with an obsequious article entitled "The Führer Protects the Law." Later in the 1930s, he popularized the Nazi doctrine of *Grossraum* (Greater Space), thereby underwriting German continental imperialism. For these acts, he came within a hair's breadth of being indicted by the allies as a war criminal.

In the West, Schmitt's rise to prominence coincided with communism's collapse. It was as though, following socialism's demise, Marxism as an analytical tool had also become obsolete. Understandably, there arose a search for new theoretical methods and models to counter global capitalism's "hegemonic" claims and practices. Partisans of the academic Left viewed Derrida's 1994 book-length study of Schmitt, *The Politics of Friendship*, as a bellwether. With the imprimatur of deconstruction's chief ventriloquist, Schmitt suddenly became fashionable — an object of left-wing intellectual chic.

Among those who flirted with left Schmittianism were the late British political theorist Paul Hirst and the former "Hegelian Marxists" associated with the social theory journal *Telos*.[3] Schmitt's wholesale cynicism concerning international law — following the Nuremburg trials and the birth of the United Nations, he famously remarked that "whoever says humanity lies" — has found resonances in Hardt and Negri's *Empire*, where human rights law is regarded as little more than ideological window dressing for the globalization agenda. Schmitt famously defined politics as the ability to distinguish friends from enemies. Well-armed with bellicose Schmittian maxims — for example, "*The pinnacle of Great Politics is the moment when the enemy comes into concrete clarity as the enemy*" — the post-Marxist Left sought to counter proclamations concerning the "end of history" with a Schmitt-inspired search for political enemies. But it is important to keep in mind that Schmitt, the Third Reich's future "Crown Jurist," developed the friend/enemy distinction for the sake of *undermining* rather than *strengthening* democracy (namely, the Weimar Republic). Is this the route that the reflective democratic Left wishes to travel?

Back in the 1960s, extremist segments of the German student Left openly flirted with Schmitt's doctrines, which confirmed their suspicions of "bourgeois democracy" (one should recall that the acronym of the German student left was "APO," or Extra-Parliamentary Opposition). Its followers were fascinated by Schmitt's notion that liberalism — the sphere of "interests" — perpetually undermines the democratic ideal of self-rule. Yet, Schmitt seems to have enjoyed the last laugh. He fraternized with the student Left with the hope that their antiparliamentary actions would lead to the declaration of a state of emergency — which is exactly what happened during the "German Autumn" of 1977: the kidnapping and murder of employers union president Hans-Martin Schleyer, the hijacking of a Lufthansa jet to Mogadishu, Somalia (both acts perpetrated by the Red Army Faction terrorists), and the mysterious deaths of Andreas Baader and Ulrike Meinhof in Stammheim prison.[4]

Those who seek to appropriate Schmitt's doctrines for the ends of the political Left must seriously weigh the risks of appropriating a *fascist* critique of democracy for *left-wing purposes*. The unambiguous lesson of the "German Autumn" is that a Left that internalizes the antiparliamentary ideology of the Far Right is flirting with disaster.

One of the major problems besetting the idea of a left-Schmittian revival was that Schmitt himself was by no means ill-disposed toward capitalism. His great aversion was toward *socialism*, whose atheistic proponents Schmitt, in a clerico-fascist spirit (Schmitt was a great admirer of the Iberian dictators Salazar and Franco), likened to apostles of the anti-Christ. It was in this vein that Schmitt was fond of citing the nineteenth-century Spanish Catholic philosopher Juan Donoso Cortès's view that the battle against atheistic socialism was not merely another political struggle, but *Armageddon*: an eschatological struggle in which the salvation of humanity itself was at stake.

The foremost exponent of the Left-Schmittian approach has been *Hegemony and Socialist Strategy* coauthor Chantal Mouffe. In her Schmitt-inspired work of the 1990s, Mouffe has highlighted the link between poststructuralism's "anti-essentialism" — the rejection of first principles and objective truth — and the political ideal of "agonistic pluralism." In Mouffe's view, poststructuralism's epistemological relativism best captures the diffuse nature of political struggle in an age of postmodern identity politics, whose standpoint has supplanted the outmoded, "foundationalist," left-wing discourse of "class." As Mouffe argues in *The Return of the Political* (1993): "In order to radicalize the idea of pluralism ... we have to break with rationalism, individualism, and universalism." "Democracy requires the constitution of *collective identities* around clearly *differentiated positions* as well as the possibility to choose between real alternatives."[5]

Yet, what exactly these "real alternatives" might be Mouffe declines to say. Indeed, one of the more frustrating aspects of her approach is that the explicit political consequences of her "agonistic pluralism" are couched in deliberate vagueness. Nor is it by any means clear that the alternatives she has in mind would necessarily be *left-wing alternatives*. After all, if one emphatically rejects the "moral baggage" of democratic universalism, as Mouffe unequivocally does, there is no compelling reason whatsoever why one should prefer *left-wing "political agon"* to that practiced by the political Right.[6] When in an article on "Radical Democracy" Mouffe openly celebrates the politics of the European Counter-Enlightenment — she claims that one need only outfit the Counter-Enlightenment standpoint with a new 'articulation' in order to make it serviceable for the ends of the postmodern left — one gains disturbing insight into her intellectual proximity to reactionary political traditions, which is one of the major perils of relying on Schmitt's intellectual coattails and pedigree.[7]

In *The Return of the Political* Mouffe repeatedly claims that one of her objectives is to counteract the "blurring of political frontiers between left and right," a practice she claims "is harmful for democratic politics, as it impedes the constitution of distinctive political identities."[8] Here, one could argue that Mouffe herself encourages this "blurring of the political frontiers" — the very tendency she warns against — by holding up a reactionary thinker like Schmitt as a model for the political Left.

One of the major dangers of uncritically relying on a framework like Schmitt's is that, in contrast to "normative" approaches that seek to place *moral limits* on political action (for example, the "deliberative democratic" model advocated by Rawls and Habermas), one risks blurring the distinction between progressive and reactionary politics. By elevating "enmity" and "antagonism" to positions of unquestioned primacy, while donning moral blinders, one risks succumbing to a moral and political free fall. Thus, in another shocking avowal of her political preferences, Mouffe singles out for praise Europe's right-wing populist parties as "the only ones denouncing the 'consensus at the center' and trying to occupy the terrain of contestation deserted by the left."[9] By ceaselessly polemicizing against the "rationalist denial of the political,"[10] Mouffe misleadingly insinuates that "deliberative democrats" such as Habermas and Rawls pose a greater threat to the contemporary Left than do figures on the right like Schmitt.

Mouffe finds Schmitt's perspective serviceable for the ends of the political Left since she fears that, following communism's eclipse, a deceptive neoliberal, antipolitical consensus has triumphed, foreclosing the prospects of authentic political struggle ("agonistic pluralism"). But it is worrisome that she seems tone deaf to the manifestly fascist resonances of his standpoint. After all, Schmitt's friend/enemy dichotomy is laden with bellicose and reprehensible social Darwinist connotations. As he remarks in *The Concept of the Political* (1927): "The word struggle [*Kampf*], like the word enemy, is to be understood in its *existential primordiality* .... The concepts of friend, enemy, and struggle receive their real meaning especially insofar as they relate to and preserve the real possibility of *physical annihilation*. War follows from enmity, for the latter is *the existential negation of another being*."[11]

Mouffe's hope is that Schmitt's rhetoric of "struggle" and "annihilation" (in German: *Kampf* and *Vernichtung*) can be domesticated for the ends of the political left. The problem is that, as the preceding quotation indicates, Schmitt's discourse tends to rule out compromises or half measures. Hence, it is difficult to envisage a tolerant or equitable assimilation of his views — an interpretation that would be consonant with the aims of the "pluralist democracy" Mouffe favors. In fact, Schmitt was such an implacable foe of liberal democracy that it is difficult to imagine *any* appropriation of his views that would enhance its fragile egalitarian potentials.

One of the major problems confronting the "left-Schmittian" paradigm is that Schmitt's vision of politics is unambiguously predicated on the "ultimate instance" of war. The political worldview he promotes is inseparable from "logics of struggle" — not in the relatively anodyne, postmodern sense of "political agon" but in the German sense of *Tod und Kampf*. Thereby, Schmitt perpetuates a bellicose German tradition, dating back to the "social imperialism" of the Bismarck era, stressing the "primacy of foreign policy." It would be flatly impossible to reconcile his views with the demands of cosmopolitan citizenship. For, according to Schmitt's perspective, the more successful international rule of law becomes, the more "the political" (in Schmitt's bloody and combative sense) is enfeebled.

Those who seek to appropriate his doctrines for left-wing ends should recall that during the 1920s, Schmitt's glorification of "emergency powers" was a none-too-subtle device for undermining the Weimar Republic's tenuous democratic legitimacy. After all, the collapse of the Weimar system was precipitated not by the Nazis per se but by radical conservatives like Schmitt who, aided by the Weimar Constitution's notorious Article 48, preferred rule by presidential decree to the uncertainties of parliamentarism.

A logical and pressing question arises: given Schmitt's distasteful political views, what might the Left have to gain from a tactical alliance with his doctrines? At this point it should be clear that the pact with Schmitt is a temptation that the Left should studiously avoid. The enticements of left Schmittianism risk bringing out what have historically been the Left's worst features: a Leninist-authoritarian subordination of morality to the imperatives of political will and a faithlessness concerning prospects of piecemeal democratic change.

Undoubtedly, the Schmittian insight that has garnered most favor among his contemporary left-wing heirs is the idea that liberalism and democracy are mutually exclusive political forms. According to Schmitt, democracy mandates an equivalence between rulers and ruled. Conversely, liberalism is a mechanism for representing *interests*, which are by definition *particular* and *nongeneralizable*. Schmitt concludes that the very idea of "liberal democracy" is a contradiction in terms, since democracy requires equality whereas liberalism is predicated on the inequalities generated by interest. In Schmitt's view, parliament is the epitome of liberal democratic duplicity. It is the scene where the claims of the "general will" are continually subverted by the interests of leading economic actors and groups.

One of the deceptive aspects of Schmitt's critique of liberalism is that it allows him to appear misleadingly as a champion of Rousseauian direct democracy — which, of course, could not be further from the truth. Instead, Schmitt openly championed the idea of "plebiscitary dictatorship" or "leadership democracy" (*Führerdemokratie*). He believed that once traditional liberal safeguards were jettisoned, the path to dictatorship would be clear. Since Schmitt tendentiously redefined democracy as the "identity of rulers and ruled," he was free to argue that the goals of democracy were better realized under *dictatorship* than under *liberalism*. The dictator was better able to represent the people's will than the corrupt trafficking in interests that predominated in parliament.

Few of Schmitt's left-wing defenders have been willing to own up to the compromising fact that Schmitt's conception of democracy was predicated on the notion of "racial homogeneity" (*Artgleichheit*). His thought betrayed a *völkisch*-racist streak — not to mention an endemic anti-Semitism — that goes far toward explaining his later partisanship for the Nazis.

But it was Schmitt's attempt to uncouple liberalism from democracy that remains the most sinister aspect of his political legacy. It is especially disconcerting to find that this move has found favor among representatives of the academic Left. His wholesale cynicism about the liberal democratic conceptions of freedom eerily complements a number of Leninist prejudices. By maligning liberalism as a fraudulent realm of "interests," Schmitt misrepresents its all-important natural law pedigree. To be sure, historically liberalism has been a mechanism for safeguarding property rights. But it has also engendered crucial components of the discourse of modern political freedom: constitutionalism; separation of powers; freedom of speech, the press, and assembly; and so forth. To dismiss these freedoms as purely "interest beholden" is misleading and shortsighted. Their preservation remains the vital precondition for any meaningful concept of "positive freedom" — the enthusiasms of civil disobedience and participatory democracy. They represent an indispensable bulwark against political despotism, including majority tyranny, as well as the necessary prerequisite for realizing the values of "strong democracy."

One could make the argument that from a political point of view the nineteenth century represented a hundred-year struggle to redeem the idea of democracy from the abuse it suffered at the hands of the Jacobin dictatorship of 1793–94. Liberalism — Benjamin Constant's "liberty of the moderns" — played a crucial role in facilitating democracy's rehabilitation as an acceptable political form. By accepting the terms of Schmitt's nihilistic critique, the Left risks surrendering valuable political gains to its adversaries on the political Right.

14

Kant at Ground Zero: Philosophers Respond to September 11

Therapeutic Philosophy

Was philosophy prepared for the events of September 11? To judge by all available evidence, the answer must be a resounding "no." For some time now, contemporary philosophy has viewed "worldliness" — the perfectly natural idea that thought should take a healthy and constructive interest in worldly affairs — as a source of contamination. Analytic philosophy's triumph in the decades following World War II meant that, henceforth, philosophy would subscribe to a primarily "therapeutic" self-understanding. Its predominant aim was to ferret out and eliminate the "pseudoproblems" that had beset the history of thought. As Wittgenstein instructed, "philosophical problems arise when language goes on a holiday."[1] According to this conception, philosophy's mission is basically a negative one: to keep language honest. Correspondingly, the history of metaphysics was written off as a history of error: an attempt to set forth claims about the ultimate nature of society, nature, and man that were simply beyond the ken of language.

Wittgenstein's approach — and the analytical method that he helped to engender, and that J. L. Austin brought to a corrosive perfection — was radically contextualist. He characterized discursive practices as "language games" and stressed the parallels between speaking a language and knowing how to "follow a rule." Yet, by virtue of collapsing the dimensions of "is" and "ought," the "real" and "ideal," this approach trivialized the demands of moral philosophy. Since, for Wittgenstein, the meaning of a word was sought in its use, his philosophy lacked a *normative* or *evaluative* dimension capable of transcending the contextual practice of this or that "language game." A thoroughgoing relativism was the consequence of this approach. How should we respond if the rules of a given "language game" were morally objectionable — the language game of ethnic cleansing, for example? Where might we look for the conceptual leverage needed to unmask egregious instances of social injustice or political domination? In what philosophical idiom might we denounce those who perpetrate crimes against humanity? On all these counts, the philosophy of ordinary language seems manifestly impotent. Wittgenstein himself owned up to the quiescent implications of his method when in *Philosophical Investigations* he confessed that the philosophy of ordinary language "leaves everything as it is."[2]

Academic philosophy's studied aversion to worldly affairs has been compounded by the requirements of professionalization. In a classic instance of "unintended consequences," young people whose "love of wisdom" inspires them to enter the field soon discover that these motivations are counterproductive: they have almost nothing to do with the demands of "philosophy as a vocation." Of course, philosophy throughout its history has often had a world-transforming function, for good or for ill: in ancient Greece, in early Christianity, in the Renaissance, in the Enlightenment. But today "engagement" is frowned upon, except as a subdiscipline of a profession. (Are you concerned about the damage to the environment? Then submit a paper to *Philosophy and Public Affairs* and then return to "real" philosophy.) It has little or no bearing on the sophisticated bureaucratic mechanisms of professional advancement. The departmental rap on "public philosophers" is usually that they are wasting their time with amateur philosophy.

A quick look at, say, the eighteenth century would show how central and fundamental the link between philosophy and public purpose was.[3] But no more. Most philosophers have become *Fachmenschen,* or "specialists," in precisely the sense that Weber feared: "Specialists without spirit, sensualists without heart, these nullities imagine they have attained a level of civilization without precedent."[4] As a result, the realm of public philosophy has been abandoned to the so-called left Heideggerians — the likes of Jean Baudrillard, Slavoj Žizek, and Paul Virilio — who have succeeded in filling the vacuum with a vengeance. Came September 11, and they quickly brought their glib up-to-the-minute postmodernist idiom to bear on the terrible events. For want of serious philosophical competition, their notions have been widely quoted, debated, and discussed.

Surely one of the "lessons" of September 11 is that in a globalized civilization lapses in "moral development" — say, the repressive and hate-filled creed purveyed by Wahhabi Islam — are liable to have unforeseeable and potentially devastating worldwide effects. In previous epochs, political deformations that occurred in this or that corner of the world could be safely ignored with only minor external repercussions. Our current state of global interconnectedness has changed all that. Who would have suspected that a relatively small group of militants based in one of the world's most backward and impoverished nations could, with relative ease, perpetrate an act of terrorism against America the likes of which we had never before seen? After all, more people were killed in the September 11 attacks than at Pearl Harbor.

What makes the interventions by the so-called left Heideggerians so odious is that their rhetoric rarely rises above the level of *Schadenfreude*. As good Heideggerians, they are simply incapable of naturally appreciating the validity and the worth of democratic political institutions — civil liberties, republican government, and self-determination. (Heidegger once remarked that from an "essential" standpoint, the Allies' triumph over fascism in World War II "decided nothing.")[5] For Heidegger, after all, the United States was nothing more than a technological Moloch: the "site of catastrophe," an extreme manifestation of civilizational *Untergang* or decline. In keeping with this perspective, the pamphlets of Žizek and Baudrillard exude a barely concealed glee over Osama bin Laden's "divine surprise" of September 2001. For Baudrillard, the attacks represented a glorious, long-awaited instance of wish fulfillment: the Al Qaeda terrorists may have perpetrated the deed, but the act itself was something the entire world had long dreamed of and desired. For the postmodernist sage, criticism of the attacks cannot mask the prodigious jubilation of seeing this world's only superpower meet with destruction: "For it is [the United States] that, by its unbearable power, fomented all the violence infused throughout the world, and thus the terrorist imagination that dwells in all of us. Haven't we dreamt of this event, hasn't the entire world, without exception, dreamt of it; no one could not dream of the destruction of a power that had become hegemonic to such a point.... In essence, it was [the terrorists] who committed the deed, but it is we who wished for it."[6]

With the publication of such texts, postmodernism's trademark cynicism about morality and democracy has reached its nadir. In late 2001, following the Afghanistan war, Baudrillard granted an interview to *Der Spiegel*. When questioned whether the removal of the Taliban from power was not in fact an emancipatory political development, he emphatically disagreed: any expression of American power was a priori condemnable. When interrogated further about whether the spread of human rights and democracy to the Middle East and the Third World was desirable, the postmodernist philosopher again replied in the negative. Human rights, he claimed, are merely a cover for superpower global hegemony: "I believe that human rights have already been subsumed by the process of globalization and function as an alibi. They belong to the juridical and moral superstructure — in sum, they are *advertising*."[7] To find a comparable instance of unadulterated nihilistic contempt for democratic norms, one would have to adduce the Nazi jurist Carl Schmitt, who famously proclaimed that "whoever says humanity lies."[8]

"There Is Nothing outside of the Text"?

Jürgen Habermas was preparing for a guest lectureship in New York when the attacks on the World Trade Center and the Pentagon occurred. Coincidentally, Jacques Derrida was also scheduled to teach in New York that fall. Since two of the world's leading philosophers would be in Manhattan a few weeks after the catastrophe, why not solicit their observations and thoughts and then publish them in book form? Thus resulted *Philosophy in a Time of Terror*.

Habermas and Derrida have for decades represented philosophical antipodes. Habermas, a self-professed child of the Enlightenment, has devoted his immense talents to recovering the progressive intellectual traditions — from Kant to the Frankfurt School — that had been brutally expunged from German soil during the Nazi dictatorship. He has consistently acted not only as a philosophical luminary but also as a vocal public intellectual — and on a number of salient occasions (notably the *Historikerstreit* of the 1980s) as the moral consciousness of his nation.[9] Few would deny that his great labor of philosophical reclamation has been remarkably successful. Several years ago he observed that the Federal Republic's singular accomplishment was to have firmly anchored Germany in the political orbit of the West, thereby ensuring an ineffaceable role for tolerance, basic rights, and rule of law.

In the academy Habermas is best known for his achievements in the field of moral philosophy. He is a highly original disciple of Kant. His unique contribution to this realm has been a variant of Kantian moral universalism known as "discourse ethics." For Kant, those actions alone count as "moral" that could withstand the test of "universalizability": that is, only insofar as I could will that in a specific moral situation every other person act as I would may my action qualify as moral. Like other philosophers, Habermas has remained mistrustful of the solipsistic implications of Kant's standpoint. He has forcefully argued that the individual subject's powers of moral reasoning need to be supplemented by a broader, communicative frame of reference. Discourse ethics holds that judgments of morality need to be redeemed by recourse to actual or hypothetical discourses with other people. In this way, moral reasoning ceases to be monological, as in Kant. In a variation on Kant's Categorical Imperative, the formula for discourse ethics runs: "Only those norms can claim to be valid that meet (or could meet) with the approval of all affected in their capacity as participants in a practical discourse."[10]

As a transcendental philosopher working in the Kantian tradition, Habermas remains acutely aware of the fallible nature of all empirical moral consensuses. Thus, even if all of the preconditions of communicative reason were satisfied (that is, assuming that norms of "fairness," "rightness," and "sincerity" were fulfilled), the result might well be flawed and require remedial discursive mediation — more plainly, it might require more discussion. Empirical results must be constantly checked against transcendental normative expectations.

By situating Habermas within the spectrum of contemporary ethical thought, one can begin to appreciate the distinctive nature of his moral "voice" as well as his distance from other, more cynical perspectives — notably that of Derrida. In view of its unflagging commitment to the primacy of the "moral point of view," Habermas's approach bears comparison to that of the late John Rawls, who is often credited with single-handedly reviving the discipline of moral philosophy. Both are ethical cognitivists. They believe that, fundamentally, moral problems concern questions of "truth." They hold that objective considerations of "right" or "wrong" are at stake, and that these considerations may be adjudicated by recourse to methods of argumentation. Conversely, the main tendencies in twentieth-century moral philosophy have been decidedly noncognitivist or "emotivist." Under the twin influences of logical positivism and the philosophy of ordinary language, philosophers have been loath to admit that questions of truth are at stake in moral judgments. Instead they have held that moral issues boil down to individual preferences — like art, they concern subjective matters of taste.

In their mutual aversion to transcendental philosophy, postmodernism and the philosophy of ordinary language climax in an ungainly ethical and cultural relativism. Both approaches entail an unqualified defense of the "other" in his or her irreducible "otherness." But what happens when the "other" in question happens to be an unregenerate fundamentalist monster — the very embodiment of political repression and religious intolerance? It is on this problem that the happy relativists founder. What we need after September 11, in other words, is a philosophy that is capable of accomplishing two ends at once. It must defend the moral legitimacy of democratic norms while at the same time respecting the realities of cultural difference. And discourse ethics is capable of satisfying both these requirements. It knows how to reconcile universal morality with cultural pluralism. Might the twenty-first century, then, be Habermasian? Only if we are lucky.

In comparison with Habermas, Derrida represents an obverse philosophical tradition: the "hermeneutics of suspicion," an avowedly anti-Enlightenment standpoint that derives from the work of Nietzsche and Heidegger. In almost every respect Derridean deconstruction could not be more unlike Habermas's veneration of "discussion oriented toward mutual understanding." Derrida made his name as a sly and indefatigable critic of Reason. In the 1940s Heidegger observed that "reason, venerated for centuries, is *the most stiff-necked adversary of thought*" — a statement that might be construed as Derrida's point of departure.[11] Heidegger famously advocated the "destruction" of Western metaphysics, and deconstruction, in no uncertain terms, picks up where Heidegger left off. In the lexicon of deconstruction, reason is incurably "logocentric": it signifies the "tyranny of the logos" and, as such, suppresses otherness, heterogeneity, and difference — concepts that, among the deconstructionist faithful, possess a type of theological sanctity. For Derrida, the trademark of Western thought, dating back to Parmenides and Plato, has been a systematic repression of marginal elements ("otherness") that fail to conform to reason's oppressive requirements: its demand for unity, totality, and sameness.

That Derrida's approach severely distorts the merits — and the history — of Western thought almost goes without saying. In the standard deconstructionist litany of incurably logocentric thinkers, Plato occupies the status of crown witness. But for anyone who has struggled with the ambivalences and the contradictions of dialogues such as the *Theaetetus* or *Parmenides*, which reveal Plato's own doubts about the irrefragability of the logos, Derrida's characterizations of Platonism are risible. Moreover, if language and knowledge are irremediably logocentric, and if understanding is merely a species of misunderstanding, then Derrida's standpoint deprives us of the means of our own liberation. Deconstruction cheerfully severs the pivotal link between insight and emancipation — a link that, from Socrates to Freud, has been central to all theories of human self-realization. When Socrates proclaimed, at the dawn of Western thought, that "virtue is knowledge," he gave voice to philosophy's central premise: that reason is the key to human flourishing, to a life well lived. By denigrating reason as "logocentric," Derrida willfully cultivates a new obscurantism. Anyone who has tried to plow through his infamously obscure texts knows exactly what this means. As one of deconstruction's French critics has aptly observed: "Deconstruction is the ruse that makes it possible to speak at the same time as there is nothing more to say."[12]

Deconstruction certainly has had a strange career. At the precise moment when Derrideanism became a dead letter in France, it was resurrected in North America. Amid the "culture of narcissism" aptly diagnosed by Christopher Lasch (among others), deconstructionist feats of interpretive bravado — its involuted "close readings" of hermetic texts — found favor among a generation of graduate students that had taken to heart Derrida's celebrated maxim *il n'y a pas de hors-texte,* "there is nothing outside the text." So deconstruction provided a fitting alibi for those who were condemned to spend the majority of their waking hours chained to a study carrel in the library.

A Dialogue of the Deaf

Since the interviews assembled in *Philosophy in a Time of Terror* were conducted in fall 2001 — prior to President Bush's January 29, 2002, "axis of evil" speech, not to mention the war in Iraq — it seemed dated by the time it appeared. At its core are the two dialogues with Habermas and Derrida, which are complemented by three interpretive essays by the Italian philosopher Giovanna Borradori. The Habermas colloquy, the book's unquestionable highlight, runs to a crisp twenty pages. The Derrida interview rambles on interminably for fifty-one pages. Lest I stand accused of misrepresenting Derrida's writerly talents, here is his response to Professor Borradori's relatively straightforward question: were the September 11 events historically unique?

> We perhaps have no concept and no meaning available to us to name ... this "thing" that has just happened, this supposed "event" ... "Something" took place, we have the feeling of not having seen it coming, and certain consequences undeniably follow upon the "thing." But this very thing, the place and meaning of this "event," remains ineffable, like an intuition without concept, like a unicity with no generality on the horizon or with no horizon at all, out of range for a language that admits its powerlessness and so is reduced to pronouncing mechanically a date, repeating it endlessly, as a kind of ritual incantation, a conjuring poem, a journalistic litany or rhetorical refrain that admits to not knowing what it's talking about. We do not in fact know what we are saying or naming in this way: September 11, *le 11 septembre,* September 11 ... The telegram of this metonymy ... points out ... that we do not recognize or even cognize, that we do not yet know how to qualify, that we do not know what we are talking

about … What remains "infinite" in this wound is that we do not know how to describe, identify, or even name it.[13]

All of this reminds me of the joke that was popular on the academic conference circuit during the 1980s: "What is the difference between a deconstructionist and a Mafioso?" "The deconstructionist makes you an offer you can't understand."

The just-cited passage reads like an exercise in self-caricature. Yet, an important philosophical issue is at stake. Deconstruction is known for fending off or keeping at bay so-called closed readings of texts: readings that would set unfair limits to "interpretive play" or (to employ one of Derrida's pet terms) "dissemination" — the inherent, unmasterable polysemy of meaning or signification. For this reason, one of deconstruction's leitmotifs is the (admittedly cumbersome) notion of "undecidability": there is no such thing as a final or definitive interpretation, only an endless proliferation of glosses and rereadings.

But this "standpoint," if one can call it that, risks degenerating into an act of intellectual bad faith. For if meaning is, strictly speaking, "undecidable," why bother taking a position at all? According to deconstruction, all truth claims are ontologically disingenuous or "false positives." Derrida's glorification of "undecidability" risks dismissing acts of judgment as such as monumental instances of bad faith. But it also underestimates our own subliminal awareness concerning the provisional nature of our everyday judgments and convictions. What is lacking in this approach is the essential distinction between warranted (or just) assertions and unwarranted (or unjust) assertions. Implicitly, we employ such criteria all of the time. Suffice it to say that language as such would "collapse" — and human sociability along with it — if distinctions of this nature proved as tenuous as Derrida suggests. After all, we employ such judgments all the time: horses have four legs, not five; the sun rises in the East, not the West; the moon is composed of rock and soil, not green cheese.

Unfortunately, the much anticipated colloquy between Habermas and Derrida, at the time the reigning titans of European philosophy (Derrida died in fall 2004), never materializes. *Philosophy in a Time of Terror* promotes itself as "an unprecedented encounter between two of the most influential thinkers of our age: here for the first time Habermas and Derrida overcome their historical antagonism and agree to appear side by side."[14] But Habermas and Derrida were not even in the same room when the interviews were conducted. In fact, they were not even on the same continent. Derrida was interviewed in New York in October 2001; Habermas was interviewed upon his return to Germany in December that same year. Instead of an historic "meeting of the minds," we are presented with a dialogue of the deaf. Borradori's repeated efforts to convince us that the two philosophers share a significant amount of common ground fall crushingly flat.

Since the interview transpired a mere three months after the events of September 11, Habermas is understandably circumspect about hazarding portentous prophecies concerning their long-term historical meanings. At the same time, as a liberal internationalist with profound Kantian allegiances, he voices significant reservations about the nature of America's response. Habermas views the strengthening of international law and related organs of international and regional governance (the United Nations and the European Union) as the most reliable bulwark against predatory state behavior. Following decades of cynicism about the viability of international institutions — a cynicism abetted by the imperatives of Cold War–induced realpolitik — the 1990s witnessed a dramatic rebirth of the cosmopolitan spirit immortalized some two hundred years ago in Kant's treatise on "Perpetual Peace." Successful instances of humanitarian intervention in Bosnia and Kosovo, "crimes against humanity" trials in The Hague (the first since World War II), a nascent International Criminal Court, and the subjection of former Chilean dictator Augusto Pinochet to the exigencies of human rights law — all of these instances denote a transformed international consensus concerning the prospects of lawful cosmopolitan governance. With some justification, scholars have referred to these developments as a veritable revolution in international governance. At issue quite simply, but momentously, is whether in the future international relations will be predicated on rule of law or, as has been true in the past, sheer force or "right of the strongest."[15]

Habermas is concerned that these inchoate strides toward a principled internationalism may be jeopardized by a new round of intemperate superpower unilateralism. Typically, declarations of war entail limited goals and relatively well-defined objectives. And the humanitarian interventions of the 1990s sought the backing of the international community. But the Bush administration's open-ended "war on terrorism" falls outside these accepted parameters, thereby potentially engendering a new wave of global political instability. Foreign nationals detained at Guantanamo Bay have been deprived of the legal safeguards commonly accorded prisoners of war. Suspected political opponents have been routinely flown to third countries where they can be interrogated at a remove from the safeguards and protections of international law. And the military tribunals contemplated by Bush and his advisers to try suspected terrorists signify another mechanism intended to circumvent the guarantees of due process. If the world's only remaining superpower regularly runs roughshod over the strictures and the provisions of international humanitarian law, where is the incentive for nations that possess weaker historical commitments to liberal values to act lawfully? Habermas's commitment to sustaining international law's moral viability parallels Rawls's attempt in *The Law of Peoples* to extend the precepts of "justice as fairness" (developed in *A Theory of Justice*) to relations among nations or peoples.

In spring 2003 Habermas published a widely discussed manifesto, cosigned by Derrida, "Our Renewal: After the War, Europe's Rebirth," which interpreted the massive antiwar demonstrations in Europe as the sign of an emergent common European consciousness. Habermas hoped that a federal Europe, united behind a common foreign policy and committed to the values of liberal internationalism, would be able to serve as an effective counterweight to the Bush administration's reckless unilateralism. In this document, written six weeks after the overthrow of Iraq's Ba'athist dictatorship in April 2003, one detects a geopolitical stridency absent in the 2001 Borradori interview:

> In this world a reduction of politics to the obtuse as well as costly alternative between war and peace does not exhaust all the options. Europe must throw its weight on the scales, both on the international plane as well as in the framework of the United Nations, in order to counter-balance the hegemonic unilateralism of the United States. Europe must bring its influence to bear on the structural design of a future international legal-political order [*Weltinnenpolitik*] — at the World Economic Summits and the Institutions of the World Trade Organization, the World Bank, and the International Monetary Fund.[16]

Yet, in view of the animosities and conflicts that have historically beset the European Union — the Nice summit on institutional reform broke down ignominiously, as did, in 2005, efforts to ratify a common European constitution; the smaller nations, a number of which supported the American campaign in Iraq, are justifiably apprehensive about being bullied in the domain of international affairs by France and Germany — one wonders whether these proposals have much of a chance to succeed. Moreover, how easy will it be to maintain a "common European consciousness" if and when there is no longer an American war to protest?

Habermas's dogged cosmopolitanism inevitably reinforces the image of the pacifist-multilateralist European recently constructed by Robert Kagan in *Of Paradise and Power*. But it would be foolish, as well as potentially self-defeating, for statesmen and policymakers to discount the German philosopher's concerns for just international governance. Since the Treaty of Westphalia of 1648, which brought the horrors of the Thirty Years' War to a merciful end, the reigning consensus in international relations has been an unyielding respect for state sovereignty, to the detriment of internationalism. The Westphalian settlement gave rise to the feast-or-famine approach of balance of power politics. It was a mechanism that enjoyed noteworthy successes, as in the relatively peaceful, one-hundred-year interregnum that began with the Treaty of Vienna in 1815. But when the system broke down, as it did in 1914, the results were catastrophic. No statesperson in his or her right mind should desire to go back down that road.

Another significant defect of the Westphalian system was that it tacitly sanctioned all manner of persecution occurring within state borders. Only with the implementation of the post-Holocaust, UN-backed human rights regime, making "crimes against humanity" an offense transcending the boundaries of state sovereignty, did the situation begin to change. Whatever the new regime's defects (most of which have pertained to a lack of capacity for enforcement), one would be hard-pressed to recommend a return to the earlier system.

Respecting the international system recommends itself on prudential grounds as well as on ethical ones. Morally speaking, such respect reinforces the ground rules of acceptable international conduct and thereby helps to curtail potential excesses on the part of rogue states and regional bullies, although no such system is flawless. Practically speaking, one of the inescapable facts of contemporary international relations is that no individual superpower can master the contingencies of an increasingly complex and unpredictable global political environment. Regional alliances are imperative, of course; but, in addition, international law provides a set of rule-governed procedures to regulate disputes that would prove too onerous to address on an ad hoc or case-by-case basis, thereby freeing up political energies for "hard cases" such as the current disputes involving Iran's and North Korea's nuclear aspirations.

In assessing the motives behind the American war on terrorism, Habermas disagrees sharply with cynics on the political Left who perceive the Bush administration's bellicosity as an unambiguous instance of self-interested *Machtpolitik*: as a grab for world mastery by an unrivaled world hegemon. Instead he understands the attitudes of the Republican administration as consistent with the values of liberal nationalism. He disagrees not so much with the administration's values — a principled aversion to tyrants such as Saddam Hussein and a desire to see democratic regimes flourish in their stead — as with its methods: an arrogant unilateralism that he perceives as ultimately self-defeating. In Habermas's view, such policies represent a classic instance of illegitimate means vitiating desirable political ends. In "What Does the Felling of the Monument Mean?," a piece written in April 2003 in the wake of the Iraq war, he articulates these objections as follows:

> World society has become too complex for it still to be steerable from some central point based on a politics of military force. The fear of terrorism experienced by the technically highly-armed superpower seems to express the Cartesian fear of a subject seeking to turn itself and the world around it into an object, in order to bring everything under control.... A nation which reduces all options to the dumb alternatives of war and peace runs up against the limits of its own organizational powers and resources. Even if this hegemonic unilateralism were realizable it would still have side-effects that would, by its own criteria, be morally undesirable. The more that political power manifests itself in the dimensions of military, secret service, and police, the more does it undermine itself ... by endangering its own mission of improving the world according to liberal ideas.[17]

By the same token, Habermas's cosmopolitanism can at times seem too rigid. His pristine view of humanitarian intervention risks foundering on the question: how should one proceed in the event that multilateral institutions break down? One could argue that the German and French refusal to join the anti-Iraq coalition was less principled than the Anglo-American military intervention — which, after all, targeted for removal one of the twentieth century's most bloodthirsty and insidious tyrants. In September 2002, Gerhard Schröder parlayed a brazen and thankless anti-Americanism into a semimiraculous electoral triumph. Across the Rhine, Jacques Chirac took careful note of the domestic political gains to be won from playing the anti-American card. Since their first priority was the eminently "realist" goal of setting limits to American geopolitical reach, France and Germany were happy to let Saddam's brutal regime off the hook, thereby forsaking — or so one might argue — the precepts of humanitarian intervention that had been put to such outstanding use in Bosnia, Kosovo, and East Timor. Nor should one forget that in Kosovo, in order to forestall genocide, NATO was compelled to act in the absence of a Security Council resolution — to act unilaterally. On that occasion it was Russia that played an obstructionist role by threatening to block UN approval through use of its veto power. Sometimes liberal nationalism is the fallback position for a dysfunctional multilateralism.

As a champion of rule of law and liberal internationalism, Habermas harbors few illusions about the morally retrograde character of the fundamentalist worldview that inspired the September 11 attacks. An ethics of tolerance appropriate to an age of globalization necessitates the ability to assume the standpoint of the "other."[18] But dogmatic belief systems of all varieties rule out precisely this capacity. Habermas views Islamic fundamentalism as a "response" to the challenges posed by modernity to the Arab world: "The West in its entirety serves as a scapegoat for the Arab world's own, very real experiences of loss, suffered by populations torn out of their cultural traditions during processes of accelerated modernization."[19] Yet unlike partisans of the "blowback" idea, who allege that on September 11 the United States merely reaped the consequences of what its foreign policy had sown, Habermas's characterization confers no legitimacy on the phenomenon that it seeks to explain. His unflagging commitment to the "moral point of view" forbids him from entertaining any illusions that one could under any circumstances justify the cold-blooded massacre of civilian innocents (at least five hundred and forty-eight of whom were in fact foreign-born).

The Hazards of "Virology"

Derrida's explanation for September 11 is decidedly more fanciful. It relies on the idiom of virology. In his view, the attacks are best described in terms of the biofeedback mechanisms of the human autoimmune system. He seems oblivious to the semantic hazards involved in trying to analyze human societies in terms of biological metaphors, which has traditionally been an essential feature of the discourse of European racism.[20]

As is well known, the autoimmune system secretes antibodies to attack unwanted foreign invaders, such as microbes. But at times the process miscarries, and the antibodies mistakenly attack the host. According to Derrida, the September 11 attacks were born of an analogous process. As the epicenter of globalization and neocolonialism, the West has become entangled in depredations and corrupt dealings well beyond its own borders. Moreover, it remains oblivious to the way the injustice and the rapacity that it has visited upon the helpless peoples of the world distort life in the Northern Hemisphere's affluent metropoles. When antibodies attack the host, they call attention to the fact that the host is diseased.

On September 11, the West at long last reaped what it had sown. According to Derrida, as a reaction to American foreign policy, the brand of Islamic fundamentalism practiced by Al Qaeda was a type of "antibody," a Western "secretion," an indigenous response to the imperiousness of American political overreach. Usually these "antibodies" thrive at the Third World sites where they are originally "secreted." But in the case at hand something went wrong. The West's usually reliable autoimmune system inexplicably miscarried, and the "antibody" known as Al Qaeda attacked its "host." The September 11 attacks thus serve as a cruel reminder of the inequities and injustices of American "hegemony." This is what the world-famous philosopher concludes:

> As we know, an autoimmunitary process is that strange behavior where a living being, in quasi-suicidal fashion, 'itself' works to destroy its own protection, to immunize itself against its 'own' immunity .... At issue is an autoimmunitary terror ... of the "Cold War,"... the formation of Arab Muslim terrorist networks equipped and trained during the Cold War.... What will never let itself be forgotten is thus the perverse effect of the autoimmunitary itself. For we now know that repression in both its psychoanalytical sense and its political sense — whether it be through the police, the military, or the economy — ends up producing, reproducing, and regenerating the very thing it seeks to disarm.[21]

From an empirical standpoint, the "blowback" argument in Derrida's assertions is untenable. It exaggerates American involvement in the anti-Soviet struggle in Afghanistan during the 1980s. To be sure, in 1986–87 the CIA provided the Mujaheddin with nine hundred Stinger antiaircraft missiles. But as Peter Bergen showed in *Holy War: Inside the Secret World of Osama bin Laden*, excessive American participation would have risked compromising the anti-Soviet guerrilla campaign as well as handing the Russians an immense propaganda coup. As Bergen concludes: "The CIA did not need the Afghan Arabs, and the Afghan Arabs did not need the CIA. The notion that the Agency funded and trained the Afghan Arabs is, at best, misleading."[22] More importantly, Derrida's wacky immunological speculations naïvely overlook the central "ethical" question: was not the goal of ending the Soviet Union's illegal occupation of Afghanistan a worthy one?

One of the unwitting merits of this book is that it demonstrates the basic incommensurability between Habermas's and Derrida's understanding of philosophy itself, despite the volume's avowed intention of "bridging the differences." Habermas remains fully committed to the central goals of normative political theory. He believes that the role of moral philosophy is to clarify the ethical presuppositions that underlie everyday social interaction. In this respect, he is a legitimate heir to the transcendental philosophy of Kant. In major philosophical works such as *Theory of Communicative Action*, he has defined the moral goal of human communication as "understanding oriented toward reaching an agreement." Transferred to the sphere of politics, this notion admirably mandates that one maximize the potentials of uninhibited discussion or public deliberation, thereby ensuring that political outcomes are fair or just. Unfortunately, in advanced postindustrial societies the constraints of "social complexity" play an increasingly dominant role, and pragmatic considerations place a premium on questions of efficiency and the role of technical expertise — in the face of which the deliberative capacities of an informed lay citizenry seem increasingly marginalized. Consequently, Habermas's political thought focuses on the extent to which "lay publics" can reclaim a deliberative role that has been increasingly usurped by experts, bureaucrats, and special interests.

What separates Habermas from postmodernists such as Derrida is a basic confidence in the capacity of democratic government to arrive at just decisions. He believes that polities founded on rule of law contain an ineradicable element of principle that distinguishes them from regimes predicated on force or interest. Democratic politics represents a perennial balancing act between the norms of fairness, usually codified in a nation's constitution, and considerations of interest or expediency that derive from the imperatives of economic and administrative life. Postmodernists are generally unmoved by norms of political fairness. Force or interest is all there is. Undoubtedly, this is one of the reasons behind Derrida's recent fascination with Carl Schmitt. "Whoever says humanity lies": this means that whoever claims to act on the basis of principle only does so the more effectively to mask his or her interests. Derrida has said that there is no such thing as a "just law." It really does not get more cynical than that.

It is on these issues that Borradori's ill-judged efforts to reconcile the philosophies of Habermas and Derrida run aground. At one point she tries to seduce Habermas into accepting Derrida's awful view that norms of "tolerance" are little more than a pretext for Western paternalism. Following Derrida's lead, she suggests that, under the cover of "tolerance," we effectively assimilate non-Westerners to our own values and belief systems. But Habermas nicely settles this hash:

> Today, for example, we encounter this paradox in the concept of "militant democracy": no freedom for the enemies of freedom. However, from this example we can also learn that the straight deconstruction of the concept of tolerance falls into a trap, since the constitutional state contradicts precisely the premise from which the paternalistic sense of the traditional concept of "tolerance" derives. Within a democratic community whose citizens reciprocally grant one another equal rights, no room is left for an authority allowed to

one-sidedly determine the boundaries of what is to be tolerated. On the basis of the citizens' equal rights and reciprocal respect for each other, nobody possesses the privilege of setting the boundaries of tolerance from the viewpoint of their own preferences and value-orientations.[23]

In other words: even if the principle of tolerance is imperiously misused in specific empirical instances, democratic norms contain a self-correcting mechanism that allows us to differentiate between a "fair-minded" and an abusive implementation of basic egalitarian precepts. While others wallow in the sophistries and cynicism of postmodernism, Habermas has remained an unwavering champion of democratic precepts and the "moral point of view."

Notes

Introduction

1. Rudolf, Carnap, "The Elimination of Metaphysics through Logical Analysis," in A. J. Ayer, *Logical Positivism* (Glencoe, Ill.: The Free Press, 1959), 60–61.
2. Cited in Karl Dietrich Bracher, *The German Dictatorship* (New York: Prager, 1970), 10.
3. On this problem, see the informative study by Jane Afary and Kevin B. Anderson, *Foucault and the Iranian Revolution: Gender and the Seductions of Islamism* (Chicago: University of Chicago Press, 2005).
4. Habermas, *Religion and Rationality: Essays on Reason God and Modernity*, ed. Eduardo Mendieta (Cambridge, Mass.: MIT Press, 2002).
5. For the relevant texts, see Derrida, "Force of Law: the Mystical Foundation of Authority," in *Deconstruction and the Possibility of Justice* (New York: Routledge, 1992); Derrida, *Acts of Religion* (New York: Routledge, 2002), and *Derrida and Negative Theology* (Albany: State University of New York Press, 1992). For an excellent critique, see Slavoj Zizek, *The Puppet and the Dwarf: The Perverse Core of Christianity* (Cambridge, Mass.: MIT Press, 2003). As Zizek observes: "The ultimate form of idolatry is the deconstructive purifying of [the] Other, so that all that remains of the Other is its place, the pure form of Otherness as the Messianic Promise. It is here that we encounter the limit of deconstruction: as Derrida himself has realized in the last two decades, the more radical a deconstruction is, the more it has to rely on its inherent undeconstructible condition of deconstruction, the messianic promise of Justice" (139).

Chapter 1

1. Benjamin, *Das Passagenwerk*, ed. Rolf Tiedemann (Frankfurt am Main: Suhrkamp, 1982), 1070. All subsequent references to this edition will appear parenthetically in text as PW.

2. For a good account, see Rolf Tiedemann, "Bild, dialektisches," in *Historisches Wörterbuch der Philosophie*, ed. Joachim Ritter (Basel: Schwab, 1971–), 919–20.
3. Susan Buck-Morss, *The Dialectics of Seeing: Walter Benjamin and the Arcades Project* (Cambridge, MA, MIT Press, 1989), 6.
4. Benjamin, *Briefe*, ed. Gershom Scholem and Theodor Adorno (Frankfurt am Main: Suhrkamp, 1966).
5. Benjamin, *Gesammelte Schriften* 4, 1, 108.
6. Adorno, letter to Benjamin, in *Aesthetics and Politics*, ed. Ronald Taylor (London: New Left Books, 1977), 128.
7. Ibid., 129–30.
8. Benjamin, *Briefe* 2, 663; See also Adorno, *Complete Correspondence, 1928–1940* (Cambridge, MA: Harvard University Press, 1999); subsequent references to this edition will appear in parenthetically in text as CC.
9. Louis Aragon, *Paris Peasant*, trans. Simon Taylor (London: Jonathan Cape, 1971), 18–19.
10. Benjamin, *Briefe* 2, 446.
11. Marx, letter to Arnold Ruge, in *The Marx–Engels Reader*, ed. Robert Tucker (New York: Norton, 1978), 15.
12. Ibid., 132.
13. Benjamin, *Briefe* 2, 524.
14. Ibid., 489.
15. Benjamin, "Surrealism," *Reflections: Essays, Aphorisms, Autobiographical Writings*, trans. Edmund Jephcott (New York: Harcourt Brace Jovanovich: 1978), 189.
16. See the testimony in *The College of Sociology*, ed. Denis Hollier, trans. Betsy Wing (Minneapolis: University of Minnesota Press, 1988).
17. For a discussion, see Richard Wolin, *The Seduction of Unreason: The Intellectual Romance with Fascism from Nietzsche to Postmodernism* (Princeton: Princeton University Press, 2004).
18. Benjamin, *Briefe*, 515.
19. Benjamin, Letter to Max Rychner, in *Briefe* 2, 524.
20. Benjamin, "Theses on the Philosophy of History," in *Illuminations*, trans. Harry Zohn (New York: Schocken, 1969), 254.
21. Ibid., 253.
22. Scholem, "Walter Benjamin," in *On Jews and Judaism in Crisis* (New York: Schocken, 1976), 254.
23. Benjamin, "Theses," 254.
24. Hegel, *Reason in History* (Indianapolis: Bobbs-Merrill, 1976).
25. Benjamin, "Critique of Violence," *Reflections*, 297, 300.
26. For example, see Giorgio Agamben, *States of Exception*, trans. Kevin Atell (Chicago: Chicago University Press, 2004).
27. Benjamin, *Origin of German Tragic Drama*, trans. John Osborne (London: New Left Books, 1977), 178.

Chapter 2

1. Adorno, Letter to Max Horkheimer, 24 March 1956, cited in Jager, *Adorno: A Political Biography* (New Haven: Yale University Press, 2004), ix. *Gunzelin, also: Text und*. See also the following remark in Adomo, *Minima Moralia: Reflections from Damaged Life*, trans. E. Jephcott (London: New Left Books,

1974), 192: "True thoughts are those alone which do not understand themselves." For a good overview of events involved in the Adorno "Jubilaum," see John Abromeit, "Remembering Adorno," *Radical Philosophy* 124 (March–April 2004). As Abromeit remarks: "Upon arriving in the mini-metropolis on the Main [Frankfurt], just asking a taxi driver to be taken to the "Frankfurt School," as some bewildered visitors have done recently, would lead only to a wild goose chase. Theodor Adorno Platz, on the other hand, does really exist. But prior to this year, one would have discovered there only a large war memorial from 1925, a concrete ping-pong table, and several benches — often littered with empty cans of beer — all surrounded by some overgrown hedges. Just a few days before what would have been his 100th, birthday, the city of Frankfurt finally decided to improve the miserable state of Adorno's official site. Beer cans were picked up, hedges trimmed, ping-pong table removed and the war monument was replaced by an artistic memorial in the form of a large desk with several of Adorno's principal works on top of it."

2. The three most notable biographies were the following: Detlev Claussen, *Theodor W. Adorno: Ein leztes Genie* (Frankfurt am Main: Fischer, 2003); Lorenz Jäger, *Adorno: A Political Biography* (New Haven: Yale University Press, 2004); and Stefan Müller-Doohm, *Adorno: Eine Biographie* (Frankfurt am Main: Suhrkamp, 2003); an English translation of Müller-Doohm's book is forthcoming with Polity Press.

3. For example, see Erich Fromm's programmatic essay, "The Method and Function of an Analytic Social Psychology," in *The Essential Frankfurt School Reader*, ed. A. Arato and E. Gebhardt (New York: Urizen Books, 1977), 477–496.

4. Alexander and Margerete Mitschlerlich, *The Inability to Mourn* (New York: Grove Press, 1975).

5. Thomas Mann, *The Story of a Novel: The Genesis of Dr. Faustus*, trans. Richard and Clara Winston (New York: Alfred Knopf, 1961), 45.

6. *In steter Freundschaft: Leo Lowenthal–Siegfried Kracaeur Briefwechsel, 1922–1966*, ed. Peter-Erwin Jansen and Christian Schmidt (Lüneberg: zu Klampen, 2003), 54.

7. For a brilliant satire of the George cult's pretensions, see Rainer Werner Fassbinder's film *Satans Braten* (Satan's Brew).

8. Adorno, *Philosophy of Modern Music*, trans. Annette Mitchell and Wesley Blomster (New York: Seabury Press, 1973), xii.

9. Ibid., xii.

10. Schoenberg, *Style and Idea* (Berkeley: University of California Press, 1984), 386.

11. Hans Heinz Stuckenschmidt, *Arnold Schoenberg: His Life, World, and Work*, trans. H. Searle (New York: Macmillan, 1978), 508.

12. See the discussion of Benjamin's *Passagenwerk* in Chapter 1.

13. Benjamin, "Surrealism: The Last Snapshot of the European Intelligentsia," *Reflections: Essays and Aphorisms, Autobiographical Writings*, trans. Edmund Jephcott, ed. Peter Demetz (New York: Harcourt Brace Jovanovich, 1978), 189; Adorno, *Notes to Literature*, 4 vols., trans. Shierry Weber Nicholsen, ed. Rolf Tiedemann (New York: Columbia University Press, 1991).

14. Cited in Adorno, *Minima Moralia*, 83.

15. Horkheimer, "Über das Materialismus," in *Schriften*, ed. Gunzelin Schmidt-Noerr (Frankfurt am Main: Fischer, 1987), 346–400.

16. Adorno, *Negative Dialectics*, trans. E. B. Ashton (New York: Seabury Press, 1973).

17. Ernst Nolte, "The Past That Will Not Pass Away," *Forever in the Shadow of Hitler: Original Documents of the Historikerstreit*, trans. James Knowlton and Truett Cates (Atlantic Highlands, NJ: Humanities Press, 1993), 18–23.

18. On this theme, see Jeffrey Herf's forthcoming book, *The War and the Jews: Nazi Propaganda during World War II and the Holocaust* (Cambridge, MA: Harvard University Press, 2006).

19. The term "redemptive anti-Semitism" figures prominently in Saul Friedlander's magisterial study, *Nazi Germany and the Jews* (New York: Perennial, 1998).

20. Jäger, *Adorno: A Political Biography*, 43.

21. See her indispensable political analysis in Rosa Luxemburg, *The Russian Revolution and Leninism or Marxism* (Ann Arbor: University of Michigan Press, 1961).

22. Brecht, *Werke* 27, 12–13; cited by Jäger in *Adorno*, 109.

23. Adorno's letter of 3 January 1963 to the Frankfurt University student newspaper, *Diskus*, is reproduced in Wolfgang Kraushaar, *Frankfurter Schule und Studentbewegung: Von der Flaschenpost zu Molotowcocktail*, vol. 2 (Frankfurt am Main, 1998), 168.

24. See Darrin MacMahon, *Enemies of the Enlightenment: The French Counter-Enlightenment and the Making of Modernity* (New York: Oxford University Press, 2001), 12: "[Today] Enlightenment bashing has developed into something of an intellectual blood-sport, uniting elements of both the left and the right in a common cause."

25. Cited in Karl Dietrich Bracher, *The German Dictatorship* (New York: Holt, Rinehart, and Winston, 1972), 10.

26. Adorno, "Education after Auschwitz," in *Critical Models: Interventions and Key Words*, trans. H. Pickford (New York: Columbia University Press, 1998), 191–204; Adorno and Hellmut Becker, "Education for Maturity and Responsibility," *History of the Human Sciences* 12(3): 21–34.

Chapter 3

1. "Zum Geleit," in J. Habermas, ed., *Antworten auf Herbert Marcuse* (Frankfurt: Suhrkamp, 1968), 10–11.

2. For a good history of the German Revolution, see A. J. Ryder, *The German Revolution of 1918* (Cambridge: Cambridge University Press, 1967).

3. *The German Artist Novel* has never been translated into English. It has been included in volume 1 of Marcuse's *Schriften* (Frankfurt am Main: Suhrkamp, 1978), 7–346. For a discussion of its basic themes, see Douglas Kellner, *Herbert Marcuse and the Crisis of Marxism* (Berkeley and Los Angeles: University of California Press, 1984), 18–32.

4. Marcuse, "Entäuschung," G. Neske, ed., *Erinnerungen an Martin Heidegger* (Pfullingen: Neske, 1977), 162.

5. For their testimonies, see Arendt, "Martin Heidegger at Eighty," in *Martin Heidegger and Modern Philosophy*, ed., M. Murray (New Haven: Yale University Press, 1978); Karl Löwith, *My Life in Germany before and after 1933* (Urbana: University of Illinois Press, 1993); Gadamer, *Philosophical Apprenticeships* (Cambridge, MA: MIT Press, 1985).

6. For an important discussion of German mandarin cultural and political attitudes, see Fritz Ringer, *The Decline of the German Mandarins* (Cambridge, MA: Harvard University Press, 1968).

7. Letter to Maximilian Beck, 9 May 1929. Cited in Douglas Kellner, *Herbert Marcuse*, 35. During 1920–21, the young Horkheimer studied with Husserl and seems to have been favorably impressed by Heidegger. As he remarks in a letter: "The more I am taken with philosophy, the further I distance myself from what is understood by that at this university. We have to look not for formal laws of knowledge, which are in the end quite unimportant, but for substantive propositions concerning life and its meaning. I know today that Heidegger was one of the most significant persons who spoke to me.... Do I agree with him? How could I, as I know only one thing for certain about him: for him the motive of philosophizing springs not from intellectual ambition and some prefabricated theory, but every day, from his own experience"; Horkheimer, *Gesammelte Schriften* 15, eds. A. Schmidt and G. Schmid-Noerr (Frankfurt: Fischer, 1985–1996), 77.

8. See Luxemburg's famous pamphlet, "The Russian Revolution," in *Rosa Luxemburg Speaks*, ed. Mary-Alice Waters (New York: Pathfinder Press, 1970), 498–540.

9. For a good discussion of these themes, see Russell Jacoby, "The Critique of Automatic Marxism: The Politics of Philosophy From Lukács to the Frankfurt School," in *Telos* 10 (Winter 1971): 119–46.

10. Marx, *Capital*, vol. 1, in *The Marx–Engels Reader*, ed. R. Tucker (New York: Norton, 1978), 32.

11. Heidegger, *Being and Time*, trans. John MacQuarrie and Edward Robinson (San Francisco: Harper & Row, 1962), 102–04.

12. Marcuse, "On Concrete Philosophy," in *Heideggerian Marxism*, ed. Richard Wolin and John Abromeit (Lincoln: University of Nebraska Press, 2005), 42. All subsequent references to this edition appear in parentheses as HM.

13. From this standpoint, Marcuse's understanding of Heidegger's methodological importance seems to foreshadow Max Horkheimer's distinction between "Traditional and Critical Theory"; see Horkheimer, *Critical Theory: Selected Essays*, trans. Matthew O'Connell et al. (New York: Herder and Herder, 1973), 188–243.

14. Marx, "Theses on Feuerbach," in *The Marx–Engels Reader*, ed. R. Tucker (New York: Norton, 1978); see also Lukács's important gloss on the Theses in *History and Class Consciousness: Studies in Marxist Dialectics*, trans. Rodney Livingstone (Cambridge, MA: MIT Press, 1971), 143–45.

15. Marx, "Theses on Feuerbach," in *The Marx–Engels Reader*, 186–87, 198.

16. See Thomas Willey, *Back to Kant: The Revival of Kantianism in German Social and Historical Thought, 1860–1914* (Detroit: Wayne State University Press, 1978).

17. See Wilhelm Dilthey, *Die Jugendgeschichte Hegels und andere Abhandlungen zur Geschichte des deutschen Idealismus* (Stuttgart: B. G. Teubner, 1959); and Michael Ermarth, *Wilhelm Dilthey: The Critique of Historical Reason* (Chicago: University of Chicago Press, 1978).

18. Marx, "Theses on Feuerbach," in *The Marx–Engels Reader*, 144.

19. For an indictment of bourgeois thought that was obviously of great inspirational value for Marcuse, see Lukács's discussion of "The Antinomies of Bourgeois Thought," in *History and Class Consciousness*, 110–148.

20. Marcuse, *Hegel's Ontology and the Theory of Historicity*, trans. S. Benhabib (Cambridge, MA: MIT Press, 1987), 251.

21. For Dilthey's belated influence on Heidegger, which had a monumental influence on the later drafts of *Being and Time*, see Heidegger, *The History of the Concept of Time*, trans. T. Kisiel (Bloomington: University of Indiana

Press, 1992). In the literature on Heidegger, this text is also known as the Kassel Lectures. For their place in the *Entstehungsgeschichte* of *Being and Time*, see Kisiel, *The Genesis of Heidegger's* Being and Time (Berkeley and Los Angeles: University of California Press, 1997), 311–420. Habermas presents a highly favorable interpretation of Dilthey in *Knowledge and Human Interests* (Boston: Beacon Press, 1971), 140–86. For an excellent treatment of the concept of historicity in Dilthey and Heidegger, see Charles Bambach, *Dilthey, Heidegger and the Crisis of Historicism: History and Metaphysics in Heidegger, Dilthey and the Neo-Kantians* (Ithaca: Cornell University Press, 1995).

22. Heidegger, *Der Begriff der Zeit* (Tübingen: Niemeyer, 1989), 25.
23. See Victor Farias, *Heidegger and Nazism*, ed. Joseph Margolis and Tom Rockmore, trans. G. R. Ricci (Philadelphia: Temple University Press, 1989). Hugo Ott, *Martin Heidegger: A Political Life*, trans. Allan Blunden (New York: Basic Books, 1993).
24. See the accounts in Kellner, *Herbert Marcuse*, 401n1, where Kellner cites Habermas as claiming that Marcuse had told him Heidegger had rejected the habilitation study; and Benhabib, "Translator's Introduction" to Herbert Marcuse, *Hegel's Ontology*, x–xi.
25. Rolf Wiggershaus, *The Frankfurt School: Its History, Theories, and Political Significance* (Cambridge, MA: MIT Press, 1994), 104.
26. Whether Heidegger actually provided the letter in question cannot be confirmed: allegedly, much of Klostermann's prewar correspondence was destroyed by bombing during World War II. For a detailed account based on documents in the Marcuse Archive, see Peter-Erwin Jansen, "Marcuses Habiltationsverfahren: Eine Odyssee," in *Befreiung Denken: Ein politischer Imperativ*, P. Jansen, ed. (Offenbach: Verlag 2000, 1990), 141–150.
27. Here, the parallels with aspects of Kojève's argument in his *Introduction to the Reading of Hegel* are striking. For Kojève, "desire" is an expression of human lack. Of course, the ultimate source of Marcuse's and Kojève's argument may have been the same: the master-slave section of Hegel's *Phenomenology of Spirit*.
28. See the discussion in Kellner, *Herbert Marcuse*, 33.
29. Friedrich Schiller, *On the Aesthetic Education of Man: A Series of Letters*, trans. R. Snell (New York: Frederick Ungar, 1965), 80.
30. See Marcuse, "Theory and Politics: A Discussion," *Telos* 58 (Winter 1978–79): 126; "At the end of 1932 it was perfectly clear that I would never be able to qualify for a professorship under the Nazi regime."
31. Ibid., 125.
32. In a number of interviews, Jürgen Habermas has claimed that he identified closely with Marcuse's intellectual path "from Heidegger to Horkheimer," since for approximately four years, he had been a "thoroughgoing Heideggerian." As Habermas continues: "It was while I was working on the concept of ideology that I came across Marcuse's early articles [on Heidegger]. There you could see the exact breaking-point between an orthodox Heideggerian and a Marxist. I still can show you the lines where Herbert made the substantive, the strategic criticism of Heidegger — namely where he rejects not just the ontological difference but the difference between history and historicity. So I can recognize my own point of departure, so to speak, from Heidegger in these texts of Marcuse"; Habermas, *Autonomy and Solidarity* (New York: Verso, 1986), 194.
33. See, for example, Leszek Kolakowski, *Towards a Marxist Humanism: Essays on the Left Today* (New York: Grove Press, 1968).

34. For more on phenomenological Marxism, see P. Piccone, "Phenomenological Marxism," *Telos* 9 (Fall 1971): 3–31 and P-A Rovatti, "Critical Theory and Phenomenology," *Telos* 15 (Spring 1973): 25–40. As Rovatti remarks, "Within certain limits there is a convergence of content in the sense that both the Frankfurt School and phenomenology were on the attack against a model of scientific development and 'bad' rationalization leading both positivism in its new forms as well as idealism to a radical crisis" (25).

35. Karl Löwith, "The Political Implications of Heidegger's Existentialism," in *The Heidegger Controversy: A Critical Reader* (Cambridge, MA: MIT Press, 1993), 173.

36. For Adorno's critical views on Heidegger, which surfaced as early as his 1931 Frankfurt University inaugural lecture, see "The Actuality of Philosophy," *Telos* 31 (Spring 1977): 120–33; see also his critical review of Marcuse, *Hegel's Ontology and the Theory of Historicity*, in *Zeitschrift für Sozialforschung* 1 (1932): 409–410. Adorno would continue his polemics against Heideggerianism in the postwar period. See *The Jargon of Authenticity* (Evanston: Northwestern University Press, 1975) and *Negative Dialectics* (New York: Seabury, 1973), 61–131.

37. The correspondence has been reproduced in *The Heidegger Controversy*, 160–64.

38. For a good account of Marcuse's attitudes towards the New Left, see Kellner, *Herbert Marcuse*, 276–319.

39. Heidegger, "The Question Concerning Technology," in *The Question Concerning Technology and Other Essays* (New York: Harper and Row, 1977), 3–35; cited by Marcuse in *One-Dimensional Man*, 153–54. To my knowledge, this is the only time Marcuse ever directly cited Heidegger following the war.

40. See Marcuse, *Technology, War, and Fascism*, ed. D. Kellner (New York: Routledge, 1998), 39–66.

41. Marcuse, *An Essay on Liberation* (New York: Penguin, 1969), 19.

Chapter 4

1. Marcuse, "The Foundations of Historical Materialism," in *Studies in Critical Philosophy* (Boston: Beacon, 1973), 3.

2. Paul Breines, "Marcuse and the New Left in America," in J. Habermas et al., *Antworten auf Herbert Marcuse* (Frankfurt: Suhrkamp, 1969), 137.

3. "Repressive desublimation" was the term Marcuse used to describe the libidinally charged relationship between consumers and their commodities. In this way, the ideology of consumerism rechanneled or "desublimated" erotic energies away from more genuine ends.

4. Habermas, "Psychic Thermidor and the Rebirth of Rebellious Subjectivity," in Pippen et al., *Marcuse and the Promise of Critical Theory* (South Hadley, MA: Bergin and Garvey, 1988), 5.

5. Ibid., 9.

6. Marcuse, *Eros and Civilization: A Philosophical Inquiry into Freud* (Boston: Beacon Press, 1966), 15.

7. Ibid., 19.

8. Ibid., 45.

9. Ibid.

10. Ibid., 49.

11. Ibid., 236–37.

12. Douglas Kellner in *Herbert Marcuse and the Crisis of Marxism* (Berkeley: University of California Press, 1984), 194.

13. Erich Fromm, "The Human Implications of Instinctivistic 'Radicalism,'" *Dissent* (Fall 1955): 344.

14. R. Tucker, ed., *The Marx–Engels Reader* (New York: Norton, 1978), 84.

15. Marcuse, "Repressive Tolerance," in *Critique of Pure Tolerance*, ed. R. Wolff (Boston: Beacon, 1965), 109–110.

16. Ibid., 111.

17. Ibid., 118.

18. Ibid., 121. Marcuse also flirted with the concept of "educational dictatorship" toward the end of his life in assessing the impact of Rudolf Bahro's book, *The Alternative in Eastern Europe* (London: New Left Books, 1978). In "Protosocialism and Late Capitalism: Toward a Theoretical Synthesis Based on Bahro's Analysis," in *Rudolf Bahro: Critical Responses*, ed. Ulf Wolter (White Plains, NY: M. E. Sharpe, 1980), he seconds Bahro's unregenerate Leninism. As Marcuse contends, echoing Bahro: "During its prepatory and transitional periods, the revolution requires a leadership that can stand up against the compensatory interests of the masses . It too must face up to the necessity of repression, repression of 'subaltern consciousness,' unreflected spontaneity, and bourgeois and petit bourgeois egoism. Obviously, at this central point, Bahro's analysis falls back on a position that has been tabooed by both Marxism and liberalism: Plato's position (an educational dictatorship of the most intelligent) and Rousseau's (people must be forced to be free) (32).

19. Marcuse, *Eros and Civilization*, 225.

Chapter 5

1. Lowenthal, *An Unmastered Past*: *The Autobiographical Reflections of Leo Lowenthal*, M. Jay, ed. (Berkeley and Los Angeles: University of California Press, 1988), 149.

2. Benjamin, *Briefe* I, (Frankfurt: Suhrkamp, 1966), 59.

3. Benjamin, "Surrealism," in *Reflections*, trans. E. Jephcott (New York: Harcourt Brace, 1978), 189.

4. Benjamin, "Program of the Coming Philosophy," *Selected Writings* I (Cambridge, MA: Harvard University Press, 1996), 101–110.

5. Benjamin, *Arcades Project*, trans. H. Eiland and K. McLaughlin (Cambridge, MA: Harvard University Press, 2000), 471.

6. Ibid., 459.

7. Lowenthal, *An Unmastered Past*, 111–112, 114.

8. See Rolf Wiggershaus, *Die Frankfurter Schule: Geschichte, Theoretische Entwicklung, Politisiche Bedeutung* (Munich: Hanser, 1986), 728; Wolfgang Kraushaar, *Die Frankfurter Schule: Vom Flaschenpost zu Molotov Cocktail* (Hamburg: Rogner and Bernard, 1998).

9. Burke, *Reflections on the Revolution in France* (Garden City, NY: Doubleday, 1961), 46.

10. See Jerry Muller, *The Other God That Failed: Hans Freyer and The Deradicalization of German Conservatism,* (Princeton: Princeton University Press, 1987); Dirk van Laak, *Gespräche in der Sicherheit des Schweigens* (Berlin: Akademie, 1993); and Adorno and Gehlen, "Sozialtechocratie," in Friedemann Grenz, *Adornos Philosophie in Grundbegriffe* (Frankfurt am Main: Suhrkamp, 1974), 225–252.

11. See Adorno's programmatic essay "What Does It Mean to Work through the Past?" in *Critical Models* (New York: Columbia University Press, 1995).
12. Kant, *Groundwork of a Metaphysics of Morals*.
13. Lowenthal, "Triumph of the Mass Idols," in *Literature, Popular Culture and Society* (Stanford: Pacific Books, 1961), 135–36.
14. Heidegger, "Nietzsche's Word: 'God Is Dead,'" in *The Question concerning Technology and Other Essays*, trans. W. Lovitt (New York: Harper and Row, 1977), 112.
15. See the biographies of Foucault by James Miller, *The Passion of Michel Foucault* (New York: Simon and Schuster, 1992), and David Macey, *The Lives of Michel Foucault* (New York: Pantheon, 1994).
16. Lowenthal, *An Unmastered Past*, 265.
17. Marcuse, "Philosophy and Critical Theory," in *Negations* (Boston: Beacon Press, 1968), 155.
18. "The specific treatment which a creative writer gives to nature or to love, to gestures and moods, to situations of gregariousness or solitude, the weight given to reflections, descriptions or conversations, are all phenomena which … are in fact genuinely primary sources for a study of the penetration of the most private and intimate spheres of individual life by the social climate on which … this life thrives." Lowenthal, *Literature, Popular Culture and Society*, 143.
19. Lowenthal, "The Sociology of Literature in Retrospect," in ibid., 168.
20. Cited in ibid., 168.
21. Jameson, "Reification and Utopia in Mass Culture," *Social Text* (Winter 1979) 144.
22. Kellner, "TV, Ideology, and Emancipatory culture," *Socialist Review* 45 (May–June 1979), 13–53.
23. *The Cultural Studies Reader*, ed. S. During (New York: Routledge, 1993), 30.
24. Adorno, *Minima Moralia*, trans. E. Jephcott (London: Verso, 1974), 25; for a good summary of developments in the field of cultural studies, see Douglas Kellner, *Media Culture: Cultural Studies and Identity Politics between the Modern and Postmodern* (New York: Routledge, 1995), 31–49.
25. Keliner, "TV, Ideology, and Emancipatory Culture," See the following critical remarks concerning trendy, academic "cultural populism" in *Media Culture*, 39. "Modes of domination are occluded, and resistance and struggle are depoliticized and rendered harmless, thus providing an ideology of 'popular culture' perfectly congruent with the interests of the powers that be."
26. See Ben Bagdikian, *The Media Monopoly* (Boston: Beacon Press, 2000) Todd Gitlin, *Media Unlimited: How the Torrent of Images and Sounds Overwhelms Our Lives* (New York: Henry Holt, 2002).
27. Habermas, "The Inimitable *Zeitschrift für Sozialforschung*, or How Horkheimer Took Advantage of an Historically Oppressive Hour," *Telos* 45 (Fall 1980): 121.

Chapter 6

1. Gadamer, *Heidegger's Ways*, trans. John Stanley (Albany: State University of New York Press, 1994), viii.
2. Heidegger, *Contributions to Philosophy: From Enowning*, trans. P. Emad and K. Maly (Bloomington: Indiana University Press, 1989), 308; cited in R. Safranski, *Martin Heidegger: Between Good and Evil* (Cambridge, MA: Harvard University Press, 1998).

3. Gadamer, *Philosophical Apprenticeships*, trans. R. Sullivan (Cambridge, MA, MIT Press, 1985), 52.

4. Dionysios was the tyrant from Syracuse in whose court Plato unsuccessfully tried to realize the doctrine of philosopher kingship.

5. Woody Allen, "Remembering Needleman," in *Side Effects* (New York: Random House, 1980), 4–5.

6. *Heidegger Handbuch*, ed. Dieter Thomä (Stuttgart: Metzler, 2003), 510–13.

7. Alexander and Margarete Mitscherlich, *The Inability to Mourn* (New York: Grove Press, 1975).

8. Heidegger, "Overcoming Metaphysics," in Wolin, ed., *The Heidegger Controversy: A Critical Reader* (Cambridge, MA: MIT Press, 1993), 68–69.

9. For more on Heidegger's postwar status, see Rüdiger Safranski, *Martin Heidegger: Between Good and Evil*.

10. Heidegger, "Nietzsche's Word: 'God Is Dead'" in *The Question Concerning Technology and Other Essays*, trans. W. Lovitt (New York: Harper and Row, 1977), 112.

11. Peter Gay, *Weimar Culture: The Outsider as Insider* (New York: Harper and Row, 1968).

12. See Victor Klemperer, *I Will Bear Witness: A Diary of the Nazi Years* (New York: Random House, 1998–99).

13. For a classic statement on this question, see Gershom Scholem, "On the German–Jewish Dialogue," *On Jews and Judaism in Crisis: Selected Essays*, ed. Werner Dannhauser (New York: Schocken Books, 1976).

14. See Isaac Deutscher, *The Non-Jewish Jew and Other Essays* (London and New York: Oxford University Press, 1968).

15. Arendt, "The Language Remains: Interview with Günter Gaus," in *Essays on Understanding* (New York: Harcourt Brace, 1995), 6.

16. Ibid., 11.

17. Heidegger, "Recollection in Metaphysics," in *The End of Philosophy* (New York: Harper and Row, 1973), 82.

18. Heidegger, "The *Spiegel* Interview," in *The Heidegger Controversy*, 91–116.

19. See Löwith, "My Last Meeting with Heidegger in 1936," in *The Heidegger Controversy*, 142.

20. Löwith, "The Political Implications of Heidegger's Existentialism," in *The Heidegger Controversy*, 182–83.

21. F. Poiré, *Emmanuel Levinas: Essais et entretiens* (Paris: Actes du Sud, 1996), 78.

22. Ibid., 81.

23. Levinas, review of Leon Chestov, *Kierkegaard and Existential Philosophy*, *Revue des Etudes juives* II, 1–2 (1937): 139–141.

24. Levinas, "Transcendence et Hauteur," *Bulletin de la société française de la philosophie*, 56 (3) (1962): 110; "My point of departure is absolutely non-theological. This is very important to me; this is very important to me. It is not theology that I do but philosophy."

25. Ibid., 141.

26. Dostoyevsky, *The Brothers Karamazov*, trans. David McDuff (London: Penguin Books, 1993), 332.

27. In *Logische Untersuchungen* II (The Hague: M. Nijhoff, 1975–84), Husserl defines *Evidenz* as "adequate perception of truth," "knowledge," "incontestable certainty," and "*adaequatio rei et intellectus*"; see 118, 122, 225.

28. "The face signifies in the fact of summoning, of *summoning me* — in its nudity or its destitution, in everything that is precarious in questioning, in all the hazards of mortality — to the unresolved alternative between Being and

Nothingness, a questioning which *ipso facto, summons me*"; Levinas, "Beyond Intentionality," in *Philosophy in France Today*, ed. Alan Montefiore (Cambridge: Cambridge University Press, 1983), 112.

29. See Levinas's characteristic critique of Husserl in "Ethics as First Philosophy," in *The Levinas Reader*, ed. S. Hand (Oxford and Cambridge, MA: Basil Blackwell: 1989), 78: "Whilst successfully isolating the idea of an originary, non-theoretical intentionality from the active emotional life of consciousness, he continues to base his theory on *representation*, the objectivizing act, adopting Brentano's thesis at this point, in spite of all the precautions he takes in his new formulation of this thesis." By the same token, Levinas's own philosophy is pervaded by "representation," albeit in the service of an approach to philosophizing "otherwise than Being."

30. See Levinas's avowal concerning Heidegger's philosophical uniqueness in *Ethics and Infinity*, ed. Philip Nemo, trans. R. Cohen (Pittsburgh: Duquesne University Press, 1985): 39–41. "In *Sein und Zeit*'s analyses of anxiety, care and being-toward-death, we witness a sovereign exercise of phenomenology …. For Heidegger one does not reach nothingness through a series of theoretical steps, but, in anxiety, from a direct and irreducible access. Existence itself, as through the effect of an intentionality, is animated by a meaning, by the primordial ontological meaning of nothingness."

31. Levinas, review of Leon Chestov, *Kierkegaard and Existential Philosophy*, 139.

32. Levinas, "Martin Heidegger et l'ontologie," *Revue philosophique de la France et de l'étranger*, 53, no. 5–6 (May–June, 1932): 395; emphasis added.

33. Heidegger, *Holderlin's Hymnen "Germanien" und "Der Rhein,"* Gesamtausgabe 39. (Frankfurt am Main: V. Klostermann, 1980), 134.

34. Susan Neiman, *Evil in Modern Thought: An Alternative History of Philosophy* (Princeton: Princeton University Press, 2001).

35. Heidegger, "Letter on "Humanism," in *Pathmarks*, ed. W. McNeill (New York: Cambridge University Press, 1998), 241.

36. Levinas, *Totality and Infinity*, trans. A. Lingis (Pittsburgh: Duquesne University Press), 21–22.

37. Levinas, "The State beyond the State," in *New Talmudic Readings* (Pittsburgh: Duquesne University Press, 1999), 92.

38. Levinas, "Ethics as First Philosophy," 76–78, 85.

39. For a classic account, see R. R. Palmer, *The Age of the Democratic Revolution: A Political History of Europe and America* (Princeton: Princeton University Press, 1959–64).

40. See Aristotle, *The Politics*, 1253 (11): "Language serves to declare what is advantageous and what is the reverse and it therefore serves to declare what is just and what is unjust. It is the peculiarity of man in comparison with the rest of the animal world, that he alone possesses a perception of what is good and what is evil, of the just and the unjust, and other political qualities."

41. The idea that Auschwitz was a crime of intellection informs the argument of Catherine Chalier's *What Am I to Do? Morality in Kant and Levinas*, trans. J. M. Todd (Ithaca: Cornell University Press, 2002), 9: "A highly civilized society produced the Shoah; the hope for a fraternal and just society gave way to the Gulag. 'Art, intellectual pursuits, the development of the natural sciences, many branches of scholarship flourished in close spatial-temporal proximity to the death camps' … The proximity between culture and horror makes the hope of seeing men bettered by education appear futile. It seems to sound the death knell of any idea of moral and spiritual progress through intellectual enlightenment." What this approach fails to explain is why the regression to

barbarism explicitly occurred in Germany and not elsewhere in the West. In other words: it fails to explore the possibility that the turn to Nazism was, to some extent, influenced by "peculiarities of German development." It also neglects to explore the Third Reich as an instance of "moral regression" rather than as the culmination of Western cultural development.

42. Adriaan Peperzak, "Levinas' Method," *Research in Phenomenology* 28 (1998), 117. "If we must avoid the entire network of [conventional] notions in speaking about the most important and interesting questions, how will we be able to treat them at all? Do we not need another experiential and conceptual framework for thinking about the non-phenomenological and non-ontological topics and themes that have emerged."

43. Levinas, "Essence and Disinterestedness," in *Emmanuel Levinas: Basic Philosophical Writings*, Peperzak et al., eds. (Bloomington: Indiana University Press, 1996), 111; emphasis added. See also the following remarks from "Ethics as First Philosophy" (82), which, employing slightly different language, convey a similar insight: "My being-in-the world or my 'place in the sun,' my being at home, have these not also been the usurpation of spaces belonging to the other man whom I have already oppressed or starved, or driven out into a third world; are they not acts of repulsing, excluding, exiling, stripping, killing?"

44. Levinas, "The Rights of Man and the Rights of the Other," in *Outside the Subject* (Stanford: Stanford University Press, 1993), 121.

45. Ibid., 122.

46. Ibid., 118.

47. See *Otherwise than Being, or Beyond Totality*, 157: "The Other and the third party, my neighbors, contemporaries of one another, put distance between me and the other and the third party."

48. Levinas, *Totality and Infinity*, 300.

49. C. Fred Alford, "Levinas and Political Theory," *Political Theory* 32 (2) (2004): 163. Alford continues (146): "The Levinas Effect [as] it has been called [refers to] the ability of Levinas's texts to say anything the reader wants to hear, so that Levinas becomes a deconstructionist, postmodern, or protofeminist, even the reconciler of postmodern ethics and rabbinic Judaism." Also see Howard Caygill, *Levinas and Political* (New York: Routledge, 2002).

Chapter 7

1. Nietzsche, *The Will to Power*, trans. W. Kaufmann (New York: Vintage 1967), 868.

2. Scheler, *Der Genius des Krieges und der deutsche Krieg* (Leipzig: Verlag der Weissen Bücher, 1915).

3. Kurt Flasch, *Geistige Mobilmachung: Die deutschen Intellektuellen und der erste Weltkrieg* (Berlin: A. Fest, 2000).

4. Frank-Rutger Hausmann, *Deutsche Geisteswissenchaft im Zweiten Weltkrieg: Die "Aktion Ritterbusch,"* 1940–1945 (Dresden–Munich: Dresden University Press, 1998).

5. Thomas Mann, *Germany and the Germans* (Washington: Library of Congress, 1945), 18.

6. Nietzsche, *Genealogy of Morals*, trans. F. Golffing (Garden City, NY: Anchor Doubleday: 1956), Chapter 2, § 12.

7. Heidegger, "Nietzsche's Word: 'God Is Dead,'" in *The Question concerning Technology and Other Essays*, trans. W. Lovitt (New York: Harper and Row, 1977), 112.
8. Suzanne Kirkbright, *Karl Jaspers: A Biography. Navigations in Truth* (New Haven: Yale University Press, 2004), 67.
9. *The Philosophy of Karl Jaspers*, ed. Paul A. Schilpp (La Salle: Open Court, 1981), 26.
10. Cited in *Der Spiegel*, November 23, 1987, 212.
11. Letter from Heidegger to Rickert, 27 January 1920, cited in Kirkbright, *Karl Jaspers*, 131.
12. Heidegger, "Comments on Karl Jaspers' *Psychology of Worldviews*," in *Pathamarks* (New York: Cambridge University Press, 1998), 13.
13. Kirkbright, *Karl Jaspers*, 131.
14. Ibid., 166.
15. Jaspers, *Philosophy of Existence*, trans. Richard Grabau (Philadelphia: University of Pennsylvania Press), 97.
16. Jaspers, *The Question of German Guilt*, trans. E. B. Ashton (New York: Dial Press, 1947), 31, 34.
17. Jaspers, "Letter to the Freiburg University De-Nazification Commission," in *The Heidegger Controversy: A Critical Reader*, ed. Richard Wolin (Cambridge, MA: MIT Press 1993), 149.
18. Jaspers, *The Question of German Guilt*.
19. *Within Four Walls: The Correspondence of Heinrich Blücher and Hannah Arendt* (New York: Harcourt Brace, 2000), 84. For an excellent commentary on Jaspers' *The Question of German Guilt* see Anson Rabinbach, "Karl Jaspers and the Question of German Guilt;" *In the Shadow of Catastrophe: Weimar Intellectuals Between Apocalypse and the Enlightenment* (Berkeley and Los Angeles: University of California Press, 1997).
20. Lukács, *The Destruction of Reason* (Atlantic Highlands, NJ: Humanities Press, 1981), 520.
21. Edgar Jung, *Sinndeutung der deutschen Revolution* (Oldenburg i. o.: Stalling, 1933); also see the discussion in Klemens von Klemperer, *Germany's New Conservatism: Its History and Dilemma in the Twentieth Century* (Princeton: Princeton University Press, 1968) Jung was the secretary of Fritz von Papen and was murdered by the Nazis on the infamous Night of the Long Knives (June 30, 1934).
22. See the discussion in Heidrun Pieper, *Selbstheit und Politik: Jaspers's Entwicklung vom esoterischen zum politischen Denker* (Meisenheim am Glan: A. Hain, 1973), 18–21.
23. Jaspers, *Man in the Modern Age*, trans. Eden and Cedar Paul (London: Routledge, 1966), 99.
24. Pieper, *Selbstheit und Politik: Jaspers's Entwicklung vom esoterischen zum politischen Denker* (Meisenheim am Glan: A. Hain, 1973), 13.
25. Jaspers, *The Idea of the University*, trans. by H. A. T. Reiche and, W. F. Vanderschmidt (Boston: Beacon Press, 1959).
26. Jaspers, Letter to Heidegger of 23 August 1933, cited in *Karl Jaspers: Philosopher Among Philosophers*, ed. R. Wisser and L. Ehrlich (Wurzberg: Königshausen und Neumann, 1993), 332–333.
27. "How Can the Universities Be Rejuvenated? Some Theses (1933)," in *Karl Jaspers: Philosopher Among Philosophers*, 315.
28. Ibid., 317.
29. Ibid 318, 319.

30. Steven Remy, *The Heidelberg Myth: The Nazification and Denazification of a German University* (Cambridge, MA: Harvard University Press, 2002), 20.
31. Jaspers, "How Can the Universities Be Rejuvenated? Some Theses (1933)," 325.
32. Ibid., 326.
33. Letter from Jaspers to Heidegger, 23 August 1933, in *Karl Jaspers: Philosopher Among Philosophers*, 335.
34. Elisabeth Blochrnann - Martin Heidegger, *Briefwechsel*, 1918–1969, ed. J. Storckmann (Marbach: Deutsche Schillergesellschaft, 1989), 61.

Chapter 8

1. For an important account of the continuities between the two major revolutions of the modern era, see Ferenc Fehér, *The Frozen Revolution: An Essay on Jacobinism* (Cambridge: Cambridge University Press, 1987).
2. Andrew Arato, "Interpreting 1989," *Social Research* 60 (Fall 1993): 611.
3. For more on these themes, see Benjamin Barber, *Jihad vs. McWorld* (New York: Simon and Schuster, 1995). See also the informative volume *Toward a Global Civil Society*, ed. Michael Walzer (Providence, RI: Berghahn, 1995).
4. Habermas, "What Does Socialism Mean Today? The Rectifying Revolution and the Need for New Thinking on the Left," *New Left Review* 183 (Sept./Oct. 1990): 8.
5. Ibid., 5. In this respect I would also take issue with the conclusion of Krishnan Kumar, who observes that the revolution of 1989 "seems peculiarly uncreative, unfertile in ideas." "The Revolutions of 1989: Socialism, Capitalism, and Democracy," *Theory and Society* 21 (June 1992): 316. Kumar goes on to attribute much of the historical responsibility for the revolutions of 1989 to Gorbachev's Perestroika (322). But whereas Perestroika may have been an important precondition of the revolutions, the self-limiting direction of their actual enactment was largely autonomous. Here, credit should be given where credit is due: to the democratic strategies and tactics of the Eastern European reformers themselves.
6. For an excellent account of the significance of the "return of the left" in Eastern Europe, see the special issue, "The Return of the Left in Central Europe?" *Constellations* 2 (April 1995). The issue contains important interviews with figures such as Adam Michnik, Janos Kis, and Claus Offe.
7. Arato, "Interpreting 1989," 620.
8. Ralf Dahrendorf, *Reflections on the Revolution in Europe* (London: Chatto and Windus, 1990), 95.
9. Francis Fukuyama, *The End of History and the Last Man* (New York: The Free Press, 1992).
10. Friedrich Nietzsche, *Thus Spoke Zarathustra*, trans. R.J. Hollingdale (New York: Penguin, 1969), 46.
11. Bruce Ackerman, *The Future of Liberal Revolution* (New Haven: Yale University Press, 1992), 14–15.
12. See the aptly titled book by Vladimir Tismaneanu, *Reinventing Politics: Eastern Europe from Stalin to Havel* (New York: The Free Press, 1993).
13. See Hannah Arendt, *The Human Condition* (Chicago: University of Chicago Press, 1958).
14. Adam Michnik, *Letters from Prison*, trans. M. Latynski (Berkeley: University of California Press, 1985), 157.

15. Ibid., 142–43. See also Jan Jozef Lipski, *KOR*.
16. Ibid., 147.
17. Tismaneanu, *The Reinvention of Politics*, 117.
18. Tismaneanu offers the following observations concerning these events: "Taking the side of the rock musicians had nothing to do with any aesthetic preference. It was a way of denying the system its right to interfere at any time and without any hesitation in individuals' lives. It was a public declaration of war against human freedom. Consequently, defending the young rock musicians meant defending the very idea of human freedom and dignity" (ibid., 146). For Havel's characterization of this group of unorthodox musicians, see his *Disturbing the Peace* (New York: Vintage, 1990), 126.
19. "Charter 77 Declaration," in Vaclav Havel et al., *The Power of the Powerless* (Armonk, NY: M.E. Sharpe, 1985), 210–11.
20. Vaclav Benda, "The Parallel Polis," in *Palach Press Bulletin* (London: Palach Press, 1979).
21. Havel, *The Power of the Powerless*, 30.
22. Ibid., 32.
23. Tismaneanu, *Reinventing Politics*, 141.
24. Havel, *The Power of the Powerless*, 40, 43.
25. See Gordon Wood, *The Radicalism of the American Revolution* (New York: Norton, 1992).
26. See Louis Hartz, *The Liberal Tradition in America* (New York: Harcourt Brace, 1955).
27. See Wood, *The Creation of the American Republic* (New York: Norton, 1969), a key text in the so-called republican revival.
28. Hannah Arendt, *On Revolution* (New York: Penguin, 1963), 213–14.
29. For a brilliant critique of what one might call "astrology as ideology," see Theodor Adorno, "The Stars Down to Earth."
30. In addition to the standard works by Riesman (*The Lonely Crowd*) and Lasch (*The Culture of Narcissism*), see also Richard Sennett, *The Fall of Public Man* (New York: Norton, 1976).
31. Max Weber, *The Protestant Ethic and the Spirit of Capitalism*, trans. Talcott Parsons (New York: Scribner's, 1958) 182.
32. Alexis de Tocqueville, *Democracy in America*; cited in Arato, "Interpreting the Revolutions of 1989," 635.
33. Tocqueville, *Democracy in America*, trans. G. Lawrence (New York: Harper and Row, 1966), 513, 516, 514.

Chapter 9

1. Epistémon (Didier Anzieu), *Ces Idées qui ont ébranlé la France* (Paris: Fayard, 1968).
2. Julian Bourg, "May 1968 and the Institution of Civil Society," paper presented at the Columbia University conference on "Liberalism's Return," April 11–12, 2004.
3. Alexis de Tocqueville, *Democracy in American*, trans. G. Lawrence (New York: Harper and Row, 1966), 513, 516, 514.
4. See Pierre Rosanvallon, *Le Modèle politique français: La société civile contre le jacobinisme de 1789 à nos jours* (Paris: Seuil, 2004), 428. I thank Julian Bourg for providing this reference.

5. See the remarks of Michael Seidman: "May was significant since it gave protesters the opportunity to begin emancipating themselves from a traditional and conservative regime." *The Imaginary Revolution: Parisian Students and Workers in 1968* (New York: Berghahn Books, 2004), 7.
6. François Dosse, *The History of Structuralism*, vol. 2, trans. D. Silverman (Minneapolis: University of Minnesota Press, 1967), 112–21.
7. See Michele Lamont, "How to Become a Dominant French Philosopher: The Case of Jacques Derrida," *American Journal of Sociology* 93 (1987), 607.
8. Dosse, *The Empire of Meaning: The Humanization of the Social Sciences*, trans. H. Melehy (Minneapolis: University of Minnesota Press, 1999), xvi.
9. Ibid., xviii.
10. Nietzsche, *The Gay Science*, trans. W. Kaufmann (New York: Vintage, 1974), para 290.
11. On this point, see Dosse, *History of Structuralism*, vol. 2, Chapter 31, "The Subject; or, The Return of the Repressed," 324–35.
12. See P. Forest, *L'Histoire de Tel Quel* (Paris: Minuit, 1995.
13. Ron Haas, "May '68 and French Cultural Revolution," paper presented at the meeting of the Society of French Historical Studies, Paris, June 18, 2004.
14. Cited in David Macey, *The Lives of Michel Foucault* (New York: Pantheon Press, 1993), 380.
15. Cited in Eric Weitz, *A Century of Genocide: Utopias of Race and Nation* (Princeton: Princeton University Press, 2003), 147. As Weitz observes: "Almost one-quarter of the one-hundred or so Cambodians sent to study in France in the late 1940s and 1950s, including Pol Pot, Ieng Sary, and Khieu Samphan, joined the French Communist Party, through which they again encountered French revolutionary republicanism but also, of course, Marxism-Leninism. In a study group, they read Marx, Lenin, [and] Stalin.... Pol Pot's first published article, in 1953, 'Monarchy or Democracy?' tellingly cited the examples of the French, Russian, and Chinese revolutions, which had overthrown corrupt monarchies and replaced them with democratic regimes."
16. Foucault, "On Popular Justice: A Discussion with the Maoists," Translated by John Mepham. In *Power/Knowledge: Selected Interviews and Other Writings 1972–1977*. (New York: Pantheon Books, 1980), 1–36.
17. Foucault, Preface to Gilles Deleuze and Félix Guattari, *Anti-Oedipus: Capitalism and Schizophrenia* (New York: Pantheon, 1977).
18. Foucault, "La Grande Colère des faits," *Le Nouvel Observateur*, 9 May 1977, 85.
19. See the discussion of these developments in James Miller, *The Passion of Michel Foucault* (New York: Simon and Schuster, 1993), 327.
20. Dosse, *History of Structuralism*, vol. 2, 336.
21. Miller, *Michel Foucault*, 315.
22. Franz Neumann, "The *Rechtsstaat* as Magic Wall," in *Rule of Law under Siege*, W. Scheuerman, ed. (Berkeley: University of California Press, 1996), 243–265.
23. Heidegger, "Overcoming Metaphysics," in R. Wolin, ed., *The Heidegger Controversy: A Critical Reader* (Cambridge, MA: MIT Press, 1993), 67–90.
24. For an excellent account and critique of this situation, see Todd Gitlin, "The Anti-Political Populism of Cultural Studies," *Dissent* (Spring 1997).
25. See the remarks in François Cusset, *French Theory: Foucault, Derrida, Deleuze et Cie. Et les mutations de la vie intellectuelle aux Etats-Unis* (Paris: La Découverte, 2003), esp. 293–96. See also Vincent Descombes, "Je m'en Foucault," *London Review of Books*, March 5, 1987; Descombes, too,

stresses the extreme "décalage" or abyss between the American and French employments of French Theory.

Chapter 10

1. See the figures cited in Pierre Moscovici, *Un An après* (Paris: Grasset, 2003), 9.
2. See Y. Mény, "La double mort de la Vième République," *Le Monde*, 23 April 2002; O. Duhamel, "L'implosion présidentielle," *Le Monde*, 19 April 2002.
3. Cited in H. Machin and V. Wright, *Economic Policy and Policy-Making under the Mitterrand Presidency 1981–1984* (London: Frances Pinter, 1985), 3.
4. Philippe Gottraux, *Socialisme et Barbarie: Un engagement politique et intellectuelle dans la France de l'après Guerre* (Paris: Payot, 1997).
5. The best discussion of these developments may be found in Pierre Grémion, *Paris-Prague: La gauche face au renouveau et a la régression tschécquehoslovakes* (Paris: Julliard, 1985).
6. For an account of *Tel Quel*'s risible political peregrinations, see Philippe Forest, *L'Histoire de* Tel Quel (Paris: Seuil, 1993).
7. See Mark Lilla, "The Legitimacy of the Liberal Age," in *New French Thought* (Princeton: Princeton University Press, 1994), 22–24. In fairness to Lilla's position, I wish to note that in his introduction, he hedges his bets by observing: "it would be mistaken to speak of anything like a liberal consensus in French political thought today ... Indeed, there is an air of strangeness, or exteriority, accompanying French analyses of liberal society, as if they were *in* liberalism yet not sure *of* it" (15–16). See also, Samuel Moyn, "Savage and Modern Liberty: Marcel Gauchet and the Origins of New French Thought," in *European Journal of Political Theory* 4 (2005), 164–87.
   For a withering critique of the liberal turn in French thought, see the articles published by Perry Anderson in the *London Review of Books*, ("Déringolade") September 2, 2004 and ("Union Sucrée") September 23, 2004. Anderson's articles were recently translated into French along with a response by Gauchet's coeditor at *Le Débat*, Pierre Nora: *La Pensée tiede, suivi de la pensée rechaufée par Pierre Nora* (Paris: Seuil, 2005).
8. See Gauchet's article on Constant in *The Critical Dictionary of the French Revolution*, ed. François Furet and Mona Ozouf, trans. Arthur Goldhammer (Cambridge, MA: Harvard University Press, 1989).
9. See Gauchet's account of his radical student days in *La Condition historique: Entretiens avec François Asouvis et Sylvain Piron* (Paris: Stock, 2003); see also Samuel Moyn, "Savage and Modern Liberty."
10. Lipovetsky, *L'Ère du vide: Essais sur l'individualisme contemporain* (Paris: Gallimard, 1983); see also Lipovetsky, *The Empire of Fashion: Dressing Modern Democracy*, trans. by Catherine Porter (Princeton: Princeton University Press, 1995).
11. Lipovetsky, "May '68, or the Rise of Transpolitical Individualism," *New French Thought*, 214–15, 216.
12. Lindenberg, *Le Rappel à l'ordre: Enquête sur les nouveaux réactionnaires* (Paris: Seuil et République des Lettres, 2002), 78–80. For more on Bataille and company, see Richard Wolin, *The Seduction of Unreason: The Intellectual Romance with Fascism from Nietzsche to Postmodernism* (Princeton: Princeton University Press, 2004), 153–186.

13. François Furet, Jacques Julliard, and Pierre Rosanvallon, *La République du centre: La fin de l'exception française* (Paris: Calmann-Lévy, 1988), 11.
14. Ibid., 137, 138, 139.
15. Tocqueville, *Democracy in America*, trans. George Lawrence (New York: Harper and Row, 1966), 27.
16. *La République du centre*, 145.
17. See the excellent account of Furet's background and development in Michael Christofferson, *French Intellectuals against the Left: The Anti-Totalitarian Moment of the 1970s* (New York: Berghahn, 2004).
18. See, for example, Pierre Bourdieu et al., eds., *The Weight of the World: Social Suffering in Contemporary Societies* (Stanford: Stanford University Press, 1999); see also, Bourdieu, *Acts of Resistance: Against the Tyranny of the Market*, trans. Richard Nice (New York: The New Press, 1999).
19. For a classic account, see Eugene Weber, *Peasants into Frenchmen: The Modernization of Rural France* (Stanford: Stanford University Press, 1976).
20. Jean-Philippe Mathy, *French Resistance: The French American Culture Wars* (Minneapolis: University of Minnesota Press, 2001), 86. See also Régis Debray, *Contretemps: Eloge aux idées perdues* (Paris: Gallimard, 1992); Alain Touraine, *Critique of Modernity*, (Cambridge: Blackwell, 1995); Luc Ferry and Alain Renaut, *From the Rights of Man to the Republican Idea*, trans. Franklin Philip (Chicago: University of Chicago Press, 1992). See also Pierre-André Taguieff, *La République menacé* (Paris: Textuel, 1996).
21. See, for example, the special issue of *Contemporary French Civilization* on "Intellectuals and the 1990s," 24 (Summer-Fall 2000); see also, Richard Wolin, "Where Have All the Intellectuals Gone?" *Dissent* (Summer 1998): 118–124.
22. Jay, "Lafayette's Children," in *Refractions of Violence* (New York: Routledge, 2003), 149–162.
23. For example, see the criticisms of deconstruction that are enumerated in the anthology *Revaluing French Feminism*, N. Fraser and S. Bartky, eds. (Indianapolis: Indiana University Press, 1992).
24. Said, *The World, the Text, and the Critic* (Cambridge, MA: Harvard University Press, 1983), 204.
25. See Alice Conklin, *A Mission to Civilize: The Republican Idea of Empire in France and West Africa* (Stanford: Stanford University Press, 1997).
26. See the account of Maurice Agulhon, *The French Republic: 1879–1992*, trans. A. Nevill (Oxford: Blackwell, 1993), 46. "In 1875 ... had not the first act of opportunism been to give in to the right on certain matters of principle, such as the maintenance of a strong presidency and the existence of an Upper Assembly?" (29).
27. Recently this thesis has been forcefully challenged by Philip Nord's book *The Republican Moment: The Struggle for Democracy in Nineteenth Century France* (Cambridge, MA: Harvard University Press, 1995).
28. Jacques Julliard, "Ou-va-est-elle, est-elle, Votre République?" *Nouvel Observateur*, 13–17 December 1989, 50–51.
29. Nicolet, *L'Idée républicaine en France: 1789–1924* (Paris: Gallimard, 1992), 512.
30. Jürgen Habermas, "Three Normative Models of Democracy," *Constellations* I (April 1994): 4.
31. Schnapper, *La France de l'intégration* (Paris: Gallimard, 1991), 81–104. See also Schnapper, "Immigration and the Crisis of National Identity," *West European Politics* 17/2 (1994): 133–35.
32. Debray, *Contretemps: Eloge aux idéaux perdus* (Paris: Gallimard, 1992), 22.

33. See two articles by Elaine Sciolino in the *New York Times*: "France Envisions a Citzenry of Model Muslims," May 7, 2003, sec. A4; "A Maze of Identities for Muslim France," April 9, 2003, sec. A3.

34. Cited in Martin Schain, "Immigrant Incorporation in France," in C. Joppke and S. Lukes, eds., *Multicultural Questions* (New York: Oxford University Press, 1999), 207. As Schain observes: "In the 1970s, when policy-makers assumed that there was a real possibility that North Africans would return home, a policy consensus developed around state aid for programmes that would encourage them ... to do so. The Ministry of National Education, controlled by the Centre-Right government, cooperated with numerous Socialist and Communist local governments in developing Arabic language classes within the normal curriculum and special language and culture classes outside of the normal curriculum" (7).

35. Michael Leruth, "The Neorepublican Discourse on French National Identity," *French Politics and Society* 16 (Fall 1998), 46–61.

36. Ibid., 59.

37. See Elaine Sciolino, "France Has a State Religion: Secularism," *New York Times*, sec. 4, February 8, 2003. Rémond observes that, "The political response is absurd and laughable. It feeds the illusion that all we have to do to solve the problem of integration is to vote through a law." Touraine told France Inter radio: "I used to always say to my foreign friends, 'France doesn't have ghettos.' Well, yes, we have ghettos." On the foulard affair, see Françoise Gaspard and Farhad Khosrokhavar, *Le Foulard et la République* (Paris: Découverte, 1995).

38. Sudhir Hazareesingh, review of Lilla, *New French Thought*, *French Studies* 51 (July 1997): 367–68.

Postscript

1. *The Mitterrand Years*, ed. M. Maclean (New York: St. Martin's Press, 1998), 51.

2. Cited in H. Machin and V. Wright, *Economic Policy and Policy-Making under the Mitterrand Presidency 1981–1984* (London: Frances Pinter, 1985), 3.

3. Berstein, "The Crisis of the Left and the Return of the Republican Model," in *The Mitterrand Years*, 82.

4. See Philip H. Gordon and Sophie Meunier, *The French Challenge: Adapting to Globalization* (Washington, DC, The Brookings Institution, 2001).

Chapter 11

1. Adam Michnik, *The New Evolutionism and Other Essays* (Berkeley and Los Angeles: University of California Press, 1985), 142–43. See also Jan Jozef Lipski, *KOR: A History of the Workers' Defense Committee in Poland* (Berkley and Los Angeles: University of California Press, 1985).

2. For a good account, see Rogers Brubaker, *Citizenship and Nationhood in France and Germany* (New York: Cambridge University Press, 1992).

3. Mussolini, *Le Socialisme* (Paris, 1933), 19.

4. For the classic account, see H. Stuart Hughes, *Consciousness and Society: The Reorientation of European Social Thought, 1890:1930* (New York: Octagon Books, 1976) ; and, more recently, J. D. Burrow, *The Crisis of Reason: European Thought, 1848–1914* (New Haven: Yale University Press, 2000).

5. See Hans Boldt, "Article 48 of the Weimar Constitution: Its Historical Origins and Implications," in *German Democracy and the Triumph of Hitler: Essays in Recent German History,* ed. A Nichols and G. Matthias (London: Allen and Unwin, 1970).

6. Mazower, *Dark Continent: Europe's Twentieth Century* (New York: Knopf, 1998), 31.

7. Quoted in M. Weil, *A Pretty Good Club: The Founding Fathers of the US Foreign Service* (New York: 1978), 171.

8. Seth Mydans, "Russians, Too, Are Warming to Autocracy," *International Herald Tribune,* April 21, 2004.

9. Warren Hoge, "Dispirited Latin Americans Tire of Democracy," *International Herald Tribune,* April 21, 2004.

10. Ibid.

11. Cited in M. Vaughan, "The Extreme Right in France: 'Lepénisme' or the Politics of Fear," in *Neo-Fascism in Europe,* ed. Luciano Cheles et al. (London and New York: Longman, 1991), 221.

12. On the Straussians, see Ann Norton, *Leo Strauss and the Politics of American Empire* (New Haven: Yale University Press, 2004) and Shadia Drury, *Leo Strauss and the American Right* (New York: St. Martin's Press, 1997).

13. Rivarol, cited in Jacques Godechot, *The Counter-Revolution: Doctrine and Action, 1789–1804,* trans. S. Annatasio (Princeton: Princeton University Press, 1981), 33.

    For a transhistorical interpretation of Counter-Enlightenment — that is, one that understands it as a perennial challenge to the hubris and pretense of wisdom and knowledge that dates back to the Bible and Aristophanes — see Mark Lilla, "Was ist Gegenaufklaerung?" *Merkur* 566 (1996), 400–411; English translation forthcoming.

14. Edmund Burke, *Reflections on the Revolution in France* (New Haven: Yale University Press, 2003), 100.

15. Lipset, Preface to Robert Michels, *Political Parties* (New York: Collier Books, 1962), 37.

16. See the classic study by Arthur Mitzman, *The Iron Cage: An Historical Interpretation of Max Weber* (New York: Grossett and Dunlap, 1970).

17. See the important critique of Weber in Wolfgang Mommsen, *The Age of Bureaucracy: Perspectives on the Political Sociology of Max Weber* (New York: Harper and Row, 1977).

18. Gerant Perry, *Political Elites* (London, 1969), 144; cited in Moses Finley, *Democracy: Ancient and Modern* (New Brunswick: Rutgers University Press, 1973), 4–5; Finley's first chapter contains an excellent comparison of ancient and modern critiques of democracy.

19. Lipset, *Political Man: The Social Bases of Politics* (Garden City, New York: 1960), 178.

20. On this point, see Joseph Stiglitz, *Globalization and Its Discontents* (New York: Norton, 2002), especially, chapters 1–2.

21. Richard Falk, *On Humane Governance: Toward a New Global Politics* (University Park: Penn State University Press, 1995), 14.

Chapter 12

1. Cited in John Merriman, *Modern Europe: From the Renaissance to the Present* (New York: Norton, 1996), 176.
2. C. V. Wedgwood, *The Thirty Years' War* (London: 1944), 526.
3. John Locke, *Letter Concerning Toleration* (Indianapolis: Hackett, 1983), 27.
4. See the discussion of Locke in Rainer Forst, *Toleranz im Konflikt: Geschichte, Gehalt und Gegenwart eines umstrittenen Begriffs* (Frankfurt am Main: Suhrkamp, 2003), 276–311.
5. Kant, *Critique of Pure Reason,* trans. Norman Kemp Smith (New York: Macmillan, 1929).
6. *Vorrede* to *Streit der Facultäten* (Berlin Edition, VIII), 316. Kant's response to Friedrich Wilhelm was often criticized for a dearth of *Zivilcourage*: "I hereby, as Your Majesty's most faithful servant, solemnly declare that henceforth I will entirely refrain from all public statements on religion, both natural and revealed, either in lectures or writings." For a discussion, see Frederick Beiser, *Enlightenment, Revolution, Romanticism* (Cambridge: Harvard University Press, 1992), 51–56.
7. Quoted by Friedrich Paulsen, *Immanuel Kant: His Life and Doctrine* (New York: Ungar, 1963), 50. For an additional account of Kant's struggles with the Prussian censors, see Manfred Kuehn, *Kant: A Biography* (New York: Cambridge University Press, 2001), 366–67, 379–82.
8. Marx, "Introduction to a Contribution to a Critique of Hegel's Philosophy of Right," in the *Marx–Engels Reader* (New York: Norton, 1978), 55.
9. For the demise of Arab nationalism, see Olivier Roi, *The Failure of Political Islam* (Cambridge: Harvard University Press, 1994). See Laurie Goodstein and William Yardley, "Bush Benefits from Efforts to Build a Coalition of the Faithful," *New York Times*, November 5, 2004. See also the important study by Ronald Inglehart and Pipa Norris, *Sacred and Secular: Religion and Politics Worldwide* (New York: Cambridge 2004). During the last twenty-five years regular church attendance in the United States has not increased at all. University Press, 2004). The authors show that, in contrast with widespread assumptions, over the last thirty years (1972–2002), weekly church attendance has declined from thirty-five to twenty-five per cent (92–93).
10. See Peter Berger, ed. *The Desecularization of the World* (Washington, DC: Public Policy Center, 1999).
11. Feuerbach, *The Essence of Christianity*, trans. G. Eliot (Amherst, NY: Prometheus Books, 1989), 31.
12. Marx, "Contribution to a Critique of Hegel's *Philosophy of Right*," in the *Marx–Engels Reader* (New York: Norton, 1978), 54.
13. Peter Berger, *The Sacred Canopy: Elements of a Sociological Theory of Religion* (Garden City, NY: Anchor Books, 1967).
14. Weber, "Science as a Vocation," in *From Max Weber*, ed. Hans Gerth and C. Wright Mills (New York: Oxford University Press) 159.
15. On this problem, see Habermas, *Theory of Communicative Action*, vol. 1, trans. T. McCarthy (Boston: Beacon Press, 1985) 247.
16. Mauss, *The Gift*, trans. I. Cunnison (New York: Norton, 1967), 74.
17. "Comprehensive doctrine" is the term used by John Rawls in *Political Liberalism* and other works to indicate a worldview that entails a determinate conception of "the good" or human excellence. According to Rawls, one of the virtues of political liberalism or "justice as fairness" is that it is (or so Rawls

claims) agnostic about conceptions of the good. Instead, it merely aims at a conception of justice that allows for a plurality of conceptions of human excellence. I do not believe Rawls's effort to separate political liberalism from liberal moral doctrine, as articulated, for example, by Kant and Mill, is successful. For political liberalism implies a distinct conception of autonomous personhood. Rawls hesitates to embrace such associations insofar as he fears that his theory could thereby be construed as embracing a "comprehensive doctrine." I do not see any way around the problem.

18. At the same time, as a Kantian, Rawls insists that the political philosophy underlying his "theory of justice," far from constituting a series of compromises, is highly principled.

19. Kant, *Critique of Pure Reason*, A 738, B 766. See the complementary remarks in his justly famous article, "Answer to the Question: What Is Enlightenment?" In this connection, one should note that in *A Theory of Justice* and other works, Rawls proposes a highly circumscribed definition of public reason. In Rawls's view, it applies only to "constitutional essentials" and "basic liberties." It does not pertain to the so-called background culture of civil society in general — the "public sphere" in Habermas's definition — where a variety of other reasons apply. The idea of public reason advanced by Kant in the passage just cited is in its generality much closer to the Habermasian conception.

20. Habermas, *Between Facts and Norms: Contributions to a Discourse Theory of Law and Democracy*, trans. W. Rehg (Cambridge, MA: MIT Press, 1994), 454, 476.

21. For a classic discussion, see John Dewey, *Experience and Education* (New York: Simon and Schuster, 1997).

22. See Stephen Holmes, "Precommitment and the Paradox of Democracy," in Jon Elster, ed. *Constitutionalism and Democracy* (New York: Cambridge University Press, 1993).

23. For a more detailed treatment, see "What Is Global Democracy?" in the current volume.

24. Habermas, *Between Facts and Norms*, 317.

25. For a spirited debate on this question, see Robert Audi and Nicholas Wolterstorff, *Religion in the Public Square: The Place of Religious Conviction in Political Debate* (Lanham, MD: Rowman and Littlefield, 1997).

26. Rawls, *The Law of Peoples* (With "The Idea of Public Reason Revisited"), (Cambridge, MA: Harvard University Press, 1999), 136–37. In an unpublished lecture, "Religion in the Public Sphere," Habermas makes an analogous point: "The self-understanding of the constitutional state has developed within the framework of a contractualist tradition that relies on 'natural reason,' in other words solely on public arguments to which all persons are supposed to have equal access ... If the principle of tolerance is to be above any suspicion of oppression in view of the limits of tolerance, then compelling reasons must be found for the definition of what can just about be tolerated and what cannot, reasons that all sides can equally accept."

27. Ibid., 144. Rawls makes a similar point: "in due course public reasons, given by a reasonable political conception, [must be] presented sufficient to support whatever the comprehensive doctrines are introduced to support." *Political Liberalism*, 2nd ed. (New York: Columbia University Press, 1996), li–lii. See also Charles Larmore's comments on the problem of the role of comprehensive doctrines in public debate in *The Cambridge Companion to Rawls*, ed.

S. Freeman (New York: Cambridge University Press, 2003), 386–87: "The mutual reassurance which comes from citizens disclosing to one another the comprehensive roots of their commitment to justice really has no place in the deliberations by which they decide what shall have the force of law. But it does have a point in the different sort of public debate I have called 'open discussion.'"

28. Habermas, "A Conversation about God and the World," in *Religion and Rationality: Essays on Reason, God, and Morality*, E. Mendieta, ed. (Cambridge, MA: MIT Press, 2002), 149. See my discussion of these themes in "Habermas and Post-Secular Societies," *Chronicle Review*, Volume 52, Issue 5, September 28, 2005, Page B16.

29. For a good discussion of this document, see Jeremy Waldron, "Religious Contributions to Public Deliberation," *San Diego Law Review* 817 (Fall 1993). The document recommends "the creation of an order that guarantees the minimum conditions of human dignity in the economic sphere for every person." It urges the nation "to make a major new commitment to achieve full employment ... with expansion of job-training and apprenticeship programs in the private sector ..." It endorses "a thorough reform of the nation's welfare and income support programs," including an increase of AFDIC aid (Aid to Families with Dependent Children) so that the level of assistance at least reaches the poverty level."

30. For a discussion of this problem during the National Socialist era, see *Betrayal: German Churches and the Holocaust*, Robert P. Ericksen and Susannah Heschel, eds. (Minneapolis: Fortress Press, 1999).

31. Benjamin, "Surrealism: The Last Snapshot of the European Intelligentsia," in *Reflections*, ed. P. Demetz (New York: Schocken Books, 1978), 192.

Chapter 13

1. Christopher Lasch, *The Culture of Narcissism* (New York: Norton, 1976); Richard Sennett, *The Fall of Public Man* (New York: Alfred Knopf, 1977).

2. Schmitt, *The Crisis of Parliamentary Democracy* (Cambridge, MA: MIT Press, 1985), 65–66.

3. For the Derridean appropriation of Schmitt, see the Winter 1992 special issue of *Diacritics* (22). See also Paul Hirst, *Representative Democracy and Its Limits* (Oxford: Polity Press, 1991); the American *Telos* circle (although, given the journal's "right turn" during the late 1980s and early 1990s, it is by no means clear that the *Telos* crowd retained any pretensions of appealing to those on the left); Chantal Mouffe in *The Challenge of Carl Schmitt* (London: Verso, 1999); *New Left Review* editor Gopal Balakrishnan in *The Enemy: An Intellectual Portrait of Carl Schmitt* (London: Verso, 2001).

4. This story is told in Jan-Werner Müller's recent book, *A Dangerous Mind: Carl Schmitt in Postwar European Thought* (New Haven: Yale University Press, 2004).

5. Mouffe, *The Return of the Political* (London: Verso, 1993), 7; *The Democratic Paradox* (London: Verso, 2000), 117.

6. *Democratic Paradox*: "The deconstructive approach reveals that the vocabulary of Kantian universalist morality ... is profoundly inadequate for thinking about ethics and politics" (135).

7. Mouffe, "Radical Democracy," in A. Ross, ed., *Universal Abandon* (New York: Routledge, 1988).

8. Mouffe, *Return of the Political*, 5.
9. *Democratic Paradox*, 7.
10. See ibid., 9: "The rationalist longing for an undistorted rational communication and for a social unity based on rational consensus is profoundly antipolitical because it ignores the place of passions and affects in politics. Politics cannot be reduced to rationality, precisely because it indicates the *limits* of rationality." As far as these observations are concerned, it would be nice to have some explanation of why exactly a politics predicated on "passions and affects" would be superior to one based on rational consensus.
11. *The Concept of the Political, trans.*, G. Schwab (Chicageo: University of Chicago Press, 1996), 33.
12. See D. Held and D. Archibugi, eds., *Cosmopolitan Democracy* (Oxford: Blackwell, 1995).
13. Mouffe, "Radical Democracy," in A. Ross, ed., *Universal Abandon* (New York: Routledge, 1988), 38–39.

Chapter 14

1. Wittgenstein, *Philosophical Investigations*, trans. G. E. M. Anscombe (Oxford: Blackwell, 1972).
2. Ibid., no. 123. One of the best critiques of Wittgenstein's philosophy of language remains Ernest Gellner, *Words and Things: A Critical Account of Linguistic Philosophy and a Study in Ideology* (London: Victor Gollanz, 1959).
3. See, for example, Habermas, "Natural Law and Revolution," in *Theory and Practice*, trans. John Viertel (Boston: Beacon, 1973).
4. Weber, *The Protestant Ethic and the Spirit of Capitalism*, trans. Talcott Parsons (New York: Scribner, 1958), 182. For an interpretation of linguistic analysis as a response to McCarthyism, see John McCumber, *Time in the Ditch: American Philosophy and the McCarthy Era* (Evanston: Northwestern University Press, 2001).
5. Heidegger, *Was Heisst Denken?* (Tübingen: Niedermayer, 1984), 68.
6. Baudrillard, "L'Esprit du terrorisme," *Le Monde*, 3 November, 2001. For the English version of Baudrillard's article, See *The Spirit of Terrorism and Requiem for the Twin Towers*, trans. C. Turner (London: Verso, 2002).
7. Baudrillard, Interview with *Der Spiegel*, no. 3, 2002.
8. Schmitt, *Der Begriff des Politischen*. (München: Duncker & Humblot, 1932), 55.
9. See Habermas, *The New Conservatism: Cultural Criticism and the Historians' Debate* trans. Shierry W. Nicholsen (Cambridge, MA: MIT Press, 1989).
10. Habermas, "Discourse Ethics: Notes on a Program of Justification," in *Moral Consciousness and Communicative Action*, trans. Christian Lenhardt and S. W. Nicholsen (Cambridge, Mass.: MIT Press, 1990), 107.
11. Heidegger, "Nietzsche's Word: 'God Is Dead,'" *The Question concerning Technology and Other Essays*, trans. W. Lovitt (New York: Harper and Row, 1977), 112.
12. Vincent Descombes, *Modern French Philosophy*, trans. L. Scott-Fox and J. M. Harding (New York: Cambridge University Press, 1980), 139.
13. Habermas and Derrida, *Philosophy in a Time of Terror*, trans. and ed. Giovanna Borradori (Chicago: University of Chicago Press, 2003), 86.

14. Here I quote from the jacket copy of *Philosophy in a Time of Terror*.
15. For two excellent accounts, see Nicholas J. Wheeler, *Saving Strangers: Humanitarian Intervention in International Society* (New York: Oxford University Press, 2000) and Richard Falk, *On Humane Governance: Toward a New International Politics* (University Park: Pennsylvania State University Press, 1995).
16. Reprinted in *Old Europe, New Europe, Core Europe: Transatlantic Relations After the Iraq War*, John Torpey et. al., eds., (London: Verso, 2005), 6.
17. Habermas, *Time of Transitions*, (Cambridge, MA.: Polity Press), 5: World society has become too complex for it still to be steerable from some central point based on a politics of military force. The fear of terrorism experienced by the technically highly-armed superpower seems to express the Cartesian fear of a subject seeking to turn itself and the world around it into an object, in order to bring everything under control.... A nation which reduces all options to the dumb alternatives of war and peace runs up against the limits of its own organizational powers and resources. Even if this hegemonic unilateralism were realizable it would still have side-effects that would, by its own criteria, be morally undesirable. The more that political power manifests itself in the dimensions of military, secret service, and police, the more does it undermine itself ... by endangering its own mission of improving the world according to liberal ideas.
18. See Habermas, *The Inclusion of the Other*, trans. C. Cronin and P. de Greif (Cambridge, MA, MIT Press, 1998).
19. Habermas, "Faith and Knowledge," in *The Future of Human Nature*, trans. Hella Beister and Max Pensky (Cambridge: Polity Press, 2003), 102 (translation altered).
20. See, for example, George Mosse, *Towards the Final Solution*: (Madison: University of Wisconsin Press, 1985).
21. Habermas and Derrida, *Philosophy in a Time of Terror*, 94, 98, 99.
22. Bergen, *Holy War: Inside the Secret World of Osama bin Laden* (New York: Free Press, 2001), 66.
23. Habermas and Derrida, *Philosophy in a Time of Terror*, 41. Habermas adds the following skeptical remarks about deconstruction's linguistic cynicism, its perception that language is a medium of (concealed) violence rather than "understanding": "Communication is always ambiguous ... But when communication gets ontologized under this [deconstructionist] description, when 'nothing but' violence is seen in it, one misses the essential point: that the critical power to put a stop to violence, without reproducing it in circles of new violence, can only dwell in the telos of mutual understanding and in our orientation toward this goal" (38).

Index

B